A COMPANION TO THE FAIRY TALE

A COMPANION TO THE FAIRY TALE

EDITED BY
Hilda Ellis Davidson and Anna Chaudhri

D. S. BREWER

First published 2003
D. S. Brewer, Cambridge
Reprinted in paperback 2006

Transferred to digital printing

ISBN 978-1-84384-081-7

D. S. Brewer is an imprint of Boydell & Brewer Ltd
PO Box 9, Woodbridge, Suffolk IP12 3DF, UK
and of Boydell & Brewer Inc.
668 Mt Hope Avenue, Rochester, NY 14620, USA
website: www.boydellandbrewer.com

A CiP catalogue record for this book is available
from the British Library

This publication is printed on acid-free paper

Contents

Abbreviations

AT	Aarne–Thompson
ETK	Evald Tang Kristensen
FFC	Folklore Fellows Communications, Helsinki
FTAW	G. Anderson, *Fairy Tale in the Ancient World* (2000)
IFC	Irish Folklore Collection, the main manuscript collection, Department of Irish Folklore, University College Dublin
KHM	Grimms' *Kinder- und Hausmärchen*
TIF	Seán Ó Súilleabháin and Reidar Th. Christiansen, *The Types of the Irish Folktale* (1963)
TR	Thompson and Roberts, *Types of Indic Oral Tales*, FFC 180 (1960)

We owe the conception of this book on the fairy tale to Derek Brewer, and we are most grateful for the support and encouragement which he has given to us throughout. In our collection of material from scholars working on the fairy tale, we have sought to give a picture of its main characteristics and regional variety, and to seek the reasons for its wide distribution and long survival.

Hilda Ellis Davidson
Anna Chaudri

Introduction

HILDA ELLIS DAVIDSON AND ANNA CHAUDHRI

> First we tell tales to children. And surely they are as a whole, false, though
> there are true things in them too.
>
> (Plato, *The Republic*, trans. A. Bloom)

What is a fairy tale? Anyone who ventures to write on this rich and complex
subject must begin with a definition of the term. This is because it is commonly
used so loosely and inconsistently, as Holbek pointed out in his *Interpretation of
Fairy Tales* (1987: 23), that 'one must sometimes doubt whether the various
authors have the same material in mind'. A distinction must be made between
the oral fairy tale, recorded with various degrees of accuracy, as delivered by a
storyteller to an audience, and the literary fairy tale, the individual creative
work of a writer. However, there is no clear-cut division between these two
types, which constantly overlap. The Danish writer, Hans Christian Andersen,
composed many memorable fairy tales, four of which appear to be popular tales
which he heard narrated and retold in his own style (Chapter Nine below). On
the other hand, there is no doubt that many features in his own tales were
brought in from popular oral tradition. We are fortunate to be able to include
here an article by Bengt Holbek, published in 1990, on this aspect of Andersen's
work. This study deserves to be more widely known because of the influence of
Andersen on the development of the fairy tale and his contribution to its
enduring popularity.

Scholars continue to argue as to how far the tales in the Grimm brothers'
collection can fairly be called oral, since they were frequently told directly to
them from memory by educated people from varying backgrounds, not
narrated by storytellers for entertainment. Moreover, the collection of the
Grimms was edited no less than seven times and the differences between
these editions are marked, with notable omissions and adaptations to accord
better with popular nineteenth-century taste. This material has been studied in
detail by Maria Tatar (1987). In Chapter Four David Blamires examines the
contribution of the Grimms to making fairy tales accessible to both children and
scholars. He points out that the fact that the Grimms 'imposed their own ideas
and views on the fairy tales they published is no different from what happens
with storytellers of any period' (see p. 82 below).

Ruth Bottigheimer, who is firmly of the opinion that the fairy tale is a
literary phenomenon, stresses a factor which she feels has been seriously

underestimated, namely that cheap printed versions of literary tales appeared frequently in the past, available to a large popular readership which would have included many professional storytellers, from the sixteenth century onwards (see Chapter Three). Few of these cheap editions survive but in their day they spread rapidly by way of book fairs, local markets and travelling pedlars, through the main countries of Europe and, in the nineteenth century, printed versions were included in school primers. In this way many famous literary works, like Apuleius' 'Cupid and Psyche', became widely known, and the sophisticated tales of Italian and French writers of the sixteenth and seventeenth centuries were passed on to readers from very different backgrounds. This type of source, like oral narratives from medieval times onwards, is now beyond recovery, but needs to be taken into account when an established tale survives through the centuries in many parts of Europe and beyond. With this evidence in mind, Bottigheimer seeks to dispel the idea that the fairy tale belongs to an ancient oral tradition of indeterminable antiquity.

There can be no doubt that the literary element in the transmission of the fairy tale is of great importance. In the case of India, for example, as Mary Brockington points out in Chapter Sixteen, literary texts have been transmitted orally, without the aid of writing, alongside what can be defined as folktales, while major literary creations contain much folk material. India has a very significant literary element in its folklore; Kenneth Jackson (1961: 31) notes the importance of the very old and extensive written compendiums of tales in India. These have been read, retold and popularised over the centuries, so that the oral tradition is full of literary influences. Jackson goes on to demonstrate a similar development in the oral traditions of Gaelic Scotland and Ireland.

There is no doubt that a vigorous two-way traffic of oral and literary tales existed in Europe from the middle ages onwards. As Marina Warner puts it (1994: 24),

> Fairy tales act as an airy suspension bridge, swinging slightly under different breezes of opinion and economy, between the learned, literary and print culture in which famous fairy tales have come down to us, and the oral, illiterate, people's culture . . . and on this bridge the traffic moves in both directions.

This constant interplay and mutual influence renders it impossible to describe the fairy tale, within the broader context of the folktale, as an exclusively literary or an exclusively oral phenomenon. It also makes it virtually impossible to date the origin of any one tale. Many fairy tales seem to retain ancient survivals; in Russian fairy tales, for example, the figure of the monstrous Baba Yaga is almost certainly a representation of an ancient goddess associated with the world of the dead. Nevertheless, this does not mean that all the stories in which she is mentioned were composed at an ancient date. On the other hand, the very structure of some tales and the vivid power of some of their characters, have guaranteed their survival through both oral and literary transmission. As Jackson (1961: 56) points out, the plot of many tales is complex and tight-knit; episodes follow each other logically, apparently insignificant details are taken up to provide a later twist to the plot. Rhythms and patterns are established, for example the use of the number three, the balance between the number of adversaries and helpers, the use of stock phrases and characters. These devices all ensure ease of transmission, whether in writing or by word of mouth, but there can also be no doubt that they greatly favour oral delivery of a fairy tale. Neil Philip makes this point very eloquently in Chapter Two below.

Graham Anderson claims in Chapter Five that, in some cases, earlier forms of famous fairy tales can be traced back to the ancient world. Evidence for story-telling there has been largely ignored because classicists and fairy-tale specialists tend to keep apart. He gives as evidence traditions and story patterns in Greek and Latin literature which bear striking resemblances to some of our most popular fairy tales. For instance, Greek stories of women dancing as Bacchantes in the woods could be the basis of tales of princesses who steal away to dance until their shoes wear out, while the story of Epimenides of Crete sleeping in a cave could be an early form of 'Rip van Winkle'. On the oral side, we have much evidence of storytellers in remote places, for instance in Denmark and Ireland, who were not likely to have been influenced by printed material. But a good story has many ways to travel. Kenneth Jackson (1961: 40) points out that some well-known tales were current in Europe by the tenth century, long before printed material developed. Many, he believed, could have been carried from one country to another during the Viking Age and the Crusades, and brought into Britain from distant regions. The amazing characteristic of fairy tales is that, in spite of the complex nature of their distribution, the essential patterns of a large number have survived for centuries over a large area of Europe and parts of Asia. The story of 'Cinderella' with its endless variations but resilient plot, a phenom-enon first revealed by Marian Cox, has been discussed by Pat Schaefer in Chapter Eight and is a striking example of how a popular tale may be welcomed and recreated in many widely differing styles in various cultures.

Although the historio-geographic method of the Finnish school, in particular the work of Antti Aarne in classifying and recording folktales, has been criticised and weaknesses have been recognised, such as, for example, the strong emphasis on oral transmission, yet Aarne's principles of folktale study are still valid. It would otherwise be very hard to account for the enormous popularity and huge geographical distribution of tales such as 'Cinderella'. References to the 1961 Index of Folktale Types are prefixed with AT throughout this book. Fairy tales dealing with the supernatural world are categorised there as *Zaubermärchen* and included between numbers 300 and 749. The advantages and weaknesses of such a system have been clearly set out by Holbek (1987: 159ff.), and again in a study of 'Snow White' by Steven Swann Jones (1983), which shows how the analysis given in the Index may be misleading because of the wide variety of motifs in different versions. Monumental and painstaking studies such as Kurt Ranke's 1934 collection and analysis of the international tale of 'The Two Brothers' show the need to collect and compare all known variants of a tale. Only then can theories be advanced as to how such a tale might have been transmitted via migratory peoples or individuals, such as traders. Application of the methods of the Finnish School should eradicate the error of selecting only certain variants of a given tale to suit certain theories. Unfortunately this rigour has not always been applied, particularly in some of the highly theoretical studies of the fairy tale, as Holbek suggests is the case in the Introduction to Alan Dundes's 1980 book *Interpreting Folklore* (see p. 9 below).

The fairy tale belongs to the larger group of folktales, traditional tales of various kinds, including animal tales, cautionary tales, religious and farcical tales, memorates and legends. There are also cumulative tales, related to fairy tales in their animation of objects and emphasis on the power of the spoken word. These are discussed in Chapter Seven by Joyce Thomas, who has shown how these apparently elementary tales for children may be works of art, a challenge to both the teller and the audience, with an undercurrent of deeper meaning. Holbek, in his far-reaching study of fairy tales, chose to deal only with oral tales, since he refused to consider as folktales 'tales known to have been re-told or tampered with by professional writers, whatever their intentions', and therefore ruled out 'texts from the *Arabian Nights*, Perrault, Andersen, even the Grimms' (Holbek 1987: 23–4). *The Oxford Companion to Fairy Tales*, on the other hand, concentrates on 'the *literary* formation of the Western fairy-tale genre and its expansion into opera, film, and other related cultural forms' (Zipes 2000: xvi).

Most writers define a fairy tale by its content. Jack Haney, in his study of the Russian Folktale (1999: 93), defined the *volshebnaia skazka* ('wondertale' or 'fairy tale') as a subgroup within the folktale (*skazka*), as a family-oriented but individually centred tale (Haney 1999: 93). The tale begins and ends within the family sphere but the hero is driven beyond the bounds of the family to seek his fortune within the enchanted realm. Within that realm the hero or heroine will be required to pass a series of tests set by adversaries and be wise enough to recognise the assistance of supernatural helpers when this is offered. The geographical settings of the tales are deliberately vague – a palace, a hut in a forest, a tall mountain – and the characters are usually known only by their functions – a king, a poor man and his wife, a princess – or else by simple names such as Ivan, or nicknames. Haney defines the Russian 'wondertale', which is his preferred term for the fairy tale, as one among some ten categories of the folktale and he stresses oral transmission as a fundamental feature of Russian folktales (Haney 1999: 4–5).

Maria Tatar (1987: 33) defines the traditional European fairy tale as set in 'a fictional world where preternatural events and supernatural invention are taken wholly for granted'. While it is included in the category of the folktale, it does not share the earthy realism characteristic of such popular stories. Instead it allows the hero or heroine to enter a world of enchantment and to encounter characters endowed with abnormal wisdom and magical powers. There is a willing suspension of disbelief and no attempt, as with legends, to claim that the story is true. Neil Philip, discussing creativity in the fairy tale in Chapter Two, suggests that it 'mediates between the life we have and the life we want'. The tales usually have a happy ending but the hero or heroine may have to overcome enormous obstacles, often by supernatural means and assisted by powerful helpers of various kinds, while other characters impose demanding tasks and threaten destruction. These figures have been discussed by Hilda Ellis Davidson in Chapter Six and may throw some light on the origin of the fairy tale. The central character is young and inexperienced and, at the opening of the tale, often in a position of apparent weakness, despised and unfairly treated.

Both Reimund Kvideland in Chapter Ten and Tom Shippey in Chapter Seventeen find that there is a core-group of familiar stories which are most popular. In *The Classic Fairy Tales* (1999), Maria Tatar deals with 'Beauty and the Beast', 'Snow White', 'Cinderella', 'Bluebeard', and 'Hansel and Gretel' in detail, tales which have occasioned a great deal of discussion in recent years, largely owing to arguments among feminists about their interpretation. The Opies, in 1974, selected twenty tales (together with four from Hans Andersen), to give a general impression of the character of fairy tales popular in Europe but there has, perhaps, been too strong an emphasis on this particular group of tales by scholars. Tom Shippey, in analysing the feminist contribution to the study of the fairy tale, points out that a very small core-group of tales has come to form an unofficial canon (p. 261 below).

A tale by someone claiming to have encountered fairies, or to know a relative or acquaintance who has done so, would not normally be described by folklorists as a fairy tale but as a memorate, and indeed in most of the so-called fairy tales fairies represented as the 'little people' play no part, as Ruth Bottigheimer points out (p. 57 below). Patricia Lysaght, in her detailed study of the international fairy tales in Ireland, chooses to use the expression 'wonder tales' to distinguish them from the many Irish stories of encounters with fairies (p. 171ff. below). Legends, unlike fairy tales, are 'told for true' and concerned with known people or places. The novella, a long tale of marvellous happenings, differs from the fairy tale in that the story takes in the human world, as in the well-known 'Sindbad the Sailor' in the *Arabian Nights.*

Fairy tales have inspired such comments as that of Schiller: 'Deeper meaning resides in the fairy tales told to me in my childhood than in the truth that is taught by life' (*Piccolomini* III, 4). James Roy King (1992: 4) claims that they challenge norms and open new possibilities. Bettelheim who, as a psycho-analyst, dealt with many seriously disturbed children during the Second World War, declared that the struggles of an apparently weak hero or heroine against odds and their eventual success in the tales enabled children to gain a new understanding of themselves and of life (Bettelheim: 1976). One reason for the enduring popularity of the fairy tale is surely the quality of fantasy. Adults and children alike know that when the words 'Once upon a time' or 'Long, long ago in a kingdom far away' open a tale, the realm of wonder and enchantment is about to be revealed. This undoubtedly accounts for the tolerance of unusual cruelty and questionable moral messages within these tales; it also accounts for the fact that generations of children have been exposed to fairy tales with no ill-effects.

We know that the tales were not originally told only to children but, as Tolkien put it (1964: 34), they were banished to the nursery when they became unfashionable, like old furniture, a process which accelerated in the course of the nineteenth century in Europe. In earlier times they were narrated primarily for the amusement of adults, often by professional storytellers, but one important source of tales from very early times was that of stories told to children by their nurses. They might also be told in the home when neighbours assembled to listen, or among groups of people engaged in dull, repetitive work such as spinning or shoemaking or some forms of agricultural labour, or among men in the army (p. 150 below). Marina Warner (1994: 23) quotes the Scottish poet Liz Lochhead:

> No one could say the stories were useless
> for as the tongue clacked
> five or forty fingers stitched
> corn was grated from the husk
> patchwork was pieced
> or the darning was done

Thus listeners of many kinds and all ages might be found listening to fairy tales.

The importance of old women, nurses, grandmothers and the like for the passing on of such tales has been discussed by Marina Warner in *From the Beast to the Blonde* (1994). Storytellers may be referred to as Mother Goose or Mother Stork, a foolish old woman who tells 'old wives' tales', but such tellers may also be seen as wise women who instil moral precepts in the young (Warner 1994: 79). Some have expressed doubt as to the importance of such old women as storytellers (Harries 1997) but the evidence for this seems convincing. The nature of the contribution made by women to the spread of the fairy tale has aroused considerable interest in recent studies and there has been a revolt against the so-called patriarchal element in nineteenth-century tales, which tended to aim at restricting women's independence and turning them into dutiful wives. Fairy tales can be turned into cautionary tales, as Maria Tatar reminds us (1987: 166) and this tendency increased as the tales began to be retold for children.

Grimm thought that fairy tales developed out of myths, while some like Mircea Eliade (1964: 201–2) felt that they were based on ancient initiatory practices. Others, like Derek Brewer in Chapter One, see them primarily as chronicling the emergence of the young from dependence on others into a new maturity, the theme of many great works of literature. Neil Philip has defined the fairy tale as 'a family drama, in which the characters, by means of a series of transformations, discover their true selves' (see p. 41 below). Whatever the reason for their appeal, such tales have proved incredibly popular and long-lived. They are found in many parts of Europe and beyond and some may be traced back into medieval times. Perhaps, as Jackson writes, 'No explanation is needed other than the fact that man has always loved stories . . . for their own sake' (1961: 43).

The links pointed out by Derek Brewer between fairy tales and the medieval romances of the twelfth and thirteenth centuries in France and England (Brewer 1980: 62ff.) have received little attention from those working on the tales, presumably because the romances, like the classics, are unfamiliar territory. Many romances, however, tell of the attainments of young heroes, of implausible adventures which include supernatural encounters, and of the winning and losing of princesses and kingdoms. They may have had an important influence on later tales narrated to humbler audiences.

There have been claims that the building elements in fairy tales go back to a more remote past in classical times or even to ancient Egypt or Sumeria, and that these may reflect early oral versions of the tales (Anderson 2000: 15). Hilda Ellis Davidson in Chapter Six has suggested that the importance of a journey into an enchanted country and the abundance of helpers in the tales from northern Europe might owe something to the traditional tales of the journeys of shamans to the Otherworld told in early times. One of the problems in considering early influences is to decide what constitutes the basis of a story. Are we to rely on the structure of the plot, even if the order of episodes and the details vary, as in the case of hundreds of surviving versions of 'Cinderella'? Or should we take into account elements in earlier tales by major poets and storytellers, such as the blinding of Polyphemus in the *Odyssey*, the adventures of the Babylonian goddess Inanna, or the tale of 'Cupid and Psyche' as told by Apuleius, as representing sources of popular fairy tales? The former assumption is based on the belief that an original form of all the known versions of a popular tale once existed somewhere in the world and that, like ever widening circles from a central point, the tales were diffused.

Theories as to where and how the most popular tales originated have been legion. At one time it was thought that they were first told in India and travelled westward into Europe. Links with Indian tales have been discussed in Chapter Sixteen by Mary Brockington. An assumption made by many scholars was that the 'folk' created its tales by a spontaneous natural process, a conception found in the writings of Jacob Grimm. A similar theory, now generally abandoned, was put forward to account for the origin of the ballad. Vladimir Propp, in his work on a selection of Russian tales (1984: 67–123), went so far as to claim that all fairy tales were of one basic structure and that this is what singles them out from folktales in general. Functions of character, he claimed, remained stable and constant elements in the tales, the basic pattern being the discovery of something lacking or a villainous act, after which help is given to the hero or heroine by a benefactor or donor. Other Soviet scholars, however, refused to view the tales as altered versions of a lost original, preferring to approach them as separate works of art in their own right. The latter view allows for much greater powers of human creativity, but Propp's approach does have merit in that it goes a long way towards defining the genre of the fairy tale within the wider context of the folktale and, as noted above, most modern writers still tend to define a fairy tale by its essential features. The problem with such an approach, however, is similar to that encountered when trying to find the earliest elements in certain tales, namely what exactly constitutes the tale?

It is only recently that the importance of the storyteller and the reaction between narrator and audience has been recognised, for it had been generally assumed by those working on folktales that storytellers among simple people merely repeated the tale as they had heard it from others, without any creative reshaping. It is remarkable that such ideas prevailed, since it has been possible, even in recent times, to attend storytelling sessions by expert narrators. A good narrator interacts with his audience and the audience, whether literate or not, is usually knowledgeable, a point made by Anna Chaudhri in her study of Ossetic narrative tradition. In the Caucasus much collecting of oral epic prose was done during the late nineteenth and early twentieth centuries. If one compares many variants of the same legend, told by different narrators, it becomes clear that some of these were particularly reputed for certain elements of their repertoire. Details could often be left out of a story or a mere allusion made to an episode, because the audience would have known it well and some narrators, often generations of one family, followed certain lines of tradition. The Andiev family of southern Ossetia, for example, were particularly noted for their tales of the Nart progenitors (Abaev 1957). These storytellings were lively occasions. The audience would sigh or laugh and no doubt nod assent to such questions as 'And who knows what happened, but when was such-and-such a hero not an unrestrained and adventurous man?' Haney (1999: 4) writes the following when considering the oral transmission of Russian folktales:

> When one considers that the telling of a traditional tale in a traditional setting was in every way a performance in Russia, it is easy to see that there could be no repetition of the tale – with its interface of narrator, text and audience in a specific setting and time. Indeed, the text invariably was a 'one-time event,' not really memorized and thus never to be repeated very exactly.

In the case of the transmission of the Russian material, the oral component is much stronger and the influence of written texts on the fairy tale would have been far more marginal than in western Europe until perhaps the mid- to late nineteenth century.

At the same time, the retelling of tales by gifted writers such as Boccaccio and Perrault for an educated audience, and by groups of sophisticated ladies in seventeenth- and eighteenth-century Italy and France, described by Ruth Bottigheimer (p. 65 below), clearly led to change and development. While the popular tale continued to develop along established lines, each country possesses its own particular history of collecting in the countryside on the one hand and of literary influences on the other. Reimund Kvideland has outlined the study of tales in Scandinavia, and Patricia Lysaght those in Ireland, in Chapters Ten and Eleven respectively. She has given an indication of the proportion of international tales recorded there, an important contribution to our knowledge of Irish fairy tales, and shown how, as in Wales, the decline of the native language played an important part. The tales from Russia have special characteristics of their own, discussed by James Riordan in Chapter Fourteen. Riordan has shown how, in marked contrast to the enthusiastic reception of the Grimms' tales in Germany, there was determined opposition in Russia to the work of collecting done by Aleksandr Afanas'ev, who died in poverty and neglect (pp. 223–4 below).

Some collectors were convinced that a study of fairy tales in their own country would help to discover and establish the national identity of its people. The Grimm brothers came to feel this as their work progressed, as did the Norwegian collectors, Asbjørnsen and Moe and others collecting tales during periods of ardent nationalism in various countries in Europe during the nineteenth century. However, as Tom Shippey points out in Chapter Seventeen, this did not happen in England, where the national identity was already firmly established. There was a lack of interest here in fairy tales, as Katharine Briggs found when working on her *Dictionary of British Folk-Tales*. The position in Wales is particularly interesting, as Robin Gwyndaf has shown in Chapter Twelve. Here strong national feeling has found expression in a multitude of local legends narrated by storytellers and collected in printed books but these have links with the international fairy tales at many points. In Ireland, as Patricia Lysaght makes clear, tales in English spread far more widely as the native language declined.

We have to recognise that, since there was constant travelling in both directions over many frontiers, fairy tales cannot be confined to any one region or race. However, national characteristics can be found at the level of language and style and in the background of the tales and sometimes in the types of supernatural beings introduced, as in the case of Russia. As von Sydow pointed out (1932/1948: 12) each tradition handed down in the tales has its own group of bearers in one particular region, but these will amount only to a small number of local people, whose quality and background needs to be taken into account.

As well as the study of individual tales and groups of tales, there is an approach to the nature of the fairy tale in general when, as Holbek puts it, it is 'envisaged as a kind of superorganic entity, or as a single gigantic growth with its roots in a misty past and its branches covering large parts of the globe, if not all of it' (Holbek 1987: 25). The way in which these tales have obstinately preserved their basic approach and general characteristics, in spite of constant movement and changing influences, is surprising and impressive, and the problem of why this should be has fascinated many writers. The study of this involves the investigation of the imagery, themes and characters of the fairy tale, as in the work of Max Lüthi and James Roy King.

This leads on to the search for meaning in the tales. This has been discussed by Neil Philip and Derek Brewer in their contributions to this book. Folklorists in general have avoided the question of interpretation of the tales, but this has been taken up by psychologists and literary critics, some of whom, according to Holbek (1992: 8) 'offered the most provocative and usually ill-founded opinions on what folktales meant'. The psychoanalytic studies of the Jungian school present the fairy tale as a source of study of the human mind, consisting of archetypal patterns which 'embody primordial images and symbols, occurring the world over and constituting man's potential to understanding himself and the world around him' (Cooper 1983: 16). While the wide and lasting popularity of the fairy tale indicates the strength of its appeal to both children and adults, the difficulty in accepting the Jungian viewpoint is that such tales are not found throughout the world. They are missing, for example, in parts of Asia and Africa and in North and South America before the coming of the Europeans and so cannot be viewed as a natural phenomenon common to all peoples at a certain stage of development.

The Freudian approach to the tales is also criticised by Holbek. He disagrees with the arguments of Alan Dundes in the introduction to *Interpreting Folklore* (1980) concerning the meaning of the tales, on the grounds that Dundes has taken selected symbols from the discipline of psychoanalysis and then forced all his evidence into the same mould. He objects to Dundes's basic assumption that a great deal of folklore is preoccupied with sexuality in its many forms, and these objections are shared by other writers, such as Lutz Röhrich (1974: 134), who criticises those who claim that one particular interpretation is the only right one, since 'many truths are better than one'. Neil Philip argues that 'The same text can be read as a spiritual allegory, as political metaphor, as psychological parable, or as pure entertainment' (p. 42 below).

Holbek himself stresses the importance of symbol in the fairy tale but in a different sense, since he sees the traditional storytellers using ready-made familiar symbols of everyday life (Holbek 1987: 318). The ogre or dragon or hostile king could represent the father opposing the hero as the wooer of his daughter, while the magical gifts the hero acquires might be seen as the natural qualities which enable him to succeed. Holbek also stresses the importance of the contrast between youth and age and rich and poor throughout the tales. But he supports Michele Simonsen when she claims:

> Meaning does not lie *in* the story, nor does it lie *in* the interpreter's head. One could say that there is never a meaning, but only one (or several) minds engaged in the process of creating meaning out of a story (1985).

As Derek Brewer emphasises (p. 25ff. below) the fairy tale lends itself to interpretation and no one intepretation is exclusively valid. The deceptive simplicity of the tales allows them to be enjoyed and interpreted in a variety of ways. Over-interpretation, however, can lead to one losing sight of the integral magic and creative force of these tales. Certainly the language of the fairy tale is symbolic; Maria Tatar points out that this constitutes one of the main differences between folklore and literature. The symbolic code of literature is private and arbitrary, whereas that of folklore is public and set down by custom (Tatar 1987: 81). Surely, however, fairy tales should not be regarded as a thinly disguised series of social or sexual allusions, although their earthy content will always have been appreciated by listeners or readers.

The development of the literary fairy tale has been discussed in the chapters by Neil Philip, Tom Shippey and Ruth Bottigheimer. Bottigheimer sees the tales of Straparola in the mid-sixteenth century as 'a quantum leap in terms of narrative significance', because he created 'coherent order from existing narrative chaos' (p. 62 below). He and Basile brought many aspects from earlier books into their popular tales, while the work of Perrault and the learned ladies in France, particularly the Countess d'Aulnoy in the seventeenth century, helped to establish the fairy tale on a firm basis. More brutal and earthy elements from folktales were brought into the Italian tales, together with a sophisticated and cynical approach, so that the scope of the fairy tale had widened considerably before the Grimms approached it in the nineteenth century. Tom Shippey shows how many well-known writers have tried their hand at fairy tales, including Dickens, Thackeray and Robert Louis Stevenson (pp. 254–4 below). However he notes that on the whole their tales were non-serious, even patronising, and they never lost sight of their own world. One interesting and little-known example in a very different vein, discussed by Neil Philip in Chapter Two, is that of the tales of Rabbi Nahman of Bratslav, told to his disciples in the Ukraine between 1806 and 1810, which he used to convey deep theological truths (Band 1978: 32ff.).

About midway through the twentieth century a new interest in the fairy tale arose and a number of writers, many of them women, began to compose tales with a different interpretation. They choose the old patterns to present new points of view, largely feminist ones and Angela Carter in particular strove to introduce fresh and disturbing features. About the same time, Tolkien in *The Lord of the Rings* supplied fairyland, as Tom Shippey puts it, 'with all the things which traditional fairy tales lack', such as history, geography, language and maps, in a work which has gained an immense and varied readership (p. 272 below).

Clearly an enormous range of problems arises from the study of fairy tales. They are very mysterious, as Holbek reminds us in the opening pages of his lengthy volume. They have a wide and long-lasting appeal to many different audiences and readers and seem to be governed by certain rules, traditions and assumptions which storytellers and their hearers still accept. The interplay between oral and literary tales, which continues unceasingly, provides endless opportunity for discussion and research and much material for controversy. It has often been suggested that the term 'fairy tale' should be replaced by a better one, since the most memorable tales that come under this heading have few fairy characters. But as Holbek concludes, after a discussion of this problem (1987: 450ff.), there seems to be no satisfactory alternative. The accepted title is a translation of *contes de fées*, used for the literary tales composed in France from the close of the seventeenth century onwards, in which fairies appear as powerful donor figures.

Alternative suggestions such as *Märchen*, 'mythical tales', 'wonder tales', 'tales of magic', 'marvellous tales', are not entirely satisfactory. *Märchen* is often used of folktales in general. Fairy tales are quite distinct from myths. Holbek (1987: 450) takes 'wonder tales' to be a translation of the Swedish *undersaga*, which means 'miracle tale'. 'Tales of magic' is a translation of *Zaubermärchen*, a term used by Aarne to suggest the use of enchantment by a supernatural power, but this is more characteristic of the legend than the fairy tale, while 'marvellous' is far too vague a term. In the case of the Russian tales, *skazka* (derived from the Russian verb *skazat'* 'to tell') is used to mean 'folktale' while those who wish to distinguish the fairy tale as a subgroup use the term *volshebnaia skazka*, literally 'wonder tale'. This would seem to be an appropriate term for the Russian tales, which do contain more vivid magical elements than their western counterparts. Nevertheless, as Maria Kravchenko points out, the use of the two terms does sometimes overlap, reminding us of the delicacy of this point of separation between folktale and fairy tale (Kravchenko, 1987: 66). In English the term 'fairy tale' is now established by long usage, although 'wonder tale' might be a more appropriate term and Holbek's objection to it is not a very serious one (1987: 450). There seems no advantage in confining the term 'fairy tale' to literary tales, as Zipes (2000: xvi) wishes to do.

In this book there is analysis of a number of problems relating to this most enduring yet flexible and elusive genre. The oral/literary question and the transmission of the tales have been discussed from different points of view. The salient characteristics and interpretations of the fairy tale have been highlighted, and close attention has been paid to regional variety. The earliest possible forms of the tales have been considered, as has the modern development and perhaps ultimate disintegration of the fairy tale.

This last point must include an appraisal of the influence of modern media and speed of transmission of information and ideas. To take but one example, nowadays it is most likely that a child's introduction to the world of the fairy tale will be watching a video of a Disney film. This must threaten the very survival of the fairy tales as we have always known them, with their reliance on the word, spoken or written. Also it must affect a child's perception of the enchanted realm, for now he or she can claim to 'know' what the witch in the 'Sleeping Beauty' or the dwarves in 'Snow White' look like. A telling of a fairy tale, on the other hand, allows the imagination full range and the images produced depend, no doubt, on the environment in which the tale is told and the emotional and intellectual stage of development of the listener. The Disney versions have fairy tales firmly planted in the age-range of young, probably pre-pubescent children, which denies their universal appeal. Additionally the power of the visual film and the moral slant of the film-maker are very influential and deprive the tales of their interesting moral ambiguity and non-judgemental tone. There is no doubt that the subject matter of the Disney films renders them very popular, which must be a tribute to the enduring quality of fairy tales, but their visual power may be shaping the future transmission, content, interpretation and ultimate integrity of this wonderful art form.

This is a depressing possibility, and we can only hope that the deep and wide-ranging appeal of the fairy tale will survive the radical changes in means of communication, just as it survived the invention of printing in the past. It seems there is a psychological need for something that only the fairy tale can give us, for all its apparent naivety, and certain facets of our imagination are left unsatisfied by other forms of literature. It has endured through enormous changes in our way of life and attitude to the world, and its patterns still influence us more than we realise. It was suggested by Hannah Betts in *The Times* of 4 April, 2002 that our reactions to the deaths of Princess Diana and the Queen Mother were influenced by the way in which their lives were felt to fit into a fairy-tale pattern. Indeed the search for a meaning behind these tales is not a pointless academic exercise. As Rabbi Nahman (Band 1978: 12) is recorded as telling his disciples, when he turned to the recital of fairy tales as a new way of teaching: 'There are in these tales that people tell lofty and hidden matters.'

References

Aarne, A. and Thompson, S. (1961/1964, 1973, 1981) *The Types of the Folktale. A Classification and Bibliography.* FFC 184. Helsinki.

Abaev, V. I. *et al.* (1957) ed., *Narty.* Moscow.

Anderson, G. (2000), *Fairy Tale in the Ancient World.* London/New York.

Band, A. J. (1978) ed. and trans., *Nahman of Bratslav: The Tales.* Mahwah, NJ.

Bettelheim, B. (1976), *The Uses of Enchantment: The Meaning and Importance of Fairy Tales.* Harmondsworth.

Brewer, D. (1980), *Symbolic Stories: Traditional Narratives of the Family Drama in English Literature*. Cambridge.

Cooper, J. C. (1983), *Fairy Tales: Allegories of the Inner Life*. Wellingborough.

Dundes, A. (1980) ed., *Interpreting Folklore*. Bloomington.

Eliade, M. (1964), *Myth and Reality*. London.

Haney, J. V. (1999), *An Introduction to the Russian Folktale*. New York/London.

Harries, E. W. (1997), 'Fairy Tales about Fairy Tales', in *Out of the Woods: The Origin of the Literary Fairy Tale in Italy and France*, ed. N. L. Canepa, 152–75. New York.

Holbek, B. (1987), *Interpretation of Fairy Tales: Danish Folklore in a European Perspective*. FFC 239. Helsinki.

——(1992), *On the Comparative Method in Folklore Research*. Nordic Institute of Folklore Papers 3. Turku.

Jackson, K. (1961), *International Popular Tales and Early Welsh Tradition*. Cardiff.

Jones, S. S. (1983), 'The Structure of Snow White', *Fabula* 24, 56–71.

King, J. R. (1992), *Old Tales and New Tales: Chasing the Bright Shadow*. New York.

Kravchenko, M. (1987), *The World of the Russian Fairy Tale*. European University Studies XVI, 34. Bern/Frankfurt/New York.

Opie, I. and P. (1974), *The Classic Fairy Tales*. Oxford.

Propp, V. (1984), *Theory and History of Folklore*, ed. A. Liberman, trans. A. and P. Martin. History of Literature 5. Manchester.

Ranke, K. (1934), *Die zwei Brüder*. FFC 114. Helsinki.

Röhrich, L. (1974), *Märchen und Wirklichkeit*. Wiesbaden.

Simonsen, M. (1985), 'Do Fairy Tales Make Sense?', *Journal of Folklore Research* 22.

Tatar, M. (1987), *The Hard Facts of the Grimms' Fairy Tales*. Princeton.

——(1999) ed., *The Classic Fairy Tales*. Norton Critical Edition. London/New York.

Tolkien, J. R. R. (1964), 'On Fairy Stories', in *Tree and Leaf*. London.

von Sydow, C. W. (1932/1948), 'Om traditionsspridning', Selected Papers on Folklore. Copenhagen.

Warner, M. (1994), *From the Beast to the Blonde: On Fairy Tales and Their Tellers*. London.

Zipes, J. (2000) ed., *The Oxford Companion to Fairy Tales*. Oxford.

1

The Interpretation of Fairy Tales

DEREK BREWER

'The logic of a fairy-tale is as strict as that of a realistic novel, though different.' (Lewis 1947: 99)

Why should fairy tales need interpretation? Are they not simple, capable of being understood by children, often fantastic, unimportant to the great literary world? And what do we mean when we speak of fairy tales? The answers are surprisingly controversial and have generated a vast secondary literature. Even the modern literary world has wakened to the power of fairy tales and has used fairy tales, often in perverted ways, to create its own peculiarly modernistic messages.

Examples of the stories we think of nowadays when we refer to fairy tales are 'Cinderella', 'Beauty and the Beast', 'Little Red Riding Hood', 'Diamonds and Toads', 'Bluebeard', 'Puss-in-Boots', 'Jack and the Beanstalk', 'Snow White and the Seven Dwarfs', 'The Frog Prince', 'Hansel and Gretel', to take only a handful of the Opies' excellent 1974 collection, *The Classic Fairy Tales*. The general characteristics of fairy tales are clear. Whether oral or printed they are not invented by any particular individual. They have the anonymity of authorship characteristic of traditional stories, described by Calvino as having that 'infinite variety and infinite repetition' common to folktale in general, for fairy tales are unquestionably part of the great worldwide body of folktale (Calvino 1982: XVIII; Jackson 1961: 5 etc.). These stories have stereotyped characters and a certain predictability of event. They embody the social wisdom of their communities and an implicit morality or didacticism. In traditional versions, that is those not retold in elaborate nineteenth-century or twentieth-century novel-like style, there is little physical description. In many tales the protagonist commits some kind of transgression, but recovers through a central 'magical' event on which the plot turns, often a form of wish-fulfilment; the hero finds his beloved, the heroine hers; or there is an unexpected escape – occasionally the ending is sad, but more often happy. The implied setting, until very recently, and in all traditional forms, is a small-scale agrarian society, unlimited wishes and limited horizons. These characteristics imply an oral origin, which has important implications for method and structure.

These apparently simple tales have been of enduring interest in many cultures over many centuries. In consequence they exist in many versions which both are and are not the same story. The question arises as to when what we call 'fairy tales' may be said to have begun. The term is a hopeless misnomer but no other such as 'wonder tale' has been generally accepted, and we must stick with the well-understood 'fairy tale', granted that few actual fairies, of whatever kind, appear. Perhaps the fairy tale as we know it took on something like its present form in the late Middle Ages, though the elements go back into antiquity.

A key turning-point in the history of the fairy tale came in French royal court circles towards the end of the seventeenth century, when some brilliant ladies conducted *salons* where the telling of what are now well-known fairy tales became fashionable (Warner 1994). Out of this improbable milieu emerged the author eventually identified as Charles Perrault (1628–1703) who published a number of tales, most notably the collection *Histoires ou contes du temps passé* (1697). Like all storytellers he adapted the tales to his audience, and from them come a long line of retellings beginning in the early eighteenth century. The Romantic Movement gave a great impetus to interest in 'the folk' as evidenced by the collections of the scholarly brothers Grimm. Throughout the nineteenth century there was growing interest among scholars and collectors throughout Europe (Dorson 1968). The most effective scientific non-evaluative study was the Finnish 'historical-geographical' school which collected and classified international tales recorded directly from oral sources, but necessarily in the early days laboriously written down by collectors who usually to some extent modified them. Such collecting culminated in the great *Types of the Folktale* completed by Antti Aarne and Stith Thompson in 1961 and many times reprinted, the indispensable basis of folktale, and consequently fairy-tale, study, with the types identified by numbers. Rarely are literary tales referred to, and the value of the list is precisely its non-evaluative non-interpretative brief summaries, which do enable some relationships between tales to be traced.

In the nineteenth century folktales, including fairy tales, were vigorously collected, especially, as far as Britain was concerned, in the Highlands of Scotland, and a series of attempts was made to interpret them and account for their wide dissemination and appeal. Some saw them as expressions of solar myths, others as expressing the 'soul' of 'the folk', told by peasants who were seen as the true representatives of society. In 1846 William Thoms invented the term 'folklore' to cover a wide range of activities of mainly those people with little formal education, and throughout the twentieth century such material was studied with increasing sophistication. An excellent brief history is given by Zipes under the heading 'Folklore and Fairy Tales' (2000: 165–70). A bewildering variety of interpretations has been offered and though the 'core' of many folktales remains astonishingly unchanged through many centuries there is a sense in which every retelling is also an interpretation.

The important point that emerges for a modern sympathetic understanding of an activity with such ancient roots is the mixture of stability and variation both in stories and in the circumstances of their telling, 'infinite variation with infinite repetition'. Fairy tales present an extraordinarily slippery phenomenon to deal with, yet they are easily recognisable. Their surface meanings are clear, but they have further depths of meaning, and valid interpretations are numerous. Fairy tales can vary in shape and style according to the period and culture in which they are found. Many details may change – even the ending may be either happy or unhappy as is notoriously the case with 'Little Red Riding Hood' – though happy endings predominate. Yet with all the changes, certain versions retain some inter-relationship, they group themselves into some kind of entity.

For many centuries fairy tales have been despised by the literati as 'old wives' tales'. More serious attacks have been made on them as corrupting the young, or even the old, by fundamentalist Christians, Marxists, feminists, modern educationalists, on a variety of grounds from corrupting the mind, promoting traditional bourgeois values, or encouraging imagination. Even these attacks imply interpretation, a perception of significance. We find controversy between those who consider themselves 'folklorists' and are concerned with collection and classification but make no value judgments, and those whom the folklorists dismiss as 'literary critics', interested in literary influences, values, structures. The folklorists often insist on the oral origin of fairy tales, as a branch of folktale. This may imply that 'authentic' fairy tales can only be 'oral', and only discussed when every variant is known, and the apparent single origin of the tale known. Literary critics accept that fairy tales, often written, and now printed, are subject to other literary factors, and may be the foundation of, or at least part of, other works, like Shakespearean plays.

Some folklorists, such as Dundes (1989) and Holbek (1987), consider as genuine only tales which have been taken down directly from a known 'genuine' teller and which must be examined in every known authentic variant. This is a counsel of perfection. Folktale study itself would have to be purely oral, for even the first transcription by however expert a scholar subtly alters the tone and cuts out the actual performance. That does not mean that we lose all the oral qualities in any kind of reportage. It is salutary to remember the case of Homer's poetry. The fundamentally oral quality of the *Iliad* and the *Odyssey* is not in doubt. It seems likely that the poems were put together from previous lays by a poet of genius. They must then have been painstakingly recorded, presumably laboriously written down to dictation, at a very early date, perhaps as early as the eighth century BC. Literary, and no doubt editorial, manipulation had already set in (Lord 1960). The same is true of the Bible. Much of the literary interference attributed by biblical scholars to 'editors' may be better considered as natural variation on the part of subsequent narrators of exactly the same kind as the variation produced by practised, or indeed unpractised, oral storytellers, and then the literary effects of writing, or later, print. There has always been an interchange between folklore and literature (Davidson 1978; Goody 1987).

It is worth asserting that the interpretation of a single version is a perfectly valid procedure, as noted by no less an authority than Linda Dégh (1990). The collection of as large a number as possible of variant versions is another important study, but of course the variants have to be identified and identification and interpretation are closely related. The different versions, although connected, may convey different meanings, yet each separate meaning may be proper to its own version. The long history of 'Little Red Riding Hood' allows a variety of interpretations according to the version discussed. It is clear that the existence of a given story in many versions is itself an important phenomenon with a meaning, or set of meanings of its own, and can be viewed much as we can view the collected works of a single author, provided we do not mythologise the collective series of authors and retellers as 'the folk'. What they tell us is something about relatively persistent common human interests.

The view that only 'oral' versions of a tale are 'authentic' may depend on the mistaken assumption that oral versions are by definition more ancient in origin, and on an unspoken, essentially Romantic, notion that only the illiterate 'folk' have imagination. Ziolkowski (1992) by contrast shows very effectively that a short Latin poem written in the first quarter of the eleventh century by Egbert of Liège, at the cathedral school of Liège, offers excellent grounds to be considered to be one of that remarkably powerful and varied yet related group of stories known as 'Little Red Riding Hood'. Some believe that while a folktale has, according to the famous Finnish School, many variants, each has a single origin and an ultimately unified identity. Certain versions may thus be dismissed as 'inauthentic' and irrelevant to the tale's true nature or meaning, as Dundes (1989: ix) dismisses some of the late-seventeenth-century versions of 'Little Red Riding Hood' by Perrault and that in the Grimm collection. Having regard to strong evidence offered by Calvino, Holbek, Campbell, Falassi and others, of narrators both illiterate and literate who have a high degree of artistry, there seems no good reason to exclude highly expert but educated narrators such as Perrault. There are a myriad of examples of all kinds of stories moving from oral to written form and back again.

With some stories it is possible to identify a 'marker', which may be a fundamental structure, or some special item. In the case of 'Little Red Riding Hood', I would suggest the first part of a fundamental identifiable structure is simply the meeting of a little girl in a red cloak with a wolf. This is just a nucleus, and needs elaboration. She 'transgresses' by delaying and then comes the 'marvel', or series of marvels. In different versions the girl may or may not escape with her life. Where wolves existed in real life they were dangerous to human beings and beasts, and they are also easily symbolised as sexually predatory men (cf. the 'wolf-whistle' and the French idiom *Elle a vu le loup!*). Inventive storytellers have gone on from there. Ziolkowski, in his article of 1992, gives evidence for arguing that the red hood is also a strong marker, but Dundes (1989) refers to a number of late oral versions where this has disappeared. The significance of the red hood has changed from being probably a red baptismal robe with magical defensive and calming properties, and in some much later versions it does not appear at all. Its appearance in other later versions has been recently interpreted as a symbol of female maturation, the onset of *menses*, and the story can be constructed in such a way, with an older girl, to make that a possible interpretation, an interesting example of the variability of story and interpretation while the actual 'marker' remains the same. In the latest version, by Angela Carter, whose writer's trademark is references to menstruation, the girl, not so little, is seduced by the wolf and goes to bed with him, the moral being that for young girls to be sexually seduced by nice strange men is really quite all right. But the ending is not always happy. In some versions, including Perrault's, the wolf eats grandmother and child, with an obvious moral, not yet to be derided in the light of some sad contemporary cases of the abduction and murder of little girls. Another variant in the seventeenth century (Verdier 1978) allows the wolf to kill the grandmother and put her blood in a bottle and part of her body in the cupboard, so that when the child comes she is led to cook and eat the remains – a symbol of how the younger generation takes over the older. The 'Fairy Play' on 'Little Red Riding Hood' by Mrs Bell (1896) offers two endings as alternatives, in one of which the girl escapes and in the other is eaten, though in either case she is a naughty silly girl.

This particular fairy tale became involved with a complex series of events in the seventeenth century in the French district of Gévaudan where several young girls were attacked and killed by what became known as 'the Beast of Gévaudan'. The story was taken up by local clergy and Parisian publishers. Various grisly variants have been located elsewhere especially by Yvonne Verdier. Here the interpretations have included assumptions that a father was the 'wolf' who raped and murdered his own daughter (Vélay-Vallantin 1998) – part of a generally feminist, anti-clerical, anti-patriarchal, anti-masculine inter-pretation. In some versions the wolf kills and partially eats the grandmother, then causes the girl to eat some of the remains, but the girl escapes by a trick. As Dundes (1989: 207) remarks, 'There is simply no end to the interpretations offered of "Little Red Riding Hood"'. Sometimes the older generation is the victim, sometimes the younger.

Confronted with such variations of structure and meaning, we need not bother with 'authenticity'. Both the general structure and the individual variant of the tale have their own validity. Egbert of Liège might have been surprised by the seventeenth-century version and its interpretation, but they are clearly related. What we have in this and virtually all fairy tales, whether oral or literary, is not one single core but a family of stories, some related more closely than others, some of the others being quite remote cousins and second cousins. Like all analogies this has its dangers in that it may wrongly suggest the existence of an 'authentic' parent-version, and thus promote value judgements privileging a supposed relation to the 'original'. Such ideas should be aban-doned.

However, we may draw some broad distinctions between mainly oral and mainly literary versions of fairy tales. In oral versions there is no single author, though a well-known teller in a settled community may have a recognisable style. The literary version, of which Angela Carter is the leading modern example, has an even more marked quality of personal authorship. But, as research has proceeded on the work of Perrault and the Grimm Brothers, it becomes clear that they too impressed their own attitude and styles on the stories they told, or rather retold, modifying them to suit the audience they had in mind. And then their tales often re-entered oral traditions. But though they have so many variations, the specific tales retain certain general patterns and an underlying structure, usually with stereotyped characters, an internal logic which is not that of the realistic novel.

While total distinction between oral and literary versions of fairy tale can be abandoned as a distraction, the defining qualities of fairy tales when told as such are to be discovered in their oral roots (much the same could be said of Shakespeare's plays). In subject matter most fairy tales, as opposed to other oral folktales, deal with some aspect of maturation of the individual, involving a 'transgression' and some appeal to the 'marvellous', giving imaginative pleasure, often wish fulfilment (Warner 1994: 25). Maturation may have originally been marked by initiation rites involving some testing, perhaps painful, experience, as some scholars believe. Although such ritual may have largely disappeared, though schools, factories, religions, etc. may retain traces, the underlying notion of maturation, powerful and widespread, certainly remains active. Nor is it 'reductive' to recognise such a general characteristic as common to many stories which work out this interesting and universal process in such a variety of ways. In style the stories are characterised by repetition with variation, told to an expectant familiar community by both good and bad storytellers, most of whom will already know at least one version of the story that is to be told.

We can normally come only indirectly at the oral root of fairy tale by necessarily literary study. Some early collectors were conscious of the problem of identifying orality, particularly the great J. F. Campbell in the Highlands. In more recent times Falassi (1980) has given a valuable account from modern Tuscany, where genuine peasant communities continued to exist until the 1970s or even later (as the present writer can testify), just as similar personal experience can testify to the survival of the Gaelic *ceilidh* in the remoter corners of Galway in the late 1940s. The notion of a 'peasant oral community' does not in the least suggest deficiencies of organisation or intelligence, nor imply illiteracy, but means a lively oral culture, a closely linked community where people have known each other for a long time, and which has long survived, barely touched by industrialisation.[1]

Falassi gives an admirable account of the rich complexity of the evening gatherings in such a community as late as the 1970s which included old and young and much varied talk and song, including stories. The range goes far beyond the fairy tales which are the subject here, but it is important to bear the general social context in mind. Falassi (1980: 30–72) also makes the point that fairy stories are not solely for children. He illustrates the interplay between audience and teller, and shows how some of the traditional stories were previously known and others not, though they follow a recognisable pattern.

---

[1] The present writer was first made aware of some forms of continuity in 1944–5 in Tuscany and the Apennines. In the farmhouses, too often alas ruined, which the advancing Allied armies occupied, one could see in the deserted hearths cooking implements identical with those to be seen in Herculaneum, overwhelmed by volcanic mud in the first century AD. In 1970 in a fertile Tuscan valley men were still ploughing with white oxen. All the occupants of the local village and farmhouses scattered over the hills within easy walking distance knew each other and were often related. In the local cemetery on the hill half the surnames seemed to be the same. The air was clear and quiet. An elderly peasant friend whom I asked about the *veglie*, the Tuscan evening gatherings recorded by Falassi, told me how enjoyable they were, though he emphasised the dancing rather than the storytelling. During the day, he said, in the twenties, the valley was full of singing. (See Falassi (1980: 110) on further social implications of this.) Radio and television finished that. My old friend and his wife in more recent times spent the evening with the television set turned on loud and even conversation was virtually impossible. In the summer of 1948, during a couple of months on the coast of Galway in an isolated cottage, I became aware of a similar community, scattered around Loch Fee, all native Irish speakers though fully bilingual who held an occasional *ceilidh* in the evening entirely in Irish. Kenneth Jackson had considerable experience of such occasions on the West coast of Ireland (Jackson 1961). But even in modern days some stable groups may develop their own personal 'folklore', e.g. large families, groups of soldiers serving a long time together, even colleges and companies, given appropriate community and continuity.

The fairy story has a moral and a clearly symbolic underlying structure. It has a message relating to attitudes maintained between the members of a family (Brewer 1980). In one story, told in 1973 (a variant of 'One-Eye, Two-Eyes, Three-Eyes', AT 511, found in Grimm 1992: 130), recorded by Falassi, the fairy (a beautiful lady) and a goat represent good, maternal figures. An aunt represents the hostile mother figure. Falassi reports the fluidity of the storytelling occasion, the recognition of variants, and at the same time the sense that one story is not another, even when elements of one get mixed with another. 'The deep structural pattern holds, then, while the surface renderings are pleasantly (if conventionally) diverse.' He remarks (1980: 55):

> It is useful to proceed in the investigation in this manner because there is ample testimony from observation that this pattern has a sense of the real with the Tuscan storyteller. On one of many such occasions three versions of the story were told by three different people, one the kind of old woman that commonly tells such stories, one an old man, and finally the grandchild of the woman who in fact was the hostess for the occasion. What was both significant and amusing in this narrative situation was that the child was able, through adept maneuvering, to tell the story more successfully than his grandmother.

Many other aspects are made clear by Falassi that are important in interpretation of fairy tales. The identification, in certain circumstances, of the teller with some character in the tale is clear. So is the symbolisation of what I called, in a book that appeared in the same year as Falassi's, 'the family drama' (Brewer 1980). On this same question of symbolism Falassi has further valuable remarks especially concerning riddles, which are closely connected with traditional storytelling. Many of the riddles told are jesting and have a sexual as well as non-sexual meaning. The sexual element is regarded as improper and not to be spoken of publicly, but of course everybody, even quite young children, realises it is there. The joke is either to trap someone into blurting out publicly what is normally private, or to be able to refer publicly and decently to what everybody knows has a private sexual meaning. The point is that the sexual meaning is fully conscious, though expression of it would offend social decorum. There is no suppressed unconscious knowledge in a Freudian sense which distorts or disturbs the personality, occasions 'anxiety', needs 'counselling' or psychoanalysis in order to be freed and discovered. Decorous expression of what is indecorous yet important is always interesting, sometimes amusing. A similar situation obtains with the underlying symbolic structure of fairy tales, well understood though implicit, and not psychopathic. The Opies claim that the perception of perfectly normal emotional tensions expressed in the explicit and implicit structures of fairy tale implies the belief, on the interpreters' part, that the tales are 'the product of psychological difficulties, and particularly, need it be added, of complexes that are sexual'; but this is to confuse such perceptions with the wilder shores of psycho-analytical theory, very comprehensively attacked in the latter part of the twentieth century by Webster (1995), Gellner (1985) and others. The Opies favour the view that no great significance has been seen in fairy tales in the past thousand years and that the only motive for telling them was for 'wonder and entertainment' (1974: 18), but the nature and sources of wonder and entertainment deserve study as much as any other aspect of human nature. Elsewhere the Opies remark more perceptively that 'Perhaps, after all, fairy tales are to be numbered amongst the most philosophic tales there are' (1974: 12).

That literacy and orality have long gone hand in hand in narrating the fairy tale is shown by the difficulty of classifying the story of 'Cupid and Psyche' by Apuleius as a very early fairy tale of the second century AD. In fact, although this story has many fairy-tale elements and is the probable ancestor of many derivative versions, it is not quite a true fairy tale. It is relatively long, written by a known author in an elaborate personalised style, with some attempt at personal characterisation of the heroine. These are not the characteristics of the typical fairy tale. Yet in 'Cupid and Psyche' the protagonist, in this case a girl, is the youngest of three daughters. Her older sisters are unkind to her. She herself is the most beautiful girl in the world, which is typical of the hyperbolical description of the heroine. The defining marvel is that she is swept off to a most beautiful hidden palace where she is served in all richness by unseen servants. A wonderful husband comes at night, whom she is forbidden to see but who is very loving. Her typically jealous siblings encourage her to transgress and break the interdiction by inflaming her curiosity. Having discovered that her husband is the beautiful young god Cupid, Psyche is banned from her home to wander the world to seek him, a kind of fairy-tale quest. Cupid's mother, Venus, appears in the mythologically unusual but typically fairy-tale role of the older woman hostile to the younger one. Venus sets Psyche apparently impossible tasks which she performs with the aid of creatures – ants, a reed, and an eagle (nature is usually on the side of the good and beautiful heroine) though in the last test, in a visit to the underworld, her fatal curiosity again very nearly leads to her destruction. Thus she is tested in a typically fairy-tale fashion. She is saved at last by Cupid himself. Jupiter, by a comically cynical device, decides that Cupid is such a nuisance that since he loves the girl he had better be tied down by being married to her. This view of marriage is at odds with the fairy tale ethos, though not with the ethos of many a folktale, which can be cynical, comic or tragic about marriage, but the underlying structure, whereby the heroine gets her man in the end and lives happily, is entirely typical.

The foregoing analysis illustrates a crucial characteristic of the fairy tale, and of folktale of which it is part. There is a general structure of the story: falling in love, a wonderful palace, a broken interdiction, a quest by the lover for her beloved, tests of persistence and endurance, magic helpers, a happy ending in marriage. All these, granted their fanciful hyperbole, are deeply rooted in the ordinary desires of ordinary people, and while specifically referring to that crucial passage in our lives from adolescence to young maturity, from singleness to union with another person of the opposite sex, including the start of a family, are easily foreseen by younger persons and reviewed with interest by the old. An interesting comparison between ancient and modern is offered by C. S. Lewis's retelling of the story of Psyche in *Till We Have Faces* (1956), in the form of a historical novel told by the Psyche figure. Although the wonders remain, they are rationalised and given a realistic but fictional setting. It is an excellent but not a great novel.

Apuleius' story reflects a very general structure of both life and the fairy tale. There is a female protagonist, a husband known and not known, a particular kind of interdiction with appropriate transgression. It shares many characteristics with other tales, but whether these came from any original tale is not a useful enquiry, because the evidence does not exist. It is enough that such tales can be grouped together at various levels of generalisation for the purpose of understanding, whether or not they are found in different languages and periods, are closer or further from the generic pattern. For some types of examination and discussion it may be useful to group many variants together: for others it will be useful to concentrate on single versions.

It is of course the 'tale type', the grouping of variants of recognisable versions of (more or less) the same general tale that is the subject of the great listing in *The Types of the Folktale*, where the story of 'Cupid and Psyche' is AT 425A, associated with AT 425B-P, a pretty example of the protean nature of the fairy tale and folktale in general. Along with the general types of the folktale go the readily observable recurrent motifs which are so to say the building blocks used to fill in the frames, listed in Thompson 1966. Motifs are highly significant for the study and theory of folktale and fairy tale because they are in their nature very different from the printed nineteenth- and twentieth-century literature which is the normal subject of literary theory. The *Types* are fluid but generally distinguishable. The *Motifs* are specific, but not tied to any particular tale, though obviously more suitable for some than for others. Obvious motifs in the story of Cupid and Psyche are the girl on the quest for her husband, the helpful animals and the envious sisters, which occur in many different fairy tales. Any reader of folk- and fairy tales recognises with pleasure these and many other old friends, which in their variety are used in many different stories. Lest this frequency and multiplicity of use of the same motif, so contrary to modern notions (though unavoidable even in the practice, if not the theory, of the modern novel) be thought to derogate from the authenticity of great literature, it should be remembered that until the seventeenth century such repetition was normal, and Homer, the Bible, the great Arthurian romances, Chaucer, and not least Shakespeare, all make use of known tale types and motifs. In English, to take specific examples nearest home, Chaucer and Shakespeare are grounded in the oral practices and themes of folktale and fairy tale for all their unquestionable literacy. Among later writers Dickens is notable for the large number of his references to, and certain similarities with, fairy tale. The oral origin of fairy tale determines its nature even after it becomes heavily modified in later practice. An illuminating anecdote was told to the present writer some years ago by the notable poet and student of gypsy lore, Hamish Henderson, who spent some time living with 'the travelling folk' who in Scotland had at that time retained their traditional Romany culture. From their camp they would go into the neighbouring town to sell such small items as clothes pegs, or with a store of traditional songs and stories which they would exchange with their customers. Without losing hold of their traditional narrative store, some of them became quite sophisticated collectors and would occasionally come back to tell him that they had 'heard a most interesting variant of Aarne–Thompson Number so-and-so today'. So much for the purity of oral tradition, but also its strength.

The massive 1987 work by Bengt Holbek emphasises the importance for scientific study of fairy tales of knowing the actual words, who is the performer, and what were the circumstances of delivery. Holbek begins from the scrupulous early recordings of the Danish teacher Evald Tang Kristensen (b. 1843), referred to as ETK. Although so long a study as Holbek's inevitably produces some self-contradictory statements it is a foundation work for further study of interpretation, covering all modern schools. ETK collected from poor country people in Denmark in the middle of the nineteenth century, when there was widespread distrust of folk- and fairy tales by the prosperous farmers, the Christian fundamentalists and some of the more-or-less educated readers. ETK's findings are of great interest, though not always widely applicable or unquestionable. He testifies to the oral nature of the tales and to the adult nature of the tellers but also to their childlike quality of mind, and there is some emphasis on children as audience. The proportion of 'carriers' of tales to passive listeners was small. Before he became known, more men told him tales than women; later more women than men, but whereas all age groups were involved in listening, the proportions of young to old and men to women varied from area to area. Considerable variation was found in the telling of what were nevertheless obviously the same tales. ETK found, as other collectors have, that the narrator to some extent identified him or herself with the protagonist (and here gender lines are easily crossed: for example, males can easily identify with Cinderella). The stories arose out of experiences and aspirations of the poor, but the defining point of the story was 'the marvellous'. Some people even believed that the fairy tale was true. In any case it provided an imaginative release, a make-believe universe, a part of day-dreaming of what might be so. The marvellous was obviously symbolic, and interpretation was variable but not mysterious.

Holbek believed, like many folklorists, that literary art is different from folktale, but here the arguments of Lüthi are stronger. The art of folk- and fairy tale is different, and not all tellers have the same degree of skill, but it is absurd to deny artistry to a well-told tale, even if the artistry is of a different nature from, for example, that of the novel. Holbek later (1987: 255) more justly claims that fairy tale is an art cultivated by the poor, dismissing the older theories that sought the origin and ultimate meaning of fairy tales in solar or other myths. While emphasising the part played by adults he argues that fairy tales have been regarded as nursery tales since antiquity, as 'old wives tales' for the children (1987: 230), while remarking that fairy tales are virtually absent from Classical and early medieval cultures. Here, however, he ignores not only 'Cupid and Psyche' but also many narratives incorporated in medieval romances and chronicles, and the kind of folklore that Shakespeare and even Chaucer drew upon, as well as the kind of evidence presented by Anderson in Chapter Five below. Holbek comments that one important aspect of the fairy tale, less often noticed, is the ability to make people laugh; the classic case is Simpleton or Dummling, the hero of the story of the 'Golden Goose' (Grimm 1992: 64; AT 571; also AT 425F where a princess is made to laugh, and AT 559).

In addition it may be noted that a number of fairy tales, notably those whose hero is a 'little tailor', are designed to make us laugh, though that does not deprive them of other fairy-tale moral messages.

The avalanche of Jungian and Freudian studies which offer psychoanalytical interpretations such as Dundes gives for 'Cinderella' (1989: 192–236) is repudiated by Holbek with some exasperation, but a useful summary of such interpretations of 'Cinderella' is given by Dundes (1989: 192–236). In opposition to such as Dundes, who is our leading exponent of psychoanalytical interpretations, Robert Darnton (1984) gives a scornful account of the psychoanalyst Erich Fromm's interpretation of 'Little Red Riding Hood', claiming that most of the details on which Fromm bases his interpretation do not exist. They may be absent from some versions but they are certainly present in others, notably the red cloak. No doubt Fromm should have made clear what version or versions he was working from, but he was not inventing them. Whether one agrees with his interpretation is another matter. The paradox here, as elsewhere, is that just as every retelling is an interpretation, so every interpretation becomes a retelling. The popularity of Bettelheim's book, whatever reservations one may have about the 'truth' of his interpretation, shows that he is at least a fine re-creator of the old stories. Egbert of Liège might even have agreed with Fromm and Bettelheim, for all three are firm believers in the symbolic importance of the red cloak.

Like many folklorists who deny literary interpretations, Holbek rejects the notion that a story may have several symbolic meanings, or several 'layers' of meaning, as the present writer claims (Brewer 1980: 24). At the same time Holbek (1987: 269–76) admits the usefulness of analysing characters in terms of the 'split', 'doubling', 'projection' (the function of one character represented in two figures, other characters representing what are in essence attitudes of the protagonist), and the family drama, which he condemns in Brewer 1980 – an interesting, if unconscious, conversion. Such analysis need not prevent us from rejecting some interpretations, whether 'psychological' or 'psychoanalytical' (the two terms are often confused) as wrong. Holbek (1987: 288) refers to 'the problems of adolescence and maturation so tangibly [sic] present in countless fairy tales' but he declares quite remarkably that they have all but escaped the notice of scholars, thus ignoring the work of Wilson (1976), Bettelheim (1976), Brewer (1980) and others, though it may be agreed that these concentrate on the fairy tale as a guide to growing up and pay too little attention to fairy tales dealing with other needs such as obtaining food and drink, and outwitting others.

Holbek rightly argues that all crises and conflicts of adolescence cannot be analysed in the framework of the Oedipus pattern and then reiterates his condemnation of 'the persistent misapprehension that fairy tales are literature for children'. The truth is that historically fairy tales are for both old and young. They are not a release from what would otherwise be unrecognised repression, and the literal surface meaning does not obscure further symbolic meanings. In any case the desire for riches, or a beautiful wife or handsome husband, expressed in fairy tales, is perfectly, literally, normal and commonplace, though such desires may be hyperbolically expressed in the tales. At the same time there are marvels and puzzles. A golden goose is an obvious marvel, not in nature, and how does a golden goose get to be in a tree before it is felled? Why do all sorts of people stick to it?[2] One of the arguments against interpretation is that 'it takes the magic out of mystery', and is 'reductive' – a frequent accusation, but for many people the charm of a puzzle depends on finding a solution, and explanations of further significance may enrich the marvel. Part of the charm of the goose is its farmyard commonplaceness, and to describe it as golden is symbolically to express its value. No mechanistic explanation of how it got into the tree is expected, nor any psychoanalytical demythologisation either. It remains a piquant image, a brilliant invention, an index of the riches that may be found in simple life in the tasks done by good-hearted young persons. It is a 'marvel' within the commonplace. When the story tells how so many usually respectable people reveal their greed or interfering nature by sticking either to the golden goose or to those already caught, it effectively ridicules them by creating such a comic marvel. Dummling, it should be noted, holds, but is not stuck to, the goose. Dummling, the previously downtrodden but kindly boy, is revealed as the hero who discovers the golden goose, values it, but is prepared to make a present of it, and is not greedy. The incongruous cluster of respectable people pulled along by the hero is a comic image of universal greed, enough to make the princess laugh, and laughter means that *joie de vivre* is returned to her. That the hero wins the princess is poetic justice. The tale is sufficiently fantastic to make no demands on belief, nor to constitute a promise that if you are kind and generous, as Dummling was to the unknown little old man at the beginning, you will inevitably be rewarded. But it is a truth, dare one say, that disinterested kindness and generosity are often rewarded, if only by internal satisfaction, and communities, like individuals, do well to foster goodness and kindness. One feels not only amused but the better for reading or hearing this story.

Holbek's solid basis in ETK's records, based on communities which were mostly poor and whose tales both reflected and offered compensation for their hard lot, cannot but remind one of that other set of documents primarily directed to similar communities – the New Testament. The fairy tales are in no sense religious or specifically Christian, but the same recognition of the harshness of life and the need for patience and goodness is explicit in the New Testament. 'We know that the whole creation groaneth and travaileth in pain together until now' (Romans 8: 22); 'For we are saved by hope' (Romans 8: 24); 'be clothed with humility, for God resisteth the proud, and giveth grace to the humble. Humble yourselves therefore under the mighty hand of God, that he may exalt you in due time' (I Peter 5: 5–6); while 'your adversary the devil, as a roaring lion [or as it might be, a wolf] walketh about seeking whom he may devour' (I Peter 5: 8); 'give, and it shall be given unto you, good measure, pressed down, and shaken together, and running over' (Luke 6: 38). These are fairy-tale themes too. In the Bible, as in fairy tales, royalty is a powerful image, and the good but ordinary person may take on royal status. There is also a central marvel, the Resurrection, as well as the miracles in both Testaments. In the Old Testament are similar stories with similar messages. Such moralities are

---

[2] A motif that is found elsewhere in folktale, e.g. 'The Tale of the Basin', AT 571A; cf. Brewer (1996: 55–8), there called more appropriately the tale of the pot – i.e. 'chamber-pot'.

not peculiar to Christians or Jews. They are common to poor agrarian communities the world over. Fairy tales are not Christian documents but many of their practical moralities coincide. The success of tricksters is more common in fairy tales, like Jack of 'Jack and the Beanstalk', but there are also successful tricksters like Jacob, David and Samson in the Old Testament. The heavenly rewards and the revelry of fairy tales occur in this world, not the next. But here we have a common quality of imagination. The immediate meaning of biblical stories is clear, but they are rich in further depths of meaning. The biblical stories, even the synoptic gospels, Matthew, Mark and Luke, like fairy tales, existed originally in oral form, transmitted by memory, and were then committed to writing, sometimes in variant versions, but with an identifiable core (Brewer, 1979).

The survival of a story orally delivered depends on the memory of the audience. It does not seem that folktales, including fairy tales, are memorised in verbal detail but according as they deal with matters of concern to the community, and in terms of stereotyped characters and narrative patterns. The pattern has its own internal logic which does not necessarily depend on material probability or a plot with strict cause and effect, as does the novel, at least in theory. The general pattern must satisfy the common desire for a marvel and a satisfactory outcome such as has been suggested above. In structural terms the most ambitious attempt at interpretation has been the analysis by V. Propp, *The Morphology of the Folktale*. This extremely influential work, based on a hundred arbitrarily selected Russian folktales, argues that there is a general narrative structure in all tales, expressed in terms of a logical sequence of functions. The functions may be expressed in many different ways, and it is claimed that they always follow in the same order, though not every function is always present. Almost all fairy tales begin with the protagonist experiencing 'a lack' and the course of the story is the liquidation of the 'lack'. The 'lack' may be one of status, like that of Cinderella. As an example of a function, the protagonist may come to a palace, or it may be a house, or a hovel, or even an empty glade in the forest. Some modifications of Propp's general formalist theory may be made, but its great value is as further illustration of the strong form of fairy tales underlying, but not reductively, the multiplicity of optional details. In the main stories a 'self-correcting tendency' has been observed amongst variants, and that in turn depends on strong stereotypes which in some way correspond to deep human needs. Such a view is nowadays challenged. Even our deepest needs are seen by some modern scholars as 'socially constructed' and the latest versions of fairy tales are indeed often so different from the traditional ones that we may have reached the end of the traditional road. Only time will tell. It may be that the latest forms of fairy tale will indeed fulfil the same social purpose as earlier fairy tales in teaching lessons, in meeting specific needs and urging socially acceptable solutions, but the personal needs and social constructs may be different. Maybe we shall see a homosexual young man setting out on a quest for his homosexual friend (a different matter from male or female comradeship), or a woman asserting her right to be a single mother. Some of the tales of brother love could be twisted, and Cinderella might successfully divorce her prince.

One aspect of the traditional tale which may well endure is the convention that the protagonist will transgress some interdiction, and by so doing find success. This may even be true of Psyche who, in a sense, had only half a marriage until she transgressed the interdiction on looking at her husband. She then had to undergo many painful trials but ended, according to Apuleius, as an immortal, enjoying a life of marriage and eternal pleasure – indeed, the name of her child is Pleasure. Bluebeard's wives transgress his interdiction to look into the 'bloody chamber' with less success. In the traditional version the last bride, though she escapes with her life, merely returns to her home. In the most modern version, however, by Angela Carter, she comes to a very satisfactory conclusion. Her mother, not her brothers, kills Bluebeard with a pistol (a 'pistol-packing momma' as an old song had it) and she ends possessing his wealth and a gentle docile blind husband. Blindness may be an image of sexual impotence and this is a feminist version, a revenge, or a 'disarming' of male sexuality. Interdictions, like a 'lack', are all part of life for everyone and fairy tales offer conveniently fictional models of how to deal with them.

The oral origin and conditioning of fairy tales make them a social phenom-enon, a shared experience, even today. They are thus conditioned by the norms of the society in which they are told, although experience shows that some ancient forms of society and ancient needs may persist remarkably to the modern day. Any modern reader of the Grimms' collection will notice how important is the subject of food (magic tables and the like), how ever-present is the forest, how far it is necessary to walk, and the passion to have children. The implicit model of agrarian society still offers plenty of scope for the expression of human needs. The nuclear family is the cast of the dramas, with the constant need of the young to go outside it to find themselves and a mate.

These general aspects and many motifs are unquestionably ancient in Euro-pean society and, as the story of Cinderella shows, are widespread throughout the world. It is now possible to summarise some of the general characteristics of the fairy tale as arising from its oral origins. In the words of Holbek, no friend to symbolic interpretation, 'Innumerable fairy tales tell us this: the human qualities of the poor and lowly are their secret powers with which all obstacles are overcome' (1987: 516). One may further add that kindness to the poor, the old, the ugly and to animals is seen as a strength. The 'passivity' of heroines, often complained about, is also a form of power. A fairy tale is likely to present the maturation of the protagonist, with whom both teller and audience tend to identify. It turns on some marvellous incident, or discovery, or gift, or information. It deals in stereotyped generalities of old and young, often implying if not revealing generational conflict. Some interdiction is often infringed, leading, though perhaps through suffering, to greater good. Many incidents are susceptible of symbolic, though not particularly mysterious, interpretation, and general sexual symbolisation. In the story of 'The Frog King', to take an obvious example (AT 440), the frog represents the repellent aspects of sexuality and the reconciling effect of love – a message similar to that of the many versions of 'Beauty and the Beast' (AT 435C). It should be repeated that such interpretations are not reductive but explanatory, relying on the fairy tale, whose narrative power beautifies and gives interest and significance to what is in itself a platitude, while the proposition's presence gives strength to the fairy tale. Nor, as Holbek points out, is symbolic meaning necessarily unconscious (1987: 580). That is one of its values. Holbek, like Falassi, rightly argues that such sexual symbolism is well understood by narrators of fairy tales (1987: 519, 521) and undoubtedly by their hearers too, and such symbolism preserves decorum and privacy.

The stereotyped characters in these tales may most usefully be regarded, from the point of view of interpretation, as projections of feelings and attitudes in the protagonist's mind (Holbek 1987: 441). Yet of course the action depends on externalisation. Although when the story is of the winning of wife or husband, the desired image may be thought to be produced within the protagonist's mind, that limitation is not what the hearer or reader should feel. The fairy story is not a solipsistic day dream, but represents a real reaching out to the external world, and to some Other (Brewer 1980: 8–11). There is a long proverbial tradition to the effect that 'if wishes were horses, beggars would ride', firmly expressing the uselessness of daydreaming in contrast to vigorous action, and clearly there is sense in this. Freud regarded daydreaming as an expression of frustration and weakness, and it may well be an expression of deprivation and lack of power, especially in the poor, as Holbek remarks. But the popularity of fairy tale, with its frequent expression of wish fulfilment (which has so often led to the condemnation of fairy tales, romance, and, when they developed, novels), reflects a deeper imaginative need, and a deeper hope. More modern scientific investigation of the working of the mind shows that daydreaming is a common human characteristic and that in many cases it strengthens the imagination, creating positive mental images, leading to more general activity. While daydreaming may be merely compensatory, or even a distraction from the necessary task in hand, it is also a valuable imaginative and intellectual resource, and the tales are not *merely* escapist. Rabkin points out (1976: 59):

> In both 'Red Riding Hood' and 'Briar Rose' we have seen that a fantastic world, a world apparently offering an escape from our own, really speaks directly to us. By making a fantastic reversal of the rules of our world and offering an ordered world, fears of maturation can be met and symbolically tamed. This quite serious purpose of escape literature is accomplished by a well-defined and highly predictive structure in cooperation with a conventional and stable style that signals the presence of the structure.

The role of daydreaming as exploring the future, elaborating the sense of possibility, has been extensively demonstrated (Singer 1981). Imaginative stories make children more imaginative, and children with low fantasy levels are less imaginative in responses to new situations and people, and are more aggressive (Singer 1981: 142–3). The importance of the projection of future possibilities in stories explains why very small children can be absorbed in, learn from, and understand, through fantasy, such real-life situations that arise in later years, as desires for food, wealth, adventure, companionship, family relations and conflicts – what Rabkin calls 'forward memory' (Rabkin 1976: 52). Such major authorities as Lüthi (1984) and Bettelheim (1976) extensively illustrate the strengthening of the imagination and of the psyche to be found in fairy tales. The specialist in the development of the child's mind, J. Piaget, claimed that the use of fantasy is to develop the child's cognitive processes by accommodation and assimilation to the structures of social reality (Singer 1981: 129).

For most fairy tales the core of what is explored is what I have called in the past the 'family drama', which is not itself a plot, but a variable structure of personal relationships through which the specific narrative weaves its way (Brewer 1980). The essential characters are the protagonist and his or her projections on parent-figures, themselves often split into, for example, good but weak father, with bad but strong wife – a stepmother, or alternatively a strong but bad father figure (he wants to marry his daughter which she does not want). Some characters are doubled, notably sibling-figures, the two ugly sisters of Cinderella being obvious examples. Within the category of doubling may be included helpful animals who obviously play the part of missing kind parent-figures. On the other hand, dragons, ogres, giants may be easily envisaged, when the protagonist is male, as hostile father figures, usually dealt with relatively easily, like the giant in 'Puss-in-Boots' (AT 545B). It should be unnecessary to add that there is no need to envisage a Freudian Oedipal complex here. Within the style of narration of these tales, based on reality but not realistically conducted, we find hyperbole, exaggeration, and repetition usually in threes, while space and time may be contracted. In a fairy tale a protagonist may serve for seven years, as Jacob first served for Leah and then for Rachel, and yet be essentially unchanged, while distance is no problem.

As works of art, fairy tales may sustain different interpretations, especially as they change in interaction with new narrators, new audiences/readers, new social circumstances. Though 'the family drama' may be the setting or background or field of action for most, there are many varieties even of that, according as the protagonist is male or female. For example, a variety of patterns have been found within the subgroup called by Heda Jason 'The Reward-and-Punishment Fairy Tale', which comprises such tales as 'Ali Baba and the Forty Thieves' (AT 676), 'The Kind and Unkind Girls' (AT 480), 'Truth and Falsehood' (AT 613) and 'The Table and the Ass and the Stick' (AT 563). She states in her preface: 'All the texts used as examples have been recorded from Jews who immigrated to Israel from Muslim countries' so there is no problem of Euro-centred ethnicity here, and the tales range in origin from Morocco to Afghanistan and the Caucasus to Yemen. Yet they possess a remarkable stability. Jason follows others in distinguishing various subgenres according to the gender of the protagonist and reveals in detail various kinds of meaning in the different kinds of tale. By so demonstrating the variety and complexity of patterns, as of complex Indian carpets, magic carpets indeed, appreciation and understanding are enhanced.

At the other extreme from such specialist analyses, it must not be forgotten that each retelling by each individual narrator is also an interpretation. There is plenty of evidence, for instance from Campbell (1860) and Philip (1992: xxii) who quotes the collector William Bottrell, and also from Falassi (1980), and A. B. Lord (1960), to show that individual narrators may think they are faithfully reproducing what they have heard, but they are not quite doing so. They are also using their own characteristic style. In this respect modern retellers like Calvino (1982), who, in his excellent introduction, explains his own methods of repeating and changing the traditional folktales of Italy, and even modern rewriters of the nineteenth and late twentieth century are only continuing, if in a more self-conscious form, a natural practice.

The apprehension in fairy tales of possibilities and fears in a mysterious world, which witness to the ineluctable optimism and anxieties of the human race, leads us to suppose on *a priori* grounds that something like fairy tales has always been a characteristic of human storytelling. Their general resemblance to, though not their identity with, myths is obvious, though the notion that they are the product of fragmented or decayed myths has long been abandoned. We receive them as once embedded in a traditional peasant culture, but surely previous nomads, and hunter-gatherers, had related imaginative needs and expressions, as we have. Traditional peasant culture has now virtually disappeared in West Europe and North America but we can trace the elements far back. 'Cupid and Psyche' has already been mentioned. Not strictly a fairy tale, it has many fairy-tale motifs. The same is true of medieval romance, with its close alliance to folktale and fairy tale in particular. The habits of mind developed in reading fairy tales and folktales are a far better preparation for reading Shakespeare than any amount of historical and social background.

England is notable in contrast with Ireland, Scotland, and the rest of Europe for the relative absence of fairy tales since the seventeenth century (but see Briggs 1970 and Philip 1992). There must have been some tales like fairy tales in English in the Middle Ages. Romances have close affinities with fairy tales, deserving more investigation than can be given here, but they were in most cases fairly directly derived from French sources. Chaucer offers an interesting test case and perhaps an early example of why fairy tales did not flourish in England. It is clear from his early works that Chaucer was much influenced by the earlier vernacular English romances, but the nearest he comes to them, and fairy tale, in his maturity is the brilliant parody 'Sir Thopas', where the hero, a milksop of a knight, has had a dream-vision of an 'elf-queen' whom he seeks to find. There is a trace of fairy tale in 'The Wife of Bath's Tale'. In this story the hero transgresses at the beginning by raping a country girl and is then condemned to death. (This is harsher than fairy tale as we know it now, but earlier forms of modern tales, such as 'Little Red Riding Hood' have some savage elements. The kiss with which the prince awakes the princess in 'The Sleeping Beauty' seems, in the earliest version, to have been a rape while she was still asleep. Two children are born and subject to gruesome ill-treatment, as we can deduce from the French romance *Perceforest*.) In 'The Wife of Bath's Tale' Chaucer satirically remarks at the beginning that while in the days of King Arthur

> Al was this land fulfild of fayerye.
> The elf-queene, with hir joly compaignye
> Daunced ful ofte in many a grene mede.
> This was the olde opinion as I rede:
> I speke of manye hundred yeres ago.
> But now kan no man se none elves mo . . .
> [the land is full of friars, etc.]
> This maketh that ther ben no fayeryes . . .
>
> (*The Canterbury Tales* III, 857–72)

There are no fairies in fourteenth-century England, says Chaucer, and perhaps implies no fairy tales. In the tale the knight, who can only escape death by finding out what women want most, after many failures, then has a glimpse of four-and-twenty ladies dancing 'under a forest side'. They disappear, leaving only a hideous old woman. The knight has to marry her to find the correct answer (which in modern terms is 'power') and she turns into a beautiful young woman and true wife. It is too sophisticated a story to count as a proper fairy tale and the sceptical Chaucer puts the fairy-tale magic in this tale 'many hundred years ago'. The contemporary author of *Sir Gawain and the Green Knight*, however, has more feeling for magic. He tells of a threateningly giant knight who is clearly a fairy-tale father figure. There is a seductive young lady, and a beheading test for the young hero Gawain. Again this is too sophisticated a narrative to be a true fairy tale, but it has close affinities (Brewer 1980). Only in the Elizabethan period do we find a few more traces of fairy tale. *A Midsummer Night's Dream* is the obvious example, but clear traces of fairy-tale structure underlie the late romances, *The Winter's Tale*, *Cymbeline*, *The Tempest*, while *King Lear* has been shown to be a special form of *Cinderella*, where the heroine is so to say displaced by the father.

A few years later both Milton (*Paradise Lost* I, 781–9, and *L'Allegro*, 101–15) and Herrick (*Hesperides*, 1648) show traces of knowledge about fairy tales, or at least, tales about fairies, but the clearest, while at the same time the most muddled, evidence of still surviving fairy tales in the Elizabethan period is in the curious jumble attributed to George Peele, *The Old Wives Tale* (Peele 1980). Peele (1556–96) was an educated man, taking his B.A. from Christ Church, Oxford, versatile and fluent in courtly plays, poems, and, it seems, in jesting, though the jest-book 'biography' *The Merry Conceited Jests of George Peele* (1607) is a collection of commonplace jests with no biographical likelihood. The latest editor of *The Old Wives Tale* believes it to be by Peele but after all the learned discussion the attribution is uncertain. Its date is probably 1593, and that date suggests as does Shakespeare's work, the familiarity of educated and courtly writers of that time with folklore, modified if not destroyed, in the seventeenth and eighteenth centuries. The play is full of fairy-tale themes. It is based, in so far as it has any coherent structure, on the type of the Grateful Dead (AT 505) in which a dead man as a ghost helps someone who has taken pity on his unburied body and buried it, but there are many other fragments from widespread tales. We have references to a story of a giant and a king's daughter (90–3) which, one character declares, would have drawn him a mile when he was a child, and traditional references, as in the title, to an old woman's tale-telling. The characters in her tale actually come alive on the stage – an interesting representation of the audience's vivid realisation of stories. We have 'Jack the Giant Killer', a magic table (AT 563), the Water of Life included in the search for the Golden Bird (AT 550) (which the text sometimes confuses with a Golden Beard), and 'Three Heads in the Well', a version of the kind and unkind girls (AT 403). All this is jumbled up with pastoral episodes, late medieval romance material and low level classical references. The whole play seems to have been thrown off as a light-hearted collection of whatever came into Peele's mind, and not a serious parody. From our present point of view the tale is a fascinating but frustrating glimpse of the wealth of earlier English fairy tale, presumably killed off by the Puritanical religion and pragmatic empiricism which became the dominant cultural forces in the seventeenth century, to make a tentative return via the French in the eighteenth century and via German in the nineteenth.

Conclusion

The general message of fairy tales which distinguishes them from most other narratives has been eloquently proclaimed by Jack Zipes (1991, 2000) in two admirable introductions to substantial anthologies. They are about growing up, finding independence and success in society. They are important instruments in 'the civilising process' because they are entertaining, variable, yet instructive. They give messages of hope, encouragement to effort, and express the ultimate goodness of life. The prevalence of the image of royalty imparts a glow, a sense of self-worth, respect for others, traditionally symbolised by royalty, whatever may be the shortcomings of actual regal persons. The fairy tale starts from the ordinariness, dullness and hardness of daily life and shows how it may be transformed. It is so far from being escapist that what is evil or hostile is represented in exaggerated or 'supernatural' forms, as witches, giants, monsters, but the protagonists may receive help from equivalent supporters, talking animals, magic gifts, etc., and in the end bravely overcome difficulties. The general pattern may be summed up as showing how the protagonist, boy or girl, usually by showing kindness, quickwittedness, endurance, grows to adulthood and achieves a mate. This, after all is what most people hope and expect from life and do to some extent achieve. It is easy to see the attraction of such lively poetic models of what is for most people an often dull workaday life. The fairy story plays a bright light on the real poetry of ordinary existence, too often dulled by use or suffering. It is also easy to see why some people despise fairy stories as being escapist or weak. 'Ours is essentially a tragic age' as D. H. Lawrence writes in the rarely noticed first sentence of *Lady Chatterley's Lover*; though this novel is in essence a fairy story about a poor boy who against all the odds, and in circumstances of high improbability, wins a kind of princess.

What happens to the fairy story in the late twentieth century has been discussed in the last chapter of this book. As traditionally known, it is usually short, although many longer narratives and later novels are based on essentially fairy story structures (Brewer 1980). The traditional European fairy story is an amalgam of many elements, some of them going back thousands of years, part of the huge body of folktale which is one of the markers of humanity. The fairy tales that we know as such seem mostly to have taken on their present form in the European Middle Ages, conditioned by an agrarian society in which men were dominant, married women's mortality high, and stepmothers common, with the nuclear family the core of society. Resources were limited. The forest had been driven back but remained both a physical and psychological dimension of the village's outer world, dangerous and attractive. Nature was close. Fairy tales evoke an anthropomorphic world where animals both tame and wild may devour or help, and natural objects, even inanimate artefacts may speak. It is a hierarchical society which takes kings and queens, princes and princesses, for granted but kings are seen as heads of households, father-figures who move about the house, and let you in at the front door, while princesses sew their own clothes. There are dangerous people: witches – old women more feared than the much rarer wicked old men – while mature men may be more dangerous to beautiful girls than the young men seen as marriageable princes. Some fairy tales recognise dangers to such an extent as to offer warnings rather than happy endings.

Not every story that has been called a fairy story should rightly be classified so, but strict criteria are impossible. Somewhere in a story should come an interdiction, a transgression and then a turning point resting on some marvellous event or feature which marks the story as in some way out of this ordinary world, yet is desired, and has a kind of truth to some illuminated view of life. Often, though not always, the marvellous event, quality or gift, comes from some normally disregarded or despised person, some poor old man, or disregarded animal, who has been treated with kindness, generosity, gentleness, by the hero or heroine. Rather remarkably, considering the originally peasant background, kindness to animals is a valued quality in fairy tales centuries before the late eighteenth century in England when kindness to animals began to be taught as a human obligation.

From Perrault onwards, reinforced by the brothers Grimm, the fairy tale has also reflected bourgeois conventions and values. These later versions are therefore less coarse, less cruel, more moral than the earlier versions which derived from a lower, harsher social milieu. Following modern intellectual dislike of the *bourgeoisie* Darnton (1984) makes a swingeing attack on the later versions, contrasting them rather too sharply with those derived from the real hardships of the poor in the *Ancien Régime* in France, when the death of children and even child murder was common among the peasantry. Here again, however, we have a confusion about authenticity. Perrault and his successors are no more unfaithful to the stories in adapting them to their social circumstances than were earlier narrators. To take another example, Shakespeare in his late romances uses fairy-tale themes to show the disruption and then the reintegration of a family through three generations, by a transgression followed by one or more marvels expressing forgiveness and love, and the maturation of the young protagonists. This is pure fairy-tale attitude and material, developed with consummate art. It is not surprising that in modern Britain, where the decay of the traditional family structure as a social norm is well advanced, modern versions of fairy tales should illustrate this decay. The fact that modern British fairy tales are often pessimistic may be the result of the decline of the culture and failure of nerve, or perhaps the result of the self-criticism which has always characterised bourgeois culture and has been so important to its success in changing itself and the world.

Whatever the answer, it is plain that there is always a case for interpretation of the fairy tale, and that retellings, which are themselves reinterpretations, along with other interpretations, are likely to flourish for some time yet. Such flourishing is the more likely for some recent developments operating in rather paradoxical combination. One is the growth of 'children's literature', itself a very large body going far beyond fairy tales but which includes many traditional fairy tales either in an earlier or transmogrified modernised form. This development comes from the association of fairy tales with children as audience or readership, despite the reiteration by scholars that fairy tales were not, at least in earlier days, meant specifically for children. Another development compensates for this emphasis on 'children's literature', namely the rewriting, and thus the reinterptretation, of fairy tales quite specifically for modern adults. Many modern versions reverse the traditional values of the fairy tales, for example the traditional, suffering, highly moral heroine may be shown as a manipulative slut etc. Another important development is the serious modern study of fairy tales by expert scholars, some of them mentioned in the present essay, and of which this whole book is an example. Although such study is an international phenomenon, it is right to point out the leading part played by scholars from the USA, such as Dundes and Zipes. To these should be added, because it will be widely used in universities of the USA, *The Classic Fairy Tales*, edited with critical introductions, by Maria Tatar (1999). One general point may be made about such modern studies: they often, implicitly or explicitly, criticise such tale-tellers as Perrault and the Grimm brothers for modifying earlier versions, and especially for being didactic and bourgeois. But of course modern studies are themselves equally didactic and bourgeois. One of the leading characteristics of the bourgeoisie is its capacity for self-criticism and change. Modern critical studies, such as those of Zipes and Tatar, are written to a noticeable political and social agenda, intended to correct earlier interpretations and retellings – for example, to restore the presentation of the active participation of women in versions of stories where it is considered such participation has been suppressed and to promote certain political views. Tatar's book is valuable in selecting six traditional tales and printing a number of historical variants, thus illustrating the variability with which a certain nucleus may be rendered and offering the possibilities of critical comparison. Two modern authors, Hans Andersen and Oscar Wilde, are also presented for critical comparison. Thus fairy tales, and the study of fairy tales, have at least achieved intellectual respectability – a very bourgeois virtue.

References

Aarne, A., and Thompson, S. (1973), *The Types of the Folktale. A Classification and Bibliography*. FFC 184. Helsinki.

Anderson, G. (2000), *Fairy Tale in the Ancient World*. London.

Bell, H. (1896), *Fairy Tale Plays and How to Act Them*. London. ('Red Riding Hood' 91–107)

Bettelheim, B. (1976), *The Uses of Enchantment: The Meaning and Importance of Fairy Tales*. Harmondsworth.

Bottrell, W. (1870–90), *Traditions and Hearthside Stories of West Cornwall*, 1870–80. Penzance

Brewer, D. (1979), 'The Gospels and the Laws of Folktale', *Folklore* 90 (i), 37–50.

——(1980), *Symbolic Stories: Traditional Narratives of the Family Drama in English Literature*. Cambridge.

Brewer, D. (1997), 'Retellings', in *Retelling Tales: Essays in Honor of Russell Peck*, ed. T. Hahn and A. Lupack, 9–34. Cambridge.

—— (1996) ed., *Medieval Comic Tales*. Revised edn. Cambridge.

Briggs, K. M. (1970), *A Dictionary of British Folk-Tales in the English Language, Incorporating the F. J. Norton Collection*. 2 vols. London.

Buchan, D. (1972), *The Ballad and the Folk*. London.

—— (1990), 'Folk Literature', in *Encyclopaedia of Literature and Criticism*, ed. M. Coyle, P. Garside, M. Kelsall and J. Peck, 976–90. London.

Calvino, I. (1982), *Italian Folktales: Selected and Retold by Italo Calvino*. London.

Campbell, J. F. (1860/1890), *Popular Tales of the West Highlands*. Facsimile repr. 1983. 4 vols. London.

Carter, A. (1979), *The Bloody Chamber and Other Stories*. London.

Crow, J. (1947), 'Folklore in Elizabethan Drama', *Folklore* LVIII, 297–311.

Darnton, R. (1984), 'Peasants Tell Tales: The Meaning of Mother Goose', in *The Great Cat Massacre and Other Episodes in French Cultural History*, 17–78. London.

Davidson, H. E. (1978), *Patterns of Folklore*. Ipswich.

Dorson, R. M. (1968), *The British Folklorists: A History*. London.

Dégh, L. (1990), 'How Storytellers Interpret the Snakeprince Tale', in *The Telling of Stories: Approaches to a Traditional Craft*, ed. M. Nørjgaard *et al.*, 47–62, esp. 48. Odense.

Dundes, A. (1980) ed., *Interpreting Folklore*. London/Bloomington.

—— (1988) ed., *Cinderella: A Casebook*. Madison.

—— (1989) ed., *Little Red Riding Hood: A Casebook*. London/Madison.

Falassi, A. (1980), *Folklore by the Fireside. Text and Context of the Tuscan Veglia*. London/Austin, TX.

Gellner, E. (1985), *The Psychoanalytic Movement*. London.

Goody, J. (1987), *The Interface Between the Written and the Oral*. Cambridge.

Grimm (1992), *The Complete Fairy Tales of the Brothers Grimm*, trans. J. Zipes. New York/London.

Holbek, B. (1987), *Interpretation of Fairy Tales: Danish Folklore in a European Perspective*. FFC 239. Helsinki.

Jackson, K. H. (1961), *The International Popular Tale and Early Welsh Tradition*. Cardiff.

Jackson, R. (1981), *Fantasy: The Literature of Subversion*. London.

Jacobs, J. (1994), *Celtic Fairy Tales* (includes edn of 1892 and *More Celtic Fairy Tales* of 1894). London.

Jaeger, C. S. (1999), *Ennobling Love: In Search of a Lost Sensibility*. Philadelphia, PA.

Jason, H. (1988), *Whom Does God Favor: The Wicked or the Righteous?* FFC 240. Helsinki.

Lewis, C. S. (1947), 'On Stories', in *Essays Presented to Charles Williams*, 90–105. Oxford.

—— (1956/1957), *Till We Have Faces: A Myth Retold*. London/New York.

Lord, A. B. (1960), *The Singer of Tales*. Cambridge, MA.

Lüthi, M. (1984), *The Fairytale as Art Form and Portrait of Man*, trans. J. Ericksen. Bloomington.

Opie, I. and P. (1974), *The Classic Fairy Tales*. Oxford.

Peele, G. (1980), *The Old Wives Tale*, ed. P. Binnie. Manchester.

Perrault, C. (1697), *Histoires ou contes du temps passé*. Paris. (Later edn P. Saintyves, *Les Contes de Perrault et les récits parallèles*. Paris, 1923.)

Philip, N. (1992) ed., *The Penguin Book of English Folktales*. Harmondsworth.

Propp, V. (1972), *Le radiche storiche dei raconti di fate*. Turin.

—— (1986), *The Morphology of the Folktale*, trans. L. Scott. 2nd edn. London/Austin, TX.

Rabkin, E. S. (1976), *The Fantastic in Literature*. Princeton.

Rooth, A. B. (1951), *The Cinderella Cycle*. Lund.

Singer, J. L. (1981), *Daydreaming and Fantasy*. Oxford.

Tatar, M. (1999) ed., *The Classic Fairy Tales*. Norton Critical Edition. London/New York.

Thompson, S. (1966), *Motif Index of Folk Literature*. Revised edn. 6 vols. London/Bloomington.

Vélay-Vallantin, C. (1998), 'From "Little Red Riding Hood" to the "Beast of Gévaudan": The Tale in the Long Term Continuum', in *Telling Tales*, ed. F. C. Sautmann, D. Conchado and G. C. Di Scipio. London.

Verdier, Y. (1978), 'Grands-mères si vous saviez . . . Le Petit Chaperon rouge dans la tradition orale', *Cahiers de littérature orale* 4, 17–55.

Warner, M. (1994), *From the Beast to the Blonde: On Fairy Tales and Their Tellers*. London.

Webster, R. (1995), *Why Freud was Wrong: Sin, Science and Psychoanalysis*. London.

Wilson, A. (1976), *Traditional Romance and Tale: How Stories Mean*. Cambridge.

Ziolkowski, J. M. (1992), 'A Fairy Tale from before Fairy Tales: Egbert of Liège's "De puella a lupellis seruata" and the Medieval Background of "Little Red Riding Hood"', *Speculum* 67, 549–75.

Zipes, J. (1979), *Breaking the Magic Spell: Radical Theories of Folk and Fairy Tales*. Texas.

—— (1983), *The Trials and Tribulations of Little Red Riding Hood: Versions of the Tale in Sociocultural Context*. London.

—— (1991) ed., *Spells of Enchantment. The Wondrous Fairy Tales of Western Culture*. New York/London.

—— (2000) ed., *The Oxford Companion to Fairy Tales*. Oxford.

—— (2001), *The Great Fairy Tale Tradition: From Straparola and Basile to the Brothers Grimm*. New York/London.

2

Creativity and Tradition in the Fairy Tale

NEIL PHILIP

Oh these folklorists! And what have they done – murder a few innocent fairy tales. (W. B. Yeats, *Collected Letters*, 1886)

Human culture exists to provide us with a context in which to live. In every culture there is a tension between the needs of the community and the needs of the individual. The fairy tale, in my view, exists as a kind of ultra-sensitive balance between these two needs. It mediates between the life we have and the life we want; between the world we inherit and the world we imagine.

Anthropologist Harold Scheub walked more than six thousand miles through southern Africa recording oral narratives. One of his key sources was the Xhosa storyteller Nongenile Masithathu Zenani, who told him: 'These are the storyteller's materials: the world and the word' (Scheub 1992: 3). It would be hard to phrase this truth more simply or more fully. From those materials has been fashioned every story ever told. 'In the beginning was the Word' (John 1: 1).

Ralph Waldo Emerson wrote that 'Every word was once a poem' (1964: 189). It would be equally true to say that every word was once a story, and that storytelling is as intrinsic to human culture as language itself. To tell a story is to interpret the world (what we experience and what we observe) through the word (what we imagine and what we perceive). All stories do this.

Fairy tales in particular seek to hold a balance between reality and dream. The realm of *Faërie*, wrote J. R. R. Tolkien (1964: 16),

> contains many things beside elves and fays, and besides dwarfs, witches, trolls, giants or dragons: it holds the seas, the sun, the moon, the sky; and the earth, and all things that are in it: tree and bird, water and stone, wine and bread, and ourselves, mortal men, when we are enchanted.

The definition of the fairy tale, as opposed to any other kind of narrative, is fraught with problems. The standard term among folklorists is the German *Märchen* which is perhaps best translated as 'wonder tale'. They are stories with an element of fantasy or magic, located in the world of 'once upon a time'.

Märchen are only one kind of oral narrative. A folklorist may collect from a single informant myths, fairy tales, local, aetiological, religious and historical legends, tales of ghosts, fairies and witches, jokes, nursery tales, and anecdotes from personal experience. The artificial dividing lines between these categories of story inevitably blur; narrators may even claim the fantastic events of fairy tales as their personal experience.

Fairy tales have also played a large role in written literature, and indeed the oral and written tale have intertwined throughout recorded history. The earliest fairy tales we possess, for instance an Egyptian version of AT 318, 'The Faithless Wife', survive precisely because they were written down.[1]

Transformation is the key to the fairy tale, and fairy tales have been endlessly transforming themselves throughout history and, by some strange alchemy, endlessly staying the same. It was Axel Olrik who, in his essay 'Epic Laws of Folk Narrative' (1909/1965), first pointed out the curious self-repairing mechanism by which fairy tales maintain their inner architecture.

Olrik's essay was the first indication that the fairy tale as a genre had a distinct deep structure which is very robust and indeed cannot be corrupted without destroying the tale entirely. This structure was charted by the Russian folklorist Vladimir Propp in his classic study *Morphology of the Folktale* (1968). Propp identified a basis of thirty-one character 'functions' that, in a particular sequence, defined the plots of all fairy tales. His work was based on the Russian fairy tales collected by Aleksandr Afanas'ev, but has proved to hold true for all fairy tales, even literary ones. Even a long literary fairy tale such as Tolkien's *Lord of the Rings* can be fruitfully analysed according to Propp's system.[2]

In this essay I intend to do as the fairy tale itself has done, and dip in and out of oral and literary culture as I please. In considering oral narratives, I wish to show that the individual storyteller is not a passive tradition-bearer, but, as Séamus Ó Duilearga (J. H. Delargy) wrote of Seán Ó Conaill, 'a conscious literary artist' (Delargy 1945).[3]

A sixteen-year-old vagrant boy in a London workhouse in 1860 introduced his carefully rehearsed version of AT 1525, 'The Master Thief', with the proud boast, 'I've told one story that I invented till I learnt it.' He launched into his narrative with a confident swagger that draws the listener immediately into the story world (Mayhew 1861):

> You see, mates, there was once upon a time, and a very good time it was, a young man and he runned away, and got along with a gang of thieves, and he went to a gentleman's house, and got in, because one of his mates sweethearted the servant, and got her away, and she left the door open.

The boy's claim to have 'invented' the story is an assertion not of authorship, but of artistry (Philip 1992: 18–20).

On the other hand, in considering literary narratives, I wish to show how the writer puts his or her originality and creativity at the service of tradition. I will argue that, in our increasingly literate culture, many of the functions of the

---

[1] AT 303, 'The Twins' or 'Blood Brothers'; cf. Lichtheim (1976), 203–11. Papyrus D'Orbiney dates from c.1200 BC. Among other ancient fairy-tale types are 'Cinderella', known from a Chinese variant datable to the ninth century AD (cf. Philip 1989: 17), and AT 425A, 'The Animal Bridegroom', known from the Golden Ass of Apuleius (cf. Swahn 1955). For a detailed discussion of the ancient and classical sources of fairy tales, see Anderson (Chapter Five) below.

[2] See Philip (1982) and Petty (1979).

[3] The entire repertoire of this fine storyteller can be found in Ó Duilearga (1981).

traditional storyteller are being absorbed and revitalised by the writer. This process is exemplified by Patrick Chamoiseau's *Solibo Magnificent* (1999) in which, as translator Rose-Myriam Réjouis writes in her afterword, 'The old storyteller makes way for a new kind of story writing.'

The incorporation into the novel's social realism of the fairy tale's dreamlike fantasy has produced a literary hybrid, known as magic realism: a kind of novel that arises from the oral tradition and aspires towards it. This style of writing was first associated with Latin American writers such as Jorge Luis Borges, Gabriel García Márquez, and Mario Vargas Llosa. Other pertinent examples include Italo Calvino, himself the editor of a notable collection of Italian fairy tales (1980),[4] and Salman Rushdie, whose response to a death-sentence from Iran for writing *The Satanic Verses* was to compose an eloquent defence of the primacy of the fairy tale, *Haroun and the Sea of Stories*.[5]

'I've always loved telling stories', the writer Bruce Chatwin told Colin Thubron. 'It's *telling* stories for what it's worth. Everyone says: "Are you writing a novel?" No, I'm writing a story and I do rather insist that things must be called stories. That seems to me to be what they are. I don't quite know the meaning of the word novel.' Chatwin's biographer, Nicholas Shakespeare, writes (1999: 10):

> Chatwin was very theatrical, but he was also deeply serious. His stories concealed as much as they revealed and he hid inside them. He talked as he wrote, to keep something at bay, with an intensity to convince whoever was listening, or reading, that his dragons were not peculiar to him. He told his stories right to the last, going up to bed, stopping on each step of the stair for five minutes, going out to the car, as he drove off, leaning out of the window, till the moment he died.

In the words of Walter Benjamin, 'The first true storyteller is, and will continue to be, the teller of fairy tales' (1968: 102).

I have defined the fairy tale as a 'family drama in which the characters, by means of a series of transformations, discover their true selves' (Philip 2000/2001: 24). While this is not wholly adequate, it does point us to a key element in the fairy tale, namely its complete faith in the transforming power of the imagination. In a fairy tale, a girl escaping from an ogre may toss a comb, or a mirror, behind her; it becomes a forest or a lake. In the logic of such a narrative, thought itself is magically potent.

The Romanian fairy tale 'The Boys With the Golden Stars' is a version of AT 707, 'The Three Golden Sons'. In it, two enchanted brothers 'with golden hair and stars on their foreheads' are persecuted by a wicked stepmother. They are

---

[4] First published in Italian in 1956, this work consciously rejects the impartiality of the scientific folklorist. Calvino, quoting a Tuscan proverb, 'The tale is not beautiful if nothing is added to it', declares 'I too have thought of myself as a link in the anonymous chain without end by which folktales are handed down, links that are never merely instruments or passive transmitters, but – and here the proverb meets Benedetto Croce's theory about popular poetry – its "authors".' The result is a book less scholarly than Crane (1885), but full of verve and delight in storytelling.

[5] This work deliberately echoes that of Somadeva's twelfth-century *Kathāsaritsāgara* ('The Ocean of the Streams of Story'), a collection incorporating many fairy tales. The standard edition is Penzer (1924–8).

murdered and buried, and from their graves spring two aspens. The trees are chopped down to make two beds. The beds are burned, leaving only ashes. The ashes are scattered to the four winds, but the two brightest sparks fall into a river, where they become two little fishes with golden scales. The fishes are caught and, when they have swum in the dew and been dried by the sun, turn once again into 'two beautiful princes, with hair as golden as the stars on their foreheads' (Lang 1901; Kremnitz 1882).

Thus, in what the nineteenth-century folklorist Joseph Jacobs called 'bright trains of images' (Jacobs 1894: vii), fairy tales unfold their deep truths about human nature and human behaviour. They move like dreams from image to image, rather than rationally from event to event, and like dreams they resist explanation. The same story can be understood in many ways, and this flexibility of interpretation is one of its central qualities. The fairy tale does not explain, it explores. As George MacDonald wrote in his essay 'The Fantastic Imagination', 'It is there not so much to convey a meaning as to wake a meaning' (MacDonald 1976: 164).

The same text can be read as a spiritual allegory, as political metaphor, as psychological parable, or as pure entertainment. My own view is that each interpretation is valid, as is each narration. The multi-layered quality of a fairy-tale text is resistant to any single simplified meaning. In his psychoanalytic study of the classic fairy tales, Bruno Bettelheim writes: 'As with all great art, the fairy tale's deepest meaning will be different for each person, and different for the same person at various moments in his life' (1978: 12). In the end no theory will outweigh the simple truth expressed by Max Lüthi: 'The fairytale is a story about people' (1984: 14).

The novelist John Buchan made a similar point in his essay 'The Novel and the Fairy Tale': 'The true hero in all the folk tales and fairy tales is not the younger son, or the younger daughter, or the stolen princess, or the ugly duckling, but the soul of man' (1931: 7). This statement may be read as a romantic encapsulation of the truth that the fairy-tale hero and heroine represent Everyman and Everywoman, or as a statement of the way in which fairy tales represent individuation as, in the words of Elliot B. Gose Jr, 'a process of magical self-transformation' (1985: 38). But there is also a deep recognition of the spiritual aspect of the fairy-tale journey.

This spiritual dimension of the traditional fairy tale was what drew one of the great storytellers to the genre, in the very same year, 1806, that the Grimm brothers began collecting their tales. Rabbi Nahman of Bratslav is a fascinating figure whose legacy has yet to be fully appreciated by the wider world. His absorbing stories are a deliberate deconstruction of traditional tale types to express his own mystical longings.

Rabbi Nahman ben Simha of Bratslav (1772–1810) is revered as a great religious teacher (Green 1992), whose inner torment was crucial to the transition between medieval Jewish thought and the modern Jewish experience. He was also an intoxicating storyteller, whose work can be compared with that of Franz Kafka and Isaac Bashevis Singer (cf. Band 1978).

Nahman was born in Medzhibozh in the Ukraine, the birthplace of the mystical Jewish movement of Hasidism, which was founded by Nahman's great-grandfather, the Ba'al Shem Tov. Hasidism is a movement which seeks ecstatic communion with God and personal redemption, through study, prayer, dance and storytelling. In the year 1806, Nahman suffered a grievous blow in the death of his infant son Shlomo Ephraim, on whom his messianic hopes were pinned. Although his key teaching was 'Never despair', he was plunged into depression.[6] He saved himself by telling stories, beautiful and complex fairy tales in which he consoled both himself and his disciples with dreams of the coming redemption. 'The time has come for me to begin telling stories', he said (Roskies 1995: 25).

The stories he told are probably the first orally related fairy tales to be recorded word-for-word as they were told, the record being made by Nahman's devoted disciple Rabbi Nathan, who printed them after Nahman's death both in the original Yiddish and in a Hebrew parallel text.[7]

It was Nahman's belief that in the original cataclysm of creation – the mystical 'Big Bang' envisioned by Isaac Luria – all the elements of the true and eternal story of redemption were scattered through the world, to be pieced haphazardly together in the form of fairy tales. 'In the tales which other people tell,' he said, 'there are many secrets and lofty matters, but the tales have been ruined in that they are lacking much. They are confused and not told in the proper sequence: what belongs at the beginning they tell at the end and vice versa' (Roskies 1995: 26).

Nahman's understanding of the way in which traditional fairy tales are constructed from the building blocks of story motifs predates that of folklorists by several generations. In 1806, the collection and study of folktales was not yet properly underway; the Grimms did not publish the first edition of the *Kinder- und Hausmärchen* until 1812, two years after Nahman's death. In any case, he was not interested in collecting and preserving traditional fairy tales, he wanted to transform them. He understood his retellings as acts of *tikkun*, that is repair and restoration. So it is always meaningful when Nahman's tales veer, as they do, from the expected pattern.

As David Roskies writes in his masterful *A Bridge of Longing: The Lost Art of Yiddish Storytelling*, the 'meaning was coded into the story's deviation from the norm' (1995: 27). One of the great pleasures of reading Rabbi Nahman's fairy tales is to enjoy the beautiful play of Nahman's mind as he takes apart the traditional fairy tale and reassembles it into something new and wonderful.

The first of his stories, 'The Lost Princess', and the last, 'The Seven Beggars', share one curious feature – they come to a close before their natural ending. This is because both could only end with the coming of the Messiah and the redemption and restoration of the world. When the stories are fully told, time will have run its course.

These intricate tales draw on the hidden traditions of the Kabbalah, but also

---

[6] Alone of all the Hasidic masters, Nahman had no successor. His followers continue to revere him as their leader, for which reason they are known as the 'Dead Hasidim'. The writer Elie Wiesel first met one of Rabbi Nahman's followers in a Nazi concentration camp. This man repeated Nahman's words to anyone who would listen, 'For the love of heaven, Jews, do not despair!' The same words were painted on a large sign in the prayer-house of the Bratslav Hasidim in the Warsaw ghetto (Wiesel 1984).

[7] Most modern commentators accept the primacy of the Yiddish text.

on the open traditions of oral storytelling. 'The Lost Princess' explores Isaac Luria's myth of creation and redemption by combining the plots of two well-known fairy-tale types: AT 301A, 'Quest for a Vanished Princess', and AT 813A, 'The Accursed Daughter'.[8] Similarly 'The Seven Beggars' is both the summation of his religious thought and a recasting of the oriental story-cycle 'The Seven Sages', which dates from at least the tenth century, and which was translated into Hebrew as 'Parables of Sandabar' as early as the thirteenth century.

This, the last and longest of Rabbi Nahman's tales, is considered by many to be his masterpiece. Certainly that was his own view. He said, 'If I only told the world this one story, I would still be truly great' (Kaplan 1983: 354). The story was begun on the night of Friday, 30 March 1810, and told in parts during the week that followed. It was told, he said, 'to tell you how people once rejoiced'. Nahman may have secretly hoped, in telling this tale in the week before Passover, at a time of high messianic hopes, that the Messiah would come and enable him to finish his story. As it is, he refused to tell the tale of the seventh beggar, or complete his frame-tale.

In many ways 'The Seven Beggars' seems an utterly original achievement. It is full of unforgettable images, such as the heart of the world which is shaped like a man crying out in anguish. Yet it has many parallels in folk literature. The essential structure of interlocking tales is borrowed from 'The Seven Sages', while the variously disabled beggars recall a fairy tale such as the Russian story, 'The Footless and Blind Champions' (Curtin 1890).

The mystical core of Nahman's tales is not superimposed on his fairy-tale models but drawn out of their essence. In a recent book, G. Ronald Murphy (2000: 26) has shown how even the Grimms saw their fairy tales as 'transcendent religious poetry', and used this sense of the tales' luminosity as one of their guidelines in rewriting them and presenting them to the world.

The fact that the Grimms' *Household Tales* are not literal transcripts of the storytelling of German peasants, but in fact highly mediated texts deriving from the narration of often middle-class storytellers, some of French descent, has been used by John M. Ellis to attack them as frauds (1983) and by Jack Zipes to arraign them for validating 'patriarchy in the family and male domination in the public realm' (1988: 34).

The Grimms themselves made no secret of the fact that they rewrote and revised their texts, but their intention was to create a simulacrum of the oral tale, not, as Perrault had done, to give it a literary varnish or, as Nahman had done, to make it their own. The great nineteenth-century collectors who did understand the importance of transcribing the exact words of the narrator, and recording details of the storyteller and the storytelling, such as Evald Tang Kristensen in Denmark (Holbek 1987) and J. F. Campbell of Islay in Scotland (1860), were consciously following in the Grimms' footsteps. Their aim was to preserve what they saw as a vanishing inheritance, as accurately and perfectly as possible. In stressing the inherited quality of the oral tradition, they tended to

---

[8] A full critical interpretation of 'The Lost Princess' can be found in Y. Elstein's doctoral thesis, *Structuralism in Literary Criticism: A Method and Application in Two Representative Hasidic Tales.* University Microfilms of Ann Arbor. See also Wiskind-Elper (1998).

underestimate the creative contribution of the storytellers themselves; even in scholarly collections, the narrators of fairy tales were often left unidentified, as if they were mere passive conduits through which the story was transferred from the ancestral past to the safe custodianship of the collector.

In fact, the tension between creativity and tradition in the fairy tale is never seen more clearly than in the different motivations of the storyteller and the folklorist. The storyteller is concerned with making the tale live in the minds of the audience. Every aspect of the storytelling, not just the words but also the timing, the pacing, the intonation, the gestures and the movements of the storyteller, is geared to this primary aim.

A vivid description by the Irish folklorist Tadhg Ó Murchú of an unnamed Kerry storyteller lists many of the ways in which an oral narrator conveys the sense of his story besides the choice of words (Delargy 1945: 190):

> His piercing eyes are on my face, his limbs are trembling, as, immersed in his story, and forgetful of all else, he puts his very soul into the telling. Obviously much affected by his narrative, he uses a great deal of gesticulation, and, by the movement of his body, hands, and head, tries to convey hate and anger, fear and humour, like an actor in a play. He raises his voice at certain passages, at other times it becomes almost a whisper. He speaks fairly fast, but his enunciation is at all times clear. I have never met anyone who told his tales with more artistry and effect than this very fine old storyteller.

The folklorist is concerned with recording this storytelling, with fixing it imperishably in the memory. The earliest recorders of fairy tales thought it was only plot that mattered. Then it was the actual words of the storyteller. Now it is the whole performance, including the interaction between storyteller and audience, and the social, cultural, and personal context of the storytelling event.

But however detailed and subtle the folklorist's account may be, it is still the record of something fixed and finished. The storyteller is at liberty at any moment to change the story in all kinds of ways; the folklorist is not. For the storyteller, a fairy tale is defined by what it may become. For the folklorist, it is defined by what it has been. A classic example of this clash of attitudes is the exasperation expressed by the Inupiaq storyteller Apákag, who was described by the ethnologist Knud Rasmussen as 'one of the most lively storytellers I have ever met'. Rasmussen remembered (1975: v, vi):

> There was one thing we never agreed upon; this was, that I must often break into the thread of the stories to write down what I should otherwise have forgotten. Apákag sometimes became infuriated and broke out, 'You ruin our stories entirely if you are determined to stiffen them out on paper. Learn them yourself and let them spring from your mouth as living words.'

The nineteenth-century folklorist Joseph Jacobs, editor of the journal *Folk-Lore* in its greatest years and one of the pioneers of folktale classification (Jacobs 1914), was virtually excommunicated from the ranks of true folklorists for daring to retell fairy tales in his own words in his books for children. Attacked by George Laurence Gomme and E. S. Hartland, Jacobs claimed 'the same privilege as any other storyteller'. But the damage was done.[9] Jacobs could not straddle the divide between folklorist and storyteller and retain the whole-hearted respect of his peers. *Folk-Lore* failed to notice his death; in his history of *The British Folklorists*, Richard Dorson excludes Jacobs from what he calls 'The Great Team', and speaks witheringly of 'Jacobs' mutilation of the tale texts for juvenile consumption' (Dorson 1968: 438). Yet in the world of children's literature, Jacobs is rightly revered as the greatest of all those who have attempted to interpret the world's oral literature for the young.

To write down an oral tale is to alter its very nature. The living word is pinned on the page like a butterfly. A spoken story is just not the same thing as a written one, and a story which might transfix its listeners could be deadly dull to read. Folklorists have tried all kinds of ways to indicate tone of voice, pace, atmosphere, audience interaction and so on, but it takes a poet's sensitivity to make it work.

One exceptional attempt to chart the music of oral narrative was Dennis Tedlock's *Finding the Center: Narrative Poetry of the Zuni Indians*. This book contains a series of oral narratives set out as free verse, with many typographical clues to tempo, intonation, and volume. In his introduction to the book, the poet Jerome Rothenburg writes: 'It's a fantastic proposition, isn't it, that the fundamental language of man (at least of the man who hasn't come to writing) isn't prose at all, but, in the way it turns upon its silences, is something more like verse' (Tedlock 1972: xii). The practice of printing oral sources as free verse, with breath-stopped lines rather like the verse of the Black Mountain School, has persisted, though not always with the eccentric readability of Tedlock's versions of Zuni stories.

The truth is, however precise a folklorist's record of a narration may be, there is always a creative interface, in which the folklorist's decisions about how to present a text to the reader, may make or mar the story. The folklorist is no more absent from this process than is the scientist from his experiment.

An interesting early example of a folklorist really making a story live on the page can be found in John Sampson's little collection of gypsy tales recorded from Wasti and Johnny Gray in Liverpool about 1890 and published as 'Tales in a Tent' (1892). Sampson, an expert on William Blake and Librarian of University College, Liverpool, was a 'Romany Rai', one of the small group of enthusiasts who, at the end of the nineteenth and the beginning of the twentieth centuries, studied and recorded the life and culture of the English and Welsh gypsies.

Sampson had an exceptional ear for the rhythm of the spoken word and transcribed the lilt of the Grays' storytelling almost as if he were recording be-bop jazz solos. Francis Hindes Groome wrote of him (1899: lv–lvi):

> He possesses the rare gift of being able to take down a story in the very words, the very accents even, of its teller. Hundreds of times have I listened to Gypsies' talk, and in these stories of his I seem to hear it again: a phonograph could not reproduce it more faithfully.

---

[9] See Gomme's Presidential Address in *Folk-Lore* V, 1894 and Hartland's hostile reviews in the same issue. A half-hearted obituary for Jacobs appears in *Folk-Lore* 65 (1954).

In Johnny Gray's 'De Little Bull-Calf' (Philip 1992: 91ff.), a combination of AT 511A, 'The Little Red Ox' and AT 300, 'The Dragon-Slayer', Sampson even left in the narrator's asides to 'my Sampson'. By including himself in the story, he brings it to life in a way that a drier presentation could never achieve.

Sampson himself, having invented a way of notating the spoken tale that captured the magic of the word in flight, then abandoned it. Having found a Welsh gypsy, Matthew Wood, who was a master storyteller, Sampson painstakingly recorded Wood's repertoire in Welsh Romani and then translated the texts into stiff, archaic English prose; but a notebook containing the memories of Esmerelda Lock, among T. W. Thompson's manuscripts, reveals that Wood habitually told his tales in English, not Romani. It was Sampson's own romantic longing that deprived us of Wood's stories as living things, not museum exhibits.[10]

Sampson's example, however, inspired marvellous transcriptions of gypsy tales by Francis Hindes Groome and T. W. Thompson. Groome's In Gypsy Tents, for instance, contains a splendid Munchhausen tale, collected from Esmerelda Lock, 'Happy Boz'll' which prompted the gypsy Lazarus Petulengro to remark to Sampson, 'Isn't it wonderful, sir, that a real gentleman could have wrote such a thing – nothing but low language and povertiness, and not a word of grammar or high-learned talk in it from beginning to end' (Philip 1992: 223).

The same remark could have been made about the gypsy fairy tales laboriously noted down in a series of numbered notebooks by T. W. Thompson, many of which remain sadly unpublished. Thompson was a chemistry master at Repton school, who first became interested in gypsy lore while an undergraduate at Cambridge. He devoted much of his spare time to its pursuit, and wrote two long essays on his collections that remain the most sophisticated account yet of the problems of collecting oral narratives in England (Thompson 1914–15; 1922).

Thompson was interested not just in the stories but in stylistics, performance and repertoire. Without recording equipment or shorthand, he was reliant on making detailed notes and then writing the story out from memory as soon as possible, but he was particular about hearing stories told more than once, and ascertaining, for instance, which elements of a story were 'fixed' and which were subject to variation. One of his most prized narrators was Eva Gray, and he also recorded stories from her brothers Reuben, Gus, Shani and Josh. The way in which his texts bring out and contrast the characters and narrative styles of these siblings is a joy. Eva, who was born in Lowestoft in 1858, was a highly regarded storyteller, and Thompson made several versions of her favourite tale, 'Doctor Forster', which is a long and circumstantial variant of AT 955, 'The Robber Bridegroom' (Philip 1992: 166).

Other gypsy storytellers recorded by Thompson speak with more flair and vivacity than Eva; her own brother Gus, 'a man of beautiful speech' (Philip 1992: 85), was much more impassioned and poetic. What she offered was a quieter

[10] Sampson published many of Matthew Wood's fairy tales in the Journal of the Gypsy Lore Society and translations of twenty-one of them in Sampson (1933/1984). Esmerelda Lock's unpublished reminiscences are in a notebook among the T. W. Thompson manuscripts in the Brotherton Collection of Leeds University Library.

kind of storytelling, in which the gradual and deliberate build-up of supporting detail draws the listener deep into the story world. Her brother Shani told Thompson (Philip 1992: 185):

> What I like about Eva is the way she can fill in as she goes along: I've never heard her equal for that. However she comes to think of it all I can't make out; and it's all so natural, so intimate like, you think she must ha' bin there and sin it all for herself from the way she pictures it. And the little sly touches she puts in; she'll make you laugh with 'em many a time they're so true on the nail.

Eva is not a showman like Gus, or Thompson's star turn, Taimi Boswell. There is no surface flash, just the relentless marshalling of necessary detail. All her storytelling skill is put at the service of the story: her gift for dialogue, for pacing, for structure is as controlled as a writer's. The passion she saved for her performance, not her language. Thompson writes (Philip 1992: 185–6):

> Eva's greatest asset . . . in producing the illusion of reality is her impassioned recital of the tale, which unfortunately cannot be conveyed in the printed text. She sweeps you along without pause from beginning to end, words pouring from her lips in a torrent, her hands, her eyes, her face, her whole body reinforcing their meaning and significance. The modulations of her voice, the mimicry, the aptness of the phrasing, you hardly notice these separately, they are so perfectly in accord with the theme.

Noting the separate repertoires and styles of the Gray siblings, Thompson wondered about the possibility of 'latter-day invention of new stories' (Philip 1992: xviii–xix):

> My chance came when Eva declared one day that out of loneliness she had an evening or two earlier told herself a 'brand new tale'. 'I med it up myself from beginning to end', she said, 'and it was a long 'un! But I sat up till I'd finished it: I couldn't give it up till I'd got everything to come right again.' What she had done, I discovered, was to invent a new plot, using incidents from *märchen* she already knew. 'I've med up many a new tale,' she said, 'when I hadn't nobody to talk to, and was feeling a bit down, but I never think nothing more about 'em, and if you was to ask me to tell you one I couldn't for the life o' me; they're all gone clean out'n my head. But the owld tales as I've know'd since I was no height, I can al'ays remember them.'

The extent to which traditional storytellers exercise this creative impulse varies from person to person. Some are highly conservative, retaining the very words and even the intonations of the story as they first heard it; some recast the story every time they tell it; others are daringly inventive, and make up the tale out of the building blocks of story they hold in their heads.

In *Memory in Scottish Storytelling*, D. A. MacDonald and Alan Bruford contrast two traditional storytellers. Alan Bruford compares five recordings of the same story from the South Uist storyteller Duncan MacDonald and finds that 'Duncan changed his words very little from telling to telling' (MacDonald and Bruford 1978: 29). A version recorded from his younger brother Neil, who also learned the tale from their father, is couched in almost the same words. Here we have a case of extreme conservatism, and there are even impenetrable passages that seem to derive ultimately from 'rote learning from a manuscript using deliberately archaic language in the way of seventeeth-century scribes' (MacDonald and Bruford 1978: 28).

Note that here, the word-for-word recitation of an orally transmitted text has its roots not in an *ur*-narration but in a manuscript, though that, in turn, no doubt derived from the oral tradition.

By contrast, Donald Alasdair Johnson, also of South Uist, told D. A. MacDonald how, when he was telling his stories, he was describing the pictures that arose in his mind, as vivid 'as if I were drawing on the wall there, how the thing was going on . . . You've got to see it as a picture in front of you or you can't remember it properly' (MacDonald and Bruford 1978: 14–15). This contrast between verbal and visual memory illustrates one fundamental difference between types of storyteller. Another is revealed in the memories of the mason turned geologist and man of letters, Hugh Miller, who recalled a stonemason from a mason's barrack in the 1820s, a middle-aged highlander nicknamed Jock Mo-ghoal ('John my Darling') (Philip 1995: xv):

> Of all Jock Mo-ghoal's stories Jock Mo-ghoal was himself the hero; and certainly most wonderful was the invention of the man. As recorded in his narratives, his life was one long epic poem, filled with strange and startling adventure, and furnished with an extraordinary machinery of the wild and supernatural . . . The workmen used, on the mornings after his great narratives, to look one another full in the face, and ask, with a smile rather incipient than manifest, whether 'Jock was na perfectly wonderfu' last night?'

This kind of free-wheeling performance has rarely been recorded, but it is an essential part of the fairy-tale tradition all the same; the way in which Jock placed himself at the centre of his narrations is not dissimilar from the autobiographical elements in the fairy tales of Rabbi Nahman and Hans Christian Andersen.

There is always a tension between the inherited and the invented in oral storytelling. In his autobiographical *Borstal Boy*, Brendan Behan gives an account of storytelling in an English young-offenders institution, about 1940. The young convicts, who had inherited no tales, drew their material from the cinema (Behan 1958: 315):

> One would say, 'Tell us a picture', and the other would begin at eight in the morning, and maybe go on half the time till the break at ten o'clock, telling it.
> A lot of the blokes went in for this telling of pictures, and if a crowd was working near him, they would all work in silence listening to a bloke a few yards away, if the story was a good one.

It would be fascinating to know what formal qualities these narrations shared with those of Jock Mo-ghoal, or with the fairy tales of the tramps in a London workhouse, reported all too briefly by Henry Mayhew, or the storytelling transportees recalled by William Henry Barker in 1852 in *Household Words*.

In her book *Interpreting Oral Narrative* (1990), Anna-Leena Siikala divides narrators into five basic types: the active narrator placing a distance between himself and tradition; the occasional narrator closely associating with tradition; the passive narrator who has internalised tradition; the active narrator who has internalised tradition; and the passive narrator placing a distance between himself and tradition. These categories give us a thumbnail sketch of the different kinds of attitude that oral storytellers may have to the same story, and therefore the different kinds of treatment they will give it.

There is also, I believe, a sixth kind of narrator, one whose imagination is so suffused in the story world that it becomes the prism through which to view the everyday world in which we live. One such was the Hungarian storyteller Zsuzsanna Palkó (Dégh 1995a). In a moving tribute to this great verbal artist, the folklorist Linda Dégh describes how Mrs Palkó, at the age of seventy-four, 'encountered face-to-face the world of fulfilment of her tales'. This was when Mrs Palkó was summoned from her remote peasant community to Budapest, to be awarded the title Master of Folk Arts (Dégh 1995b: 93):

> Throughout her stay in the city, she identified her tale concepts in real life, matching reality against the background of a deeper, subjective truth. 'This is where Little I Don't Know could have lived', she whispered. 'His palace is just like the one in which King Lajos was reared . . . and, oh yes, there is the telephone, like the one the palace guard had at the gate when he reported to the king that a guest was arriving, but he didn't know if it was an emperor or a king . . .' Mrs Palkó actually found reinforcement for her belief in the miraculous world of the tale by discovering and identifying experienced miracles of the city.

There is a similarity here with the world view of Hans Christian Andersen, who entitled his autobiography *Mit Livs Eventyr* ('The Fairy Tale of My Life') and constantly referred his real experience to the fairy-tale world. Andersen is an intriguing figure in terms of this essay because by rights he should have turned into a tradition-bearer like Mrs Palkó or the Danish narrators recorded by Evald Tang Kristensen. Instead he absorbed the tradition and, like Rabbi Nahman, transformed it in his own soul into something new and strange.

Born in Odense in 1805, and raised in poverty, he was determined from an early age to be an artist. The path he was to tread was laid out for him like a magic thread in a fairy tale. He told his mother, 'First you go through terrible suffering, and then you become famous.' As a child, Andersen was a favourite with the old women in the spinning room of the local pauper hospital-cum-asylum, where his grandmother was employed to take care of the garden. He entertained them, and they 'rewarded my eloquence by telling me tales in return; and thus a world as rich as that of the Thousand and One Nights, was revealed to me' (Andersen 1975: 8). He also heard traditional fairy tales told during the annual hop harvest.

A handful of Andersen's stories are based on these tales – 'The Princess on the Pea', 'The Wild Swans', 'What Father Does Is Always Right' – but most are entirely original. They are highly individual, quirky tales, brilliant balancing acts of absurdity and common sense, fantasy and reality, tragedy and comedy. A surprising number of them end unhappily, and even if the characters achieve their desire, the story may end on a wistful note. Andersen is a poet of longing and unfulfilment; the master of the dying fall.[11]

He was the first writer to adapt the storytelling techniques of the oral tradition to express the intimate secrets of his life and thoughts, and he did so because, like Mrs Palkó, the magical realities of the fairy-tale world provided him with the yardstick by which he measured his experience.

Andersen was first and foremost a storyteller. Edvard Collin, the son of his mentor Jonas Collin, described his storytelling style (Bredsdorf 1975: 300):

> The tale went on all the time, with gestures to match the situation. Even the driest sentence was given life. He didn't say, 'The children got into the carriage and then drove away.' No, he said, 'They got into the carriage –"Goodbye, Dad! Goodbye, Mum!" – the whip cracked smack! smack! And away they went. Come on! Gee-up!'

Hans Christian Andersen's fairy tales very quickly established themselves as classics, even in the clumsy early English translations which captured little of his crisp, colloquial style (Alderson 1982). His influence on the literary fairy tale has been profound; it can be felt, for instance, as early as 1857 in several passages of Dickens's *Little Dorrit*.

In Britain, the fairy tales of Oscar Wilde, Mary de Morgan, Laurence Housman and the like are suffused with Andersen's spirit. Wilde's 'The Fisherman and his Soul', for instance, reworks and intertwines the themes of two of Andersen's tales, 'The Little Mermaid' and 'The Shadow' (Philip 1994).

In America Andersen's influence was just as deep, permeating through the translations and original stories of Horace Scudder to writers such as Frank Stockton, Howard Pyle, Will Bradley, and Laura E. Richards. But in the development of the American fairy tale there was another influence just as important: America itself.

There was a hunger in the new country for a new kind of fairy tale. It is typified by the attitude of the king in Arlo Bates's 1877 story 'The King and the Three Travellers' (Philip 1996: 155). The three travellers offer to tell the king 'strange and unheard tales'. He replies, 'If you can tell stories worth hearing, you are indeed welcome. The court storyteller has just been banished for presuming to tell the same story twice' (Bates 1877).

In 1901, L. Frank Baum boldly published a book entitled *American Fairy Tales*, in which he unashamedly set wonder tales in the streets of Chicago. He wanted to create, he said, fairy tales that 'bear the stamp of our own times'. In 'The Wonderful Wizard of Oz' and its many sequels, the American 'can do' spirit prevailed. In 'Ozma of Oz' (1907), Princess Langwidere asks Dorothy, 'Are you of royal blood?' Dorothy's confident reply is, 'Better than that, ma'am. I come from Kansas.' In the land of Oz, Baum created a fairyland shaped to the imaginative needs of the American child. The novelist Frank Buechner writes in his memoir *The Sacred Journey* of the powerful hold Oz held over him as a sick child in the 1930s (Buechner 1982: 14):

[11] The best collection of Andersen's tales in English is R. P. Keigwin (1982). Other good translators include Reginald Spink, Brian Alderson, Naomi Lewis. The Haugaard (1974) edition contains all 156 tales but the translation is untrustworthy.

I lived, as much as I could be said to live anywhere, not in the United States of America but in the land of Oz. One Oz book after another I had read or had read to me until the world where animals can speak, and magic is as common as grass, and no one dies, was so much more real to me than the world of my own room that if I had had occasion to be homesick then, it would have been Oz, not home that I would have been homesick for as in a way I am homesick for it still.

To create a fairyland that America's children could be homesick for; this is, as Baum touchingly wrote, 'as great an achievement as to become President of the United States' (Philip 1996: 156).

After Baum we begin to find a new kind of fairy tale emerging in America. The feminist fairy tale, for instance, can be said to have begun with B. J. Daskam's 'The Little Princess of the Fearless Heart' (1907).

The American fairy tale truly came of age in Carl Sandburg's *Rootabaga Stories*, the first volume of which was published in 1922; a typical Rootabaga tale is called 'The Two Skyscrapers Who Decided to Have a Child'. Sandburg, a distinguished poet, understood that true American fairy tales had to be couched in the rhythms of American speech. He wanted, he said, to write fairy tales 'in the American lingo' (Sandburg 1993). Both in language and in invention, Sandburg's fairy tales have a robust sense of the vital forward movement that is at the heart of American culture.

The moment in 'How They Broke Away to Go to the Rootabaga Country' when Gimme the Ax and his children sell all their belongings for 'spot cast money' and buy railroad tickets 'to go away and *never* come back' is the moment the American fairy tale, initiated by such writers as Washington Irving and Nathaniel Hawthorne, finally came of age. 'To go away and *never* come back': this is a true fairy-tale choice, but not one found in the European tradition.[12]

Over the course of the twentieth century, many writers incorporated both the stylistic and the symbolic characteristics of the fairy tale into their work. Where a nineteenth-century writer such as Charles Dickens, whose imagination was suffused with fairy tales, keeps the stream of fairy-tale references in his fiction submerged beneath the text, magic realist novelists such as Angela Carter deliberately keep the fairy-tale model in the reader's mind.

As well as writing novels deeply influenced by the traditional fairy tale, Angela Carter edited two fine anthologies of fairy tales in 1990 and 1993, and in her collection *The Bloody Chamber*, reworked the fairy tales of Charles Perrault with breathtaking audacity. *The Bloody Chamber* and similar works, such as Emma Donoghue's *Kissing the Witch* (1997), represent a particular fascination with the fairy tale among women writers, and a desire to reclaim its secrets from what can be seen as the patriarchal world view of male collectors such as the Grimms. Women poets, in particular, have used the fairy tale as a frame of emotional and psychological reference. The poems of Edith Södergran (1984), for instance, tremble on the edge of turning into fairy tales. Twenty-eight contemporary women writers explore their attitudes to the fairy

---

[12] For the American fairy-tale tradition see Lanes (1971), Sale (1978), White (1989) and Philip (1996).

tale in a stimulating collection of essays, *Mirror, Mirror on the Wall* (Bernheimer 2002).

Just as writers are increasingly placing a sense of orality at the heart of literature, so too a new generation of oral storytellers has arisen as tradition-bearers for the global village. The storytelling movement in Great Britain, for instance, is a rich and thriving multicultural community with room for both traditional storytellers, such as the Scottish traveller Duncan Williamson, and new-age oral performers such as the movement's linchpin, Ben Haggarty.[13] For an audience listening to them work their magic, the difference between the storyteller who has inherited his tales and the one who has acquired them is irrelevant. As Harold Scheub writes, 'Storytellers have always been innovative, and they have always been imitative.' He quotes a San storyteller: 'A story is like the wind: it comes from a distant place and we feel it' (Scheub 1992: 1–2). A story is indeed like the wind. To try to define it more closely than that is as pointless as trying to catch the wind in your hand. All we can do is be eternally grateful that, in Rabbi Nahman's play on the wording of the Hebrew of the Torah, God resolved, when creating mankind: 'Let us make man with an imagination.'

References

Afanas'ev, A. (1945), *Russian Fairy Tales*, trans. N. Guterman. New York.

Alderson, B. (1982), *Hans Christian Andersen and His Eventyr in England*. Wormley.

Andersen, H. C. (1855/1975), *The Fairy Tale of My Life*. London.

Aylwin, T. (1992), *Traditional Storytelling and Education, Incorporating an Update of the 1990 Directory of Storytellers*. London.

Band, A. (1978) ed. and trans., *Nahman of Bratslav: The Tales*. Mahwah, NJ.

Bates, A. (1877), 'The King and the Three Travellers', in *St Nicholas*. New York.

Baum, F. J., and MacFall, R. P. (1961), *To Please a Child: A Biography of L. Frank Baum*. Chicago.

Baum, L. F. (1900), *The Wonderful Wizard of Oz*. Chicago

—— (1901), *American Fairy Tales*. Chicago.

—— (1907), *Ozma of Oz*. Chicago

Behan, B. (1958), *Borstal Boy*. London.

Benjamin, W. (1968), 'The Storyteller: Reflections on the Work of Nicolai Leskov', in *Illuminations*. New York.

Bernheimer, K. (2002) ed., *Mirror, Mirror on the Wall: Women Writers Explore Their Favorite Fairy Tales*. New York.

Bettelheim, B. (1978), *The Uses of Enchantment: The Meaning and Importance of Fairy Tales*. Harmondsworth.

Bredsdorf, E. (1975), *Hans Christian Andersen: The Story of His Life and Work*. London.

Buchan, J. (1931), *The Novel and the Fairy Tale*. English Association Pamphlet 79. London.

Buechner, F. (1982), *The Sacred Journey*. London.

Calvino, I. (1956/1980), *Italian Folktales*, trans. G. Martin. New York/London.

Campbell, J. F. (1860), *Popular Tales of the West Highlands*. 2nd edn. Paisley/London.

---

[13] For the British storytelling revival, see Aylwin (1992); for the storytelling movement in the United States and its relation to the oral tradition of the Appalachians, see McCarthy (1994).

Carter, A. (1979), *The Bloody Chamber and Other Stories*. London.

—— (1990), *The Virago Book of Fairy Tales*. London.

—— (1993), *The Second Virago Book of Fairy Tales*. London.

Chamoiseau, P. (1999), *Solibo Magnificent*, trans. R.-M. Réjouis and V. Vinokurov. London.

Crane, T. C. (1885), *Italian Popular Tales*. London.

Curtin, J. (1890), *Myths and Folk-Tales of the Russians, Western Slavs and Magyars*. Boston.

Daskam, B. J. (1907), 'The Little Princess of the Fearless Heart', in *St Nicholas* 36. New York.

Dégh, L. (1995a), *Hungarian Folktales: The Art of Zsuzsanna Palkó*. Jackson.

—— (1995b), 'The World of European Märchen-Tellers', in *Narratives in Society: A Performer-Centered Study of Narration*. Helsinki.

Delargy, J. H. (1945), 'The Gaelic Storyteller, with Some Notes on Gaelic Folk Tales' (Sir John Rhys Memorial Lecture), *Proceedings of the British Academy XXXI*.

Donoghue, E. (1997), *Kissing the Witch: Old Tales in New Skins*. London.

Dorson, R. M. (1968), *The British Folklorists: A History*. London.

Ellis, J. M. (1983), *One Fairy-Story Too Many: The Brothers Grimm and Their Tales*. London/Chicago.

Emerson, R. W. (1964), 'The Poet', in *Essays and Poems*, ed. T. Tanner. London.

Gose, E. B. (1985), *The World of the Irish Wonder Tale: An Introduction to the Study of Fairy Tales*. London/Toronto.

Green, A. (1992), *Tormented Master: The Life and Spiritual Quest of Rabbi Nahman of Bratslav*. Woodstock, VT.

Groome, F. H. (1899), *Gypsy Folk Tales*. London.

Haugaard, E. (1974), *Hans Andersen: The Complete Fairy Tales and Stories*. London.

Holbek, B. (1987), *Interpretation of Fairy Tales: Danish Folklore in a European Perspective*. FFC 239. Helsinki.

Jacobs, J. (1894), *More English Fairy Tales*. London.

—— (1914), 'Some Types of Indo-European Folktales', in *The Handbook of Folklore*, ed. C. S. Burne. London.

Kaplan, A. (1983), *Rabbi Nachman's Stories*. Jerusalem.

Keigwin, R. P. (1982) trans., *Hans Christian Andersen. Eighty Fairy Tales*. New York.

Kremnitz, M. (1882), *Rumänische Märchen*. Leipzig.

Lanes, S. G. (1971), 'America as Fairy Tale', in *Down the Rabbit Hole: Adventures and Misadventures in the Realms of Children's Literature*. New York.

Lang, A. (1901), *The Violet Fairy Book*. London.

Lichtheim, M. (1976), *Ancient Egyptian Literature: A Book of Readings, II, The New Kingdom*. Berkeley.

Lüthi, M. (1984), *The Fairytale as Art Form and Portrait of Man*, trans. J. Erikson. Bloomington.

MacDonald, D. A., and Bruford, A. (1978), *Memory in Scottish Storytelling*. Edinburgh.

MacDonald, G. (1908/1976), 'The Fantastic Imagination', in *A Peculiar Gift: Nineteenth-Century Writings on Books for Children*, ed. L. Salway. Harmondsworth.

Mayhew, H. (1861), *London Labour and the London Poor, III: the London Street-Folk*. London.

McCarthy, W. B. (1994), *Jack in Two Worlds: Contemporary North American Tales and Their Tellers*. Chapel Hill/London.

Murphy, G. R. (2000), *The Owl, the Raven and the Dove: The Religious Meaning of the Grimms' Magic Fairy Tales*. New York/Oxford.

Ó Duilearga, S. (1981), *Séan Ó Conaill's Book: Stories and Traditions from Iveragh*, trans. M. MacNeill. Dublin.

Olrik, A. (1909/1965), 'Epic Laws of Folk Narrative', in *The Study of Folklore*, ed. A. Dundes. Englewood Cliffs, NJ.

Penzer, N. M. (1924–8) ed., *The Ocean of Story*. 10 vols. London.

Petty, A. C. (1979), *One Ring to Bind Them All: Tolkien's Mythology*. Birmingham, Alabama.

Philip, N. (1982), 'Children's Literature and the Oral Tradition', in *Further Approaches to Research in Children's Literature*, ed. P. Hunt. Cardiff.

—— (1989), *The Cinderella Story*. Harmondsworth.

—— (1992), *The Penguin Book of English Folktales*. Harmondsworth.

—— (1994), *The Fairy Tales of Oscar Wilde*. London/New York.

—— (1995), *The Penguin Book of Scottish Folktales*. Harmondsworth.

—— (1996), *American Fairy Tales: From Rip Van Winkle to the Rootabaga Stories*. New York.

—— (2000/2001), 'The Cinderella Cycle', programme note for Rossini's *La cenerentola*. Royal Opera House, Covent Garden. London.

Propp, V. (1928/1968), *The Morphology of the Folktale*, trans. L. Scott. Austin, TX.

Rasmussen, K. (1932/1975), *The Eagle's Gift: Alaskan Eskimo Tales*, trans. I. Hutchinson. New York.

Roskies, D. G. (1995), *A Bridge of Longing: The Lost Art of Yiddish Storytelling*. Cambridge, MA.

Rushdie, S. (1990), *Haroun and the Sea of Stories*. London.

Sale, R. (1978), *Fairy Tales and After: From Snow White to E. B. White*. London/ Cambridge, MA.

Sampson, J. (1892), 'Tales in a Tent', *Journal of the Gypsy Lore Society* 3.

—— (1933/1984), *Gypsy Folk Tales*. London.

Sandburg, C. (1922), *Rootabaga Stories*. New York.

—— (1993), *More Rootabagas*, with foreword by G. Hendrick. New York.

Scheub, H. (1992) ed., *The World and the Word: Tales and Observations from the Xhosa Oral Tradition*. Madison/London.

Shakespeare, N. (1999), *Bruce Chatwin*. London.

Siikala, A.-L. (1990), *Interpreting Oral Narrative*. Helsinki.

Södergran, E. (1984), *Complete Poems*. Newcastle upon Tyne.

Swahn, J.-Ö. (1955), *The Tale of Cupid and Psyche*. Lund.

Tedlock, D. (1972) trans., *Finding the Center: Narrative Poetry of the Zuni Indians*. New York.

Thompson, T. W. (1914–15), 'English Gypsy Folk-Tales and Other Traditional Stories', *Journal of the Gypsy Lore Society*, new series vol. 8.

—— (1922), 'The Gypsy Grays as Tale-Tellers', *Journal of the Gypsy Lore Society*, 3rd series, vol. 1.

Tolkien, J. R. R. (1964), *Tree and Leaf*. London.

White, M. I. (1989), *Before Oz: Juvenile Fantasy Stories from Nineteenth-Century America*. Hamden, CT.

Wiesel, E. (1984), *Souls on Fire and Somewhere a Master*. Harmondsworth.

Wiskind-Elper, O. (1998), *Tradition and Fantasy in the Tales of Reb Nahman of Bratslav*. Albany.

Zipes, J. (1988), *The Brothers Grimm: From Enchanted Forests to the Modern World*. London/New York.

3

The Ultimate Fairy Tale: Oral Transmission in a Literate World

RUTH BOTTIGHEIMER

The term 'fairy tales' connotes tales about fairies such as 'The Yellow Dwarf' as well as fairy tales like 'Cinderella' and 'Puss-in-Boots'. Tales about fairies and fairy tales differ considerably from one another. After a brief introduction, this article will deal chiefly, but not exclusively, with fairy tales.

Tales about fairies treat fairyland and its fairy inhabitants (e.g. elves, kobolds, gnomes, leprechauns, fairies) as well as the complex relationships that develop between fairies and human beings. Narratively elaborate and lexically rich, tales about fairies and fairyland typically include lengthening episodes such as entering a meta-human kingdom through a familiar and apparently ordinary aperture (well, cave, tree, or door in wall).

Fairy tales are commonly narratively and lexically simple, may or may not include fairies, unfold along predictable lines, with magically gifted characters attaining their goals with thrice-repeated magical motifs. They integrate fairy-tale motifs familiar throughout the western world, such as specific magical objects (rings, wands) and magical transformations (in appearance, size, and ability to understand the language of animals). Fairy-tale themes are similarly simple: a rise from poverty to wealth, marriage above one's class, and a triumph of good over evil, or of apparent weakness over overwhelming strength. The episodes in fairy tales are formulaic: quests, tasks, trials, enchantments, curses, and travelling with supernatural swiftness from one place to another. The characters are rarely distinguished in personal terms: good girls and women are kind, beautiful and industrious; good boys and men are handsome, benevolent and equally hardworking. Witches, stepmothers, occasional ogres, and frequently cannabalistic giants, who are all uncompromisingly murderous, comprise the company of the wicked.

As individual narrative elements fairy-tale motifs, themes and episodes each have long documentable histories in European literature. When the first fairy tales in the Western world were published in the *Piacevoli Notti* ('Pleasant Nights') of Giovan Francesco Straparola in Venice in 1551[1] they included magic rings, good and evil, tests and trials set by wicked antagonists, and exotic forms of transportation, including dragon-drawn chariots. Many such motifs came

---

[1] The title page is dated 1550, but the colophon date of January, 1550 indicates that the year of publication was 1551 by modern calendar reckoning.

into the Mediterranean narrative world in story collections from Western Asia. *Kalila wa Dimna*, known in Europe as *The Fables of Bidpai*, influenced European narrative tradition, as did the story collection *Disciplina Clericalis* by Petrus Alphonsus, while courtly romances such as *Perceforest* with its 'Sleeping Beauty' plot embedded piecemeal, and the *Gesta Romanorum* with its samplings from the Bible, religious legends and the *Barlaam and Josaphat* romance, were among the earliest books published. All appeared before 1500 and all contained fairy-tale elements which nourished subsequent fairy-tale collections. Other fairy-tale motifs, themes and episodes entered the fairy-tale narrative tradition from *fabliaux*, courtly romances, and stories from Latin classics such as Ovid's *Metamorphoses* and Apuleius' *Golden Ass* (Clausen-Stolzenburg 1995: 333). Thus the simple existence of motifs such as magic rings, magic chariots, and tests and trials are in themselves insufficient proof for a long-ago existence of the fairy tales in which those motifs now appear.

'Fairy tale', despite its clearly demarcated genre boundaries, has a problematic terminological history. Storytelling, as an engrossing human activity, has been reported or recorded in most human cultures in every age. The fact that brief narratives of all sorts are called *Märchen* in German, and that the Grimms *Kinder- und Hausmärchen* has commonly been translated as the 'Grimms' Fairy Tales', has led to a widespread misunderstanding that the *Märchen* told by peasants and villagers, through the medieval and into the early modern period, were themselves 'fairy tales'. Indeed, the German folk narrativist, Rudolf Schenda, concluded that fairy tales had historically formed no part of peasants' and villagers' storytelling (Schenda 1986; 1993). Nonetheless, past and present scholars commonly assume that references to *Märchen* in former ages indicate the presence of 'fairy tales'.

The *Metamorphoses* of Ovid and the *Golden Ass* of Apuleius both incorporate instances of magic, which has led many scholars to cite the two authors as waystations in an oral transmission of fairy tales from the ancient to the modern world. Both ancient authors, however, followed rules very different from those evident in fairy tales. Ovid's 'Pyramus and Thisbe' is in no sense a fairy tale, nor is Daphne's magical transformation into a tree. Neither do Ovid's notations of Medea's rejuvenating brew, magic herbs and chariot-pulling flying dragons, nor Jason's serpent's teeth form part of a fairy-tale narrative. The same is true of Apuleius' *Golden Ass*, originally entitled, like Ovid's work, *Metamorphoses*. The dead are revived, an unfaithful lover is turned into a beaver, witches try to seduce handsome young men, a man is turned into a frog, and the narrator becomes an ass. Each of these narratives, whether allusive or fully developed, incorporates and expresses a belief system based on powerful gods and goddesses. In formal terms, some aspects of such stories form parallels to tales about fairies, cobolds, goblins and their brethren that were composed a millennium later, but they remain distinctly mythological rather than fairy-tale-like.

It is well known that fairy tales, i.e. those classified as AT 300–749, were not documented before the invention of the printing press in the mid-1400s. Committed oralists understand this absence of documentation as *prima facie* evidence for unlettered survival and oral transmission of tales from antiquity to modern days. That view should be much weakened by the fact that examples of a demonstrable oral genre, the *Schwank*, can be documented from the modern period back to the early Middle Ages and, in some cases, to earlier periods (Köhler-Zülch 1989: 198). It beggars belief that scribes would have noted one genre and not another in their casual doodlings in the margins of medieval manuscripts. The differential documentation of the *Schwank* and the fairy tale require that the role of print in the history of fairy tales be considered seriously.

In England more than in other countries there is abundant evidence that, in the sixteenth, seventeenth and eighteenth centuries, large numbers of city and country people believed in fairies, fairyland and fairy lore. In their lives the activities of 'little people' accounted for whatever was inexplicable in daily life, whether cows sickened, babies were born malformed, or keys suddenly disappeared. In the English environment, however, references to fairies tended to be anecdotal rather than narrative, with few, if any, orally recorded tales about fairies with sustained plots.

One tale from Apuleius' *Golden Ass*, 'Cupid and Psyche', achieved fame among folk narrativists, because of its similarity to 'Beauty and the Beast' stories which appeared more than one thousand years later. Because the publishing history of this gripping story was either unknown or ignored, the absence of medieval documentation fostered and furthered notions of the tale's oral transmission over centuries. On the other hand it is well known that Apuleius' work was rediscovered by Giovanni Boccaccio, who began to disseminate its contents to correspondents in the fourteenth century, that some two hundred years later, 'Cupid and Psyche' was published in Latin and distributed throughout western Europe in hundreds of identical print copies and that, within a few more decades, the story began to appear in the vernacular. These facts plausibly account for the sudden documented appearance of stories of the 'Cupid and Psyche' type in literate Europe in the late Middle Ages and the early modern period.

A further objection to the concept of long-term oral transmission of entire tales was raised by Albert Wesselski, when he demonstrated that even a well-known fairy tale such as 'Sleeping Beauty' could not be transmitted without significant alteration (Wesselski 1931: 127–31). It is hardly surprising that people should not be able to remember fairy tales accurately, which are longer and much more detailed than jokes and anecdotes.

Fairy tales, as we have come to know them in the modern world, resulted from multiple intersections of technological, commercial, and social processes – printing, publishing, book distribution, and story dissemination – with a series of named authors, the most important of whom were the Italians Giovan Francesco Straparola and Giambattista Basile, the French Countess d'Aulnoy and Charles Perrault, and the Germans Jacob and Wilhelm Grimm and Ludwig Bechstein.

Once the technology of printing became established, a newly and quickly developed international book trade distributed its goods. In terms of story dissemination, books were able to perform far more efficiently than single storytellers could ever do. For instance, books that were displayed and sold at the Leipzig book fairs found their way all over Europe. Printers in Lyons produced for the local market, but they also printed books sold in France,

England, Germany, the Netherlands, or Italy. Venice, Italy's print centre, printed books for an international buyership, as well as for readers all over the Italian peninsula.

Among the earliest narrative works to be printed were Latin editions of the *Gesta Romanorum*, Apuleius' *Golden Ass*, and Petrarch's *Griselda*, all of which were soon translated into other languages, in the process of which national differences were introduced to make narratives acceptable to the local expectations of different communities.

It is a sad fact of printing and publishing history that the most popular and widely read books are precisely the ones which are today the least recoverable. In terms of ordinary experience this means that a book's selling out quickly indicated that its contents satisfied public taste and that, if the price could be lowered, new readers in the next lower tier of consumers could be expected to buy that cheaper reprint. Lower prices could be achieved by using cheaper paper and ink. Book-buyers themselves could keep the price of acquisition low by not having the book's folded sheets bound but by sewing them together themselves. At the point at which pages were torn, dog-eared or illegible, a book became a paper source for a household use and would disappear leaf by leaf. We know of many such cheaply priced books from publishers' catalogues but a cheap edition that survives to the present day is rare. The fragility of popular books and their resulting disappearance resulted in an absence of tangible evidence. As long as publishers' catalogues remained unknown, oralists could reasonably argue in favour of oral tale transmission to account for the existence of the same or similar tales over long periods of time. Studies of popular reading, however, provide mounting evidence that renders obsolete general theories of oral transmission as well as correlative theories like Walter Anderson's 'Self Correction' (Anderson 1951).

Booksellers in large cities like Venice, London and Paris could, and did, specialise, so that people in search of amusing tales could find what they wanted in a known shop, where a variety of printed, folded, and unbound sheets lay ready for sale, title pages beckoning with decorative woodcuts and descriptions of a book's contents. Country people who lived far from towns had two options: they could seek out cheap books from bookstalls at local fairs on any of the many appointed market days each year or they could await the arrival of a colporteur, the pack-carrying pedlars of western Europe. In England in the sixteenth, seventeenth and eighteenth centuries, every village, no matter how remote, was visited by a pedlar who sold chapbooks, along with pins, ribbons and other lightweight household desirables. The chapbooks, printed in London's centre of cheap print in St Mary's churchyard and on London Bridge, brought urban-produced tales to the countryside quickly and efficiently. Exactly the same process took place in Germany and France.

In the nineteenth century, as public schooling for the poor was instituted across Europe, one country after another, beginning with Germany, included fairy tales in reading primers for school pupils. Thus schools delivered fairy tales to children at an impressionable age and drilled them into their heads by memorisation, the standard teaching method of the time.

The most cherished traditional vision of tellings of fairy tales centres on evening work sessions. Evening work gatherings, referred to as *veillées* in French or *Spinnstube* in German, are known to have taken place but, according to Rudolf Schenda, there is no evidence that fairy tales formed part of *veillée* tale-telling. Indeed, morally outraged contemporaneous defenders of public virtue accused *veillée* tale-tellers not of talking about prohibited magic, but of using filthy language and of telling obscene stories.

Throughout northern Italy in the late middle ages municipalities hired *contastorie* ('storytellers') or *cantastorie* ('story-singers') to present chivalric epics in public spaces; they used printed sheets which they sold at the conclusion of their performances. Embedded in their narratives were magical motifs that would eventually be absorbed into the soon-to-emerge genre of fairy tales, along with magical episodes and characters such as ogres, flying horses and fairies (Petrini 1983). Street theatre was an effective means of spreading a knowledge of classic stories. Ones with action-packed plots could be, and were, enacted by puppets, marionettes, or humans in public performances accessible to every social group. *Lionbruno* with its seven-league boots and cloak of invisibility provides an apposite example. Performed by story-singers and enormously popular in the 1400s, it was 'one of the first secular works in the vernacular to be printed' in Italy (*Lionbruno* 1976: 5). In Venetian dialect in 1476, the printed page assumed that the story-singer would sing directly from its words (*Lionbruno* 1476/1976: [12], [13], 27, 28):

> inel secondo cantar ue diroe
> cio che al caualier so incontrato
> de lion bruno e deto il primo cantare
> christo ne ainte e la sua dolce mare

In the second canto I will tell you what befell the knight, for the first canto about Lionbruno has now been told. May Christ and His sweet Mother help us.

> la bella historia y rima fiorita
> al nome dioio so voglio cominciare
> de lion bruno lo secondo cantar
> Signori io ne disse ne laltro cantar
> co[n]me lion bruno dal demonio sca[n]poe
> di ponto in po[n]o ne co[n]rai prima
> co[n]me a gra[n]de honore al patre ritoanoe
> e li ue disse come il lirob stimop
> comme madonna aquilinallo lassoe . . .

My Lords, I told you in the other canto how Lionbruno escaped from the demon. From point to point I related in verse how he returned to his own country in great honour, and I told you, as the book relates, how Madonna Aquilina abandoned him.

Here a book clearly preceded the performance.

Literary 'academies' for the elite provided a second known venue at which fairy tales were performed. In the seventeenth century, and possibly also in the sixteenth, leisured men of privilege gathered to amuse one another and to admire one another's verbal cleverness. Giambattista Basile is known to have presented his fairy tales one by one at the Accademia degli oziosi in Naples; Charles Perrault at the Académie française. Similarly Mme d'Aulnoy, as well as other women in her literary milieu, occasionally told tales about fairies in Mme de Lambert's salon in Paris.

Lionbruno, the first coherent tale of magic, began with a poor boy, included an eagle that carried a boy through the air, a magic ring, and a purse ever full of florins. But when the hero transgressed his beloved enchantress's injunction not to speak of her, he lost her and his magic (*Lionbruno* 1476/1976). In the tale's second part, a cloak of darkness and seven-league boots helped him regain his otherworldly wife, achieve happiness, and attain perfect love. In both parts, Christian practices and images accompanied the plot.

Some three generations later Giovan Francesco Straparola (c.1485–c.1557) stepped into a richly appointed narrative world. The evident sources for his collection, *Le Piacevoli Notti*, reveal extensive personal knowledge of nearly every book of tales printed from Boccaccio's Tuscan ones to Girolamo Morlini's Latin ones, including Boiardo's *Orlando inamorato*, Ariosto's *Orlando furioso* and the *Historia de Lionbruno*.

His composition of the first European fairy tales in the middle of the 1500s represented a quantum leap in terms of narrative significance, because as far as magic plots were concerned – with the single exception of *Lionbruno* – he was the first to create coherent order from existing narrative chaos in magic tales. Ariosto's *Orlando furioso*, for instance, had flying horses, but the plot within which they appeared careered back and forth, with bits and pieces of various characters' quests and contests following hard upon one another at a frantic pace. The tale of 'Sleeping Beauty', translated from the French and published in Italy in the 1550s, did not stand alone as a coherent tale, but deposited its plot in fragments within the larger, and interminable, romance in which it was embedded.

In addition to the many tales he borrowed, Straparola used known plots, motifs and episodes to construct a series of fairy tales about heroes and heroines who, displaced from the royal courts of their birth, undertook tasks, trials and quests to regain their royal status. These I term 'restoration tales', many of which have survived, whole or in part, to the present day and can be found in the Grimms' tales.[2]

Straparola invented a second set of fairy tales, which I call 'rise tales'. These directly addressed urban social and economic conditions as experienced by Venetian artisans, craftsmen, and small merchants of his day (Bottigheimer 1994). In earlier rags-to-riches tales, such as England's tale of 'Dick Whittington', a cat had achieved wealth for its poor master by an extraordinary feat, namely eating all the rats of an entire kingdom, but in the first story of the eleventh night, Straparola's magically intelligent and articulate cat, who was, he told his

---

[2] Livoretto and Bellisandra's tale in *Pleasant Nights* (night 3, story 2) recurred as *Ferenand getrü un Ferenand ungetrü* (*KHM* 126); *Biancabella* (3, 3) returned as Mme d'Aulnoy's *Blanchebelle*, and *Guerrino* (5, 1) is well known both as Mme d'Aulnoy's 'Prince Guerini' and the Grimms' 'Iron John' (*KHM* 136).

readers, a fairy in disguise, arranged a royal marriage through which the hero became wealthy. This was the last and the most successful of Straparola's handful of modern rise tales, which also included 'King Pig' (night 2, story 1), 'Lazy Peter' (3, 1), 'The Magic Doll' (5, 2) and 'The Tailor's Apprentice' (8, 5).

In each of Straparola's rise tales a desperately poor girl or boy, through magic, married royally and became rich, a plot that was impossible in Venice where, some two decades before, new legislation forbade marriages between nobles and non-nobles. Straparola's authorial response was to set his rise tales in lands as distant as those in which his restoration tales took place, making it clear that a poor boy or girl's marrying into a noble family was a stroke of fortune that was not to be expected in Venice.

Straparola's tales exemplified all of the publishing and distribution processes discussed above. *Pleasant Nights* was published at least twenty times in Italy, beginning in 1551. Its ten-year copyright in his own name probably passed to his printer, Comin da Trino, at his death. Upon its expiration other printers produced Straparola's tales in a variety of formats until, with censorship and suppression begun by various Indexes in the late 1500s, it was quashed entirely in the early 1600s by the Italian Inquisition.

Straparola's book passed to France within a few years of its initial Venetian printing, long before it was prohibited by the Inquisition. In France it was translated, printed in Lyons, Paris and Rouen, and distributed to French readers from the 1550s until 1615, providing a ready source for France's later authors of tales about fairies, as Mme de Murat readily admitted in the 'Avertissement' of *Histoires sublimes et allégoriques* (1699). In the eighteenth century, Straparola's tales were printed twice more in France, in 1726 and 1739–49.

In Spain Straparola's tales were given a permission in 1569, and they were published in Baeça, Saragossa, Madrid and Granada (Senn 1993). Their Spanish published life was brief, however, with the book falling early to the iron hand of the Spanish Inquisition.

Within Italy the distribution of Straparola's books can only be surmised. Because Venice was Italy's centre of printing in the 1500s, it exported books to the whole of the peninsula, and because Comin da Trino, as one of Venice's largest printers, participated in this distribution system, he very likely sent *Pleasant Nights* to Naples, with whose booksellers Venetian printers had close ties.

Straparola's fairy tales provide a base line in the history of European fairy tales. The brutal content of several of his tales retained and reflected the roughness of *fabliaux* precursors, and as taste changed, so did fairy-tale content. The first stage in those changes can be readily discerned in Basile's tales, where personal filth and social meanness shifted from the story's heroes onto the frame tale's parodic narrators.

Giambattista Basile (1575–1632) began and ended his life in the then Spanish-governed Kingdom of Naples, but he passed several years in Crete and Venice. In Crete, at that time an outpost of the Venetian empire, Basile enjoyed the society of members of Venice's ruling families and was a member of the Accademia degli stravaganti. Subsequently he moved back and forth between the ducal court of the Gonzagas in Mantua, where he was honoured and advanced, and Naples, where he was also entrusted with governmental responsibilities and where he eventually remained.

Basile was one of the many writers in the Neapolitan dialect (Basile 1932; 1979: xxxvi–xxxix). N. M. Penzer concluded that Basile was working on his collection of fifty novellas in 1616 and continued perhaps as late as 1626 (Basile 1932; 1979 xliii). After Basile's death in 1632, friends published his fifty tales under a pseudonym, with the title the tales had originally borne, *Lo cunto degli cunti*. Dedications on the first, second and fifth days spoke of the entertaining style of the tales, and said nothing to suggest that the substance had derived from 'the people', as has so often been asserted. Basile's compositional practice fitted well with pre-copyright notions of authorship, in which giving an existing story a new form conferred 'authorship' on the stylist. As Straparola can also be shown to have done, Basile may have turned to available story collections, including, perhaps, Straparola's own, for plots, which he then tricked out in Baroque *bizarrerie*. Certain it is that his plots include themes from classical mythology, late Roman adventure novels, medieval courtly epics, episodes from the Renaissance Orlando cycles, motifs from north Italian novellas, quotations from contemporaneous Neapolitan literature (in particular references to street minstrels and story-singers), as well as scenes, monologues and dialogues from baroque performances in the Teatro San Carlino and the farces of Neapolitan street theatre. In other words, Basile's tales clearly and unambiguously display book culture as well as piazza culture (Schenda 2000: 486–7, 489). Schenda's informed assessment of Basile's sources offers a far more sophisticated understanding than Penzer's belief that 'Basile culled his tales directly from the people, as is attested by the virgin freshness of their form' (Basile 1932: lxxii).

The humour of Basile's tales derives from their multiple inversions. Forty-nine tales (the fiftieth is the frame tale itself) are told not by incarnations of beauty and virtue, as in all previous European tale collections, but by urban uglies whose job it is to amuse a villainous deceiver in the final days of her pregnancy. The collection's great distinction is that it is the first to include magic tales unmixed with other subgenres. The path by which some of its tales entered Perrault's collection may have been either fortuitous, due to his niece's possible acquaintance with them from Paduan intermediaries (Gicquel 1998: 116), or structural, due to street puppet performances by Italian troupes in French cities like Paris, or from a book itself. As a book, the *Pentamerone*'s historical importance was limited in its own day: it had far fewer printings than Straparola's *Pleasant Nights*. Basile's stories re-emerged transformed in tales composed by Charles Perrault ('Cinderella', 'The Fairies', 'Sleeping Beauty', 'Little Thumbling'), Mme d'Aulnoy ('Finette Cendron'), Mlle de la Force ('Persinette') and Mlle L'Héritier ('The discreet Princess', 'The Enchantments of Eloquence', 'Ricdon-Ricdon'). The *Pentamerone*'s appearance in the *Bibliothèque Universelle des Romans* in 1777, eased other stories of Basile into the German world of print, whence they eventually made their way into the Grimms' collection.

In a rush of imaginative creativity, several French authors took up the genre of the fantastic in the 1690s and early 1700s, the most influential of whom was Marie-Catherine Jumel, the Countess d'Aulnoy. In 1690 she published a classic tale, *L'Île de la félicité*, the hero of which moved between the mortal real and the immortal fairy world and ultimately fell to strangulation by Father Time. A few additional tales, such as 'The Yellow Dwarf' were equally dystopic, but for the most part the heroes and heroines of her *Contes des fées* (1697–8) and *Nouveaux contes ou les fées à la mode* (1698) negotiated successfully among fairy helpers and hinderers and ended happily wedded. Mme d'Aulnoy's fairyland is an independent kingdom, often in fundamental competition with, or opposition to, the earthly interests of a tale's hero or heroine. Tradition-bound, Mme d'Aulnoy sought her plots from earlier publications (e.g. Straparola's *Pleasant Nights*), embellished them with baroquely florid details, introduced intersecting subplots, and often embedded the whole within frame narratives. As is frequent with women writers, Mme d'Aulnoy's tales about fairies included many strong heroines, of whom Finette-Cendron is a good example. As far as Mme d'Aulnoy's sources are concerned, Jacques Barchilon noted that it is impossible to disentangle material that might have come from popular tradition from Mme d'Aulnoy's own creation (1997: xxxvi), a view that vitiates the credibility of often-cited folk sources for her tales.

Mme d'Aulnoy's books were published in full several times in France and entered the *bibliothèque bleue*, often in abridged form. In Germany her tales were occasionally published together with Perrault's but they had a far greater success in England, where *L'Île de la félicité* was translated almost immediately (1691), and her other tales were translated on three separate occasions for three different classes of buyer: first for an elevated social class, again for the middle classes, and finally for a simple readership. In each of these forms her tales were published numerous times within the first half of the eighteenth century. Eventually all but two of her tales dropped from sight, leaving 'The Yellow Dwarf' and 'The White Cat' to enter the ranks of children's literature in the late 1700s, where they remained well into the 1800s.

The fairy tales of Charles Perrault (1628–1703) were distinguished by the fact that all appeared freestanding, without the literary device of a framing tale. Perrault also utilised a simpler vocabulary than either Mme d'Aulnoy or Basile, and his uncomplicated linear plots proceeded to endings embellished by socially acceptable morals. Like the Grimms' *Tales*, Perrault's collection was slow to catch on, for in France the upper classes initially preferred the ornate language and construction of Mme d'Aulnoy's tales. Many editions of Perrault's tales were published in the Netherlands, presumably for export, some of which must have gone to France, while others found their way to the French-reading upper classes of Austria, Hungary, Germany, Poland and Russia.

In language, structure and moral stance Perrault's fairy tales resembled *bibliothèque bleue* publications, and his tales were adopted entire into the realm of cheap print. In small octavo editions, Perrault's words and phrases spread to the farthest reaches of France's borders in the eighteenth and nineteenth centuries. The process was so effective in creating a common national fairy-tale culture that nineteenth-century informants were able to recount 'Red Riding-Hood' in very much the same language as that in which Perrault had originally published it. Folklorists have seized on France's national knowledge of 'Red Riding-Hood' as evidence for both an existence and a stability of oral tradition, with Anderson's theory of self-correction to account for the phenomenon of peasants telling Perrault's tales in Perrault's language two hundred years after their initial publication. The real national memory, however, is far more likely to have resided in the unvarying texts of cheap publications read by generation after generation.

French fairy tales arrived in Germany in several waves. The first comprised French language books published in France or the Netherlands, which are still to be found in the holdings of princely libraries all over central Europe, and especially in Germany. The second was the publication of such tales in word-for-word translations by German publishers, which resulted in a very small group of books. In the third, and by far the largest and most influential wave, German publishers edited the word-for-word translations and retailed them to a German public hungry for new narratives.

The first major translation of French fairy tales into German was Saal's *Abendstunden* ('Hours at Dusk'), closely followed by the 1761 *Cabinet der Feen* ('Chamber of Fairies'). After an interval of a generation, Friedrich Justin Bertuch published *Blaue Bibliothek aller Nationen* ('Blue Library of all Nations') in 1790–7, which consciously imitated the style of France's *bibliothèque bleue* and included tales from Mme d'Aulnoy, Perrault and subsequent fairy-tale authors, as well as oriental tales.

The period of almost forty years between the 1761 and the 1790 translations from French was filled by German-produced fairy tales in the French style. Manfred Grätz demonstrated in his study of the shift from tales about fairies to folk fairy tales in the period of the German Enlightenment, that the adaptation of French tales could be divided into three stages: the first, awkward word-for-word translations from French into German; the second elegant and often altered versions that retained evidence of their French origins; the third completely Germanised versions. This string of developments was followed by German-produced imitations and newly created tales that dipped into the repertoire of French and oriental magic objects and episodes of enchantment. Grätz concludes that this flood of translations and imitations, manifest everywhere in Germany, makes untenable the assumption that German fairy tales (*Märchen*) were transmitted orally and unnoticed (Grätz 1988: 166, 267). The detailed documentation of Grätz's study makes it the most important single study of the history of fairy tales in the last fifty years but it remains untranslated and relatively unknown outside Germany.

The German literary market was saturated with books of fairy tales, and the dates of their publication bear witness to the process of the continuous development of a market for such tales in Germany. Gottlieb Wilhelm Rabener published the first literary tale about fairies in German in 1755; nine years later Christoph Martin Wieland put fairies into stories about Don Sylvio de Rosalva; in 1777, Wilhelm Christhelf Siegmund Mylius produced three fairy tales by the French Count d'Hamilton in a form and context that promoted the assumption that they had originated in an ancient oral folk tradition. Johann Gottfried Herder took up Mylius's fictive contextualisation and gave it a theoretical form that has continued to be invoked by students of German fairy tales to this day. His concept of *Volkspoesie* ('folk literature') appeared in 1778, and Johann Karl

August Musäus incorporated that vision almost immediately into his *Volksmärchen der Deutschen* ('Folktales of the German People') of 1782–7. Christoph Wilhelm Guenther then built upon Musäus's erroneous notion and claimed a falsified folk origin for his *Kindermärchen aus mündlichen Erzählungen gesammelt* ('Children's Tales Gathered from Oral Tellings') published in 1787, as did Benedikte Naubert in her *Neue Volksmärchen der Deutschen* ('New Folktales of the Germans'), dated 1789–93. Despite their claims, the tales in both Guenther's and Naubert's books consisted of lexically and narratively elaborate literary fairy tales of the sort that flourished among Germany's leisured women readers of the eighteenth century and that bore no resemblance to oral narratives collected in the field.

Enlightentment educators had damned fairy tales as undisciplined and non-rational products of anti-intellectual imaginations. Influential German Romantics such as Karl Teuthold Heinze (1765–1813), Clemens Brentano (1778–1842) and Achim von Arnim (1781–1831) responded in opposition, expressing a deep sympathy for fairy tales. German Romantic poets such as Novalis (1772–1801), Ludwig Tieck (1773–1853), Carl Wilhelm Salice Contessa (1777–1825), Friedrich de la Motte Fouqué (1777–1843), E. T. A. Hoffmann (1776–1822) and Christian August Vulpius (1762–1827) reproduced the style of Mme d'Aulnoy in their literary fairy tales, as did even the lion of German classics, Johann Wolfgang von Goethe (1749–1832), in his tale *Das Märchen*.

Underlying both public discourse and private thought in the early nineteenth century was positivism, a system of thought that posited an unbroken chain of historical and intellectual tradition. Once oral tradition had been asserted, positivism encouraged a belief in continuous oral tradition. Schooled in Greek and Latin classics, Germany's Romantics could not help seeing resemblances between contemporary tales like 'Beauty and the Beast' and ancient ones like 'Cupid and Psyche'. With no knowledge of the publishing history of the late 1400s, when printers had resuscitated 'Cupid and Psyche' and distributed it Europe-wide, the Grimms further developed Herder's proposition of *Volkspoesie* into a theory that accounted for narrative similarities in tales separated by centuries. Persuaded that fairy tales themselves were a genuine genre of 'the folk', Jacob and Wilhelm Grimm began collecting tales from young ladies (*sic*) among their middle-class and town-dwelling friends in Kassel.

The Germanies in which the Grimms began collecting tales were saturated with stories that had begun arriving from France when their informants' grandparents and parents had been young. The Grimms themselves, however, had been reared in an elite tradition that eschewed frivolous reading, and they did not recognise some of the early contributions to their collection for the French-influenced narratives that they were. The result was that the first volume of their first edition (1812) included Perrault's 'Bluebeard' and 'Puss-in-Boots' in language that (in translation) was nearly identical to that in which it had first appeared in Paris in 1697. Realising that Perrault's French could not represent the German folk spirit, Wilhelm quickly excised these two tales from the Second Edition of 1819.

Stories in the second volume of the first edition of the Grimms' *Tales* (1815) drew heavily on the repertoire of Dorothea Viehmann, a marketwoman from a village near Kassel. More proletarian in outlook, this volume far undersold the first volume.

The *Circular of the Wollzeiler Society* (1815), fostered by Jacob Grimm, gave international impetus to the project of collecting a broad variety of oral genres and it provided the Grimms with collaborators all over the Germanies. Philip Otto Runge composed and contributed two early dialect tales, whose sophisticated metaphors and similes expressed a refined literary artistry, which further augmented the growing belief in the remarkable verbal skills of the 'people'.

Positivism generally held that the closer one approached the origins of a process, in this case the telling of a tale, the more pure, the less uncontaminated the product was. To enlarge their collection, Wilhelm and Jacob Grimm therefore turned to sixteenth- and seventeenth-century German tale collections. These, however, retained far more of their rough misogynistic *fabliaux* ancestry than had the French tradition. Such values informed Wilhelm's continuous editing of the *Tales*, an inclination that can be traced in tale after tale, and with particular vividness in *Marienkind* (*KHM* 3: 'Mary's Child'). There the girl-protagonist's isolation, sufferings, and punishment increased from edition to edition, with even the tree in the tale's illustration becoming increasingly foreboding as it was visually edited from a foliage-covered shelter to a spikily and threateningly dead tree.

Wilhelm Grimm had identified the *Tales* as a nation-forming project from the beginning, and patriotic school teachers, university professors and poets were among their earliest and most vocal supporters. As intellectuals and politicians struggled to form a unified nation from the disparate Germanies in the course of the nineteenth century, school teachers became an essential part of the process of incorporating some of the Grimms' tales into school primers, which effectively disseminated knowledge of the tales from the Grimms' collection to the nation's children and seeded the broad population with a knowledge of 'folk fairy tales' into which later collectors would dip and from which they would find proof of the existence of a continuous oral tradition.

Germany's book-buying public, as opposed to its teachers and poets, was middle class and had largely been brought up according to Enlightenment ideals. Contrary to a widespread assumption, they did not buy the Grimms' *Tales* in large numbers. Volume One of the First Edition, the most literary, the least folk and the most bourgeois, sold better than any other imprint during the Grimms' lifetimes and for a long time afterwards – three hundred copies a year for three years. Volume Two of the same edition sold at an overall rate of seventy-five copies a year. The sad story continued with the First Small Edition which sold at an overall rate of 187 copies per year, even though it was both illustrated and cheap. When given a choice in the mid-1800s, Germany's book-buying public overwhelmingly preferred the fairy tales of the Grimms' competitor, Ludwig Bechstein.

In 1845 Ludwig Bechstein (1801–60) published *Deutsche Märchen* ('German Tales'). In many respects his fairy tales were a reaction against the Grimms' *Tales*. In his foreword he humanely inveighed against the [Grimms'] practice of maligning stepmothers, whose situation he found difficult enough without adding fairy-tale attacks. The children in his tales tended to be plucky seekers for assistance rather than passive recipients of magic help. Sisters and brothers aided each other in stories that typically concluded with families happily and affectionately reunited. Bechstein's tales far outsold the Grimms' *Tales* from every point of view until the 1890s.

In the 1890s three processes intersected, dooming Bechstein's *German Tales* and raising the Grimms' *Tales* to national preeminence. The first was stylistic: Bechstein's literary style had fitted a benevolently humorous middle-class literary pattern. It had suited the taste of its own generation perfectly, but by the 1890s had become outdated and outmoded, whereas the style of the Grimms' *Tales*, crafted slowly and steadily until it approximated German usage in its deepest structure, remained recognisably usable. The second, the lapse of copyright, threw the Grimms' *Tales* open to every publisher in the Germanies in 1893. Enormous changes had taken place between 1850 and 1900, including the growth of an urban proletariat. The time was ripe to provide Grimms' *Tales* in a variety of forms in order to sell the book in the many different markets that now existed. In addition, Bechstein's tales were attacked by influential educators in the 1890s as unsuitable for children, while the same critics were simultaneously celebrating the Grimms' *Tales* as a perfect vehicle to inculcate Germanic values in the German folk.

Since the time of the Grimms, oralists have posited an undocumented oral transmission of fairy tales, because no available evidence could account for the otherwise incomprehensible process by which plots and language could make the leap from one location to another, from one country to another, and from one language to another. The Grimms themselves favoured the view that all fairy tales had originated at a certain point (monogenesis) and had spread outward from that point, accreting plot elements that changed them from their original state as they became ever more distant from their point of origin. Theories of oral diffusion that were consistent with monogenesis asserted a quasi-arithmetical pace of narrative change as a tale diffused itself outwards. Such thought required that the tale geographically and historically most distant from its point of origin be the most different from the original version. But as studies of colonial cultures developed, they disclosed once again the power of books, rather than oral transmitters, to diffuse plots, characters, and language from French and German cultural centres to colonies in, for instance, south-east Asia and east Africa.

When late-nineteenth-century folklorists recognised the existence of similar or identical tales far distant from one another, they concluded that the similarities they observed were inconsistent with monogenesis. They proposed a theory of polygenesis, and to justify so unlikely an idea, turned to emerging views of the human psyche that posited identical or similar emotions in people in widely differing societies. Polygenesists concluded that identical psychological needs would generate identical stories, with the same plot, characters and language, something that every scholar of narrative recognises as an impossibility and that common sense must reject.

Oral transmission, the central tenet of fairy-tale research for two centuries, was based on the gaping absence of evidence. Adherence to this outmoded theory continues because principles derived by folklorists from non-literate societies, where oral transmission of tribal histories clearly exists and has existed, are inappropriately applied to literate societies where the written and the printed word has acted as a transmitter and regulator of fairy-tale transmission.

References

Anderson, W. (1951), *Ein volkskundliches Experiment*. FFC 239. Helsinki.

d'Aulnoy, M.-C. Countess (1697–8/1997), *Les Contes des fées*, ed. P. Hourcade, intr. J. Barchilon. Société des textes français modernes. Paris.

Basile, G. (1932/1979), *Pentamerone*, trans. B. Croce and N. M. Penzer. Westport, CT.

Bottigheimer, R. B. (1994), 'Straparola's *Piacevoli notti*: Rags to Riches Fairy Tales as Urban Creations', *Marvels and Tales* 8.2, 281–96.

—— (2002), *Fairy Godfather: Straparola, Venice and the Fairy Tale Tradition*. Philadelphia

Clausen-Stolzenburg, M. (1995), *Märchen und mittelalterliche Literaturtradition*. Heidelberg.

Gicquel, B. (1998), 'Les *Contes* de Perrault: réception critique et histoire littéraire', in *Tricentenaire Charles Perrault: les grands contes du XVIIe siècle et leur fortune littéraire*, ed. J. Perrot. Paris.

Grätz, M. (1988), *Das Märchen in der deutschen Aufklärung: von Feenmärchen zum Volksmärchen*. Stuttgart.

Köhler-Zülch, I. (1989), 'Bulgarische Märchen im balkanischen Kontext und ihre Stellung in der internationalen Erzählüberlieferung', in *Kulturelle Traditionen in Bulgarien*, ed. R. Lauer and P. Schreiner. Göttingen.

The Story of Lionbruno (1976), / *Historia de Liombruno* (1476). Toronto Public Library.

Petrini, M. (1983), *La fiaba di magia nella letterattura italiana*. Udine.

Schenda, R. (1986), 'Telling Tales – Spreading Tales: Change in the Communicative Forms of a Popular Genre', in *Fairy Tales and Society: Illusion, Allusion and Paradigm*, ed. R. B. Bottigheimer. Philadelphia.

—— (1993), *Von Mund zu Ohr. Bausteine zu einer Kulturgeschichte volkstümlichen Erzählens in Europa*. Göttingen.

—— (2000) ed., *Das Märchen der Märchen. Das Pentamerone*. Munich.

Senn, D. (1993), '*Le piacevoli notti* (1550/53) von Giovan Francesco Straparola, ihre italienischen Editionen und die spanische Übersetzung *Honesto y agradable entretenimiento de Damas y Galanes* (1569/81) von Francisco Truchado', *Fabula* 34, 45–65.

Wesselski, A. (1931), *Versuch einer Theorie des Märchens*. Prager Deutsche Studien 45. Reichenberg.

4

A Workshop of Editorial Practice: The Grimms' Kinder- und Hausmärchen

DAVID BLAMIRES

The most famous collection of fairy tales the world over is that made by Jacob and Wilhelm Grimm (1785–1863 and 1786–1859) and published under the title *Kinder- und Hausmärchen*, 'Children's and Household Tales' (hereafter *KHM*). The first edition appeared in two volumes dated 1812 and 1815, and six more editions, each different from the others, followed during their lifetime: 1819–22 (second), 1837 (third), 1840 (fourth), 1843 (fifth), 1850 (sixth) and 1857 (seventh). The seventh edition is the basis of virtually all subsequent printings of the tales in German. Here the tales are numbered 1–200, but with an additional item, 151*; no. 38, 'Die Hochzeit der Frau Füchsin' ('The Wedding of Mrs Fox'), consists of two separate items, while no. 39, 'Die Wichtelmänner' ('The Goblins') and no. 105, 'Märchen von der Unke' ('Tales about the Toad') are both divided into three parts. At the end of the collection ten *Kinderlegenden* (pious tales for children) are added. This makes for a total of 216 items. But in the forty-five-year-long process of editing many more tales were collected. Some of them were new; others were alternative versions of already known tales, while thirty-four items printed in the 1812 volume were removed from subsequent editions. The mass of material thus published is very extensive. The numbering of the tales up to 200 clearly had some sort of symbolic significance for Wilhelm Grimm, who was responsible for editing the collection from 1819 onwards. It was not until 1850 that the collection amounted to two hundred items, exactly twice the number of tales in Boccaccio's *Decameron*, that most influential late medieval collection of popular story material. Also in that same year of 1850, Friedrich Heinrich von der Hagen (1780–1856), appointed first Professor of German at the newly founded University of Berlin in 1810, published a collection of one hundred medieval German tales entitled *Gesammtabenteuer*, clearly emulating Boccaccio. Wilhelm Grimm and von der Hagen were elected members of the Prussian Academy of Sciences in Berlin in 1840 and 1841 respectively, so one can perhaps infer that Grimm was aiming to outdo his colleague.

Both Boccaccio and von der Hagen were writing or collecting material designed for an adult readership. The Grimms, on the other hand, were concerned with traditional tales for children, a form of literature hitherto neglected or looked down upon by intellectuals in Germany and circulating, so they believed, chiefly in oral form. Initially they were not aiming at producing a book for children but rather at rescuing from oblivion stories that were part of a rapidly disappearing popular tradition. Their scholarly enterprise was all of a piece with their preoccupation with medieval literature, language and mythology. Indeed, the annotations that they made to the tales they collected frequently drew attention to parallels between fairy-tale motifs and aspects of mythology.

The Grimms were pioneers in the scholarly study and collection of what they referred to in the preface to the first edition of *KHM* as 'these innocent household tales' (Rölleke 1986: I, vi). That is what made them different from their literary predecessors and contemporaries who also published versions of the same kind of traditional material. (I shall come back to the question of definitions in due course.) The late eighteenth and early nineteenth century in Germany was not short of books presenting *Märchen* in a variety of formats to the middle-class reader, but these books were decidedly literary, rather than scholarly, in character. Foremost among them was J. K. A. Musäus's *Volksmährchen der Deutschen* ('Popular Tales of the Germans') published in Gotha in five volumes between 1782–6 (Musäus 1977), in which the author retold in a discursive, ironic and linguistically ambitious style some fourteen tales that were not wholly German by origin nor all traditional tales. Musäus himself makes the point, in a prefatory letter to a friend, that he was writing for adults (Musäus 1977: 12):

> Popular tales, however, aren't children's tales either, for a nation doesn't consist of children, but mainly of grown-ups, and in ordinary life one usually speaks differently with them than one does with children. It would therefore be a mad idea if you supposed that all *Märchen* ought to be told in the tone that Mother Goose uses for children.

Many other writers of the time shared Musäus's view that fairy tales were not specifically designed for children and Goethe, Wieland and the Romantics followed him in composing *Märchen* for adults. Benedicte Naubert followed up Musäus's popularity by producing *Neue Volksmährchen der Deutschen* ('New Popular Tales of the Germans') published in four volumes between 1789–93 in Leipzig (Zipes 2000: 335–6).

Individual *Märchen* for children, however, were included in a number of eighteenth- and early-nineteenth-century collections.[1] Several of these collections were mentioned, mainly dismissively, by the Brothers Grimm in the preface to the first volume of the first edition of the *KHM* (Rölleke 1986: I, xviii–xix). The Grimms do not spell out the precise grounds for their objections, but one can fairly assume that they had to do with expansive or elaborate treatments of the plots and with the invention of superfluous detail. That,

---

[1] Schummel, J. G. (1776–8) *Kinderspiele und Gespräche* ('Children's Games and Conversations') 3 vols. Leipzig. Günther, C. W. (1787) *Kindermährchen aus mündlichen Erzählungen gesammelt* ('Children's Tales collected from Oral Narratives'). Erfurt. The anonymous (1791–2) *Ammenmärchen* ('Nurses' Tales'). Weimar. Münch, J. G. (1799) Das *Mährleinbuch für meine Nachbarsleute* ('The Book of Little Tales for my Neighbours'. Leipzig. The anonymous (1801) *Feen-Mährchen* ('Tales of the Fairies'). Braunschweig. Grimm, A. L. (1809) *Kindermährchen* ('Children's Tales'). Heidelberg.

however, was the style of the time and can be seen in other countries too, as, for example, in Thomas Crofton Croker's *Fairy Legends and Traditions of the South of Ireland* (1825–8). The Grimms were breaking new ground by concentrating on simplicity of expression and clarity of structure.

The fascinating thing about the Grimms' enterprise of producing the *KHM* is that we are able to follow the whole process from their initial impetus and researches right through to the definitive edition of 1857. With most other editors of fairy tales, by contrast, we have simply a final printed edition, so their methods of working are less transparent. The two brothers were indefatigable letter-writers, so often personal documentation of details about particular tales and informants can be found in their correspondence. They sent their manuscript collection of tales in October 1810 to their friend, the Romantic poet Clemens Brentano (1778–1842), who was interested in using them for a project of his own which, however, never came to fruition. Prudently, the Grimms had made a copy for themselves, which was used for printing the first edition of the *KHM* and then destroyed. Brentano never returned the original and, decades later, it was found among his posthumous papers and has been edited at least twice (Lefftz 1927; Rölleke 1975). This gives the earliest documentation for some forty-six items, not all of which got into print. In addition to this, there is extant Wilhelm Grimm's personal copy of the two volumes of the first edition of the *KHM*, which contains his autograph notes and emendations of the text for the second edition (Brüder Grimm-Museum, Kassel). This wealth of material allows us an unparalleled insight into the brothers' working methods.

Jacob Grimm was a student at the University of Marburg from 1802 to 1805, Wilhelm following him from 1803 to 1806. There they became acquainted with Brentano and his sister, Bettina and subsequently with Brentano's friend, Achim vom Arnim (1781–1831). Although the Grimms studied law at Marburg with Friedrich Karl von Savigny (1779–1861), they were both passionately involved in reading and rediscovering older German literature. It was in this capacity that they were drawn into contributing material to Arnim and Brentano's influential 1806–8 collection of popular songs, *Des Knaben Wunderhorn* ('The Boy's Magic Horn'). The first volume of that work concluded with an essay by Arnim, in which he declared the aim of collecting and publishing 'the faith and knowledge of the people, what accompanies them in pleasure and death, songs, legends, sayings, stories, prophecies and melodies' (Rölleke 1987: I, 413). Encouraged by both Arnim and Brentano, the brothers embarked on collecting stories and legends from 1807 onwards, though with no clearly formulated idea of publication. They were happy to let Brentano have the fruits of their labours in the manuscripts that they sent him in October 1810, but in March 1811, when he had failed to do anything about them, they set about working on the material with a view to publishing a volume of their own (Rölleke 1985: 1160).

The 1810 manuscript, sometimes known as the Ölenberg manuscript from the abbey of Ölenberg in Alsace, where Brentano's posthumous papers came to rest (it is now in the Fondation Martin Bodmer, Cologny, Geneva), represents the earliest stage of the Grimms' collection. This heteregeneous assemblage of material gives the lie to the popular conception of the two brothers busily going round Hessian villages taking down fairy tales from elderly peasant men and women. The first thing to strike home is the proportion of items taken from literary sources – thirteen out of forty-six. These go back as far as Martin Montanus's *Wegkhürtzer* (1557), but include material as recent as Albert Ludwig Grimm's *Kindermährchen* (1809). There is a preponderance of items from the period from 1790 onwards. Three are derived directly or indirectly from French material: 'Von der Nachtigall und der Blindschleiche' ('The Nightingale and the Slowworm'), no. 38, 'Der Drache' ('The Dragon'), no. 20, 'Murmelthier' ('Marmot'), no. 37, while 'Der Mond und seine Mutter' ('The Moon and his Mother'), no. 36, goes back to a German translation of a passage from Plutarch. Thus already the Grimms make plain their interests in both the historical and comparative aspects of the fairy tale. Though their focus was on German material, it was far from exclusive. Perhaps this is why the word *Deutsch* does not figure in the title of their book. The notes they added to the printed texts from the first volume of the first edition onwards indicate their continuing concern to place what they collected from oral sources within as comprehensive a framework as possible.

As to the orally collected tales in the manuscript, the Grimms' informants were not of peasant stock, but chiefly educated middle-class young women from the Grimms' own social circle. The largest number of tales came from the Wild family in Kassel – Dorothea Catharina (Frau Wild, 1752–1813), Lisette (1782–1858), Gretchen (1787–1819), Dortchen (1793–1867), who became Wilhelm Grimm's wife in 1825, and Mie (1794–1867). Herr Wild was an apothecary and both he and his wife came from Swiss families. Then there were the three Hassenpflug sisters, Marie (1788–1856), Jeanette (1791–1860) and Amalie (1800–71), whose parents had moved from Hanau to Kassel in 1798–9. Their mother was of Huguenot stock and there was a strong tradition of speaking French in the family (Rölleke 1975: 391). A few other tales came from Friederike Mannel (1783–1833), the daughter of a pastor from Hilmes, near Hersfeld. It is possible that another tale came from the Ramus sisters, Julia (1792–1862) and Charlotte (1793–1858), daughters of the French pastor in Kassel. So much for the manuscript and core of the first volume of the first edition.

As far as the second volume is concerned, we have to contend with the figure of Frau Dorothea Viehmann, described in the preface to that volume as 'a peasant woman from the village of Zwehrn near Kassel, through whom we received a considerable portion of the tales communicated here, which are thus genuinely Hessian, along with several additions to the first volume'. However, research has shown that Frau Viehmann was also of Huguenot descent. As John M. Ellis, summarising the results of Georg Textor's investigations of 1955, puts it (1983: 32):

> Dorothea Viehmann's first language was French, not German, and she was a member of the large community of Huguenots who had settled in the area, in which the language of church and school was still French. She was not a peasant but a thoroughly middle-class woman; she was not an untutored transmitter of folk tradition but, on the contrary, a literate woman who knew her Perrault; she was not a German but of French stock.

It is impossible to account for the discrepancy between the Grimms' claim in their preface and the facts that Textor uncovered. Some scholars, like Ellis, regard the Grimms as disingenuous or even duplicitous not only in regard to Frau Viehmann's background, but also in their claims about methodology.

The French connections have been emphasised a good deal recently, under-mining the common opinion that the Grimms' collection is peculiarly German and free from any foreign influence. We need to remember, however, that Perrault composed only eleven fairy tales, eight in prose and three in verse. Only two items in the Grimms' manuscript – 'Dornröschen' ('Thorn Rose'), no. 19, and 'Prinzessin Mäusehaut' ('Princess Mouseskin'), no. 35 – betray a strong resemblance to tales by Perrault ('La Belle au bois dormant' and 'Peau d'âne' respectively). Similarly, out of the twenty-five items supplied by Frau Viehmann only two – 'Der arme Müllerbursch und das Kätzchen' ('The Poor Miller's Son and the Cat') and 'Sechse kommen durch die ganze Welt' ('Six travel through the whole World') have clear parallels in Madame d'Aulnoy's 'La Chatte blanche' and 'Belle-Belle ou le chevalier fortuné'. The 1812 volume also included 'Der gestiefelte Kater' ('Puss-in-Boots') and 'Blaubart' ('Bluebeard'), both pro-vided by the Hassenpflugs, but they were eliminated from subsequent editions because of their close correspondence to Perrault's 'Le Chat botté' and 'La Barbe bleue'. This helps to put in perspective the French contribution to the Grimms' collection. The only remaining problem case is perhaps 'Rothkäppchen' ('Little Red Riding-Hood'), which appears to be a conflation of Perrault's 'Le Petit Chaperon rouge' with 'Der Wolf mit den sieben jungen Geißlein' ('The Wolf with the Seven Little Kids').

To return to the Grimms' manuscript, Heinz Rölleke has shown that the collection sent to Brentano must have consisted of fifty-three items (Rölleke 1975: 15). These can be broken down into the broad categories of the Aarne–Thompson classification of folktale types as follows: eight animal tales, thirty-seven tales of magic, one tale of the stupid ogre, two novellas, one cumulative tale and four tales that do not fit the classification. This last group includes one aetiological tale, 'Der Mond und seine Mutter' ('The Moon and his Mother'), one that might fit somewhere among AT 275–99, 'Blutwurst', and two religious tales similar to those collected later as *Kinderlegenden*, namely 'Armes Mädchen' ('Poor Girl') and 'Von dem gestohlenen Heller' ('The Stolen Penny').

Overwhelmingly, therefore, the emphasis in this *ur*-collection lies on tales of magic, that is, fairy tales in the narrower sense of the term. Approximately seven tenths of the tales are fairy tales. It is interesting to compare this with the 1857 edition of the *KHM*, where the proportion of fairy tales in this sense is about half. Already the *ur*-collection contains versions of such famous fairy tales as 'Allerleirauh' ('All Kinds of Fur'), 'Die zwölf Brüder' ('The Twelve Brothers'), 'Brüderchen und Schwesterchen' ('Little Brother and Little Sister'), 'Hänsel und Gretel' ('Hansel and Gretel'), 'Der Froschkönig' ('The Frog Prince'), 'Fundevo-gel', 'Die goldene Gans' ('The Golden Goose'), 'Rumpelstilzchen' ('Rumpelstilts-kin'), 'Sneewittchen' ('Snow White'), 'Aschenputtel' ('Cinderella') and 'Der goldene Vogel' ('The Golden Bird'). What we must remember, though, with regard to these manuscript versions is that they are not verbatim records of an orally performed tale, but more like plot summaries. Some are very brief indeed; others needed very little editorial treatment before being printed in the 1812 volume. In this initial collaboration, Jacob seems to have played the leading role: some twenty-nine tales were collected by him in comparison with Wilhelm's eighteen. Friederike Mannel and Jeanette Hassenpflug wrote down one tale each, while the origin of four others is not clear.

Not all this manuscript material was used for the first edition. It represents only the first stage of the Grimms' collection, since they continued their work after sending this preliminary material to Brentano. By the time they were ready to move towards their own publication they had amassed many more tales, including some that they considered better versions of tales they already had. So seven items (nos. 13, 20, 22, 29, 32, 36 and 46) found a place only in the notes to the 1812 volume, supplementing these better versions. Three tales were not published at all (nos. 23, 31 and *vor* 48). The first two had been excerpted from printed sources, while the third, 'Vom König von England' ('The King of England'), was probably eliminated because of its close similarity to the story of 'The Three Sisters' from the *Thousand and One Nights*. The Grimms did not want to include tales that they ultimately considered literary in presentation and style. They were looking for material, whether in printed sources or in contemporary oral form, that was simple and unpretentious and could be regarded as reflecting the ideas, tastes and aspirations of ordinary people.

The preface to the 1812 volume of the KHM begins with a comparison from the world of nature. The persistence of fairy tales (in the broader sense) among the peasantry is seen as analogous to that of ears of corn that escape the destructiveness of storms and flourish by hedgerows and on the edge of fields, where they are carefully gathered by 'poor, pious hands', taken home and provide nourishment through the winter.

> Seats by the stove, the kitchen range, attic stairs, holidays still celebrated, pastures and forests in their quietness, above all the unsullied imagination, these were the hedges that kept them safe and passed them on from one era to another.

The Grimms make high claims about their presentation of the tales:

> We have taken pains to present these tales in as pure a manner as was possible. In many one will find the narrative interrupted by rhymes and verses that sometimes even alliterate, but are never sung while the story is being told, and these very tales are the oldest and best. No detail has been added or embellished and altered, for we should have been afraid of enlarging stories that are so rich in themselves with analogies or reminiscences taken from them; they are not to be fabricated.

The latter part of this claim has proved very contentious, since the comparison of printed tale with manuscript format has shown that, in a number of instances, the Grimms did alter and embellish not merely unimportant or trivial details but also critical events or aspects of a tale. We shall need to take our consideration of changes as far as the second edition (1819), since the issues are not entirely straightforward. Let us turn now to some examples.

'The Frog Prince or Iron Henry', placed first in the collection from 1812 onwards, derives from a manuscript summary by Wilhelm Grimm headed 'Die

Königstochter und der verzauberte Prinz, Froschkönig' ('The King's Daughter and the Enchanted Prince, Frog King'), which he expands to about twice that length. The manuscript starts by referring to the protagonist as the youngest daughter of the king, while the printed texts make the fact known only through the frog's appeal to her in what is printed in verse format: 'King's daughter, youngest one, open up for me, don't you know what you said to me yesterday by the cool water of the fountain? King's daughter, youngest one, open up for me.' But in neither manuscript nor printed text is there any allusion to other sisters.

In the 1812 text the princess offers 'everything, my clothes, my jewels, my pearls and everything in the world' for the return of her lost golden ball, while the manuscript says nothing. The manuscript has the frog offering to fetch it 'if you will take me home with you'. This the 1812 text expands to: 'but if you will take me as your companion and I sit next to you at table and eat from your little golden plate and sleep in your little bed and you respect and love me'. The 1819 version is even more specific: 'if you will take me as your *friend and* companion, I shall sit at your table *at your right side*, eat *with you* from your little golden plate, *drink from your little goblet* and sleep in your little bed' (my italics).

Th climax of the tale comes when the princess flings the frog at the wall, which the manuscript presents as: 'However, when he hit the wall, he fell down into the bed and lay in it as a young, handsome prince, and the princess lay down with him.' The 1812 text is slightly different: 'But the frog did not fall down dead, but when it came on to the bed it was a handsome young prince. He was now her dear companion, and she respected him as she had promised, and they fell contentedly asleep together.' The 1819 version is again more specific: 'But what fell down was not a dead frog, but an alive young king's son with beautiful and kind eyes. He was now, rightfully and according to her father's will, her dear companion and spouse. Then they fell contentedly asleep together.' The sequence of changes made between the manuscript and the 1819 text make ever clearer the nature of the marriage contract and the father's role in determining his daughter's future. In the manuscript it is the frog that takes the initiative and states his conditions for fetching the golden ball for the disconsolate princess, while in the 1812 text, it is the princess who weeps and laments and declares what she will give in order to get her ball back.

Some of these changes Wilhelm Grimm must have made quite consciously, but possibly not all of them. It is only when we know about them that we can properly assess the significance of the final text of 1857, which is not so very different from that of 1819. All of the German texts are content with the prince falling into the princess's bed and the two going to sleep together, but the first English version of the tale, by Edgar Taylor (1823), could not cope with it and changed the ending completely. Taylor has the frog sleep on the princess's pillow for three nights, 'but when the princess awoke on the following morning, she was astonished to see, instead of the frog, a handsome prince gazing on her with the most beautiful eyes that ever were seen, and standing at the head of her bed'. There is no flinging against the wall and no prince and princess sleeping together in bed. The English reading public would have thought it immoral (Blamires 1989; Sutton 1990), but it caused no problems in Germany.

A fairy tale that did cause problems in its first printed state was 'Rapunzel'. This derives from a story by Friedrich Schultz included in his *Kleine Romane*, which in its turn goes back to the fairy tale 'Persinette' by Mademoiselle de la Force (Rölleke 1980: III, 447). 'Rapunzel' is now mainly known in a version in which the heroine incriminates herself by asking her godmother why the latter is so much heavier to pull up into the tower than the young prince who is up in a moment. This poorly motivated incident features in all the editions of Grimm from 1819 onwards, but the 1812 text is much more convincing. There, after the prince has been visiting for some time, Rapunzel asks her godmother why her clothes have become so tight and don't fit any more. This allusion to premarital pregnancy was severely criticised, so Wilhelm Grimm removed it from subsequent editions. The fact of pregnancy remains in the story, since Rapunzel gives birth to twins while the prince, blinded from his fall from the tower, wanders around miserably in the forest; but it is not talked about.

Another fairy tale that undergoes far-reaching changes between manuscript and printed text is 'Snow White'. Not until the 1819 edition do we get the figure of the wicked stepmother; up to that point it was Snow White's own mother who was her jealous persecutor. In the manuscript she takes her daughter into the forest to pick red roses and abandons her, hoping wild animals will eat her. In the 1812 text she orders a hunter to kill Snow White and bring back lung and liver as proof. In the manuscript it is Snow White's own father who finds her supposed corpse in the glass coffin when he returns from abroad. The doctors in his entourage bring her back to life, she is taken home and married to a handsome prince. But already in the 1812 text, Snow White in her coffin is given to a prince who has fallen in love with her beauty, and she comes back to life when an irritated servant knocks the body and dislodges the poisonous piece of apple from her throat. This latter motif is removed from the 1819 text, so that the apple is dislodged as a result of servants merely stumbling while carrying Snow White. In every version Snow White is a passive victim whose only activity is keeping house for the seven dwarves. The main interest of the tale lies in the figure of the wicked (step)mother, and it is noteworthy that the Grimms' predecessor, Musäus, in his version of this fairy tale, concentrated virtually all his attention on the stepmother and made her name, Richilde, the title of his complex ironic story.

The changes in textual form do not depend solely on Wilhelm Grimm's whim, but on new variants of the tale with which he had become acquainted. The manuscript version came from the Hassenpflugs, while the altered ending given in 1812 derives from Ferdinand Siebert, a young theologian and student of German philology, who provided the Grimms with several tales. The further change to Snow White's restoration to consciousness in the 1819 text comes from a variant provided by Heinrich Leopold Stein (Rölleke 1980: III, 465). The change of mother to stepmother, however, seems to be Wilhelm Grimm's own and to reflect a peculiarly protective and idealised view of the mother figure.

As the Grimms continued collecting tales, principally from oral sources and from people outside their own immediate circle, they constantly encountered variant versions of tales that they already knew and thus had to make some judgement about how to treat them. What they did was to follow the practice then employed in editing medieval texts. Scholars attempted to reconstruct the original form of a work on the basis of a comparison of extant versions varying in date, dialect, substance, vocabulary, aesthetic skill and so on. In this way a 'critical' text could be established. When the Grimms had variants of fairy tales they tended to construct composite texts. They would choose a variant with the most coherent plot structure as the basis, but modify or amplify it with details taken from other variants. Because they were also interested in things like proverbs, traditional verses and folk customs, they often included them, where appropriate, in particular tales. As they became more familiar with the structural features of fairy tales, they tended to standardise patterns such as threefold repetitions of actions or the protagonist being the youngest of three siblings of the same sex. Often the reason for editorial changes in the form of a particular tale from, say, the first edition to a later one, was that the brothers had been provided with a new variant which they considered better than what they previously possessed. The rejected variant was often, but not invariably, relegated to the notes that the Grimms appended to their texts from the first edition on. By the time of the second edition they had so much material that the notes formed a separate volume published in 1822. A third edition of the notes, greatly expanded, was published in 1856. It is thus possible, in some cases, to locate discarded versions of a tale in these notes.[2]

A particularly striking instance of the substitution of a new text occurs with 'Der Eisenhans' ('Iron John'), a composite standard German text that replaced, as late as 1850, the Low German 'De wilde Mann' ('The Wild Man'), which had reached the Grimms via the Haxthausen family from Paderborn and been included in the KHM from the 1815 volume of the first edition up to 1843. The Low German text, which is simpler, rougher and only about half the length, but more difficult of access owing to its dialect form, was completely supplanted; it was not included in the 1856 edition of the Grimms' notes. The new version is more literary and, in the complexity of its plot moves, somewhat akin to an abbreviated Volksbuch. This new text has recently attracted considerable attention through Robert Bly's interpretation in Iron John: A Book about Men (1990).

Another tale that underwent a similar process of substitution is 'Der Räuberbräutigam' ('The Robber Bridegroom'), a disturbing tale analogous to the English 'Mister Fox'. The manuscript version, written by Jacob and taken from Marie Hassenpflug, is basically a plot summary mixing past and present tenses and has a princess and a prince as its key figures. The 1812 text expands the narrative, which it gives entirely in the past tense, increases the mood of fear and gives the supposed dream sequence in full. The atmosphere of suspense is very striking. However, the version printed in 1819 is quite different and compounded of two other variants from Hessen, contaminated with some details from the 1812 text. We now have a miller's daughter and a would-be bridegroom of unspecified background, though supposed to be wealthy. The latter marks his bride's path through the forest with ashes, whereas the prince had tied ribbons to the trees. On arrival at the lonely forest house, the miller's

---

[2] Rölleke reprinted the 1856 edition in his three-volume Reclam edition of 1980.

daughter is warned of danger by the voice of a bird in a cage, not simply by the old woman housekeeper. This is the only non-realistic element in the story. In the manuscript and the 1812 text, the robbers murder the princess's grandmother, while in the 1819 version, they murder 'another young woman', first making her drunk with white, red and yellow wine, before hacking her body into pieces and salting it. The horror is intensified through this clearer alignment of the robbers' victim with the protagonist of the story. Presumably also Wilhelm Grimm preferred a miller's daughter to a princess because it fitted better with the belief in the popular origins of the fairy tale. Further, mainly stylistic alterations were made to the story for the 1837 edition.

Several other tales show comparable kinds of changes in textual form from the manuscript or the first edition onwards, among them 'Rumpelstilzchen', 'Das Mädchen ohne Hände' ('The Girl without Hands') and 'Der Jude im Dorn' ('The Jew in the Brambles'). With the majority of the remaining tales, however, the changes tend to be verbal or stylistic rather than centring on content. The main criticisms that had been levelled at the 1812 volume when it first appeared focused on style and presentation, which were felt to be rough and unpolished. Both Brentano and A. L. Grimm mentioned Runge as a model that ought to have been followed (Rölleke 1985: 1162–3). Philipp Otto Runge (1777–1810), a leading Romantic artist, had provided the Grimms with two Low German tales – 'Van den Fischer un siine Fru' ('The Fisherman and his Wife') and 'Van den Machandel-Boom' ('The Juniper Tree') – that were printed in the 1812 volume and quickly achieved great popularity. Oddly enough, these texts were also subjected to verbal and orthographical changes from the fifth edition (1843) onwards, as Wilhelm Grimm tried to iron out variations that went back to two different versions that Runge himself had made (Rölleke 1980: III, 449–50). A Low German dialect form was nonetheless retained, and indeed the 1857 edition contains twenty-one tales in a variety of dialects. Runge's two tales were narrated in a simple, straightforward manner but certain episodes were made more immediate through the use of dialogue and lines of verse. 'The Juniper Tree', for example, is famous for the song that Goethe included in *Faust*, in which the murdered boy, in the form of a bird, recounts what has happened:

> Min Moder de mi slacht't,
> min Vader de mi att,
> min Swester de Marleeniken
> söcht alle mine Beeniken,
> un bindt se in een siden Dook,
> legts unner den Machandelboom;
> kywitt, kywitt! Ach watt een schön Vagel bin ick!

> My mother slew me,
> My father ate me,
> My sister Marleeniken
> Sought all my bones
> And bound them in a silken cloth,
> Put them under the juniper tree;
> Kywitt, kywitt, what a beautiful bird I am!

The inclusion of verse material is something that we find in about a quarter of all the tales (53 items) in the 1857 edition.

The 1812 volume was experimental. The Grimms were trying out the material they had collected and it presents a considerable variety of kinds of tale as well as modes of narration. When it came to revising the collection for the second edition of 1819–22, a great deal was altered. Nineteen texts were entirely eliminated, while fourteen were removed to the notes. From the 1815 volume five were eliminated, and two removed to the notes. The differences in the changes made to the two volumes demonstrate how much the brothers had learnt between 1812 and 1815. They had realised from their own continued collecting, as well as from the reactions of friends and critics, that some of their tales could be replaced with better versions, while some were more appropriately removed altogether. Among the latter perhaps the most striking excision affected the two versions of 'Wie Kinder Schlachtens miteinander gespielt haben' ('How Children Played at Butcher Together'), a gruesome tale of children playing at butcher, in the course of which one little boy has his throat slit. Both versions have literary sources that go back to the sixteenth and seventeenth centuries respectively, though Wilhelm Grimm claimed he had heard it from his mother as a child (Rölleke 1980: III, 520–1). Other tales, such as 'Der gestiefelte Kater' ('Puss-in-Boots'), 'Blaubart' ('Bluebeard') and 'Die drei Schwestern' ('The Three Sisters'), were excluded because of their closeness to Perrault's 'Le Chat botté' and 'La Barbe bleue' and Musäus's 'Die Bücher der Chronika der drei Schwestern'. The fifth edition (1843) included a story entitled 'Die Erbsenprobe' ('The Pea Ordeal'), which was removed from subsequent editions because of its dependence on Andersen's 'The Princess on the Pea'. A few other tales were omitted because they were more like legends than fairy tales. All this omitted material is of interest, but it is accessible only in the first edition or in the appendix to a modern scholarly edition such as Rölleke's 1980 edition or in the English translation by Ruth Michaelis-Jena and Arthur Ratcliff (Grimm 1956/1960).

The biggest change in the presentation of the KHM occurred between the first and the second edition, but further smaller changes took place all the way through to the seventh edition of 1857. New tales were added, better versions were substituted, and stylistic improvements and other verbal alterations were made. These changes, beginning already in 1819, turned the collection increasingly into a work calculated to appeal to a child readership, while at the same time maintaining an ambitious basis in the production of 'better' texts of individual tales and the provision of a scholarly commentary. Through the removal of morally questionable elements from certain stories and their alignment with the values and feelings of the middle class, including their attitudes towards religion and gender roles, the Grimms created a work of immense appeal. While the complete collection was perhaps dauntingly long, a selection of fifty tales, attractively illustrated by their younger brother, Ludwig Emil Grimm, created a more accessible 'small edition' that went through ten editions from 1825 to 1859, the year of Wilhelm Grimm's death, and had reached thirty-six editions by 1887 (Gerstner 1982: 351).

Many people referring to the KHM today are unaware of the textual history of the collection and are apt to make pronouncements on the basis of slender or fragmentary acquaintance with the material. If they rely on translations the situation is increasingly fraught, as many translators have made modifications of their own to their chosen text. There is also a tendency among some writers to judge the Grimms with the hindsight of 150 or more years of critical experience and then to blame them for not occupying the critical positions of today. But the Grimms were men of their own era and reflected, consciously or unconsciously, the accepted social, moral and religious standards of their day. Maria Tatar and Ruth Bottigheimer have skilfully laid these standards bare, particularly in respect of the Grimms' understanding of gender roles. The fact that the brothers imposed their own ideas and views on the material they published is no different from what happens with storytellers of any period. Scholars may construct what they believe to be the 'original' or base-text of a particular tale, but each storyteller, whether in speech or in print, creates his or her own narrative. Only with printed texts do we approach standardised forms. But anyone who examines different translations of the same base-text will see that changes occur here too. Moreover, even with one and the same text, we can see how different illustrations can create varying interpretations and reader reactions.

There is in fact no form of a fairy tale that can be regarded as normative, since the storytelling tradition is a process in which tales are constantly reinvented. We may imagine that in going back to the earliest examples we are getting closer to a hypothetical 'original', but we have no means of knowing what may have preceded those earliest extant examples in oral tradition. In recording in print different versions of orally current tales, usually through intermediaries, the Grimms were, as it were, making snapshots of a living, developing tradition (though, ironically, they thought it was actually dying). They themselves contributed to this living tradition through the work they published in the seven editions of the *KHM*. It thus seems fruitful to regard these editions as a workshop of editorial practice, the progressive shaping of contemporary and historical folktale material so as to make it simultaneously available to child readers of their day and the world of scholars too.

References

Aarne, A., and Thompson, S. (1981), *The Types of the Folktale. A Classification and Biography*. FFC 184. Helsinki.

Blamires, D. (1989), 'The Early Reception of the Grimms' *Kinder- und Hausmärchen* in England', *Bulletin of the John Rylands University Library of Manchester*, 71.3, 63–77.

Bly, R. (1990), *Iron John: A Book about Men*. Reading, MA.

Bottigheimer, R. B. (1987), *Grimms' Bad Girls and Bold Boys: The Moral and Social Vision of the Tales*. New Haven/London.

Ellis, J. M. (1983), *One Fairy Story Too Many: The Brothers Grimm and Their Tales*. Chicago/London.

Gerstner H. (1982) ed., *Grimms Märchen: die kleine Ausgabe aus dem Jahr 1825*. Dortmund.

Grimm, J. and W. (1956/1960), *New Tales from Grimm*, trans. R. Michaelis-Jena and A. Ratcliff. Edinburgh/London. (First published as *Grimms' Other Tales*. London.)

Lefftz, J. (1927) ed., *Märchen der Brüder Grimm: Urfassung nach der Originalhandschrift der Abtei Ölenberg im Elsaß*. Heidelberg.

Musäus, J. K. A. (1977), *Volksmärchen der Deutschen*. Munich.

Rölleke, H. (1975) ed., *Die älteste Märchensammlung der Brüder Grimm*. Cologny/Geneva.

——(1980) ed., *Brüder Grimm, Kinder- und Hausmärchen: Ausgabe letzter Hand mit den Originalanmerkungen der Brüder Grimm*. 3 vols. Stuttgart.

——(1982) ed., *Brüder Grimm, Kinder- und Hausmärchen: nach der zweiten vermehrten und verbesserten Auflage von 1819*. 2 vols. Cologne.

——(1985) ed., *Kinder- und Hausmärchen gesammelt durch die Brüder Grimm: vollständige Ausgabe auf der Grundlage der dritten Auflage (1837)*. Frankfurt.

——(1986) ed., *Kinder- und Hausmärchen gesammelt durch die Brüder Grimm: vergrößerter Nachdruck der zweibändigen Erstausgabe von 1812 und 1815*. 2 vols. Göttingen.

——(1987), *Des Knaben Wunderhorn: alte deutsche Lieder gesammelt von Achim von Arnim und Clemens Brentano*. 3 vols. Stuttgart.

Sutton, M. (1990), 'A Prince Transformed: The Grimms' "Froschkönig" in English', *Seminar* 24.2, 119–37.

Tatar, M. (1987), *The Hard Facts of the Grimms' Fairy Tales*. Princeton.

Taylor, E. (1979) trans., *Grimms' Fairy Tales*, illustrated by George Cruikshank, reproduced in facsimile from first English edn. 2 vols. London.

Zipes, J. (2000) ed., *The Oxford Companion to Fairy Tales*. Oxford.

5

Old Tales for New: Finding the First Fairy Tales

GRAHAM ANDERSON

There is a general assumption, certainly among children's writers and also among both classicists and folklorists, that fairy tales should be seen as a relatively recent phenomenon (e.g. Opie 1974 *passim*; Purkiss 2000 by implication). Certainly one might be tempted to say this of such products as the Harry Potter books written specifically for a children's market by literate adults. But magically escapist plots of stories that could be told to, or adapted for, children are very old indeed (Thompson 1946: 272–82). This is fairly widely known or suspected in a very general way, but seems not to be widely cared about, and there has been hitherto little detailed treatment of specific examples. Just how old are 'Cinderella', 'Snow White' and 'Goldilocks and the Three Bears'? If you ask such a question, people might well wonder why you should want to know: have scholars not got better things to do than try to put a timetable on what 'everybody knows' is timeless? Either we feel that such information is really unknowable anyway, or we somehow hope it will turn out to be so. Professional folklore scholars have gone at least part of the way to putting some kind of date on some tales: for close on ninety years there was known to be a 'Cinderella' story in ninth-century China, though 'Goldilocks' has been pushed back no further than 1830, and the very name Goldilocks may be no older than the twentieth century. Many fairy tales seem no older than either eighteenth-century France, or the Renaissance at most.

The way scholarly enquiry has developed over the past two centuries has meant that classicists do not generally study fairy tales, and fairy-tale specialists do not study the ancient world. The result is that, outside a very narrow range of specialisms, there is only token, grudging or misleading information that fairy tales existed in classical antiquity at all. We are told that very popular tales which might have been so described are really either myths or migratory legends, or that they are not really 'our' fairy tales, which are so to speak the inviolable preserve of the Renaissance or just before. There is a sense that because the trail tends to peter out at the end of the Middle Ages, there is likely to be little or nothing beyond the earliest point of observation; or that if there is, it must somehow be someone else's province. Most recently we might note that a professional account by a modern literary specialist, Diane Purkiss (2000), does include a detailed investigation of the equivalents of fairies in the ancient world, but offers no acknowledgement of the existence of 'Cupid and Psyche', if only to discount its status as a fairy tale, as some still do. This is unfortunate, since

folklore studies have made such progress on the geographical front: if a
Patagonian peasant breathes a word of 'Cinderella', then there will be an
anthropologist on hand to explain whatever 'equivalent' there might be in the
tale as a counterpart to the glass slipper. But if a 'Cinderella' is found, let us say,
in an author of the early Roman Empire, there is more likely to be a classicist
prepared to explain why this is not really *our* 'Cinderella', and why any
references to it are fanciful, approximate or misguided.

Let us recapitulate, then, what is agreed: a small cache of 'modern' fairy tale
from antiquity is indeed known. Apuleius' 'Cupid and Psyche' (second century
AD) commands general agreement as having fairy-tale quality of some description; if this is not a 'real' fairy tale then nothing else is likely to be. But what else
is there? H. J. Rose (1958: 286–304) drew up a tiny (and muddled) check list of
transmitted tales and motifs, tied persistently to a long-outdated indexing
system, through which it is not possible to make substantial comparison. The
implication was quite clearly that these were so much nonsense anyway. But
textbooks continued to echo the claim that the first 'Cinderella' occurred in
ninth-century China, that 'Snow White' is not found before the Grimms, that
'Jack the Giant-Killer' comes from Renaissance chapbooks, and so on.

In what follows I wish to illustrate briefly a number of different approaches
that can be followed to enlarge the canon of ancient fairy tale very substantially.
First of all we need a flexible working definition of fairy tale that will include
narratives of a 'Cupid and Psyche' type and exclude others, with a reasonable
degree of common sense. A tale is likely to turn out to be a fairy tale if the
following conditions are fulfilled: (a) it is a clear example of Aarne–Thompson
types, especially those listed between AT 300 and 749; (b) it approximates to
examples of fairy tale in the standard collections of Straparola, Basile, Perrault
and the Grimms; (c) the removal of expurgations or cultural modifications of a
characteristic type would turn it into a children's or nursery tale; (d) it 'has the
feel of a fairy tale', however we might succeed in defining it. This last category is
not nearly so absurd, approximate or irresponsible as it seems: there may be
fairy tales which would have reached Basile or the Grimms if they had not
simply died out or been modified out of recognition; there must, theoretically at
least, be fairy tales which for some reason did not survive the ancient world, but
which cannot be excluded from the genre just because they are difficult or
impossible to classify on any current system. Let us test our criteria on an
example (Diogenes Laertius I, 109):

> Epimenides of Crete was serving as a shepherd. While he went to look for a
> lost sheep he went into a cave and fell asleep. When he awoke and could not
> find the sheep, he went home and found someone else in his house; only his
> brother, now an old man, was able to tell him that he had slept for fifty-seven
> years.

The story in this form belongs to the third century AD. It is, as far as it goes, the
story of 'Rip van Winkle', and not 'The Sleeping Beauty' as Rose claims (1958:
293). Do we call it historical legend because the person to whom the experience
is attributed in this case actually existed and the location is precise? Or do we
call it fairy tale because of the element of the supernatural involved? Com-

parison with 'Rip van Winkle' may help: there is no funny little man to ask a favour of him, as there is in Washington Irving's story[1] and no other world (we are not told of any dream during the interval). But the reason there is none is that Diogenes Laertius saw the story as biographical legend; he may well have abridged precisely the decisive fairy-tale element out of the tale. I should unhesitatingly include it as it stands in an anthology of ancient fairy tale, but with these reservations duly expressed. It seems as clear a 'take' of 'Rip van Winkle' as we shall get, and proves that there was an almost fully developed version of this story in classical times.

To ask what the ancient world had by way of fairy tales is seldom done. It is all rather like asking whether madmen have normal dreams – we are assumed to have no way of entering a closed world. People who wrote ancient literature, be they Æschylus, Ovid or Plato, have little interest in such supposed trivia, where they see fit to mention it at all, and the rich repertoire of myth is an 'adults only' affair. But there are traces. In my 2000 study, *Fairy Tale in the Ancient World*, I have set out to look at the evidence for some two dozen modern fairy-tale types. The method is to build up a short profile of the tradition of each tale as it has emerged in modern times, and to match this flexible framework with examples and fragments of tales drawn most often from unfamiliar corners of the ancient world and from often quite obscure mythographers and ancient commentators. This makes it possible to recognise tale after tale, though often the details of ancient texts turn up in the sort of modern examples furthest removed from the polite world of Perrault's prettified and sanitised versions which so often set the standard for modern retellings. It is worthwhile to draw up a brief repertoire of 'classic fairy tales' to see how many can be found in classical antiquity in at least some form. Without making unduly precise distinctions between folk- and fairy tale, I suggest the following list, by no means intended as complete. Nor can it be claimed that the level of correspondence is consistently striking in every case. The traditional earliest dating is followed, where appropriate, by one revised in the light of ancient texts:

Fairy tale	Traditional earliest dating	Revised earliest dating
Cinderella	9th century Chinese	Sumerian; Herodotus/ Strabo (*FTAW* 27ff.; 39f.)
Snow White	Grimm; cf. Basile, 1634	Ovid; Greek Chione-texts (*FTAW* 46–57)
Puss-in-Boots	Straparola, 1553	Hyginus, 2nd century AD (*FTAW* 173–6)
Rumpelstiltskin	Basile; L'Héritier, 1696	Ancient: Lucian, *Fugitivi*; Chryse legends; Ancient Egyptian analogue (*FTAW* 138–42)

[1] In *The Sketch Book* of Geoffrey Crayon, Gent (1819–20).

Fairy tale	Traditional earliest dating	Revised earliest dating
The Frog Prince	Petronius, 1st century AD	Homer, *Odyssey* 6 (*FTAW* 176ff.)
Hop-o-My-Thumb	'Ino and Themisto' (Hyginus, 2nd century AD)	No change
Sleeping Beauty	Basile; Perrault	Chloris-Niobe legend, Homer onwards
Jack and the Beanstalk	18th century	'Gilgamesh and the Huluppu-Tree' (*FTAW* 187)
Blinding the Ogre	Homer, *Odyssey* 9	No change
Aladdin	Galland's source for his 18th-century translation of the *Arabian Nights*	Gyges-legend (*FTAW* 105ff.)
Cupid and Psyche	Apuleius, 2nd century AD	Hittite analogues (*FTAW* 63–9)
Innocent Slandered Maid	*Count of Ponthieu's Daughter* (Medieval French) (cf. Brunel 1923; Matarasso 1971)	Herodotus; Chariton (*FTAW* 86, 89)
Little Red Riding Hood	Egbert of Liège; Perrault	Pausanias; Thetis-legend (*FTAW* 92–7)
The Foolish Wishes	Phaedrus, 1st century AD	No change
King Thrushbeard	Grimm	Sumerian, 'Enlil and Ninlil' (*FTAW* 188ff.)
Six around the World	*Argonautica*	No change
Bluebeard	Late medieval?	Ancient Minos-legend (*FTAW* 98f.)
Twelve Dancing Princesses	Grimm	Melampus-legend (*FTAW* 119–21))
Alcestis	Greek tragedy	No change
Hansel and Gretel	Grimm	Philostratus (3rd century AD) *Life of Apollonius* 4.25
The Emperor's New Clothes	*El conde Lucanor*, late medieval	Lucian, 2nd century AD
The Pied Piper	Historical legend after 1284 AD	Laomedon texts; Moses and Pharaoh (*FTAW* 134f.)
The Sorcerer's Apprentice	Lucian	No change
The Magic Cockerel	Modern Low Countries	Lucian (*FTAW* 107ff.)
The Obstacle Flight	Argonautica (*FTAW* 73–6)	Sumerian, 'Inanna and Enki'
Kind and Unkind Girls	Perrault	Menander, Ovid (*FTAW* 178–82)
Dragon-Slayer	Bellerophon, Perseus, Peleus, Homer onwards	No change
Avoiding Destiny	Oedipus legend, classical	No change
Men into Swine	Gilgamesh	No change
Journey to the Other World	Gilgamesh	No change

Of the thirty tales listed, no fewer than twenty should be redated, of which only two are redatings within antiquity itself. Some of any such list leaves room for disagreement, in at least several cases very considerable. But the cumulative case is still a substantial one: if this 'spread' of materials is recognisable, then we are entitled to claim that the kernel of the modern western European repertoire, including no fewer than seven of the eight Perrault tales, and all but three of the tales designated as 'Classic Fairy Tales' by the Opies, are actually ancient. We should note as a caveat that several of the texts only make sense in a reconstruction from two or more partially interlocking versions. Each case needs to be assessed on its own merits, but the general trend is scarcely in doubt.

Why, and in what sense, are ancient tales likely to be 'different' from their modern counterparts? In some cases we should be tempted to feel that differences are minimal, and it is only sheer familiarity with a text in some completely different context that makes it difficult to recognise a variant. Denys Page (1972), in discussing the *Odyssey*, deals with Circe, the Lotus-eaters and others, but not with Nausicaa. Yet what fairy tale entails a princess going to the waterside and disturbing a strange creature with her ball, only to find him in due course transformed into a handsome prince? This is already a form of 'The Frog Prince' (AT 440), which has well-established variants where a kelpie or bogle or similar creature plays the part of the frog. Odysseus, unrecognisable and horrifying because of the brine, is awakened by the girls' loss of their ball, and is then totally transformed into a supposed marriage prospect, to the princess's delight. Of course Odysseus does not marry her, but the fairy tale has been neatly adapted into a gentle domestic comedy of manners just as surely as several other folk- or fairy-tale episodes that follow.

Or again, where should we look, for example, for an early specimen of 'My Mother Slew Me, My Father Ate Me'? We need look no further than the book of Genesis: all we are told is that 'the voice of thy brother's blood crieth unto me from the ground' (4: 10). If the Genesis author had added something like 'And he said, "My brother slew me"', the identification would have been much easier. And that is a reminder that often what sticks in our mind is the more variable and incidental component in a tale. We tend to know 'Cinderella' by the glass slipper, not by the really significant bride test, of which this is only an apparently invented variant; we remember 'Snow White' by the magic mirror's question and the seven dwarves; the 'Pied Piper' as much by his uniform as his function; 'Puss-in-Boots' by the boots rather than the outline of the plot. Indeed 'All the better to eat you with', 'Who's been sleeping in *my* bed' and 'You *shall* go to the ball' tend to be more immediate indicators of their respective tales than Aarne–Thompson or Proppian analysis: a reminder of the power of the heard or spoken punch line.

Sometimes a new ancient version will contain a combination of standard variations in both detail and structure. Perhaps the most surprising 'new text' of ancient fairy tale concerns the gods who build city walls for a king, then cause him to lose the city's children when he refuses to pay. One of the gods is Apollo, a lyre-player rather than a piper, and a god who controls mice rather than rats, but the overall story-pattern is clear enough, even if we have to combine

Apollo's exploits with mice from a different text with the rest of the narrative (Strabo 13.1.48; Apollodorus 2.5.9; 2.6.4). Even the little boy who survives is there – the future King Priam of Troy, long before the building of Hamelin, let alone the Pied Piper. Apart from substitutions in matters of minor detail (the task, the role of the vermin, the musical instrument, the precise fate of the children), the ancient version we have is also complicated by a double action: Laomedon refuses to pay first Poseidon and Apollo, then Heracles, and suffers on each occasion. What we have runs to two creditor gods functioning together as a pair; it would be no surprise if we were to find a version where the traditional rule of three applies, where Laomedon would double-cross gods on three separate occasions, losing say his daughter Hesione, the rest of the girls, then the male children of Troy at the three stages. Nor can we be accused of distorting or manipulating a sequence of coincidences in widely scattered texts: the account of Moses and the Egyptian plagues produces much the same story, even if we have ten plagues when three or even one would have done (Exodus 5–12).

Other examples, however, offer more fundamental differences: we have a girl whose sandal is delivered to a Pharaoh by an eagle, before the familiar Cinderella slipper test. She has a past, not in the hearth first and foremost, but as a slave-girl and a courtesan (Anderson 2000: 27–8); this is obviously an adult tale when Strabo tells it in the Augustan age, and the first casualty of adapting such stories for children is the sex life of the heroine. But we have another Cinderella who rolls in cinders before an angel tells her to put on a wedding garment and marry the biblical Joseph, this time with only a faint echo of the slipper test.

Sometimes the changes are still more disturbing: in our Hellenistic version of this 'Joseph and Asenath' tale, the heroine is totally pure; but a medieval rabbinical version has the heroine born out of the rape of Dinah (Anderson 2000: 33–7). The realities of an adult sexual world are never too far from the surface. So again, when Chione ('Snow-girl') is visited by someone in the guise of an old woman and, on a second occasion, put to sleep, it is not for murder but for rape. And the jealous 'other woman' who tries to kill her is the goddess Artemis. Moreover, she succeeds where the wicked queen fails and Chione is really killed (Anderson 2000: 46–9). But can we afford to disqualify a 'Snow White' simply because it does not end 'happily ever after'?

Sometimes speculation by modern fairy-tale specialists that a tale is symbolically sexual turns out, as here, to be literally true. Take the case where an athlete, not a huntsman, rescues a girl who is about to be deflowered by a wolf-spirit, which he drowns; the spirit had been stoned for rape in a former life. Deaths by stoning and drowning are found in a Grimm version of 'Red Riding Hood'; but here they are already in Pausanias (6.6.7–11) in the second century AD.

Often we may be inclined to suspect a total difference in narrative priorities in dealing with very similar material. Where a tale is told or partly told, in Ovid's *Metamorphoses*, for example, then the chances are that a version will be selected that seems to end in an irreversible metamorphosis rather than our conception of a happy ending; where it is told as local tradition, history or even epic, it is likely to be purged of just those elements that would clearly identify it as a fairy tale in the first place.

Another obvious difference in the surviving ancient tales is that the moral fulcrum is often differently adjusted. In the case of 'Cinderella' it is more or less constant, whatever the telling: we approve of rags to riches and we are meant to approve aristocratic marriage. But it is a different matter in Ovid's version of the story of Chione (*Metamorphoses* 11, 295–345), where, in effect, the girl herself seems to be punished by Artemis for boasting of her seduction, and this trend runs through several 'Snow White'-related tales as well. On the other hand, in 'Puss-in-Boots' it is the protagonist's mother who is the enabling figure of the fox, and the hero is being legitimately restored to his kingdom, not gaining one by fraud (Anderson 2000: 175–6).

Another aspect is that ancient institutions such as oracles and sacrifice tend to be handled somewhat differently: consultation at Delphi tends to be routine in polytheist versions of tales, and characters perform sacrifices as a matter of course, rather than having to be begged by talking cattle to kill them and perform whatever task with the bones. Moreover, ancient practice relating to the exposure of infants with birth-tokens tends to give several plots at least a somewhat different alignment. When slippers are circulated at the end of Longus' 'Daphnis and Chloe' (4, 34–5), they are not to identify the bride as such, but to match her to her parents (Anderson 2000: 146).

Sometimes we are left without a single complete 'take' of the characteristic elements of a given tale in one single surviving version. The results are less clear, and least rewarding where the arguments are most complex: we have to struggle quite hard to see Bluebeard in King Minos, largely because the configuration of evidence is so frustrating. But he does have a purple lock, he was a sea-king, no woman could survive a night with him and he locked the living in with the dead – all in different stories. Or again, we might ask 'Was there a Red Riding Hood? And if so, was she in a fairy tale?' We need to arrive at some kind of formula for 'Red Riding Hood' itself: girl or child victim, preferably connected in some way with the colour red, predatory wolf, threat to eat the child, victim's escape, champion, death of wolf by stones/drowning. The grandmother and the location seem inessential to me, though they are material to most modern versions. We have a number of traces or hints. There is the episode where the sea-nymph Thetis encounters a wolf and changes it into stone. Petrifaction is just as much 'death by stones' as putting them in the wolf's belly. But, as it stands, that is probably not enough. What changes this story, to my mind, is another feature which we know from elsewhere about Thetis, namely that she was capable, among a repertoire of metamorphoses, of changing both into fire and into a cuttle-fish, which has a sac emitting reddish-brown dye. Both give us an unexpected application of red to her nature, the latter perhaps even the 'red hood' itself. Let someone object that this is over-ingenious and out of context and we can still point out other such connections: she galvanises her children with fire, has a close association over a number of years with Hephaestus and gives her son the pseudonym Pyrrha, before sending 'her' to another wolf-figure, King Lycomedes ('Wolf-sly'). A fire-girl who turns a wolf to stone is a minimalist Red Riding Hood to me.

But let us not multiply approximations: we actually have a case noted by Pausanias, where a girl is brought to the house where a spirit with a wolf-name (Lykas) is due to mate with her, then after a year discard her; a passing athlete rescues her and drives the wolf-spirit into the sea; it had formerly experienced death by stoning after a rape. Nothing red here, and still no grandmother, but this is a reasonable version, only slightly dislocated, of one story, translated into the terms of ancient religious terminology and expectation. And we have the case of the child disgorged alive from the belly of the child-eating monster, the Lamia: some Italian versions still have this substitution of cannibal monster for the wolf. We should have to be perverse and hypercritical to say that there is no relationship between ancient wolf-and-children stories and 'Red Riding Hood'. We should also have to acknowledge that there are indeed sexual implications to the story, and we should be very cautious indeed about any claim that this story did not exist in any form in antiquity (Anderson 2000: 92–7). The suggestion that it did should make us all the more inclined to acknowledge the late medieval version reported in the *Fecunda Ratis* of Egbert of Liège in the early eleventh century,[2] in which the red garment is a baptismal dress of red wool which, as a Christian talisman, protects the little girl from being eaten by the wolf-cubs. The importance of this contribution to the wider tradition is that it actually offers other than a purely decorative point to the red garment, and once this is realised, the great chronological gulf between ancient 'takes' and Perrault is suddenly much reduced.

In searching for the possible fragments of an ancient tale, it is particularly crucial to take into account the bizarre episodes (especially in early modern versions) that tend to be edited out. Current forms of 'The Sleeping Beauty' avoid the episode of the prince raping the girl at the castle in the wood (Basile) or the variants on her rival (the prince's wife or mother) eating the heroine's children (Basile, Grimm). Yet it is these elements which are most likely to receive emphasis in at least some ancient versions. How, in the first place, can we hope to find a Sleeping Beauty where no one suspects she exists? In this case, one of the defining features is the 'freezing' of the whole country at the point when the girl is put to sleep. This in itself is not significant, but it will become so when tied to the motif of a curse on a child whose mother has offended a goddess. This conjunction occurs in the story of Niobe: as a result of her boast that she has more children than Leto, Artemis kills all her daughters and Zeus changes all the inhabitants of Thebes to stone, except for Meliboia who is spared and changes her name from Meliboia ('Sweet-voice') to Chloris ('Pale green'); she later marries Neleus ('Cruel man'). We are not told in any extant version that she sleeps for a long time surrounded by vegetation, but the change of the name at the correct point in the story implies as much: she herself is now the colour of vegetation itself. We are left wondering, and are not told, how Neleus deserves his name too. So far we have a Sleeping Beauty, as far as she goes. But there is one more piece which will connect us to another form of the tale. Chloris in Homer indicated the nightingale, and we have another story of a Nightingale-

---

[2] Rejected by Delarue (1951: 221–8) but see the discussion by C. Vélay-Vallentin in Sautmann *et al.* (1998: 275ff.).

girl in comparable circumstances. Philomela is raped by a king while shut up in a place in a wood, and the consequence is that the outraged woman's sister kills his child and serves it up as a meal. The coherence of these two stories with Basile's Sleeping Beauty, 'Sun, Moon and Talia', soon becomes clear.

Chloris	Philomela	Basile/Grimm
Royal mother Niobe boasts about her beautiful daughters		King and queen offend a vindictive fairy
Jealous goddess kills them at home in the palace		She vows to kill their daughter
One daughter, Meliboia, escapes by praying to the goddess's mother		Daughter is spared thanks to good fairy
She is spared but now called 'Green-Girl' (Nightingale)	Heroine is called Nightingale	
The city's inhabitants are turned to stone		The city's inhabitants are immobilised
	She is raped in a building in an ancient wood	Sleeping princess is raped in the middle of a wood
Chloris later marries Neleus		Princess marries king
	She and the king's wife cook the king's son, whom he eats	King's wife prepares to cook king's children

Here we can see that the two nightingale stories are really variants of a single one, and that the story of Philomela-Procne has lost its beginning. The connections of the modern tale with nightingales is shown by the following Armenian version (Downing 1972: 46–50):

The mistress of the Nightingale-of-a-thousand-voices sleeps and wakes alternately for seven days on end; a king's son finds her after an obstacle course (river, flower, animals, gate); he kisses the girl and steals the nightingale; one of his brothers is turned to stone in a palace where all the courtiers are of stone, and the youngest brother duly disenchants them all with a magic whip. After a failed attempt by the other brothers to claim to have stolen the nightingale, the youngest brother proves that it was he who stole it and kissed the princess and claims her as his bride.

There seems to be some intrusion from the tale of 'The Two Brothers' here, but the symbolic theft of the nightingale at the point of kissing the sleeping girl corresponds neatly to the concerns of the ancient tale-complex.

Sometimes examples of tales need to be traced over several very different genres in order to form an overall picture of the variants available in antiquity. It is generally taken for granted that 'The Emperor's New Clothes' (AT 1620), now routinely incorporated in fairy-tale collections and children's literature, is a product of the Middle Ages. A version of the familiar outline of the oral tale is found in Juan Manuel's classic collection *El conde Lucanor* in the fourteenth century, long before its appearance in Hans Andersen. But an earlier recension has been identified, which again has been traced back no further than the Middle Ages, and in which the story concerns not a weaver of invisible clothes but a painter of invisible pictures (Uther 1993: 7.852ff.). The latter offers to paint a grandee but declares that only persons of noble birth can see the painting; the grandee of course 'sees' the invisible picture and only his jester declares that it is not there. This is the version told at some length in chapter 27 of *Till Eulenspiegel*. The basic formula at least, and the connection with a context of pictures, is much older. The core of the tale is a pretence by flatterers that a powerful person's appearance is other than it actually is; the pretence is maintained until someone at the bottom of the social heap, with nothing to lose, tells the truth.

Lucian tells such a story about Pyrrhus of Epirus, according to which Pyrrhus fancies that his appearance is like that of Alexander the Great, when in fact portraits betray that it is opposite to that of the outstandingly handsome Alexander. But his courtiers and toadies maintain the fiction, until an old foreign woman is asked by the king whom he most resembles; portraits of Alexander, Cassander and other worthies are displayed. The woman, undaunted, replies that he most resembles Batrachion ('Little frog') the Cook; and indeed there was a cook in her home town of Larissa whom Pyrrhus resembles (*Adversus Indoctum* 21). Lucian introduces the story as an exemplary anecdote in an invective pamphlet, firmly in the context of the 'real world'. Obviously the detail of the flattery is different from that in both the story of the invisible pictures and that of the invisible cloth, but the tenor of the anecdote is exactly right: the courtiers will be regarded as fools if they do not fall in with their deluded leader's vanity. The honest informant need not be a child, as in Hans Andersen; Juan Manuel offers instead a negro, in a medieval Arabic society likewise bottom of the heap; Lucian's old lady, female and foreign, is exactly right for the role of an outsider who has no place to maintain in the social hierarchy of the royal entourage.

A parallel occurs even earlier in Aesopic literature, a suitable conveyor of what is obviously popular anecdote material. In the *Life of Aesop* 112–15, Aesop himself is invited to the court of the king of Egypt. The king dresses himself and his courtiers, no fewer than three times, in pretentious clothes and colour-schemes, asking the slave what the king is like; Aesop pretends to flatter ('the king is like the moon' etc.); only after the third time does he take his foolish host down a peg by saying that his *own* master, the king of Babylon, can be compared to powers still greater (Zeus himself). Once again Aesop's character is right: although by this time he is presented as an international celebrity on account of his wisdom, he has just been released from prison and is, in any case, an ugly ex-slave who naturally plays the role of a professional joker; indeed much of the humour of the *Life* depends on his 'nothing-to-lose' attitude.

I know, however, of no parallel to the motif of 'royal nudity exposed' in extant Greek and Roman literature. But one parallel can be strongly suspected in what is lost. The story of Rhampsinitus as told by Herodotus (2, 121) is generally recognised as a selection of episodes from the 'Master-Thief' cycle. In some modern oral variants from the Near East, a rival king challenges Master-Thief's father-in-law, the king of Egypt. In the ensuing contest Master-Thief cons him into believing that he and his wife are about to die; they are to go naked into coffins and come out and dance when they hear music. They come out of their coffins and dance naked at the rival royal court until, presumably, they recognise the trick. The context is of course parallel to the royal rivalry between King Lycurgus of Babylon and the king of Egypt that forms the setting of the Aesop story above. But it is still not possible on this evidence to do more than suspect that ancient variants of the Aesopic and Herodotean forms of the tale actually presented a king naked at court.

There is also, however, a quasi-historical account of an incident in which a king behaves in a publicly exposed manner and is then brought back to his senses; the story is foretold by an outsider when the king's usual consultants are found wanting. I suspect that it has not been spotted because any context in which it occurs is presented either as serious history or religious propaganda. The episode is the madness of Nebuchadnezzar, as told in the Book of Daniel 4 and elsewhere in a variety of Jewish-related sources till the end of antiquity. The king has a vision that he is given the mind of a beast and put out in the field; none of his seers and astrologers tells him the meaning of the dream. Only Daniel, a Hebrew and therefore an outsider, is apparently willing to do so, and he foretells that the king will lose his kingdom and his reason and be treated as an animal, before recovering his kingdom when he accepts the Lord God. The dream is then described as actually taking place. It seems to be implied clearly enough, though not explicitly stated, that the king is naked: he is to be 'wet with the dew of heaven' during his animal interlude; and he is said to resemble an ox down to the navel and a lion below, a detail which suggests that his actual body must be exposed to view. The Hebrew who cures him of his madness (again an outsider and so bottom of the heap) should once again have had to bring him to his senses by telling him, 'Your Majesty, you have nothing on', when evidently none of his Babylonian courtiers could dare to do so. We are not told this in so many words in any of our versions; rather we are told that many people went to see the king, but that Daniel stayed away and prayed to God on the king's behalf. But once more the various essentials are in the right relationship to one another, and Daniel's direct involvement with the king is variously implied by the logic of the tale.

What we still lack is the motif of conmen who take money for something that is invisible. My colleague, Dr Christopher Chaffin, reminds me that the motif at least (though not the intention) exists in ancient popular literature: in the apocryphal Acts of Thomas, King Gundaphorus is promised by Thomas to build a palace; as he builds it in heaven and not on earth, it cannot be seen. This is of course the opposite of our motif: the invisible palace is the real one but Thomas *appears* to be a conman, selling invisible palaces.

We can see then, that in this one instance, variants and motifs of the tale can turn up in canonic biblical texts, apocryphal Acts and pagan historical exempla or comic joke-book alike. A generally popular feel to an entertaining satirical and cautionary tale ensures its incorporation in a broad variety of cultural contexts.

Some other material is quite unmistakably fairy tale, but can be extremely hard to classify: a reference preserved only in scholia to Statius and cited by Rose (1958: 340B) in an unindexed addendum runs as follows (Scholiast on Statius, *Thebaid* 8, 198):

> A man called Patron takes in a lost child Smikros ('Tiny'). Smikros and his friends find a swan and wrap it and present it to Patron. On being unwrapped the swan has turned into a woman, who commends Smikros to his master, who marries him to his own daughter.

This tale is neither 'Tom Thumb' nor the 'Swan Maiden', but is very clearly using pure fairy-tale material in a correct and convincing way: thanks to his good deed to the Swan-girl, the insignificant foundling is rewarded with a prosperous marriage (cf. Basile's 'Nenillo and Nenella', where Nenillo is found hiding in a wood by a king and is eventually married to a nobleman's daughter).

There is one further frustrating exhibit, whose analogues I do not wish to push too hard. A goddess comes along to talk to three very hairy one-eyed monsters in their workplace; at the tender age of three, on a previous occasion, she had sat on the knees of one of them and had pulled out a patch of hair from the monster's chest. Here, in Callimachus' version of what we might call 'Golden Artemis and the Three Cyclopes' (Hymn 3), we do not quite seem to have arrived safely and unequivocally at 'The Three Bears', but we are certainly looking at a facetiously told nursery-type tale, from which characters were used, on the author's admission, by nurses as bogey-men to scare young naughty children, as 'The Three Bears' might properly be felt to do. Indeed we could note that the Cyclops is a fruitful figure of fairy tale: the 'hospitality-violated' theme is, after all, central to our first Cyclops story, that in *Odyssey* 9. The Cyclops offers an unusual 'Beauty and the Beast' sketch in Lucian's first 'Dialogue of the Sea-Gods', where Galatea defends her ugly suitor against the sneers of her sister sea-nymph, Doris (Macleod 1961: 178–83). We should not be prepared to draw a chronological line under 'Goldilocks' at the beginning of the nineteenth century.

If all this material was on hand, why was there no ancient Perrault? Why do the many extant collections which include fairy-tale material seem to do so so sparingly? One reason for the lack of a comprehensive fairy-tale collection is that people might have had difficulty in reading it and preferred to rely on oral transmission anyway. There was no need for a book of nursery tales, since the nurses knew the tales already and had learned them from whoever had nursed them.

On the other hand, the kind of compilations which yield material more or less at random, such as exemplum books, *Variae Historiae*, collections of *mirabilia* and the like, have much wider agenda. The limitations of Phlegon's work, which yields us most of the tale of Philinnion (Hansen 1996), is a case in point: the rest of the work comprises a random collection of miraculous material or curious facts. We should perhaps note that our most likely source of ancient fairy tale is a genre of which much is known but very little survives complete: the Athenian satyr-drama repertoire had a good deal of the wherewithal and at least some of the spirit of fairy tale (Sutton 1980: 145–59), though how exactly the repertoire aligned with that of the modern genre we cannot be certain.

On the other hand, we should note that there *existed* a virtually unrecognised anthology of children's stories in antiquity. Almost no one working on the modern fairy tale is likely to have heard of Philostratus; and yet in his *Eikones* ('Portraits') we have a collection of some forty brief descriptions of narrative paintings *addressed to a ten-year-old boy*. Most of them might be used to suggest that the diet of such a person in antiquity was not at all like that of the reader of Perrault. But one of the episodes is the forerunner of a satyr-tale by Straparola; one is a giant-killing tale of Heracles; one an episode in the Argonautic cycle ('Six around the World'); a further two deal with the adventures of sets of dwarves (one analogous to Gulliver in Lilliput). We should also note that the sequence of spinning-women's stories told by the Minyadæ in the first half of Ovid's *Metamorphoses* IV offers a sequence of folktales: 'Pyramus and Thisbe' explains the blood-red colour of a plant; 'Leucothoe and Clytie' offers similarity to AT 480, 'The Kind and the Unkind Girls'; and 'Hermaphroditus and Salmacida' is a story much like the Hylas tale. The last thing Ovid aims at is documentary realism, but even this obvious artifice for linking metamorphoses is a reminder of the conditions under which oral material is both transmitted and irretrievably lost.

Enough has been said to suggest the potential of this and related lines of investigation. The results favour explanations based on diffusion rather than polygenesis, though in no case can we be confident of having the very first version of any tale. But the field is so sparsely explored and so readily dismissed that it is still routinely possible to add more than a millennium to the life of a fairy tale.[3]

References

Anderson, G. (2000), *Fairy Tale in the Ancient World*. London.

Brunel, C. (1923) ed., *The Count of Ponthieu's Daughter*. Paris.

Delarue, P. (1951), 'Les Contes de Perrault et la tradition populaire', *Bulletin folklorique d'Île-de-France*.

Downing, C. (1972), *Armenian Folk Tales*. Oxford.

Dundes, A. (1982), *Cinderella: A Folklore Casebook*. New York.

FTAW = Anderson 2000.

Hansen, W. (1996), *Phlegon of Tralles' Book of Marvels*. Exeter.

—— (2002), *Ariadne's Thread: A Guide to International Tales Found in Classical Literature*. Ithaca, NY.

Macleod, M. D. (1961) ed. and trans., *Lucian 7*. Loeb Classical Library. Cambridge, MA.

Matarasso, P. (1971) trans., *Aucassin and Nicolette and Other Tales*. Harmondsworth.

---

[3] Since writing the above I have had a chance to see Hansen's *Guide to International Tales found in Classical Literature* (2002) which appeared only as this paper was going to press. This excellent compendium goes far towards collecting together the materials so long neglected, but concentrates on a much more general spectrum of popular materials, including joke-tales and fables. Much work still remains to be done on the recognition of well-known fairy tales.

Opie, I. and P. (1974), *The Classic Fairy Tales*. Oxford.

Page, D. (1972), *Folktales in Homer's Odyssey*. Cambridge, MA.

Purkiss, D. (2000), *Troublesome Things: A History of Fairies and Fairy Tales*. Cambridge.

Rose, H. J. (1958), *A Handbook of Greek Mythology*. 6th edn. London.

Sautmann, F. C., Conchado, D., and Di Scipio, G. C. (1998), *Telling Tales: Medieval Narrative and the Folk Tradition*. London.

Sutton, D. F. (1980), *The Greek Satyr Play*. Meisenheim am Glan.

Thompson, S. (1946/1977), *The Folktale*. Berkeley.

Uther, H.-J. (1993), 'Kaisers neue Kleider', in *Enzyklopädie des Märchens*, vol. 7, 852–7. Berlin.

Zipes, J. (2001), *The Great Fairy Tale Tradition: From Straparola and Basile to the Brothers Grimm*. New York/London.

6

Helpers and Adversaries in Fairy Tales

HILDA ELLIS DAVIDSON

I

One well-established pattern found in the fairy tale throughout Europe and beyond is that of various characters offering help to the hero or heroine, while others seek to destroy them. The helpers may be either animal or human, dolls or inanimate objects, the dead or supernatural beings, although deities and recognised supernatural powers, such as are found in myths and legends, do not normally appear in the fairy tale. The intervention of the helper is essential to the plot, since this is what usually ensures that the final outcome is a happy one – marriage, reunion with brothers or sisters, husband or wife, or the winning of a treasure or a kingdom – while the destroyers are finally exposed and punished. For all their importance, few attempts have been made to analyse helpers or adversaries in any detail, and it seems worthwhile to pursue the subject further, since the conflict between these opposing forces for the destiny of hero or heroine is clearly of primary importance for our understanding of the tales.

Helpers in animal form include birds, fishes and insects, and these have no obvious parallels in heroic literature, myths or legends. In many cases the help is given in response to generosity on the part of the central character, who then achieves success against apparently insuperable odds (AT 534). In the Grimms' tale of 'The Queen Bee' (1944: 317), a very simple story, this forms the basic plot. When three brothers set out to seek their fortunes, the two elder are going to destroy an ant-hill, thinking it would be amusing to see the ants scurrying about in terror. But the youngest, Simpleton, prevents them, insisting: 'Leave the creatures in peace. I will not allow you to disturb them.' He similarly stops them from killing two ducks on a pond, and breaking into a bee's nest for honey. To deliver a castle from enchantment, they have to find a thousand pearls scattered in the moss, recover a key from a lake, and declare which of three sleeping princesses has eaten honey. The two elder brothers fail, but the ants, the ducks and the queen bee solve the problems for the youngest son when his turn comes. In the Russian tale 'Emelya the Simpleton', a pike found in the water pail addresses the youngest brother (Afanas'ev 1945: 47):

'Simpleton, do not eat me; put me back into the water and you will be happy!'
The simpleton asked: 'What happiness will you give me?' 'This happiness I'll

give: whatever you say will come to pass. For instance, say now: By the pike's command, by my own request, go, pails, go home by yourselves, and stand in your accustomed place.'

This formula 'by the pike's command' is found in other tales, indicating that help from a fish was a familiar concept.

The heroines in the tales also gain animal helpers through generosity, and sometimes their consideration for inanimate objects stands them in good stead (AT 480). In a Russian tale, 'Baba Yaga' (Afanas'ev 1945: 363), a cruel stepmother sends the heroine to the terrible Baba Yaga the Bony-legged to ask for a needle and thread, hoping that she will devour the girl. However her aunt counsels her to tie the birch tree with a ribbon when it lashes her face, oil the gate when it creaks, throw bread to the fierce dogs, and give ham to the cat when it attacks her. The cat offers her good advice when Baba Yaga has gone out and gives her a magical comb and towel to help her to escape, while he answers his mistress in a human voice to make her think the girl is still in the hut. When Baba Yaga scolds and beats him, he retorts: 'I have served you so many years and you have not given me even a bone; but she gave me a piece of ham.' The dogs, the gate, the birch tree and her servant all answer her similarly, and when she pursues the girl the magic towel becomes a river, and the comb a forest blocking her path, so that the heroine reaches home safely (AT 313H).

In a Swedish tale, 'The Two Chests' (Blecher 1993: 305), the girl pushed down a well by her wicked stepmother enters another world. Here a fence asks her to step over it gently since it is old and fragile, a cow offers milk and tells her to put the pail back on its horn, and an oven full of cakes tells her to eat as many as she wants but to take none away. When she accedes to these requests, the oven tells her: 'This will serve you well' (AT 480). Later an old cat tells her how to carry water in a sieve, and how to choose the right chest from an old man, and avoid being beaten afterwards. When she returns home with a chest full of gold and jewels, the stepmother sends her own daughter down the well, but she ignores all advice, gets severely beaten and comes home with a chest of toads and snakes. The moral given at the end is 'He who listens to good advice is all the wiser for it.'

In these two tales the cats are more than grateful creatures helping with their special skills, for they give wise advice and magical gifts. Such animal helpers often accompany the hero on his travels, and in a number of tales, such as 'Puss-in-Boots', a cat by its cunning procures riches and a splendid marriage for him (AT 545). He may also be assisted by a marvellous talking horse, of exceptional size and strength, as in a Norwegian story, 'Dapplegrim' (Dasent 1908: 272). Here the horse gains his qualities as the result of the slaughter of many foals, so that the mares all nourish him with their milk. Such steeds may be bought, received as gifts, or won from some supernatural owner. They recall some of the famous steeds in heroic epics, but possess more wonderful powers.

In the Russian tale 'The Gold-Bristled Pig, the Golden-Feathered Duck, and the Golden-Maned Horse' (Afanas'ev 1945: 533), the dead father comes out of his grave and rewards the youngest son for his vigil there by blessing him and giving him three horse-hairs. The youth goes into 'the forbidden meadows' (no explanation is given of these), and singes the hairs, crying out: 'Magic steed, horse of my need, blessing of my father! Stand before me as a leaf before grass.' Flames stream from the mouth of the wonderful horse, and smoke from its ears, and when the hero creeps inside the left ear he can eat and drink his fill, while on entering the right ear he receives a many-coloured garment and appears as a splendid hero. He accomplishes mighty deeds with his horse's help, and finally marries the princess.

Sometimes the steed appears at first of little worth. In an Irish tale, 'The Story of Conn-eda' (Yeats 1973: 275), a 'great Druid' advises the hero to take 'yonder little shaggy steed'. We are told: 'It would be tedious to relate the numerous adventures he had with the little shaggy horse, which had the extraordinary gift of speech, and was a *draoidheacht* (magic) horse throughout the journey.' This horse also had special treasures in its ears, from one of which the hero takes a bottle of *íce* (translated 'all-heal'), equivalent to the 'water of life' which plays a part in many tales, and a small wicker basket holding meat to pacify fierce serpents. Another example of an apparently humble steed is found in the Russian gypsy tale 'The Enchanted Hinny', a hinny being the offspring of a stallion and a donkey (Riordan 1986: 7). The tiny hinny, tied to a horse's tail, is bought by a gypsy for his son. It saves him from his stepmother, carries him up into an enchanted kingdom, and helps him to win a princess for his bride.

A wolf or fox may replace the horse as a helpful steed for the hero (AT 550 IV). In 'Prince Ivan, the Firebird and the Gray Wolf' (Afanas'ev 1945: 612), a wolf devours the hero's horse, but then takes its place, giving his rider good advice, which he does not always follow. When he obtains the horse with a golden mane, he foolishly takes the golden bridle as well, in spite of the wolf's warning (Afanas'ev 1945: 617):

> 'Oh, young lad, Prince Ivan', said the gray wolf, 'why did you not heed my words, why did you take the golden bridle?' 'It is true, I am guilty before you', answered Prince Ivan. 'Well, let it be so!' said the gray wolf. 'Sit on me, the gray wolf; I will carry you where you have to go' . . . and he ran as beasts run in fairy tales, so that in a very short time he arrived in the kingdom of Elena the Fair.

After the wolf has helped Ivan to procure the princess, the horse and the firebird he seeks, it leaves him, but then his wicked brothers come up when he is asleep and cut him in pieces, and the wolf returns to restore him with the water of life. However once Ivan wins his bride it drops out of the story, with no indication as to why it has served the hero so faithfully. But in a similar tale in the Grimm collection, 'The Golden Bird' (Grimm 1944: 272), and a Norwegian one with the same title (Asbjørnson and Moe 1960: 49), the fox which replaces the wolf as helper has been rejected by the two elder brothers and welcomed by the youngest. After helping him to succeed, it begs to be killed, and in the Norwegian version is then freed from enchantment. In the German version the hero cannot bear to kill his benefactor, and so the fox leaves him, but comes to his rescue later after his brothers have pushed him down a well, and finally persuades him to cut off its head. It is then revealed as the princess's brother, of whom we have heard nothing hitherto.

An animal helper who is a human being seeking freedom from enchantment is found in a number of tales (AT 314). Such a character may be clumsily introduced, as in 'Snow-white and Rose-red' (Grimm 1944: 558), where a mother and daughters befriend a bear, and gold is glimpsed under its fur. In the Irish story of Conn-eda referred to above, however, there is a moving account of the hero reluctantly killing his helper, an exception to the usual lack of emotion in the fairy tales commented on by Tatar (1987: 78). The little shaggy horse tells his rider to kill him with a knife taken from his ear, and then to flay him and wrap himself in the skin. The lamentation and tears of the hero are described at length, but all ends well when he drives off the birds of prey from the remains of the horse, and pours some of the 'all-heal' on them. The king's brother then appears, and the whole adventure is said to have been planned by his sister, so that he can be freed from enchantment by a wicked druid.

In a further group of more moving tales, the bird or animal which helps an ill-treated girl is linked in some way with her dead mother. The Grimms' version of 'Cinderella' (1944: 121; AT 510) begins with the death of the loving mother, and when the girl is oppressed by a cruel stepmother, she asks her father for the first branch which knocks his hat on his way home, and plants this on her mother's grave. She waters it with her tears, until it grows into a fine tree on which a little white bird perches. The bird brings Cinderella all she wants, and provides her with wonderful dresses. She is also able to call on pigeons, doves and other birds to perform tasks imposed on her by the stepmother, while two doves inform the king's son of the deceit of the wicked sisters. There is another bird donor in 'The Juniper Tree' (Grimm 1944: 220; AT 720), a powerful tale where a little boy is murdered by his stepmother and cooked for his father to eat (see p. 110 below). He appears as a bird on the tree under which his weeping stepsister, tricked into believing she has killed him, has buried his bones. The bird sings a song telling of the crime, and gives gifts to the father and stepsister, but drops a millstone on the wicked stepmother, after which it is miraculously restored to human form.

Help from the dead mother in animal form is implied in the Russian tale, 'Burenushka, the Little Red Cow' (AT 511A). Maria, the ill-treated stepdaughter, half-starved and in rags, is sent out every day to look after a little red cow (Afanas'ev 1945: 146):

> The princess went to the open field, bowed to Burenushka's right leg, ate and drank her fill, and dressed in fine attire. All day long, dressed like a lady, she tended Burenushka. At the end of the day, she again bowed to the little cow's right leg, removed her fine attire, went home carrying her crust of bread, and put it on the table. 'How does the slut keep alive?' wondered Yagushka.

The stepmother's two daughters, one of whom has one eye and the other three, are sent to spy on her, and the second discovers her secret, whereupon the stepmother persuades her husband to slaughter the cow. Maria begs for some of the entrails, and a bush with sweet berries grows from this where little birds perch, singing 'songs of kings and peasants'. A prince asks for a dish of berries from the tree, and since the birds prevent the sisters from picking them, he meets and marries Maria. The Grimms have a similar tale, 'One-Eye, Two-Eyes and Three-Eyes' (1944: 585), but here there is no stepmother, and this prevents us from connecting either the woman who comforts the heroine or the goat which gives her food with her dead mother In an Irish version of 'Cinderella', 'Ashey Pelt' (Briggs 1970: 137), recorded in the 1890s by a woman from Ulster, the helper is a black ewe who came 'from under the grey stone in the field'. This is not said to be the dead mother of the oppressed girl, but the story begins: 'My Grandmother, she told me that in them auld days a ewe might be your mother. It is a very lucky thing to have a black ewe', so this is clearly the implication.

A variation on the theme of the continuing influence of a mother parted from her daughter is found in 'The Goosegirl' (Grimm 1944: 404; see p. 112 below), where a wicked maid-in-waiting, a convincingly evil figure, usurps the place of the royal bride (AT 533). The aged mother of the princess sends her away to be married in a distant kingdom, riding a horse called Falada, which can speak. She gives her daughter a white handkerchief on which there are three drops of her own blood, but by ill chance the girl drops this in a stream, and so is left with no defence against her companion, who makes her exchange clothes and takes Falada away from her. The maid poses as the princess and asks the prince to have Falada killed, since she is afraid the horse might betray her. The princess, who is working as a goose-girl, gives the knacker a gold piece to fasten the horse's head over a gateway in the town, and there she addresses it as she passes: 'Alas, Falada, hanging there!', to which the head replies:

> 'Alas, young Queen, how ill you fare!
> If this your mother knew
> Her heart would break in two.'

The boy whom she helps with the geese hears these words and tells the old king, who discovers the deception and restores the heroine to her rightful place as his son's bride, condemning the waiting-maid to death.

In the Russian tales the mother may leave a little doll behind instead of an animal to help and protect her daughter after her death, as in the tale of 'Vasilisa the Beautiful' (Afanas'ev 1945: 439). Her dying mother hands her the doll from under the coverlet, saying:

> 'Together with my maternal blessing I leave you this doll. Always keep it with you and never show it to anyone; if you get into trouble, give the doll food and ask its advice. When it has eaten, it will tell you what to do in your trouble'.

When her father marries again and she is cruelly overworked by her stepmother and stepsisters, jealous of her beauty, she keeps the choicest food for her doll and tells it her troubles, and it performs all the hard tasks laid upon her. While the girl's father is abroad, the stepmother moves near the hut of Baba Yaga, and often sends Vasilisa into the forest in hope that she will be devoured by that sinister figure, known 'to eat human beings as if they were chickens', but the doll gives her good advice and keeps her away from the hut.

However one autumn night the stepmother provides only one candle for the girls to work by, tells her daughter to snuff it out as if by accident, and insists that Vasilisa shall go to Baba Yaga and ask for a light. In her terror she consults the doll, and owing to its good advice survives unhurt. The doll carries out the tasks imposed on the girl, cooking food for Baba Yaga, cleaning her hut, and saying each evening: 'Fear not, Vasilisa the Beautiful! Eat your supper, say your prayers, and go to sleep; the morning is wiser than the evening.' Vasilisa makes the right replies to Baba Yaga, who finally asks her: 'How do you manage to do the work I set for you?', to which she answers: 'I am helped by the blessing of my mother.' At this Baba Yaga shrieks out in rage: 'Get you gone, blessed daughter! I want no blessed ones in my house!' and pushes her out of the gate, with a light in a skull for her stepmother. She finds the house still in darkness when she returns home, and the skull burns up her stepmother and sisters. Later the doll makes a wonderful loom for Vasilisa, on which she weaves such marvellous linen that it brings about a marriage with the Tsar, and we are told that she carried her doll in her pocket till the end of her life. Here the dead mother's blessing, expressed through the doll, is sufficiently powerful to defeat the evil Baba Yaga.

In 'Prince Danila Govorila' (Afanas'ev 1945: 351), four dolls placed in corners of the room enable the heroine to escape from a forced marriage with her brother. Dolls are also found in Greek and Turkish tales of the Patient Griselda type (AT 887), where a doll comforts the unhappy wife (Bettridge and Utley 1971). They could be based on the little household guardians in the shape of stuffed rag dolls or wooden figures, made by relatives of the bride and taken away with her to her new home, or left with her mother until she expects her first child. These were kept in the women's section of the house among various Turko-Tatar peoples (Davidson 1998: 126ff.).

Human helpers are often left unspecified beyond such vague descriptions as an old woman, an old man with a white beard, a grey man, or a druid in the Irish tales. They are usually elderly rather than young. They often appear when the hero or heroine is in despair and ask why they are weeping, and it is clearly wise to tell them. In the Russian tale 'Ivan the Peasant's Son and the Thumb-sized Man' (Afanas'ev 1945: 262), Ivan at first repulses an old man and then thinks: 'Why did I offend him? Old people know a great deal', goes back and apologises: 'Grandfather, forgive me, I offended you because of my own grief.' In the Swedish tale of 'The King's Hares' (Blecher 1993: 128), the two elder brothers repulse a poor old woman, but the youngest greets her, gives her food and is given a magic whistle which enables him to catch the hares.

It is often not clear whether such helpers are supernatural beings. An example of this is the old woman who suddenly appears uninvited to a queen unable to bear children (AT 711), as in the Danish tale of 'King Wivern', thirteen different versions of which are discussed by Holbek (1987: 46off.). She tells the queen what to do to have a child, and the instructions vary, but the common factor is that the queen does not follow them fully and so gives birth to a dangerous wivern (serpent). In Holbek's first version an old woman appears later to tell the girl who is to be married to the wivern how to disenchant him, but it is not clear if this is the same old woman, and no version identifies the queen's helper.

The story of 'The Grateful Dead' (AT 507A), when a dead man comes to the help of the hero who paid for his burial, is a widespread folktale (Gerould 1908). In a Norwegian tale, 'The Companion' (Asbjørnsen and Moe 1960: 84), a peasant boy sells everything and sets off to seek a princess whom he has seen in a dream. He comes upon the body of a man who was executed for watering down wine, preserved in ice because no one will bury him, and pays for the burial out of his scanty means. Then he is overtaken by a man offering to serve him, though the youth protests that he cannot pay him: 'You need a servant you can rely on in life and death. If you won't have me as a servant you can take me as a companion.' He proves a wonderful helper, overcoming evil trolls and gaining magical gifts for the hero, who finds and wins his princess. After the horrible troll who gained power over her is slain by the Companion (AT 507), the hero has to disenchant her by a cleansing process like that in the Danish tales of 'King Wivern'. He promises his Companion half of all he gains in the next five years, and when the time comes divides his possessions between them, but the Companion then demands half of his young son. The hero is about to cut the child in two when his helper seizes the sword and prevents him, tells him that he is the man whom he had buried, and departs for the heavenly kingdom (AT 506V). In a similar tale from Sweden, 'Little Hans' (Blecher 1993: 25), the hero meets two ghosts fighting in a churchyard over an unpaid debt, and settles it himself. His helper ensures that he wins the riddle contest imposed by the princess, again under the power of a troll, but here there is no final test of the hero, and Little Hans simply reveals his identity and departs. Hans Christian Andersen has retold the tale of the Grateful Dead first under the title 'The Dead Man', and then as 'The Travelling Companion' (Holbek 1990: 168ff.).

This motif was certainly a familiar one in sixteenth-century England, since it provides the main plot of George Peele's *Old Wives' Tale*, a comedy thought to have been composed in the early 1590s (Binnie 1980: 5). Peele's plot contains a number of fairy-tale motifs, such as a maiden 'white as snow and red as blood', two contrasted sisters, the water of life, the magic table providing meals and so on, and the hero pays for the funeral and burial of a dead man, and is joined by a young lad offering to serve him, who frees the heroine from evil enchantment. He then calls on the hero to share his bride by cutting her in two, but having 'tried his constancy' prevents him from carrying out the deed, and leaps down into the ground. The old woman, Madge, who introduces the play makes sure that the audience gets the point: 'O, man, this was the ghost of the poor man that they kept such a coil to bury; and that makes him to help the wandering knight so much.' The concept of the grateful dead is evidently an ancient one, found in the Book of Tobit in the Apocrypha, and also in Ancient Greece (Davidson, forthcoming). Although the companion of Tobit's son Tobias is not a dead man, but the Archangel Raphael, the reason why he comes to help Tobias is because his father Tobit has buried a number of murdered Jews. Tobias marries a rich kinsman's daughter enchanted by a demon lover, and his supernatural helper overcomes the evil power, as in later versions of the tale.

Helpers who are clearly supernatural beings abound in the tales. Sometimes they are vague and unspecified, described as little men, dwarves or 'earthmen', as in the Grimms' tale 'The Three Little Men in the Wood' (Grimm 1944: 78). Here dwarves help the ill-treated stepdaughter who befriends them, and in 'The Two Kings' Children' (51) the princess summons earthmen to perform difficult

tasks. A Danish storyteller, Ane Dorotea Jensdatter, used dwarves as supernatural helpers in a number of tales, but the term seems to be employed vaguely:
'It appears that Ane Dorotea likes the appellation *dwarf* and that she uses it for
all kinds of extraordinary beings', suggests Holbek (1987: 522). Other terms used
rather casually are giants, hags and sorceresses, normally hostile characters, but
supernatural figures can be ambivalent. We find a three-headed dragon in the
Russian tale, 'The Three Kingdoms' (Afanas'ev 1945: 49) offering help: 'Come
with me', says the obliging monster, 'I will lead you. We shall see whether you
can get a bride', and he lowers the hero into a hole leading to an enchanted
kingdom. The dragon never reappears, but in the same tale the hero is helped by
a giant, who sends him to Baba Yaga, and she allows him to use her eagle to
return home, so that in this case help is obtained from a series of normally
destructive powers. In 'Elena the Wise' (Afanas'ev 1945: 545), an evil spirit
released from a tower proves a powerful helper, although continuing to wander
about the world doing mischief, 'as is the custom of evil spirits'. Evidently when
the plot requires a helper, either an anonymous figure or any recognised
supernatural one will serve the required purpose.

Another type of helper is the ogre's wife or the evil sorcerer's daughter, who
conceals hero or heroine when the monster returns home, and sometimes
obtains an essential secret from him while the hidden visitor listens. These
may not necessarily be characters from the supernatural world, since ogres often
carry off princesses, but we are seldom told much about them, In two stories in
the Grimms' collection, 'The Devil with the Three Golden Hairs' (1944: 151) and
'The Devil and his Grandmother' (56) the helper is the grandmother of the Devil.
In the first tale she sits in a large armchair and 'did not look so very wicked', and
she hides the hero in the folds of her gown. An example in a popular English
fairy tale of this type of helper is the ogre's wife in 'Jack and the Beanstalk' (Opie
1974: 162; AT 328). Here the giant has a series of treasures, and his wife helps
Jack three times to carry these off, in spite of her husband's anger over the thefts.

While many of the supernatural helpers in the tales have no special indi-
viduality, there are others who are more arresting figures. Princesses whose
fathers have supernatural powers may help the hero to perform tasks, or use
their own magic skills to escape with their lovers. One such is the 'Mastermaid'
in Asbjørnsen's collection (Dasent 1908: 71), who wins the contest in magic with
her father and escapes with the prince. Other female supernatural helpers seem
to be based on earlier beliefs in protective female guardian figures whose
memory has lived on in popular tradition, such as Frau Holle in the German
tales. Jacob Grimm in *Teutonic Mythology* recorded folklore concerning Holle,
Holda, Berchta and other female powers associated with both agriculture and
spinning, who assisted young wives and helped with child-bearing. The widespread traditions concerning such figures in Germany, Austria and Switzerland
are brought out in an important monograph by Waschnitius (1913), and these
support Grimm's claim that we have memories here of ancient local goddesses.
(Davidson 1998: 66; 104–7).

In the tale of 'Mother Holle' (Grimm 1944: 133) we have the familiar motif of
the cruel stepmother, who forces the heroine to spin outside by a well until her
fingers bleed (AT 480). Trying to wash her shuttle, she drops it into the well and

in desperation jumps down after it. She arrives in a fair enchanted country, passing an oven where the bread asks to be taken out, and an apple tree calling for its apples to be shaken off. After complying with these requests she reaches the house of Mother Holle, an old woman with large teeth, who however greets her kindly, asking her to work for her and shake the bed till the feathers fly, to cause snow on earth. The girl works faithfully and well, and leads a happy life with never an angry word, eating 'boiled or roast meat every day'. However, Mother Holle can also be ruthless. She rewards the girl with a rain of gold, but when the lazy sister, sent down by her mother to get a similar reward, ignores the oven and apple-tree and proves an incompetent servant, Holle sends her home drenched in pitch. The folklore about Holle and other similar figures shows them encouraging good work by girls and women who spin, and meting out punishment to lazy and careless workers.

On the other hand there is a popular tale of three ugly old women who help a lazy girl who refuses to spin to make a successful marriage (AT 501). In the version from Selkirk in Scotland (Briggs 1970: 303), a feckless girl because of her mother's boasting is faced with a huge pile of flax to spin into yarn. Habitrot, the ugly old woman who comes to her help, lives under the roots of a tree, and can be seen through a hole in a stone. The laird is so impressed by Habitrot's work that he marries the girl, but she is saved from a dismal future of endless spinning when Habitrot arrives at the wedding with two companions. She has deformed lips, the second woman a flat thumb, and the third a splay foot, and when the laird hears that these are the results of spinning, he vows that his wife shall never touch a spinning wheel again. In the Grimms' tale, 'The Three Spinners' (Grimm 1944: 83), the girl's rescue depends on her willingness to invite the hideous old women to the wedding, calling them her aunts, and this also happens in a Norwegian version, 'The Three Aunts' (Dasent 1908: 193), where the heroine is called upon to spin flax, produce linen and make it into shirts.

The fairy godmothers in Perrault's tales, who sometimes replace the dead mothers of afflicted heroines, may have been influenced by such stern but benevolent female guardian figures as Frau Holle. In 'The Sleeping Beauty' (Opie 1974: 81), the godmothers invited to the christening of the baby princess do not bring material gifts, but are clearly bestowing her destiny upon her (Davidson 1998: 152). At the time when Perrault was writing, the Christian godmother bore some likeness to earlier supernatural guardians, since she was a donor of gifts, benefactor of the family and associated with the Otherworld. Godmothers are rare in the Grimms' tales, but one brings up a motherless girl in 'The Spindle, the Shuttle and the Needle' (Grimm 1944: 764), leaving her a house and spinning equipment which results in her marriage with a prince (AT 585).

Another possible use of earlier supernatural figures can be found in a number of Norwegian, Swedish and Russian tales, although not in the Grimms' collection. Here there are three helpers, usually sisters of great age, though in one Norwegian tale, 'The Three Princesses of Whiteland' (Dasent 1908: 181), they are three brothers, and brothers again give help in a Scottish tale, 'Greensleeves' (Briggs 1970: 296). Three giant brothers, ruling animals, birds and the winds, are brought into 'The Lost Princess', one of Rabbi Nahman's tales (see pp. 43–4), so that the motif must have been known in the Ukraine in the eighteenth century (Band 1978: 58ff.). The hero seeks out these characters to find the way to a distant land, and they consult the animals, birds or fishes over which they rule (AT 400). Finally some very ancient creature, perhaps a frog or eagle, returns from a long journey there, and acts as guide to the hero. The theme of the most ancient creature which can supply information is a very old one, found in the tale of 'Culhwch and Olwen' in the Welsh *Mabinogion* which goes back to the eleventh century, and even earlier in fourth-century material from India (Jackson 1961: 76–7). That of the three ancient characters, each older than the previous one, is a separate motif (AT 400: 'Man on the Quest for his Lost Wife'), not found in eastern sources, and in some of the European tales it is they who summon the animals for questioning.

An interesting example is found in the Norwegian tale of 'Farmer Weathersky [*Verskegg*] (Dasent 1908: 185), where the so-called farmer carries off Jack, whose father was seeking to apprentice him to someone who would teach him to be master of all masters (AT 325). Farmer Weathersky declares that he is at home north, south, east and west, and rides through the air in a sledge, while his dwelling is surrounded by dead bodies, and he can pursue fugitives in the form of a hawk. Dasent (1908: cxvii) suggests that he is 'one of the ancient gods degraded into a demon shape', and the hawk shape and the corpses, as well as the fact that he teaches cunning, suggest vague memories of Odin. Three ancient sisters help the father to recover his son. The first of them is an old hag with a nose so long that she can use it to draw water from a well. Jack's father gives her some tobacco and stays the night in her hut, and she lends him a horse and sledge and sends him off to her sister three hundred miles away. This old hag, again drawing water with her nose, tells him that she rules all the fish in the sea, and plays her pipe to summon them, but none of them know where Farmer Weathersky can be found. She sends him to another sister, six hundred miles away, who uses her long nose to poke the fire, and she summons all the birds of the air. After a long delay the eagle arrives from Farmer Weathersky's house, and at his mistress's command takes Jack's father there. They carry off a hare from the stable, which turns back into the lost son when sprinkled with Christian mould from the churchyard. Farmer Weathersky pursues his lost apprentice in various shapes, finally becoming a cock, but Jack, who has learned magic skills from his former master, becomes a fox and bites off the cock's head.

Another example is found in a Swedish tale, 'The Castle East of the Sun and West of the Wind' (Blecher 1993: 176), where the hero, a miller, meets three old sisters described as troll-women. The first summons with her pipe all the fish in the sea, the second all the animals on earth, and the third all the birds of the skies. When the eagle is missing, she blows on her pipe in anger, 'so sharply that the foundations of the mountains shook, and the sound echoed in all the corners of the world'. He finally appears and abjectly begs her forgiveness, knows the castle the miller is seeking and carries him there, clearly terrified of offending his mistress further. In 'Prince Vilius' (Blecher 1993: 185) it is a princess who encounters three sisters ruling over bears, lions and birds, and an old falcon who knows the way.

Three ancient women are also found in a number of Russian tales, though their connection with wild creatures is not always mentioned. There is an old woman in 'Go I know not whither' (Afanas'ev 1945: 513) who rules over animals and birds, while in 'The Maiden Tsar' (229) Baba Yaga has two sisters, and while the third is whetting her teeth to devour the hero, he summons all the birds with her horn, and one helps him to escape. The link with Baba Yaga, thought to be based on memories of an ancient goddess (see p. 118 below) may be significant. The conception of a mistress of wild creatures, well established in the Norwegian and Swedish tales, must surely originate in memories of the hunting goddess, who protected the creatures of the wild, and gave those who gained her favour good fortune in hunting (Davidson 1998: 13ff.). There is evidence for such beliefs over a long period in northern Europe, and popular traditions about such figures survived in Scandinavia well into the twentieth century (Hultkrantz 1961).

A few further examples of supernatural helpers might conceivably be based on earlier beliefs. A motif known in the sixteenth century in England is that of heads rising out of a well, which give help if kindly treated. (AT 480 VI). In Peele's *Old Wives' Tale*, two such heads appear, and one sister smashes her pitcher on the first, while the other sister does what they ask, and combs out gold and corn from their hair into her lap. Anne Ross (1967: 110) claimed that this is based on memories of the cult of the head among Celtic peoples in pre-Christian times; but it is not found to my knowledge in either Scottish or Irish fairy tales. Moreover, as Jacqueline Simpson (1963–4: 47ff.) has pointed out, both the English tale of the Queen of Colchester from a chapbook (Opie 1974: 156), and a Norwegian folktale, 'The Bushy Bride', offer close parallels to the episode in the play. These heads are bestowers of bounty after the fulfilment of a strange ritual, rather than guardians of holy waters like those in the saints' legends discussed by Ross.

There are also occasional examples of help from the personified forces of nature (AT 400V, 425IV). In the Russian tale 'Jack Frost' (Afanas'ev 1945: 366), the frost is charmed by the lovely girl whom her stepmother has put out in the cold to die, and marries her, providing her with rich clothes and furs. The North Wind gives magic gifts in 'The Lad who went to the North Wind' (Dasent 1908: 228), and advice and help in 'The Three Princesses of Whiteland' (181), while the winds and the sun and moon help the heroine in 'The Singing, Soaring Lark' (Grimm 1944: 399). In tales of the 'Cinderella' type, where the helper provides dresses to enable the heroine to regain her true status and meet the prince (AT 510B), these are often compared to the sun, moon and stars. Here cosmic and domestic backgrounds are linked to suggest gifts from the world of nature, bringing beauty to the heroine (Tatar 1987: 118). Lüthi (1984: 188) claims that the world of nature in the fairy tale is less dangerous and hostile than that of the home.

Thus beside animal and human helpers in the tales, it must be recognised that we have some with supernatural powers, who appear to go back to earlier traditional beliefs. Holbek (1987: 437) prefers to see the helpers as aspects of the hero, and the gifts as indicators of his physical or mental qualities, following Propp's suggestion that the hero might function as his own helper, but this does not satisfactorily account for the variety of helpers depicted. Before drawing any conclusions however, we must consider the destructive figures opposed to the helpers, who also play an essential part in the tales.

II

The list of those who obstruct, attack or seek to destroy a hero or heroine is shorter than that of the helpers. The threat of hostility may come from members of the family, jealous companions, tyrannical rulers, or powers from the Otherworld, destructive by nature. While there are many animal helpers, no serious threat comes from hostile animals, apart from occasional fierce beasts on guard, usually placated by a timely gift of food, or evil characters who have temporarily taken on animal form. Monsters such as many-headed dragons, serpents or trolls who carry off princesses seldom show hostility to the hero until he attacks them.

The most familiar human figure who represents evil in the tales is the stepmother. Instances of her cruelty, greed and malice have already been given, and she often destroys the helpful animal which has fed and aided her stepdaughter (p. 102 above). Occasionally it is the natural mother who treats one child unkindly, and the Grimms changed some of these to stepmothers (Tatar 1987: 35), but stepmothers feature as evil characters in tales from many countries (AT 510). The cruelty varies from continual scolding and imposing unreasonable tasks on the stepdaughter to half-starving her, or sending her out in the cold (AT 403). In the Grimms' tale, 'Three Little Men in the Wood' (1944: 78), the stepmother drives the girl out in mid-winter in a paper frock and with only a piece of hard bread to eat, and forbids her to come home without a basket of strawberries. In 'Jack Frost' (Afanas'ev 1945: 366), where again the heroine is sent out to die of cold in the forest (p. 109 above), there is a vivid description of the stepmother's persecution:

> No matter how hard the stepdaughter tried, she was always in the wrong. Yet the truth of the matter was that the stepdaughter was as good as gold; in the proper hands she would have been like cheese in butter, but in her stepmother's house she bathed in tears every day. What could she do? Even an angry wind subsides at last; but when the old woman got angry she never quietened down, she would hurl one insult after another, and her mouth was so full of venom that her teeth itched.

Another convincing picture of evil is given in 'The Juniper Tree' in the Grimms' collection (AT 720; p. 102 above). Here the stepmother hates her little stepson, thinking that he will always get in the way of her own daughter and inherit his father's property:

> . . . and the Evil One filled her mind with this till she was quite wroth with the little boy and she pushed him from one corner to the other and slapped him here and cuffed him there, until the poor child was in continual terror, for when he came out of school he had no peace in any place.

The woman's own daughter supports the boy, and when her mother gives her an apple out of a chest, she asks 'Is brother not to have one too?' This makes her mother angry, and when the boy comes home, he exclaims 'Mother, how dreadful you look!' She offers him an apple from the chest, and when he bends down to take it out, slams down the heavy lid so that his head is cut off and falls among the apples. Yet this does not exhaust her villainy; she props him up with his head in place and an apple in his hand, and when Marlinchen her daughter is alarmed by his silence, tells her to give him a box on the ear. His head flies off, and the child blames herself for his death:

'Marlinchen', said the mother, 'What have you done? But be quiet and let no one know it; it cannot be helped now, we will make him into black puddings.' Then the mother took the little boy and chopped him in pieces, put him into the pan and made him into black puddings; but Marlinchen stood by weeping and weeping, and all her tears fell into the pan and there was no need of any salt.

The dish is served for supper, and the father eats heartily, declaring 'You shall have none of it. It seems to me as if it were all mine.' Thus the woman has not only committed a crime against her stepson, but also against her own daughter, whom she is said to love, and the boy's father, deceiving him into eating his own son. Such an impression of innate evil as is conveyed here in a couple of pages would be hard to equal. Other versions, such as one from a fourteen-year-old boy in Scotland (Briggs 1970: 378), in which the stepdaughter is the victim and there is no brother, are less powerful, though there may be grisly details such as the little girl's finger found in the pie given to the father to eat.

Another instance of evil conduct by a stepmother is found in the tale of 'Vasilisa the Beautiful' (p. 103 above), where she breaks the sacred rule of never extinguishing the last light in the house, so that she can send Vasilisa to Baba Yaga for a light, hoping that she will be devoured. She and her two daughters receive their due punishment when the house is burned down. Stepsisters are less active in evil-doing than their mothers, but marked out by their spitefulness, envy and lack of sympathy for others. They pay dearly for this because they fail in the tests put upon them when they leave home, and are left smeared in pitch, unattractive to look at, or dropping snakes and toads when they open their mouths.

Sometimes, as in versions of 'Cinderella', they are beautiful but heartless. In the Grimms' version (1944: 121) they delight in humiliating their stepsister:

They took her pretty clothes away from her, put an old grey bedgown on her, and gave her wooden shoes. 'Just look at the proud princess, how decked out she is!' they cried, and laughed and led her into the kitchen.

Not only is she given all the hard work to do, but the sisters deliberately add to this by malicious tricks like emptying peas and lentils into the ashes. However they too pay dearly for their unkindness; their cheating over the slipper is betrayed by the pigeons which help the heroine, and in the second edition of the Grimms' tales these peck out their eyes. Very occasionally such sisters repent of their conduct, when treated generously by the heroine, as in 'One-Eye, Two-Eyes and Three-Eyes' (Grimm 1944: 585), whereas the evil stepmother is neither forgiven nor converted. Her usual fate is to die a cruel death, perhaps put into a barrel filled with spikes, or torn apart by horses.

Another evil woman in the tales is a member of the husband's family, perhaps his mother or sister, who resents his marriage with the heroine, and steals her children. One particularly monstrous example is found in 'The Mother-in-Law', an incomplete story in the first edition of the Grimms' tales, later omitted. Here the king's mother imprisons the queen and her two young sons when the king has gone away to war, intending to have them cooked, to satisfy her craving for human flesh. The woman with cannabalistic instincts who seeks to devour the heroine or her children is balanced by the male ogre desiring to eat the flesh of the hero, as Maria Tatar (1987: 133ff.) has shown. She may also appear as the evil power in the forest, as in 'Hansel and Gretel' and the tales of Baba Yaga.

Occasionally the wrong-doer is the queen's wicked stepsister who comes to help at the birth. The young wife is accused of devouring the child, or of giving birth to an animal, and a letter announcing the birth of a fine child to the king may be altered to deceive him. When this happens several times his wife is condemned to death, but the children are finally produced unharmed, and it is the plotter who comes to a painful end (AT 451). This motif is very effectively used in the Norwegian tale 'The Twelve Wild Ducks' (Dasent 1908: 51), where the wicked old queen is said to be the stepmother of the king. The young queen is unable to defend herself, because she has to stay silent until she has finished spinning and weaving clothes for her twelve brothers, turned into wild ducks, in order to free them from enchantment. She finishes the last garment as she is about to be put on the pyre, and the ducks reappear as princes. The king to his joy hears the true story, and his three lovely children are found playing in a snake-pit unharmed.

Christian figures are occasionally brought into the tales. In 'Our Lady's Child' in the Grimms' collection (1944: 230) the Virgin Mary is surprisingly given the role of the stealer of children, in order to punish the girl she fostered for opening a forbidden door in heaven and refusing to confess her fault (AT 710). She is only saved from the pyre at the last moment when she repents, and her children are then restored. Maria Tatar (1987: 26) gives this as an example of excessive punishment for slight wrongdoing, characteristic of the moral emphasis brought into the tales when adapted for children, but the use of the usually benign figure of the Virgin here is exceptional.

There is also the substitute bride, who usurps the place of the rightful princess. One outstanding example is the maid-in-waiting who accompanies the heroine in her journey to the kingdom of her betrothed, in 'The Goosegirl' (p. 103 above). In a Russian version 'The Merchant's Daughter and the Maidservant' (Afanas'ev 1945: 327), the heroine is sent off to be married to a king. Her servant, who resembles her in appearance, is 'full of spite', and she gives her mistress a sleeping potion, cuts out her eyes and puts them in her pocket, and then takes her place as a bride. The blinded girl is helped by an old man who makes two wonderful embroidered crowns, for which he demands two eyes in payment from the false queen, so that the heroine's sight is regained. The queen then has her cut to pieces and takes out her heart, which she rolls into an egg. When a wonderful garden grows where the girl is buried, she has it cut down and it turns into stone. But there the king finds a handsome boy, who weeps bitterly and will not be comforted until the queen gives him the egg from her pocket, whereupon he runs joyfully back to the garden and the true bride is restored to life. While the setting of these tales is very different, with the loss of the horse Falada and the princess as goosegirl in one case, and the blinding of the merchant's daughter and the unexplained episode of the handsome child in the other, the basic pattern of the maid's wicked spite and ruthless cruelty is present in both.

Sometimes it is the stepsister who usurps the place of the king's young wife, as in 'The White Duck', a tale recorded by Kristensen in Denmark (Holbek 1987: 528). The banished wife visits the palace kitchen in the form of a duck, and eventually the king cuts a cross on the duck's beak, restoring her to human form (AT 403V). The stepmother may turn the queen into an animal or bird, as in the Swedish tale 'Little Rose and Big Briar' (Blecher 1993: 208), where she becomes a golden goose. Here and in other tales the bird speaks a verse, asking how things go on without her:

> Does my linden tree play?
> Does my nightingale sing?
> Does my little boy cry?
> Does my husband ever smile?

She is able to return three times, and on her final visit is released from enchantment.

So far all those seeking to destroy the heroine are women, and it has been noted that siblings of the same sex are in general hostile figures in the tales, while those of the opposite sex are helpful (Brewer 1980: 9). There are however tales of a murderous bridegroom, as in the English story 'Mr Fox' (Briggs 1970: II, 446), which apparently predates Perrault's 'Bluebeard' (Opie 1974: 103–4; AT 312, 955). Here the heroine visits the house of the mysterious man whom she has promised to marry, and discovers that he has murdered many former brides. Next day, at the breakfast to celebrate the signing of the marriage contract, she relates all she has seen in the form of a 'bad dream', and produces the hand of the last woman murdered, whereupon Mr Fox is killed. In a similar tale recorded by the Grimms, 'The Robber Bridegroom' (1944: 200), a bird gives the intended bride warning when she visits the house, and an old woman helps her to escape.

In Perrault's 'Bluebeard', the motif of the breaking of a taboo is introduced (Opie 1974: 103). The young wife opens a forbidden door, finds the remains of previous murdered wives and cannot remove telltale bloodstains from the key, but is rescued from death at the last moment by her brothers. An interesting variant on this is 'Fitcher's Bird' in the Grimms' collection (1944: 216), where the heroine survives by her own efforts. Her two sisters are killed by the murderer, but she restores them to life and keeps the egg given to her unblemished, so that the evil wizard has to agree to marry her. She sets up a skull wreathed in flowers in an upper window in her place, covers herself in honey and rolls in feathers. Thus she gets away unrecognised, and her brothers set fire to the house. There is a link here with a very different motif (AT 1091), that of a husband deceiving the devil by disguising his wife as a strange creature after she has rolled in tar and covered herself with feathers (Spring 1988: 139). These tales of a murderous bridegroom do not end in a happy marriage, but the girl saved from death returns to her own family.

The human characters who most frequently seek to destroy the hero are his two elder brothers (AT 550). The youngest brother is often despised when young as a simpleton or a lazy lad, and later his brothers become bitterly jealous of his successes. They may murder him while he sleeps (p. 101 above) or cut the rope when they are hauling him up from the enchanted land below the earth, as in 'The Gnome' in the Grimms' collection (1944: 420). Here the little man who helps the hero warns him against his brothers, and after Hans has saved three princesses from many-headed dragons and had them drawn up, he remembers the warning and puts a stone in the basket. His brothers cut the rope, and conclude that he is dead. In 'The Water of Life' (Grimm 1944: 449), the elder brothers steal the healing water won by the youngest, and substitute salt water for it, so that they can cure their sick father and he will be put to death for making his illness worse (AT 551).

While the heroine may be replaced by a false bride, a coward may falsely claim credit for the hero's achievements (AT 300). In the Swedish tale of 'The Three Swords' (Blecher 1993: 145), a tailor offers to save the king's daughters from three many-headed trolls. He cowers in terror when the monsters arrive, but afterwards claims to have slain them. In a Russian tale, 'The Bold Knight' (Afanas'ev 1945: 314), an 'envious fellow' cuts off the head of the hero who has slain the dragon and throws his body into the sea, but the princess restores her deliverer with the water of life.

The hero may also be threatened by the king whose daughter he hopes to marry; the king imposes task after task upon him with the threat of death should he fail. In the Russian tale 'Go I Know Not Whither' (Afanas'ev 1945: 504) the king and his steward seek to destroy the archer Fedot, because they both desire his beautiful wife (AT 465). They are aided by the evil Baba Yaga, but she is outdone by Fedot's wife, who possesses magic skills. When he is to be sent out in a rotten ship manned with drunken sailors to obtain a golden-horned stag from the thrice-tenth kingdom, his wife simply sends two attendant spirits for the stag and tells Fedot to return. He is then ordered to 'go I know not whither, bring me back I know not what'. The spirits cannot help in this case, and Fedot's wife tells him the journey will take eighteen years, but gives him a ball to roll before him to show the way. He is helped by his wife's mother, who consults the birds, animals and fishes over which she has power, like the supernatural sisters in other tales (p. 107 above), and sends an ancient frog with him on his journey. It carries him over a river of fire to a door in a mountain, where an invisible helper procures magic gifts for him and takes him home to his wife, living as a dove during his absence. The archer defeats and kills the king, and takes over the kingdom. Here the hostile king loses kingdom and life, but similar figures trying to destroy the hero may escape unharmed. In one Swedish tale of this kind, 'The Boat that Sailed on Both Land and Sea' (Blecher 1993: 105), the story ends:

> This time the king had to keep his word. Since he was very greedy, he figured that he couldn't have a better son-in-law, so he lived on the money the boy had given him, and the boy and the princess took over the kingdom.

Sometimes the villain is the master who takes a youth as his apprentice (AT 325). In 'Farmer Weathersky' (p. 108 above) the mysterious figure who refuses to release the youth clearly possesses supernatural powers. In the Russian tale 'Magic' (Afanas'ev 1945: 399) there is a similar figure called a magician, and in both cases the apprentice finally destroys his master and marries his daughter. In a Danish story recorded by Kristensen (1490: 'The Transformation'), there are no indications of supernatural powers, although plenty of fantasy, and Holbek interprets it as 'the apprentice's daydream, seeing the master tailor as representing the father of the girl whom the hero wants to marry' (1987: 562).

In some tales it is the princess herself who seeks to destroy the hero who comes to win her. This may be due to natural perversity or conceit, because she has never been beaten in a riddle contest or war of words (AT 851). In the Swedish tale, 'The Princess who always had an Answer' (Blecher 1993: 103), the princess decides that 'if she was to have a husband, he had to be even cleverer than she'. There are also tales where she mocks her suitors, but is made to regret it by a man of strong character, the motif of the taming of the shrew, as in 'Prince Greenbeard' (Blecher 1993: 132; AT 900). Sometimes however she has a demon lover, who eggs her on to destroy her suitors, and finally has to be killed, while she may need cleansing to restore her to normality (AT 507). In 'Little Hans' (p. 105 above), she flies by night to the Brocken, where her troll lover gives her an object to think of next day which he is sure the hero will fail to guess, but his Companion steals the object and gives it to the hero, and on the third occasion when she has been told to think of the troll's head, cuts it off. The princess is devastated, and we are told that 'everyone felt that she must be punished for the evil she had done'. On the advice of the Companion, she is put into boiling water and then whipped for three days with hazel sticks, after which 'she became a good and decent person again'.

The ogres and trolls who play a large part in the tales have no individual characteristics, and are mainly distinguished by their stupidity and thirst for human blood. On many occasions the giant suspects that there is a man in the house, but his wife allays his suspicions by assuring him that a bird has dropped a bone, or strangers have passed by. The rhyme he speaks is preserved in various forms in English tales of giants, such as 'Jack and the Beanstalk'; a version from Massachusetts dated 1794 (Opie 1974: 63) runs:

> Fee, Faw, Fum.
> I smell the Blood
> Of an Earthly Man,
> Let him be alive or dead,
> Off goes his Head.

In an Irish tale, 'Iolann Airiminic' (Ó Duilearga 1981: 31), the ogre declares: 'Foo, foo, foo, I get the scent of an Irishman on the truthful sod!', and in one from Norway, 'Soria Moria Castle' (Dasent 1903: 396), a troll exclaims: 'Hutetu! What a smell of Christian man's blood!' In Russian tales there is a slightly different formula: 'I smell a Russian bone', says the Baba Yaga (Afanas'ev 1945: 351), or 'Fie, Fie! Of a Russian bone not a sound was heard, not a glimpse was seen, and now a Russian bone has come to my house of its own free will' in 'The Frog Princess' (122).

It seems to be mainly male blood which tempts giants, since they keep beautiful maidens captive, and it may be these, rather than the giant's wife, who conceal and befriend the hero. Whirlwind in the Russian tale 'The Three Kingdoms' (Afanas'ev 1945: 375) behaves like a giant, and has a series of captured queens immured in various castles whom he visits at regular intervals. Here, and in other tales, the hero is given a special strength-giving drink by the captured queen, and the tubs are then reversed so that Whirlwind drinks the water of weakness instead.

There are however a number of individual destroyers hostile to men and women alike. Although many-headed dragons are fairly conventional figures, Zmei ('dragon') in the Russian tales appears as a supernatural character who has links with Otherworld powers. Like the ogres, he kidnaps queens and princesses, and in 'Ilya Muromets and the Dragon' (Afanas'ev 1945: 567), visits a princess in her own home and 'withered her young life; she was completely worn out'. He can take on human form as in 'Dawn, Evening and Midnight' (Afanas'ev 1945: 457), and may ride a wonderful horse, or rest his head in the princess's lap. In 'Prince Ivan and Byely Polyanin' (Afanas'ev 1945: 475) he is said to rule in the enchanted thrice-tenth kingdom. Sometimes there are three dragons, said to come from the Black Sea. In 'Ivan and the Cow's Son' (Afanas'ev 1945: 234) they are married to the daughters of Baba Yaga, themselves destructive beings. Indeed the females connected with these dragons may prove more deadly than the males. In 'Two Ivans' (Afanas'ev 1945: 463) their sister takes on the form of a lioness and destroys both heroes in revenge for the killing of her brothers. In 'Ivan the Peasant's Son' (Afanas'ev 1945: 262) the dragon family consists of a twelve-headed dragon with three dragon sons, and his wife and three daughters-in-law plan unsuccessfully to avenge their killing on the hero. In 'Nikita the Tanner' (Afanas'ev 1945: 310) the hero overcomes the dragon and then agrees to divide the earth with him. The dragon ploughs a furrow from Kiev to the Caspian Sea, said to be seen to this very day: 'those who do not know what it is, call it the rampart'.

The relationship between the dragon family and a tiny man, said to be thumb-sized, is not clear. He has an enormously long beard or moustache, is extremely strong and usually hostile to the hero, bringing threatening messages demanding a princess for the dragon, as in 'Prince Ivan and Princess Martha' (Afanas'ev 1945: 79). In 'Ivan the Peasant's Son and the Thumb-sized Man' (Afanas'ev 1945: 262) he steals the hero's horse and demands a princess in exchange, and also bites off the hands and feet of a champion. However he is an ambivalent figure, since in 'The Milk of Wild Beasts' (Afanas'ev 1945: 304), where he is called Little Fist, he appears from the bones of a bullock who has helped the hero and his sister and then commanded them to slay him. Little Fist supports Prince Ivan against his treacherous sister, and when Ivan marries a champion maiden who tries to murder him, he beats her until she becomes a reformed character.

Another mysterious figure is Koshchey the Deathless. He is chained in a locked room by the heroine in 'Maria Morevna', and released by Prince Ivan out of pity; whereupon he carries off Maria Morevna. Koshchey can overtake all those escaping from him because of his wonderful horse, given to him by the Baba Yaga, but the hero manages to steal a 'mangy colt' from her, which finally kills Koshchey with a blow from its hoof. Koshchey behaves like a giant, declaring that there is a Russian smell in the house when the hero arrives, but is reassured by Maria Morevna: 'You have been flying through Russia and you yourself have become full of it.' The same dialogue takes place between Koshchey and Vasilisa Kirbitievna in 'Koshshey the Deathless' (Afanas'ev 1945: 485). When the hero arrives to rescue his bride, Vasilisa discovers that Koshchey's death is hidden in a coffer buried under an oak, which contains a duck inside a hare, so the deathless one's life is finally ended (AT 302). However he, like the dragons, has dangerous sisters, who arrive in the form of twelve doves, and attempt to kill the hero.

Thus there are several supernatural male figures in the Russian tales who appear as characters of some power in the underworld, familiar to the story-tellers and their audiences, but not found in the German or Scandinavian tales. The outstanding hostile figure in the Russian tales however is the Baba Yaga, whom many have thought to be based on memories of an ancient goddess. She is connected with the dragon family and with Koshchey the Deathless. She appears as a terrifying old woman who inhabits a hut in the forest which revolves on chicken or dog legs. In 'BabaYaga' (Afanas'ev 1945: 194) we are told: 'Her head was in front, her right leg was in one corner and her left leg in the other corner', while her nose may grow into the ceiling, so that she fills the hut like a corpse within a coffin. In many stories however she is active, using her long nose to poke the fire, and her iron teeth, sharpened on a file, to devour young and tender victims. Occasionally she roasts them in her oven, like the witch in 'Hansel and Gretel' (Grimm 1944: 86; AT 327A), but this may be a later addition to the tale; in 'Prince Danila Govorila' (Afanas'ev 1945: 351) she is pushed in herself, as in the Grimms' tale, though she somehow manages to escape.

Baba Yaga journeys through the air in a mortar, which she drives along by her pestle, sweeping behind her with a broom. To enter or pass through her hut the right formula must be used as it is by the heroine in 'Prince Danila Govorila': 'Little hut, little hut, stand the old way with your back to the woods and your front to me.' To survive a visit to Baba Yaga one must know the correct way to deal with her. In 'The Sea King' (Afanas'ev 1945: 427) the prince demands that she gives him food and questions him later, and she meekly agrees to this and later gives him help. She is sometimes said to own a herd of marvellous horses, and Koshchey the Deathless claims to have gained his wonderful steed by guarding these for three nights.

The most detailed account of Baba Yaga comes in the tale of Vasilisa the Beautiful (p. 103 above), which brings out something of the terror evoked by the monstrous creature. When the heroine, sent by her stepmother to get a light, is approaching the hut, she sees a horseman all in white, on a white horse, galloping past her, and then one all in red. The hut is surrounded by a fence of human bones, with skulls on the spikes with eyes which gleam in the darkness, and mouths with sharp teeth 'in place of a lock'. Then a black horseman gallops in through the door of the house, and a terrible noise is heard as Baba Yaga drives up in her mortar, and confronts Vasilisa. She agrees to give her a light if she will work for her, and the girl accomplishes the heavy tasks set her with the help of her wonderful doll. Mysterious hands come to grind the wheat which she has sorted out, but the girl wisely refrains from asking questions about these, though she learns that the three horsemen are Baba Yaga's faithful servants, bringing night and day. When asked how she managed to complete her tasks, Vasilisa gives the right reply, saying that she has the blessing of her dead mother, for this causes Baba Yaga to drive her out in fury, giving her one of the skulls as a light.

Reasons for suggesting that Baba Yaga might be based on memories of an earlier goddess are her powers over the light and the dark, as well as over the strange hands that grind the wheat. While magical helpers are a commonplace in the fairy tale, it is implied that the hands are of a different order, on no account to be mentioned. Propp believed that she had connections with the goddess ruling the creatures of the wild (Kravchenko 1987: 189), and there are sometimes three sisters, all called Baba Yaga, who share such powers (p. 116 above). Her strange hut on chicken legs, for which no convincing explanation has been given, may be seen as a point of entry to the Otherworld, perhaps to the world of the dead. There has been much argument as to whether she is a matriarchal figure; though Propp denied that she had a husband or children, these do sometimes appear in the tales. Theories of Russian scholars, summarised by Kravchenko (1987: 167ff.), tend to ignore the fact that additional motifs and traditions must have been introduced into tales about Baba Yaga over centuries of storytelling, accounting for some contradictions. However her dual nature, making her at times a good counsellor and helper although her destructive aspect is predominant (p. 109 above), is in keeping with the character of the powerful hunting goddess of early times (Davidson 1998: 25ff.). Kravchenko (1987: 186-7) sees a link between the Baba Yaga and the Maiden Tsar who appears in a number of tales, a somewhat Amazonian figure who takes part in battles and may destroy unsuccessful suitors. Such figures however are found elsewhere in western Europe, especially in Scandinavia, whereas the Baba Yaga is a character confined to the Russian fairy tales.

Conclusion

Looking back over the impressive array of helpers, it seems that those who come to assist hero or heroine have two main purposes. One is to act as guide to the Otherworld, providing the means to reach the desired goal, and the other to offer food, magical gifts, practical help and advice. While the first might seem to relate mainly to the hero and the second to the heroine, there are exceptions to this. The women undertake arduous journeys as well as tasks about the house, climb glass mountains, fall down wells or are lost in the deep forest, while magic tablecloths or food from a horse's ear are often essential for the survival of the hero. The Otherworld may be reached through the air, perhaps on a magic horse or an eagle's back, or by descending into the earth, and the general impression is of a land of richness and beauty, where enormous distances may separate one kingdom or supernatural being from another. Helpers often give the adventurers a ball to roll before them to show the way, or seven-league boots to take them swiftly over the countryside, or a steed of some kind to carry them to the next stopping place.

There is emphasis on the remoteness of the place to be reached and the difficulty of finding the way there, so that the counsel of wise animals or supernatural beings may be necessary. Some helpers however are not encountered in the Otherworld, but may appear in the home, or be helpful relatives, neighbours or passing strangers. Trees may spring up in the familiar world on which helpful birds perch, or the grave of a dead parent may be the place where help is procured. Sometimes after the quest is accomplished the helper entreats the hero to slay him, so that he can resume human form.

When we search for the source of evil in the tales, we find it not so much in the Otherworld as in the human characters in close contact with the hero or heroine. Stepmothers, mothers-in-law, jealous siblings, envious colleagues and greedy servants are the ones who commit ruthless crimes against the innocent, together with tyrannical rulers. There are also women who are 'enchanted', perhaps by a demon lover, and must be rescued and cleansed to recover their full humanity. Human characters can restore and save the apparently doomed, and the water of life bring about the resurrection of hero or heroine. Crimes and deeds of violence can be undone, and just as a prince cut to pieces or thrown into the sea can be brought back to life, so the heroine's hands which have been cut off can be replaced, and her lost eyes restored. In very few of the tales does evil finally triumph, and when this does happen, it is through the intervention of supernatural destroyers (p. 116 above). It is common for the evil-doers unwittingly to pronounce their own death sentence (Lüthi 1984: 131).

Both helpers and adversaries can be supernatural figures, and this is an important point to be recognised. We cannot assume that the fairy tales originated in myths, as was argued by Grimm and others in the nineteenth century, for there is no convincing evidence for this, but it seems possible that the tales contain memories of earlier traditions of journeys to the Otherworld and communication with the dead, as well as those of supernatural powers who may guide or hinder. There appear also to be memories of a female guardian figure protecting women and girls, and of supernatural rulers of the wild creatures. Such helpful yet dangerous figures were known early in northern Eurasia, and this gives a possible explanation of the strong emphasis on animal helpers in the tales. While not found in the northern myths or in tales of gods and heroes, they are encountered in earlier shamanistic tradition, since the shaman depended on such helpers for his journeys to the Otherworld, and his spirit guides were in the form of birds or animals (Eliade 1960: 94ff.). The strong emphasis on long and perilous journeys in the tales is characteristic of shamanistic tradition, as are the episodes in which the journeying figure is maimed or killed and then restored to life and health. In the initiatory dreams of a shaman he may be cut to pieces, cooked and eaten or swallowed by a monster, and such dreams are accepted as evidence that he is destined to be a shaman (Krippner 1989: 382). It is generally agreed that shamanism formed part of the hunting culture in northern Europe and Asia, as Hultkrantz (1961: 47) and others have shown, and it seems possible that earlier accounts of shamans' journeys have influenced the patterns of the tales.

At the same time many helpers and adversaries could represent familiar human figures in the world of the storytellers and their audiences. The wicked king or ogre could be equated with the heroine's father showing hostility to the suitor, as has been convincingly argued by Holbek (1987: 426–7), while the unkindness of stepmother and mother-in-law was notorious in a world where frequent deaths in childbirth led many fathers to remarry, and young wives often entered unfriendly households (Davidson 1998: 127ff.) However the supernatural elements in the tales should not be neglected, They are particularly powerful in the Russian tales, where Baba Yaga plays a frequent part, together with the dragon figures who fluctuate between monsters and rulers of Other-world kingdoms. Baba Yaga seems sometimes to be related to the mistress of the animals, while showing characteristics of the goddess of the hearth and of the dead (Davidson 1998: 181). However, the purpose of the fairy tales is not to present these supernatural figures as central characters in the plot, since they are only important for the part they play in the destiny of hero or heroine. They are not seen as invariably good or evil, as are the human characters. Figures like stepmothers, vicious servants or jealous brothers may turn to destructive supernatural beings to assist them in their malicious intent, but it is they who commit the crimes and are incapable of remorse.

As opposed to this impression of evil close at hand, the positive side of human relationship comes out strongly in pictures of heroic loyalty. The possibility of willing self-sacrifice, as in the tales of sisters determined to disenchant their brothers almost to the point of their own destruction, is an important element in the tales. So too is the motif of the necessary killing of the faithful helper, and the readiness to sacrifice wives or children to save the hero's deliverer. Lack of morality in the tales has often been stressed, and the hero may cheat, steal or use cunning to succeed, or the heroine seek to destroy her suitors. Nevertheless there is a firm sense of responsibility for others, and of the necessity to face up to the issues of life and death when the crisis comes. The tales are more than entertaining accounts of successful wooings transformed into a magical framework. It has been claimed with some justification that they give a picture of youth attaining maturity, learning to make lasting relationships and to become independent and responsible (Brewer 1980: 7ff.). Yet they are by no means tedious moralising tales, even if there have been attempts to turn them in this direction, particularly when adapting them for children in the nineteenth century. Much of the vitality which saves them and has assured their survival over the centuries comes, surely, from the rich tapestry of helpers and destroy-ers which extends the action into the realms of the Otherworld.

References

Afanas'ev, A. (1945), *Russian Fairy Tales*, trans. N. Guterman. New York.

Anderson, G. (2000), *Fairy Tale in the Ancient World*. London.

Asbjørnson, P. C., and Moe, J. (1960), *Norwegian Folk Tales*. New York.

Band, A. J. (1978) ed. and trans., *Nahman of Bratslav: The Tales*. Mahwah, NJ.

Bettridge, W. E., and Utley, F. L. (1971), 'New Light on the Origin of the Griselda Story', *Texas Studies in Language and Literature* 13, 152–208.

Binnie, P. (1980), *The Old Wives' Tale*. The Revel Plays. Manchester.

Blecher, L. T. and G. (1993), *Swedish Folktales and Legends*. New York.

Brewer, D. (1980), *Symbolic Stories: Traditional Narratives of the Family Drama in English Literature*. Cambridge.

Briggs, K. M. (1970), *A Dictionary of British Folk-Tales*. 4 vols. London.

Dasent, A. J. (1903/1908) ed., *Popular Tales from the Norse*. Edinburgh.

Davidson, H. E. (1998), *Roles of the Northern Goddess*. London.

—— (forthcoming). 'The Grateful Dead', in *Supernatural Helpers*, ed. A. Chaudhri and H. Ellis Davidson. Durham, NC.

Eliade, M. (1960), *Myths, Dreams and Mysteries*, trans. P. Mairet. London.

Gerould, G. H. (1908), *The Grateful Dead: The History of a Folk Story*. Publications of the Folklore Society 60. London.

Grimm, J. and W. (1944), *The Complete Grimm's Fairy Tales*, trans. M. Hunt, revised J. Stein. New York.

Holbek, B. (1987), *Interpretation of Fairy Tales: Danish Folklore in a European Perspective*. FFC 239. Helsinki.

—— (1990), 'Hans Christian Andersen's Use of Folktales', in M. Nøjgaard *et al. The Telling of Stories: Approaches to a Traditional Craft*. Odense. (Reprinted as Chapter 9 of the present volume.)

Hultkrantz, Å. (1961) ed., *The Supernatural Owners of Nature*. Stockholm.

Jackson, K. (1961), *International Popular Tales and Early Welsh Tradition*. Cardiff.

Kravchenko, M. (1987), *The World of the Russian Fairy Tale*, trans. P. Lang. European University Studies, series 16: Slav Language and Literature 34. Berne/New York.

Krippner, S. (1989), 'The Use of Dreams in Shamanic Traditions', in *Shamanism Past and Present* 2, ed. M. Hoppál and O. von Sadovszky. International Society for Trans-Oceanic Research. Budapest.

Lüthi, M. (1984), *The Fairytale as Art Form and Portrait of Man*, trans. J. Erickson. Bloomington.

Ó Duilearga, S. (1981) ed., *Seán Ó Conaill's Book: Stories and Traditions from Iveragh*, trans. M. MacNeill. Dublin.

Opie, I. and P. (1974), *The Classic Fairy Tales*. Oxford.

Riordan, J. (1986) ed. and trans., *Russian Gypsy Tales*, collected by Y. Druts and A. Gessler. Edinburgh.

Ross, A. (1967), *Pagan Celtic Britain: Studies in Iconography and Tradition*. London.

Simpson, J. (1963–4), 'Mimir: Two Heads or One?', *Saga-Book of the Viking Society* 16.1, 41–53; 'Note on the Folktale Motif of the Heads in the Well', *Saga-Book* 16.2–3, 248–50.

Spring, I. (1988), 'The Devil and the Featherly Wife', *Folklore* 99, 139–45. London.

Tatar, M. (1987), *The Hard Facts of the Grimms' Fairy Tales*. Princeton.

Waschnitius, V. (1913), *Perht, Holda und verwandte Gestalten.* Sitzungen der Kaiser-
lichen Akademie der Wissenschaften (Philos./Hist.) 174. Vienna.
Yeats, W. B. (1973) ed., *Fairy and Folk Tales of Ireland.* Gerrards Cross.

7

'Catch if you can': The Cumulative Tale

JOYCE THOMAS*

What follows is a rumination upon the cumulative tale, its characteristics, its appeal and its relation to the fairy tale. As with the latter, cumulative tales span ancient to modern times and are found in virtually all cultures. No doubt their popularity owes much to the manner in which they invite audience participation; that invitation is one of a playful mnemonic challenge posed to both the tale-teller and his or her audience. As a formula narrative, the cumulative tale or song follows a traditional, readily discernible pattern of repetition, of accumulating characters, objects, actions, that are repeated with each new addition of character, object or action; this repetition may follow a linear chronology from the first introduced to the last, or it may backtrack from the most recent to the first. Rather like a constructed tower of cards, the tale extends itself until it reaches the inevitable collapse – at its best, a resounding memory-racking crescendo of accumulations, which then abruptly stops. With the cumulative tale, the repetitive pattern takes precedence over the plot or, some might say, *is* the plot. Essentially, the tale exists to add to or multiply itself via those accumulations.

Probably most of us are acquainted with a cumulative song or two, such as the widely distributed 'The Twelve Apostles', performance-rich 'Old Mac-Donald Had a Farm', and seasonable if rather irksome 'The Twelve Days of Christmas'. In *The Folktale* Stith Thompson (1977: 230–3) briefly discusses 'the principal cumulative tales', which he indicates as including 'The Death of the Cock', 'The Death of the Hen, 'The Fleeing Pancake' or 'The Gingerbread Man', 'The Fat Cat', 'The Fat Troll' or 'The Fat Wolf', 'The Goat Who Would Not Go Home', 'Stronger and Strongest' (a literary narrative), 'The Cock's Whiskers', 'How the Mouse Regained Its Tail', 'Pif Pof Poltrie' and 'The Horseshoe Nail'. As Thompson notes, this list is by no means complete. Indeed this writer would at least like to add the German 'The Louse and the Flea', the Italian 'The Cock and the Mouse', the Irish 'Munachar and Manachar', the West African 'Why Mosquitoes Buzz in People's Ears' and the Ashanti 'Talk'.

The cumulative tale is also known as a chain tale, one based upon 'a characteristic series of numbers, objects, characters, days of the week, events,

*Portions of this essay were initially presented at a panel of the Northeast Popular Culture Association Meeting, October 1989; and again at the children's literature panel, Northeast Modern Language Association convention, April 1991.

etc., in specific relation' (Leach and Fried 1984: 207). *Funk and Wagnall's Standard Dictionary of Folklore, Mythology and Legend* gives the example of the story of the origin of chess, which advances by means of numbers in geometric progression: the inventor of chess asks in payment one grain of wheat for the first square of the board, two for the second square, four for the third, eight for the fourth, and so on (Leach and Fried 1984: 207). Likewise, the nursery song 'Solomon Grundy' represents a versified chain tale. Its strictly linear design is that of a series of interdependent parts, perhaps intended to teach children the days of the week, if not something about human life's abbreviated condition (Baring-Gould 1967: 105):

> Solomon Grundy
> Born on a Monday,
> Christened on a Tuesday,
> Married on a Wednesday,
> Took ill on a Thursday,
> Worse on Friday,
> Died on Saturday,
> Buried on Sunday.

Clearly, though the cumulative tale or song qualifies as a formula tale and a chain tale, the latter narratives need not be cumulative, for they lack the requisite repetition of accumulated elements.

Probably the most popular cumulative tale throughout Europe and America is that of the renegade pancake or corresponding fleet-footed gingerbread man. In a number of respects this story exemplifies the cumulative tale; certain of its features are also commonly seen in other folktale types, especially the *Märchen*, wonder or fairy tale. Thus, it offers itself as a playful and meaningful case study.

To begin, there is the aspect of its antiquity. As with many other folktales, shadows of distant times, cultures and literatures are cast by the cumulative tale as a type, which dates in printed form back to at least the Indian *Pañcatantra*, compiled about the fifth century AD (Thompson 1977: 231). While of the past, this particular tale of 'The Pancake' exhibits an intriguing modernity as well, thanks to its appeal, to its 'translation' into the form of children's picture story-books, and to its use as part of the child's introduction to language. Even today some cultures retain customs of pancake contests, tosses and rolls. In the case of 'The Gingerbread Man', the protagonist (not to mention entire gingerbread families) has been transported outside his tale to take up independent existence as the cookie-effigy we consume. The flight from consumption, of course, constitutes the tale's core while imbuing the narrative with a fascinating play upon language and some related oral aspects.

Gingerbread man or boy or pancake, the protagonist may change form, may change his mode of propulsion – from running on two flat feet to rolling on a crisp edge – but remains the same basic figure, the same bit of animated matter, animated batter. In keeping with other cumulative tales, the action grows through a successive accumulation of players, building to the inevitable climax in which the full sequence of characters and events is repeated. One hallmark of such tales is that virtually anyone, knowing the formulaic pattern (which does not take long to recognise), can recreate the tale's core action after hearing the final formula. One has merely to backtrack, unwind the thread bound around the narrative's spool.

Here, approaching the tale's end, the pancake recites its chain-linked flight to the gander (Thompson 1968: 430):

> When I have run away from Goody Poody and the goodman and seven squalling children, and from Manny Panny, and Henny Penny, and Cocky Locky, and Ducky Lucky, and Goosey Poosey, I must run away from you too, Gander Pander.

As with rote learning of vocabulary or multiplication tables, the tale tests one's memory and linguistic facility, with both the tale-teller and the audience participating in the test. Tension mounts with the building blocks of actors: how long can the narrator sustain the thread she is spinning before memory falters, the action snarls? How long can the audience remember and repeat that thread? The tale truly engages us through its tension and test. It is a game and challenge; few people, once perceiving the narrative formula by which it operates, can help becoming a participant in it.

The tale's narrative simplicity – its adherence to a set formula embracing both action and structure – and its conjoined challenge posed to both narrator and audience, constitute much of its appeal. That simplicity, that test of memory, and the overall accompanying playfulness are characteristic of the cumulative tale as a type. A single, simple action sets the formula in motion, then builds upon it via the process of incremental repetition, in which the original cause is not so much complicated as added on to. The formula's simplicity entices us into participation; at the same time, as each new actor enters the sequence of repetitions, even simplicity comes to pose a challenge. The playful aspect of this challenge is further evidenced here in the nursery-like names of our characters: Goody Poody, Manny Panny, Henny Penny, Cocky Locky, Ducky Lucky, Goosey Poosey, Gander Pander, all are children's nursery appellations, appealing in their sounds, the musical rhythms of rhyme, alliteration and assonance. Such rhythms aid recall and serve as the mnemonic, poetic stepping stones between and among characters. Here, the individual noises of the individual names playfully, musically, combine in a fugue of pursuit, a versified litany of flight. One can easily imagine the tale's audience, children or adults, chanting this litany in unison with the narrator's, with the pancake's, voice. Another aspect of this playful challenge is seen in the rather paradoxical effect of the accumulations: while each added character increases the difficulty of one's remembering the full catalogue of figures (let alone remembering them in correct sequence), each addition also functions as an added 'beat' or 'measure' by which the narrative extends itself. The more one adds, the more rhythm is generated, which then may aid the storyteller's memory.

The tale is not over when the pancake or gingerbread man mouths the last formula. That string of pursuers ends when the pancake omits the last character encountered, Piggy Wiggy (or the gingerbread man omits the fox), who, deceiving the pancake, is able to eat it, closing the tale with 'Ouf, Ouf' grunts of oral satisfaction. Like the cancelling zero in multiplication, the pig's eating of his doughy prey dissolves all actors. Addition and multiplication function here as the mathematical analogues of the verbal narrative: they help create, sustain, and extend the pursuers, while the pig's maw, the opened 'O' of his 'Ouf, Ouf' devouring mouth, uncreates and cancels the pancake and, therefore, all pursuers. What remains is the grunting pig, who orally and aurally closes, punctuates, the action, rather like a burped full stop.

Given the tale's playful challenge (akin to a riddle's), its formulaic structure, the 'poetry' of the characters' names, one might view this narrative as a sort of disguised incantation, one that inevitably conjures linguistic and folkloric elements. As with any number of fairy tales, 'The Pancake' rises from an animistic base: the world, including non-human and even inanimate matter, is 'animated', invested with intelligence, emotion, reason, speech. In keeping with such animism is the anthropomorphism of talking animals that one sees so frequently in beast and fairy tales. Further, there is the belief in the magic and power of language. As the early Hebrews depicted Yahweh creating the universe by voicing each cosmic element, so the tales employ language on the basis of a fundamental law of magic: the word does not only refer to the thing it represents, but actually is the thing or has the potential to become it. The world, after all, is but one letter removed from the word – a fact the goodwife should have remembered at the tale's inception.

Indeed, one sees that the pancake is a creation of both batter and language. Our tale opens with the good housewife frying pancakes for her children, only this time she puts new milk into the batter. It continues with her pacifying her children, each of whom begs to be fed, by saying: 'Wait a bit till it turns itself . . . only look how thick and happy it lies there.' The story's double mention of 'new milk' suggests the importance of this ingredient, a breaking of the wife's usual recipe of old milk. New milk is fresh, nearer its original life source, and thus transmits life by means of contagious magic. Something more, however, is needed for the pancake to assume, or act upon, that life. That something comes with the wife's leavening pronouncement, wait until it 'turns itself'. Her simple slip of the tongue – a mere grammatical error transposing the object of the action into the subject – creates the live pancake. Thus, via the alchemy of her recipe and spoken words, the wife in the kitchen assumes the role of a creating, if ignorant, god: not Adam emerging from the dust, but the pancake rising from the griddle is the result.

In addition, the wife ascribes human emotion to her creation: it looks 'happy'. It is a single step from this ascription to the pancake's hearing the wife, knowing what lies in store for it, becoming frightened, struggling to escape from the pan and as a consequence turning itself, frying more and, finally, jumping out and rolling away. One is struck by the detailed and rather logical sequence of actions the narrative delineates. Step by step the batter frying in the pan acquires life, becomes self-animating (that agonising birth struggle in the pan-womb) and completes itself, to roll out of the door. Not only does the wife's grammatical slip of the tongue convey life, it is the pancake's hearing of the family's intentions that propels it into action. Thus, linked words and actions set the tale moving, to be continued throughout the pancake's flight.

As the pancake rolls, it encounters the string of would-be eaters like a microcosm of the farmyard: wife and children and husband, man, hen, cock, duck, goose, gander, pig. Now the pancake, the one anomalous bit of matter within so much, is the star in the spotlight. In keeping with the tale's opening, it flees as the object of the pursuers' desire – that bit of matter and grammar running amuck – while simultaneously functioning as the subject of the action. Indeed, the pancake is the character who speaks most in every verbal exchange along the way and who voices the mnemonic formula that animates this cumulative tale. Each character who encounters the pancake initiates a conversation with it, beginning by saying 'Good day' and continuing with the oh-so-polite request: 'My dear pancake, don't roll so fast, but wait a bit and let me eat you.' That 'bit', of course, is an intended bite. The manner in which the pancake, 'dear pancake', is addressed is suspicious at best. Though newborn, our pancake is not quite as naïve as Adam and Eve. It responds to such would-be persuaders with its ever-growing formulaic catalogue, ending on the declaration, 'I must run away from you too.' In stating the situation and adding on the next player it encounters – man or hen, cock or duck, goose or gander – the pancake retains the power of the spoken word as a creator of reality. So long as it follows this formula, it is safe: 'I must run away from you' becomes the reality. (Truly the pancake is the child of the vocalising goodwife.)

Wisely, the pig never says he wants to eat the pancake. Instead, he suggests they walk together in the wood. In a typical scenario, the pig offers to ferry the pancake across a brook by having it sit on his snout, and then be swallowed 'in one gulp'. The pig *does* ferry the pancake across the water, though the vehicle is that of his own round belly. In a nice twist, the cancelling 'zero' of the pig's mouth takes back the live 'O' of the rolling pancake; the story comes full circle by way of the mouth, and all narrative 'rounds' cease.

This use of language as a creator of reality, this portrayal of the word as ineluctably linked to the world, is, of course, as old as spoken story itself. Innumerable fairy tales employ this motif for part, if not all, of their action, from 'The Frog Prince','The Goose Girl' and 'The Gallant Tailor', to 'The Singing Bone' and 'Rumpelstiltskin' or 'Tom Tit Tot' – these last two being especially noteworthy for their depictions of the connection between words and deeds, words and identity. Incantations, prophecies, oaths, unwitting verbal promises and self-punishments, even characters' attributive names, are common manifestations in fairy tales of 'word magic'. Certainly the belief in the inherent power of words comprises a significant portion of many tales' underlying folklore.

It is also a belief that finds an apt voice in the storyteller herself whose own voice has, after all, called the narrative's world into being. As that vocal creator, she is also one who may well be proficient in the varied voices which can help animate a tale. Orally transmitted tales often rely on the speaker's changes in voice to indicate such narrative elements as foreshadowing, threat, different characters, changes in action, and atmosphere or emotional undercurrents. Such vocal alterations also serve to sustain audience interest while providing another sort of 'story rhythm'. While some cultures may produce speakers who tell their tales in a flat monotone, as with certain Native American tribes, the majority of storytellers appear to place a high value on voice and, by extension, on voices.

One need merely try reading aloud a representative tale like Grimm's 'The Goose Girl' to appreciate how one's own vocalisations help to resuscitate the page-bound text. In print, of course, those changes of voice and emphasis are indicated by such devices as quotation marks, punctuation, italics, and rhyme.

Which brings us back to 'The Pancake', a simple tale that yet manages to boast, in addition to a combined chorus of human pursuers, seventeen distinct voices: the narrator, the seven children, the good wife or Goody Poody (not atypically, the goodman husband is silent), the Pancake, Manny Panny, Henny Penny, Cocky Locky, Ducky Lucky, Goosey Poosey, Gander Pander, and Piggy Wiggy. Not all of our tale's challenge lies in its test of memory. As one character after another is added to the action, one voice after another is likewise added. The action is that of accumulation and repetition, which assumes the form of dialogue as the pancake encounters first one and then another character on its journey. The dialogue itself is formulaic and essentially the same until the final encounter with the pig. The extra task the tale-teller has set herself is that of mouthing the same words – 'Good day, pancake'; 'My dear pancake, don't roll so fast, but wait a bit and let me eat you' – with the different voices of a man, hen, cock, duck, goose, gander. As we have seen, the pig does not participate in this formulaic exchange, though he nonetheless speaks as the seventh, success-ful consumer. Orally then, the pig's change in voice and pattern of dialogue indicate and anticipate a change in action.

The seven characters the pancake encounters on the road are themselves anticipated in the seven children of the opening. This opening is itself both a cumulative and a chain tale in miniature, as each hungry child begs his or her mother for 'a bit of pancake' and the noun of 'mother' is modified each time by one more adjective as the tale progresses from the second to the seventh child, whose 'formula' is 'dear, good, kind, nice, sweet, darling mother'. Here, the distinction between one child and another – themselves little more than numbered flatterers, as befits the chain tale – comes with the added adjective, the word to which the tale-teller might most want to give emphasis. Though this prologue is not particularly necessary to the main narrative, it does serve purposes one often sees with prologues in the fairy tale, for it functions as both an orientation to, and a representation of, what is to come. Then again, the children's repeated pleas and mounting flattery may be said to be the initial cause of all that ensues: they not only begin the tale's cumulative action, but they also are the repeated voice(s) that prompt the mother into her vocalisation which, in turn, is the aural ingredient, oral leavening, which causes the pancake to rise from the pan.

Perhaps more so than many other types of folktales, cumulative tales demand to be spoken, to be heard. The tale's test of memory is lost upon the silent reader of its text, since everything is on the page in front of one. Likewise, the plays upon the voices of characters (how might a duck sound? a goose?) is lost when muffled by print. Not unlike the pancake (and how would *it* sound?), these are stories that require vocalisation to come to life, require both a speaker and an audience. This dependence upon vocalisation goes even further in making the cumulative tale especially popular with children as well as tale-tellers, and hearkens back to the time when story was solely oral. 'The Pancake' is notable for the manner in which it weaves concerns of voice and language about its cumulative nature and its oral motifs.

Clearly, language itself functions as a sort of player in this tale. That words and voice represent so vital an aspect of the tale is all the more appropriate in the light of those oral motifs. Cumulative tales often portray a desired creature whose fate is to be eaten. The seven children initiate that fate through their vocal request for the pancake, which request, they say, is prompted by hunger. While the wife's spoken, prophetic words help generate the pancake, further action is generated with each encountered creature's spoken intent to eat the fugitive food – a 'bit of pancake' now becomes 'wait a bit'. Ultimately the tale intentionally consumes itself by having its principal player consumed. In every sense, the mouth propels the tale as well as ends it: hence the tale's rather odd status as a self-generating story that exists in order to self-destruct.

Cumulative tales frequently make use of food and eating in their narratives. While 'The Pancake' and 'The Gingerbread Man' portray their protagonists as being chased by would-be eaters and ultimately swallowed, the popular Scandinavian tale 'The Fat Cat' reverses roles: now it is the cat who eats everything with which he comes in contact, from gruel and pot, five birds, seven dancing girls, a lady and her pink parasol, on to a parson and his crooked staff. As drawn by illustrator Jack Kent (1971) in the picture story-book version, the cat grows, plumps and swells, until it assumes the proportions of a furry, feline giganticism (indeed, here one sees an example of the verbal rather successfully rendered visual). In proper cumulative style the cat repeats the formula of its devouring progress with each new encounter, and predicts the imminent future to its next morsel by proclaiming, 'Now I am also going to eat YOU.' The cat's literal and linguistic gluttony ceases when the woodcutter simply states 'No', thereby negating, breaking the formula with a single syllable's noise, that 'No' being similar to the nullifying 'Ouf' of the pig's opened mouth. The engorged victims are then released by the woodcutter as he performs a caesarian section (yet another motif shared with other folktales) on the 'little cat'.

Analogues of this tale appear in India, Russia and East Africa, two popular versions being 'The Fat Troll' and the corresponding 'The Fat Wolf' (Thompson 1977: 231). The Troll or Wolf eats a watcher's five horses, followed by the watcher himself, the master, his wife, servant, daughter, son and dog, always adhering to the repeated, cumulative list and verbal threats seen in 'The Fat Cat'. This time, however, it is a cat who steps in to stop the other's devouring path when she scratches him open and releases the victims.

While the cat's, the wolf's, the troll's bellies motivate their bulimic progress, the manner in which they ingest the world via their mouths and spoken words is of interest. The cat, in fact, seems suspiciously suggestive of a young toddler moving through its environment by putting everything in its path into its mouth. The literal 'mouthing' of objects is not mere idle, oral curiosity, but a means of physically knowing those objects, of understanding the world by tasting it, 'gumming' it, if not directly ingesting it (though very real dangers do reside therein). Understanding requires that we make the unfamiliar somehow familiar, the unknown known; that we make it a part of ourselves. The object the eye apprehends as unknown is made known by means of the mouth – at first literally, in an impossible 'Fat Cat' mimicry of assimilation; then symbolically, through words, the meaningful noises of things. Thus language, in replacing the thing proper, allows us to ingest, to know, the world. It assumes the form of what one might term 'symbolic cookies', perhaps less tasty, but surely more practical morsels.

What is perceived as most desirable is, of course, all the more delectable: hence such popular appellations as 'honey', 'sweetheart', 'babycakes', 'sugar', 'sugarplum', all accorded to both child and adult. In this respect 'I love you' translates to 'I could eat you', and we all assume the potential roles of both lover and beloved, devouring Fat Cat and fleeing gingerbread man or woman. That 'dear' pancake's flight is thus not only a flight from the physical hunger of its pursuers, but also a flight from their physical desire, the love that would consume the object of desire. Somewhat uncomfortably, one is reminded of the children at the opening of the tale, coaxing their mother with flattery: 'dear, good, nice, sweet', like so much icing on the cake. Fortunately their words replace what could be human food in what is a safe act of metaphoric cannibalism, just as our spoken love and fond nicknames help satisfy our appetites, our gingerbread desires to possess and consume.

Perhaps not coincidentally, whether speaking of food or its emotional counterpart, one often sees it accompanied by violence. With the cumulative tale, food may lie at the action's centre or along its path and, not infrequently, it is linked with violence. In 'The House that Jack Built', the narrative centrepiece is that of the rat that ate the malt that lay in the house that Jack built. Move to the final formula, and one has (Opie 1997: 271–2):

> This is the farmer sowing his corn,
> That kept the cock that crowed in the morn,
> That waked the priest all shaven and shorn,
> That married the man all tattered and torn,
> That kissed the maiden all forlorn,
> That milked the cow with the crumpled horn,
> That tossed the dog,
> That worried the cat,
> That caught the rat,
> That ate the malt
> That lay in the house that Jack built.

Both 'How the Mouse Regained its Tail' and 'The Old Woman and her Pig' depict a series of exchanges, many violent, many involving food, as with the latter's formula: 'Cow give milk for cat; cat kill rat; rat gnaw rope; rope hang butcher; butcher kill ox; ox drink water; water quench fire; fire burn stick; stick beat dog; dog bite pig; pig jump over stile' (Thompson 1977: 232).

In the Irish 'Munachar and Manachar', it is Manachar's eating of raspberries – 'as many as Munachar used to pick Manachar used to eat' (Cole 1982: 232) – that begins Munachar's cumulative quest to find a 'gad' to hang Manachar, and that leads him from rod to axe to flag to water to deer to hound to butter to cat to cow to threshers to miller . . . While Munachar's progress from one to another does not entail any violent action, the story ends with him returning, gad in hand and ready to hang Manachar, only to find that Manachar had burst – a just fate bestowed upon this raspberry-glutton, if not on the fat cat and troll of the previous tales. The English 'Henny Penny' of the-sky-is-falling renown employs the memory test, an accumulation of animal characters with tongue-twisting nursery names, and violent beheadings for all but Henny-Penny (Jacobs 1967: 113–16).

Violence and death are certainly part of the folktale tradition and all the more likely when a tale of any type treats animals and food, for then the basic dynamic of predator and prey asserts itself. Also, while violence and death are popular motifs in fairy tales, they may find even greater acceptance when presented within the context of non-human characters such as the doomed pancake. An entire group of cumulative tales treats the death of an animal; no doubt 'The Fat Cat' and similar tales might just as easily have once ended with the devourer's demise and the subsequent release or escape of his engorged victims, as seen in some versions of 'Little Red Cap'. In *The Folktale*, Stith Thompson refers to 'The Death of the Cock' as being especially popular, and to the widely distributed 'The Death of the Little Hen', dating back to the *Pañcatantra*. In the former, the cock chokes to death while the hen seeks aid from such helpers as a stream, tree, pig, miller, baker; in the latter, the hen chokes while the cock rushes from spring to bride to willow – not a long sequence but, thanks to narrative repetition, long enough for the hen to expire. Grimm's version of this tale also sees a quasi-cumulative or chain ending in which the hen's funeral processes as fox, wolf, bear, stag, lion, 'and all the beasts of the forest' get into the carriage (Grimm 1972: 366). It ends in total devastation with the deaths of a straw, six mice, a coal and all the animals inside the carriage. Only the cock escapes to bury the hen, after which 'he died too, and everyone was dead'.

Other cumulative tales cited by Thompson follow a similar end-of-the-world pattern approximating to a micro-Ragnarok. Their apocalyptic endings, in which every or nearly every character is destroyed, multiply the single death of the pancake or gingerbread man while also serving purposes similar to that lone death: namely to climactically, absolutely, irreversibly end the story. In the case of 'The Pancake', this is accomplished by removing the desired object from the action. In the case of tales like 'The Death of the Little Hen', in which accumulated characters cannot as easily be dispersed, the chain itself is destroyed; indeed, excepting the cock, all members of the funeral procession are 'swallowed' by the water when they fall into the stream and drown. After the narrator's painstaking task of generating, constructing and sustaining the cumulative pattern of characters and actions, the casual manner in which the creation is 'deconstructed', terminated, is quick and striking: 'and everyone was dead' – truly, the end.

Such endings do work as an effective counterpoint to the chains that have preceded them. All that narrative rhythm, all that tension mounting as one tries to remember the sequence and wonders how long the game will go on, is simply, suddenly, stopped. The tale-teller's mouth closes in silence, that final full stop of death. Many folktales conclude with death for the wicked and life for the good. Often the wicked are disposed of in a similar, matter-of-fact fashion, while it is understood that, with them thus removed, the good will prosper and 'live happily until their lives' end'. However, with these particular cumulative tales, virtually all characters, who are essentially 'innocents', non-entities, the shadow plays of story, may be summarily dispatched. Again, one sees that the cumulative tale's repetitive pattern takes precedence over all else.

Though 'The Pancake' and 'The Gingerbread Man' do not overtly subscribe to this apocalyptic vision, one might catch a glimpse of it behind the action's flight and pursuit. The desire for food motivates all characters except the pancake, whose desire is to escape being that food. What begins innocuously and routinely enough in the kitchen with the mother's preparation of a meal for her family, turns nightmarish when the food's sensibilities are awakened (how quickly 'happy' is replaced by 'frightened' in the narrative). Rather like a chicken running to escape its fate of becoming Sunday dinner, the pancake flees to the outside. Not only is it pursued by the goodwife's world it sought to leave behind, but it discovers that everyone it encounters is a creature of appetite who entertains the same designs on it. Clearly the pancake is at the bottom of the food chain, as befits its origins of milk and grain.

The string of pursuing would-be devourers is even more interesting when viewed as a microcosm of the farmyard: hen, cock, duck, goose, gander, pig – all domesticated creatures – are part of the food chain controlled by the human. In tale versions that see the pig replaced by a fox, the tensions between tame and wild are also enacted, following nature's timeless script of predator and prey. To be sure, the food chain of eaters that chase the pancake offers an amusing image, suggestive of the stuck-together characters in the fairy tale 'The Golden Goose'. One might visualise them engaged in some sort of fantastic dance, some rumba across the countryside's hills and dales, with the lead dancer being the pancake or, even better, the gingerbread man. Replace that lead figure with the skeleton of Death, however, and all changes: now a horrific silhouette of gyrating forms chisels itself against the darkening skyline like a medieval woodcut, the figures seem less voluntary participants than ones being pulled along, and we recognise the *danse macabre*. Inevitably, every one of those hungry links in the chain will trip into the grave's maw to be devoured by other hungry things. And how could it be otherwise, given the interdependence of those links, and of the tale's cumulative parts?

So we have fate as death, we have pursuers and flight, we have food. It does not take much to draw some parallels between the fleeing pancake or 'dough boy' and certain grain and harvest rituals cited in *The Golden Bough* (Frazer 1922: 493–500, 508–18). Like so many fairy tales culled from the past, this particular folktale yields intriguing associations with related folklore and symbolism. Of interest is the custom, formerly practised in much of eastern and western Europe, of bundling the last sheaves of wheat or corn sometimes into a human effigy known variously as the Old Man, Old Woman, Maiden, Boy or Child. Frazer notes how the corn spirit, fleeing before the reapers as they cut the grain, runs away to seek refuge beyond the fields, and is pursued by the reapers or harvest revellers. Its fate ranges from that of being saved through the winter to being torn apart on the threshing floor, a throwback to similar rituals of

Dionysus and Osiris. More pertinent are the dough humans made from the last of the harvest grains, effigies which were then eaten by the household or villagers. Ingestion of the baked effigy represents ingestion of the grain spirit, most often linked by contagious magic to acquiring that spirit's life source, health and fertility. Frazer further notes how such material creations might once have had human blood (in the more distant past, human flesh and bone) mixed into their recipe as part of their efficacy. Gingerbread humans in the form of small cakes or bread loaves might be one manifestation of this, while numerous pancake rituals were once popular, with the tossing and rolling of a pancake being a common game. Perhaps, just perhaps, the gingerbread man survives as a vestige of earlier folk practice, both in his human form and flight . . . though one hesitates to suggest that he represents an indisputable rendition of the sacrificed, eaten god or human. Though as an aside, one might speculate that the 'new milk' which first confers the potential for life may at some earlier time have been human blood or the milk of a nursing woman, as both fluids were considered to possess and confer magical, life-giving properties. Perhaps the cook's own milk or blood accidentally dripped into the batter?

A bit of batter mixed with milk, with blood, proffers *golem* possibilities. The *golem* in Hebrew lore indicates an incomplete or not fully formed thing, like an embryo. Its inert mass assumes form and life – most typically, as an automaton servant to a great rabbi – when animated by a charm, a charm of language, whether that of a spoken spell or one of the names of God inscribed on a paper and inserted into its mouth or head. Several tales of the *golem* depict it running amuck in the vein of 'The Sorcerer's Apprentice' until the master can stop it by voicing the right words, whereupon it collapses back into its original formlessness. Given its incomplete nature, the *golem* contains full potentiality. It can assume horrific or comedic possibilities, running the associative spectrum from Frankenstein's creature to such cinematic silliness as *The Blob* and *Attack of the Killer Tomatoes*. The latter film reflects well the fantastic and comic strains inherent in the animation of mundane foodstuffs, particularly if that food is non-animal. Horror, disease and guilt too readily accompany the animal, as in Homer's magnificent portents of Helios' slaughtered kine lowing on the spits. Even vegetable matter might get out of hand, as the film *Day of the Triffids* shows. But batter seems safe enough. The gingerbread man may be a human effigy, but remains a cookie. It would require a supreme leap of imagination to shudder at the prospect of *Attack of the Gingerbread Men* (unless one is a baker) or, less plausibly, *Attack of the Pancakes*.

Still, that runaway cookie or pancake as a piece of out-of-control dough fleeing from its normal role as food, rolling across the countryside, in effect thumbing its nose at the human's empirical and hungry world, can be a disquieting figure, as already suggested. In throwing our known, familiar world topsy-turvy, it suggests the trickster archetype. Like that famous trickster Brer Rabbit, it moves through a world whose basic law is that of eat or be eaten, a world where fleetness (of foot, of brain) alone ensures survival. Like Brer Rabbit, like all tricksters, it can as easily lose as win. Thus, during the 1960s, *San Francisco Chronicle* cartoonist Dan O'Neill, in his Odd Bodkins creation, drew the gingerbread man as a running African-American pursued by unknown adversaries whose voices boomed across the strip's panels, threatening to catch and eat the gingerbread man. Like Ralph Ellison's 'invisible man', the flat, one-dimensional figure kept on running, occasionally threatening his pursuers with a bad case of heartburn should they catch and eat him. As with the more popular fairy tale, even the cumulative tale can serve as a vehicle for contemporary recastings, even a gingerbread man can provide a criticism of a society that consumes its minority citizens. And, discerning his somewhat tongue-in-cheek use, one approves this play upon the familiar form just as one applauds the classic fairy tale's recastings by writers like A. S. Byatt and the late Angela Carter.

As we have seen, even the modest cumulative tale shares many characteristics with its fairy-tale kin: characteristics such as simplicity of style, plot, character and setting; a penchant for abbreviated, climactic endings; the motifs of magic, animism, folklore, food, violence, animals; an attention to voice and language as a creator of reality; a predilection for wonder, for marvel, for entertainment woven from the twin threads of the serious and the playful. Above all, the cumulative tale revels in the pure pleasure of playing with memory, with language, and with narrative's basic building blocks.

One of the finest examples of such pleasure and play is that of the Ashanti 'Talk' (Yolen 1986: 246–8). It begins with a farmer going into his garden to dig some yams. As he digs, the yam speaks, criticising him for never having weeded it, then ordering him to leave it alone. The farmer then turns to his cow and asks if she said anything. She does not respond, but his dog does, telling him that the yam spoke and wants to be left alone. From this opening the narrative advances through the standard accumulating sequence of encounters that is then summarised to the tribal chief near the tale's close: the farmer tells of the talking yam, dog, tree, branch and stone; the fisherman he has encountered tells of his talking fish trap, the weaver of his talking bundle of cloth, the bather of the talking river. Unable to believe them, the chief dismisses the farmer, fisher, weaver and bather. The story ends with the chief shaking his head and mumbling to himself: 'Nonsense like that upsets the community', followed by one last voice: 'Fantastic, isn't it?' his stool said. 'Imagine, a talking yam!'

'Talk' runs a mere two printed pages in length yet contains fourteen voices, nine of which are non-human: the yam, dog, palm tree and branch, stone, fish trap, bundle of cloth, river and stool. The farmer, fisherman, weaver and bather retell their respective segments of the story by repeating the voices of these non-human speakers. The teller of this particular tale, therefore, faces some fascinating tests. True to the tale's cumulative nature, the test of memory remains; the multitude of voices simultaneously strains memory and poses the challenge of conveying or taking on each speaker's individual, unique sounds. Particularly challenging are the sounds of the non-human, ordinarily inanimate representatives of the world: one cannot help but wonder what a yam might sound like (perhaps somewhat mealy-mouthed and low to the ground?), what a bundle of cloth might sound like (surely calico would sound differently from plain, crude cotton?), what the river, the stone, the stool would sound like? As with similar tales, we see characters and their voices accumulate, only to end in an abrupt fashion; likewise, we have the motifs of food and the threat of physical violence when the man cuts the branch with the intent of whipping his dog because it had not spoken before and because he did not like its 'tone'.

What makes 'Talk' an outstanding cumulative tale is its vocal variety, its use of voices within voices, and the fact that the story truly *is* its title: talk – as plot, as character, as challenge to the teller, as entertainment for the audience – is the tale's *raison d'être*. The speaking non-human world spurs the humans, investing the action with drama, drama derived from the non-humans' uninvited participation in a conversation. The joke (if joke it is) is that those participants, whether animal, vegetable or mineral, have ears which overhear us and tongues with which to respond, if they so choose. As with the pancake, the everyday matter of a yam and a palm tree, a trap and a bundle of cloth, a stone and a stool, turns man's world topsy-turvy, and it does so by way of speech: 'Everything began to talk!' the farmer exclaims. While the non-humans that speak to the farmer seem antagonistic or critical, the fish trap, cloth and river appear to be more interested in the chain of events – more interested than are the fisherman, weaver and bather. Their non-human responses are voiced as questions or commentary upon the situation. The same is true of the stool which agrees with the chief: 'Fantastic, isn't it? Imagine, a talking yam!' Aptly, the story ends where it began, with the yam, though it also leaves us anticipating the next set of reactions spurred by our speaking stool.

Even as vocalisation and reaction to it make up 'Talk's' talk, silence also has a role. Indeed the opening scene is almost as interesting for what is not said, as it is for the verbal yam. Why does the farmer turn to the cow and ask if she said something? While we can deduce why she does not respond (her mouth is full; she is an uncommonly polite bovine), we cannot help wondering whether she would speak if she were not engaged in chewing her cud. And then, what would she say? The narrator's own silence concerning why the farmer addresses his cow taunts us with possibilities, not the least of which is that the farmer, even if amazed, appears to expect the cow to have spoken, whereas a talking yam is out of the question.

This play upon speech and silence represents a type of dialectic, a dialectic that extends into that of the expected and the unexpected. Mostly, the non-human world is expected to be quiet; when it violates that human expectation, the men become agitated, run away, feel the need to tell others of their experience, which telling then elicits the next set of human and non-human vocalisations. Interestingly, the human listener more often than not treats what he is being told as unremarkable – 'Is that all?' 'That's nothing to get excited about' – or as incredible, as 'nonsense'. By contrast, it is the non-human fish trap that responds with interest – 'Did he take it off the stone?' – while the cloth and the river respond with apparent understanding – 'If it happened to you, you'd run too!' Again, as with other cumulative tales, the spoken word functions as a prediction of action when those very words cause the men to run away. They also ensure that each non-human speaker, by virtue of having participated in the conversation, will become part of the story in a double sense: first as the original speaker, and later as a character and a voice within each man's respective tale. At the end, the chief mumbles 'nonsense' and the stool agrees. At least these two speakers are in accord; thus the tale concludes, even as we suspect that the stool, rather like a prodded atom, is about to set off the next chain of reactions.

Of course, both the cumulative tale and the fairy tale explore tensions generated between the expected and the unexpected, the human and the non-human, speech and silence; the former is more playful in its explorations, the latter more serious. Yet no matter how playful, there is a serious stratum beneath; no matter how serious, there is the element of play, for both are ingredients of art, of craft, of storytelling. Whether cumulative or fairy tale, the folktale plays out its dialectic of expectations, of voice and silence, that is as familiar to us as words and the spaces between, as what is spoken and what is not, as life's first yowling intake of breath and death's sighing into quietude. God decreed, 'Let there be . . .'; the tale-teller proclaims, 'Once upon a time' and the Twelfth Wise Woman speaks a hundred years' sleep for Briar Rose; the foolish little man sings his name is Tom Tit Tot, a mute maiden knits her brothers nettle shirts, seven hungry children clamour after one fleet pancake, a yam complains, a cow chews. The voice that is the tale stops when memory falters, when language fails. Its dialectic concludes, to be continued with the next inspiring encounter of world and word: muse-struck, the stool exclaims: 'Imagine, a talking yam!' Imagine, indeed.

References

Baring-Gould, W. S. and C. (1967), *The Annotated Mother Goose*. New York.

Cole, J. (1982), *Best-Loved Folktales of the World*. Garden City, NY.

Frazer, J. G. (1922), *The Golden Bough*, abridged edn. New York.

Grimm, J. and W. (1972), *The Complete Grimm's Tales*, trans. M. Hunt and J. Stern. New York.

Jacobs, J. (1967), *English Fairy Tales*. New York.

Kent, J. (1971), *The Fat Cat*. New York.

Leach, M., and Fried, J. (1984) ed., *Funk and Wagnall's Standard Dictionary of Folklore, Mythology, and Legend*. New York.

O'Neill, D. (1969), *Hear the Sound of My Feet Walking, Drown the Sound of My Voice Talking*. San Francisco.

Opie, I. and P. (1997), *The Oxford Dictionary of Nursery Rhymes*. Oxford.

Thompson, S. (1968), *One Hundred Favorite Folktales*. Bloomington.

——(1977), *The Folktale*. Berkeley.

Yolen, J. (1986) ed., *Favorite Folktales from Around the World*. New York.

8

Unknown Cinderella: The Contribution of Marian Roalfe Cox to the Study of the Fairy Tale

PAT SCHAEFER

I never could repeat a story without giving it a new hat and stick.

(Sir Walter Scott)

There once was a very rich man who had a beautiful daughter called Snow-White Maiden. After the death of his wife, he married Frizzle, or Bald-Pate, who had two daughters of her own, Fair Maid and Swarthy Maid.

It had been announced that the king's son was to attend church. Every person, young or old, wished to see him, including Fair Maid, Swarthy Maid and Frizzle, or Bald Pate, their mother. The Snow-White Maiden wished to go as well but as she was held in such low esteem amongst her half-sisters and their mother, they endeavoured to keep her in the background. She was made to do every difficult and menial task until her fingers ached. When she asked to go and see the Prince, her sister, Swarthy Maid, said that she could not come as it would only bring disgrace upon the family to have such an undesirable creature accompany them.

When they left to go, 'Cantrips', or Trouble-the-House, a little woman of the fairy race, came in where Snow-White Maiden was and said to her, 'You have not gone with them?'

'No', she replied, 'they would not allow me to accompany them. How could I go when I am so unkempt, unclad, untrimmed and unshod?'

'You will go', said Cantrips, 'and you will see the king's son as well as they do.' She laid a wand of enchantment over Snow-White Maiden, and made her a woman so beautiful and graceful as no eye ever saw or ear ever heard report of one so perfect. Her wealth of hair reached from the crown of her head to her heels. Her dress dazzled like sunlight. A golden shoe shone on one foot and a silver one on the other. Three starlings twittered on each shoulder.

'Should you become thirsty, put your hand to your mouth and wine and honey will flow from your fingers. When you enter the church, you must take a seat near the door, and do not wait for the close. I will give you a steed and a bridle; when you put the bridle on, the steed will bring you here before others can move.' With that Cantrips struck the wand of enchantment on a rock near the threshold, and it became a noble black steed that could ride the waters of the deep blue sea as if it were smooth fertile land . . .

The tale continues as the king's son is completely overwhelmed by the heroine's beauty; however, she does as Cantrips has directed and returns home before the others. The episode is repeated, although this time as she leaves the church the king's son is able to snatch the golden shoe from Snow-White Maiden's right foot. The search for the owner of the shoe leads the king's son to the heroine's house. She is hidden under a washtub, but at last makes her presence known and appears before the king's son in all her finery. They are to be married, and Fair Maid accompanies them as Maid of Honour.

As happens in a number of stories, there is an extension to the tale. Fair Maid and Snow-White Maiden are walking beside the loch when Fair Maid pushes the heroine into the water. Snow-White Maiden is captured by 'Great Beast Senselessness' who keeps her captive. Three times she is allowed to go on to the shore to warm herself; the third time the king's son and the townsfolk are lying in wait, and they kill the beast and rescue Snow-White Maiden.

This early Gaelic tale is to be found in *The Celtic Magazine* (Sinclair 1888: 454–93) and might never have been brought to notice had it not been for Marian Roalfe Cox and her book, *Cinderella*, published in 1893. It was the first comprehensive, comparative study of a folktale. The tale given above is no. 27.

Born in 1860, Marian Emily Roalfe Cox was a Londoner. She became a reclusive, unassuming person who was home-educated; an industrious individual, yet always hampered by delicate health. At a time when the education of women was ill provided for, the knowledge she attained was truly remarkable. She spoke modern Greek and read the classics in the original. She was familiar with several European languages. Literature, music and science were also of great interest to her, yet she spent most of her life looking after her parents, or they after her. Charlotte Burne remembered in her *Folk-Lore* Obituary for Miss Cox (1916: 434–5): 'the pale, fragile-looking girl, who, closely chaperoned by her dignified early Victorian mother, was a regular attendant at the [Folk-Lore Society] meetings'.

Miss Cox joined the Society in 1888, and immediately let it be known that she wanted to be involved in work on its behalf. At first she began writing tabulations of folktales accompanied by extensive bibliographical information. The thoroughness with which she did these must have set a formidable example for others to follow. Her first tabulations appeared in the *Folk-Lore Journal* (1889: 1–57): eighteen tales which covered fifty-seven pages, far more than her colleagues were to produce. In the 1890 volume of *Folk-Lore* (1890: 123–8), Cox more than laid the groundwork for what was to come. Her tabulation of 'Cinderella' or 'Aschenputtel' from Grimms' *Household Tales*, translated by Margaret Hunt (1894: 93–100), was exceptional. Under the heading 'Remarks by the Tabulator', she listed numerous variants, perhaps the initial collection of material for inclusion in the book which was to come.

After a short time the Society Council asked if she would undertake a project of classifying and analysing variants of the story of 'Cinderella'. It was then that she began the first major investigation of a single folktale. She recorded the 345 variants in 535 pages, and completed the work in under four years.

Cox had the full backing of the Council, and was aided in her quest by several international scholars whom she thanked warmly at the end of the Preface. Since this was a first attempt, there was no criterion to follow. She decided on a division of her material into five parts: (a) Cinderella; (b) Catskin; (c) Cap o'Rushes; (d) Indeterminate (Tales containing incidents [motifs] common to the aforementioned groups); and (e) Hero Tales, in which the protagonist is male. The tales were numbered and abstracted, with further development in the tabulations or summaries. Geographical and chronological details were given along with a bibliography. Both Preface and Notes were considerable, giving a vast amount of information.

One of the most remarkable yet expedient additions that Cox included at the end of her Notes was a second bibliography consisting of eighty-nine titles, books that she had consulted and found to be of no use for her work: 'It may save other Students trouble to give the following list of books which have been found to contain no Cinderella variants' she stated (Cox 1893: 529), a rare gesture of assistance to future persons doing research on the subject.

The Introduction by Andrew Lang was to create quite a stir. Cox lavished gratitude on him for enriching her work: 'so strong a prop to support so weak a burden'. She said she would never be sorry that Cinderella had so noble a godfather: 'I leave it to [his] honourable survey.' (Cox 1893: lxix). It must have been discouraging to her, however, when Lang began (Cox 1893: vii):

> In fulfilment of the Rash Vow of Folk-lore, I offer a few words on Miss Cox's collection of *Cinderella* stories. On the first view of her learned and elaborate work I was horrified at the sight of these skeletons of the tale.

He famously claimed that 'a naked and shoeless race could not have invented Cinderella' (Cox 1893: x). After only four pages of a seventeen-page introduction, he states: 'Being unable to throw any more light on *Cinderella*, I may take advantage of the opportunity to show what I think about Popular Tales, their origin and diffusion, as, from certain criticisms, my position seems not to have been understood' (Cox 1893: xi). Thus having given the book and Miss Cox a complimentary nod, he used this opportunity to reply to, and expound on, the argument he was having with other folklorists, including Emmanuel Cosquin, Joseph Jacobs and William W. Newell.

Controversy over the diffusion of folktales continued with 'Cinderella' in the middle of the debate. Jacobs, Lang and Nutt put forth their beliefs in articles in volumes four and five of *Folk-Lore* (1893–4). Newell entered into the heated discussion when he wrote his review of the book from America in the *Journal of American Folk-Lore* (1893: 159–61). Cox did not enter the fray. A succinct but more detailed account of the debate is covered in Richard Dorsons's book, *The British Folklorists* (1968: 304–10).

Within her 345 variants, Cox began with the first ones known to her at the time: the 1558 story by Jean Bonaventure Des Periers (234), Basile's 'La Gatta Cenerentola', 1636 (18), and Perrault's 'Cendrillon', 1697 (91). It is the Perrault variant which it seems appropriate to compare with some of the other tales in her first category ('Cinderella'). Ask any adult or child to tell the story of 'Cinderella', and it is most likely that you will be given the version of Perrault, with two ugly sisters, fairy godmother, glass slippers, the ball, the precise time of midnight, the mice, rat, lizards and pumpkin. Even Beatrix Potter was influenced by Perrault in her retelling of 'Cinderella' (Linder 1971: 364–74), although it was much lengthier. There were rabbits to pull the carriage, Cinderella lived in the Kingdom of Nowharra, and the glass slippers were precisely size two and a half.

As Stith Thompson wrote (1946: 127):

> The version of Perrault is so familiar through two hundred and fifty years' use as a nursery tale that we are likely to think that all the details he mentions are essential. Some of them, as a matter of fact, are practically unknown elsewhere.

Neil Philip elaborates this (1980: 133):

> The *Cinderella* we know is not the open-ended *Cinderella* of Marian Cox's study, subtly modulating according to time, place and culture, but a narrowly orthodox creature based on the literary interpretation of Perrault's; often the *Cinderellas* offered in popular fairy-tale books are retellings of retellings of retellings of translations of 'Cendrillon'.

This was true in 1980, and one need only look at most of todays's newly published collections and single picture-book editions to see that the trend continues.

To compare some elements that are more common in versions other than that of Perrault, the glass slipper would be an obvious start. Cox mentions in her Notes that in only six variants can she find this type of footwear; the majority seem to be of gold. There are also slippers of silver, pearl-embroidered, silk, with diamonds, and even in a striking combination of red, white and green. Some are simply described as 'spangled with jewels', 'matchless', 'sun shoes', sandals, clogs and boots. In a Danish variant (62), the heroine wears galoshes over her gold shoes to protect them from mud. The fitting of a ring or glove, or the loss of such items as a bracelet or earrings, may be substituted for the shoe motif.

Most Cinderellas go to church as the 'meeting-place' (Cox's term), most likely because it is a place where people congregate. A stranger can see and be seen, particularly a beautiful young woman or a king's son. There are other venues, including festivals, fetes, balls, the theatre, a party, the races, the dancing-green, and in the town. To return precisely at midnight is rare. Most often the heroine is warned simply to leave before the others, and given the means of returning home rapidly.

There are few fairy godmothers, as help usually comes from animals, super-natural beings, or inanimate objects. Helpful animals are usually substituted for a dead mother or father, and may take the form of cows, calves, sheep, lambs and birds. Dogs, fish, frogs and toads, and even the more unusual white bear, ermine, wolf and eel appear. Supernatural help includes that given by little old women or little old men, the dead mother or father, or even trees: hazel, willow, oak, lime, and birch, or fruit-bearing ones, apple, pear or date. There are also trees that laugh, treasure trees, wishing trees, and the great wonder tree of Tjalindo-lindo with a trunk of iron, blossoms of gold, and fruit of diamonds. Rods, switches and magic wands appear, as do nuts, either undesignated kinds

(125), or the specific almond, filbert or walnut (72), or three walnuts (244). One of the most unusual items to aid the heroine is a sword (268), which not only provides clothes and shoes but carries out any order given to it.

It is usually footwear which is found by the pursuer and taken round to discover its owner. Sometimes 'all young women' are summoned to the palace or some other specific location. The shoes have been accidentally dropped, or left behind because of tar, pitch, mud, wax, or even honey being spread about. In other variants the slipper has been taken by a bird and the heroine has yet to be involved in the action. Rhodopis, an early Egyptian princess, mentioned by Cox (Note 48), had her sandal snatched by an eagle as she bathed in the river. The eagle deposited the tiny sandal in the lap of the king, who then had the owner found and made her his wife. Two variants (68, 69) from Vietnam are similar, with a crow replacing the eagle; in one from India (235), a prince finds the slipper himself while travelling through the jungle. One of the strangest situations is in 'The Brother Ram', an Armenian tale (8), when the king's horses come upon a gold shoe in a stream and refuse to drink. This incident also appears in the story 'Conkiajgharuna' (Wardrop 1894), the Georgian Cinderella which Cox mentioned later (1907: 208).

Beginnings are sometimes unusual. Generally the heroine is of royal birth or 'the daughter of a gentleman'; certainly most are not poverty-stricken. However in 'Finette Aschenbrödel', a German tale (56), the king and queen are reduced to poverty and must earn their living by making nets to catch fish and birds. The king loses his kingdom and becomes a forest ranger in a Slovakian version (32). 'Ashey Pelt', an Irish variant mentioned by Cox (1907: 208), begins: 'Well, my grandmother she told me that in them auld days a ewe might be your mother'. In a Portuguese variant (89), 'The Hearth Cat', a widowed schoolmistress wishes to marry the father of a pretty pupil to whom she promises porridge and honey every day if the girl will persuade her father into the marriage. The father orders boots of iron for himself and declares he will only marry when they turn to rust. The girl puts them in water every day, so that they fall to pieces and the marriage takes place. 'Aschengrübel', a Swiss variant (254), begins with both parents dying, leaving their daughter nothing but 'a wonderful scintillating dress and a testament', but a dowry hidden in a book reveals that she is heiress to a great estate.

Denmark produced several unusual Cinderellas during this period, many from the eminent folklorist and collector Evald Tang Kristensen. In 'The Little Gold Shoe' (61) the father, a farmer, is dying. He gives his eldest daughter the farm, his second daughter all his money, and the youngest a little dog and a lime tree in the garden. In order that the heroine may go to church, the dog performs all her tasks, while the lime tree provides her with a black silk dress, black gloves and shoes, and a splendid chariot. On the following Sunday she goes to church all in white, and on the third in yellow and gold. As she is escaping home, the prince seizes her gold ring and shoe. A magpie later reveals all. In another Danish variant, 'The Golden Shoe' (65), the two elder sisters are reading a newspaper at home and see the announcement that all young girls between eighteen and twenty years of age must appear at the castle on a certain day to try on the shoe. They are both too old, but they make the attempt. From the Danish scholar Grundtvig's unpublished collection, 'The White Dog' or 'Put-in-Pot' (40) is a combination of 'Cinderella' and 'Rumpelstiltskin': the heroine must discover the dog's name or forfeit her twin sons.

In the Swedish tale of Benjamin Thorpe, 'Crow-Skins Maria' (119), Maria follows her sisters to the palace where the king's son is to choose a wife. The sisters had given the girl a 'soporific' (*sic*) potion in order to leave without her. They come upon an apple, a plum and a pear, and each pleads for their help but is treated roughly. Maria, on the other hand, picks them up and takes them with her, and from them receives magical help.

An early Scottish 'Cinderella' appeared in the *Archaeological Review* (Blind 1889: 24–7), entitled 'A Fresh Scottish Ashpitel Tale' (4). The story begins in the usual way: following the death of a gentleman's wife, he marries a widow with two daughters. Given a thimbleful of broth, a grain of barley, a thread of meat and a crumb of bread, his own daughter is sent into the field to watch the sheep, and there encounters a little black lamb. The girl is hungry, so the lamb tells her to put her finger into its ear and see what she can find. A good dinner is the result. The stepmother becomes suspicious when the girl seems to thrive on so little. She discovers her secret, and the lamb is killed. The distraught girl is approached by a little old woman, who advises her to collect all the lamb's bones and bring them to her. The girl finds all but one shank bone. On Sunday the others attend church while the girl is left behind to cook the dinner. The black lamb suddenly comes limping in and tells her to dress and go to church while it prepares the meal. She puts on her dress and a pair of pretty glass slippers. In church she is seen by the young Prince, but she leaves early and he fails to find her. The same happens on the following Sunday, but this time the girl loses a slipper, and the Prince finds it and proclaims that he will marry the girl whose foot fits it. He goes to the heroine's house and one of the stepsisters declares she can wear the slipper, chops off her toes and heel and gets it on.

The prince is taking her back to the castle when a raven warns him:

> Haggit-heels and Hewed-toes
> Behind the young Prince rides.
> But Pretty-foot and Bonnie-foot
> Behind the cauldron hides.

He discovers his mistake and returns the stepsister. He finds the girl behind the cauldron, and she changes into her dress and gets the other slipper. As they pass the first tree, the raven sings:

> Pretty-foot and Bonnie-foot
> Behind the young Prince rides.
> But Haggit-heels and Hewed-toes
> At home with Mama bides.

Here there are similarities to the Grimms' 'Aschenputtel' (37) in the rhymes, the birds and the mutilated foot. Perrault is represented by the glass slippers. But the story also has a quality of its own, in the heroine watching sheep in the field, the appearance of the little black lamb and advice of the little old woman. Food supplied from the animal's ear (the familiar 'ear cornucopia'), and the killing of a helpful animal are found in many variants (AT 511A). This story is peculiar in that its history can be traced back through several generations to at least the mid-eighteenth century, and was only committed to writing in 1888. Part of the interest and indeed charm of Cox's book is that its tabulations or summaries can be read with enjoyment. The inclusion of quotations and accompanying rhymes make them more complete.

Regarding the Hero Tales, Cox stated (lxvii):

> A selection has been made with a view of embracing as many as possible of the separate incidents which are met with in stories of the 'Cinderella' type. These examples are given merely for purpose of comparison.

A young man, usually the idle third son, who stays by the hearth all day, becomes the hero, albeit sometimes a reluctant one. The dead father appears as the supernatural helper in 'Der Aschentagger', a tale from Austria (341). Hansl, though never anxious to move from the hearth, is the only one of three brothers brave enough to visit his father's grave at midnight, as they have been instructed to do, and his father gives him a bridle, a whip, and a Spanish staff. In order to win the king's daughter for a wife, the contestants have to scale a great wall of rock. Hansl accomplishes this with the aid of his father's gifts, together with a dappled steed and suit of silver armour, although during the second contest he is wounded in the foot. The king himself attends him, wrapping his own handkerchief round the wound. Hansl is later identified by means of this, and becomes the king's son-in-law.

A variant from Hungary, 'Aschenbrödel' (338) is almost identical to 'Cinder Jack' mentioned by Cox in Note 76, also of Hungarian origin (Jones and Knopf 1889). The tale begins with the eldest of three brothers sent to guard vineyards which are being trampled overnight. He and the second brother fail after confrontation with a toad, which offers help in return for a piece of cake, but is refused. Aschenbrödel, the youngest, who spends his time among the ashes, succeeds because he feeds the toad, and is given a copper, a silver, and a gold switch to tame the horses causing the damage, and to cause them to appear at his command. He tells no one the secret of his success. The king then organises a competition for the hand of his daughter. He places three fir poles, of increasing height, in front of the church, the first bearing a sprig of golden rosemary, the second a golden apple, and the third a gold silk kerchief, and anyone who can take these with one spring of his horse shall wed his daughter. All fail until a knight in copper armour on a copper horse arrives and is successful. In the second contest the winner is a knight in silver armour on a silver steed, and in the third a knight in golden armour on a golden steed. Each time the brothers return to tell what has happened. Aschenbrödel tells them he already knows because the first time he had watched from the top of a fence (this is pulled down); then from a stable (this is demolished), and finally, from the top of a house (the roof is taken off). He is revealed as the knight in each contest, weds the princess and inherits the kingdom. The motif of observance from a number of heights is found in several of the 'Cinderella' tales.

In 'Das Rosenmädchen', a German tale (324), the hero seeks the rose-girl whose castle is guarded by a dragon. Bees lead him there, and he becomes the gooseherd. With a magic wishing-bell which produces magical attire, he goes three times to balls which he knows the girl will attend. She falls in love with him, and her mother advises her to put pitch in his hair so that he can be identified. Finally a variant from Ireland is mentioned in Note 72 (Cox 1893: 522) which had been published in the *Folk-Lore Journal* (Britten 1883: 54–5). Jack, who is minding cows for a king in Ireland, fights and slays three giants. He then saves the king's daughters from a sea serpent. Before each skirmish, he goes to one of the giants' houses, where he finds clothes and a horse as well as a bottle labelled: 'Whoever would take one drop of this stuff would have three times as much strength.' At the third and final encounter with the monster, the third princess snatches one of his blue glass shoes. The king celebrates the killing of the serpent with a ball, and brings in the shoe to find its owner. Jack is finally called in from the kitchen, and the shoe fits perfectly.

There are more motifs of the Cinderella story which could be mentioned, such as the variety of tasks presented, the different means of survival with the aid of a helpful animal, including the obtaining of food and other objects from its ear, spies sent to discover the source of food, and the magic flight with an animal's help. However those mentioned above give some idea of the more unusual aspects of the tale.

The variety and expanse of the stories which Cox and her colleagues discovered are truly amazing when one considers the lack of modern technology. After such extensive research it is surprising, as Archer Taylor pointed out (Dundes 1982: 115–28), to note 'the failure of Miss Cox's *Cinderella* to stimulate further investigation. Scholars did not discuss the tale for a generation, and when they did they made no use of her book.' W. R. S Ralston (1879) had written about 'Cinderella', and Cox refers to this in her Preface and Notes; however it was not until the twentieth century that interest in the story resulted in several articles and books. Anna Birgitta Rooth's book, *The Cinderella Cycle*, was first published in 1951, and is the second large-scale comprehensive study of the Cinderella story. Her investigation contains almost twice as many variants as those of Cox. The format and development of the tale types are organised differently, but to all intents and purposes it is an extension of the earlier work. In her introduction Rooth wrote:

> When first reading Marian Roalfe Cox's *Cinderella* I was deeply impressed by the immense material collected, the skill and thoroughness with which Miss Cox retold more than 345 Cinderella tales.
>
> The aim of Miss Cox's investigation was not to come to any conclusions about the development of the Cinderella story. Her intention was only to give a collection of Cinderella tales grouped in some natural types. As a starting-point for further studies in the subject, her work about Cinderella is most important to students of folktale.

Rooth refers to many of Cox's variants throughout her own expansive survey of the story. In 1977 she published *Askungen*, a short book in Swedish with sixteen

Cinderella stories from Europe and Asia. There is a commentary, including a discussion of names, and several pages of maps showing the geographical distribution of the motifs.

Articles also appeared concentrating on specific locations around the world: China, Ireland and Africa. Three studies were on the Cinderella story in China; R. D. Jameson's 'Cinderella in China' (Jameson 1932) contained the earliest Chinese version of the tale. Yet it was Arthur Waley's inclusion of the same story, in his study entitled 'The Chinese Cinderella Story' (Waley 1947), which provided the better translation, and his discussion is the more useful. 'Yeh-hsien' is thought to be the earliest datable version of the Cinderella story, written down in the ninth century AD from its narrator, Li Shih-yuan.[1] Waley follows the story with detailed explanations of various incidents. The third study is Ting's 'The Cinderella Cycle in China and Indonesia' (1974), presented at the Finnish Academy of Science and Letters on 12 March, 1973.

'Cinderella in Ireland' by Reidar Th. Christiansen appeared in *Béaloideas* 20 in 1950, following the publication of Rooth's monograph. Christiansen felt that the Irish material was much better represented in her book than in that of Cox. However he went on to state that:

> *Cinderella*, written in 1893 by Marian Roalfe Cox, was in itself a great achievement with the 345 variants from every part of the world, summarized and systematically arranged according to the various redactions. Miss Cox's book will, therefore, always remain an indispensable preliminary to any further studies in this cycle, one of those most universally popular, so that during the 60 years since its appearance many times as many versions are on record.

'Cinderella in Africa', by William Bascom, was published in 1972, and was based on a paper given at the annual meeting of the American Folk-Lore Society on 10 November 1968, at Indiana University. He discusses several African 'Cinderella' variants, most importantly a translation by Neil Skinner of 'The Maiden, the Frog, and the Chief's Son'. Many elements in this particular story are strange, yet it is recognisable as a 'Cinderella' variant. He mentions the 'two intensive, comparative studies', that of Cox and 'Anna Rooth's extension and amplification of Cox's study'. Bascom goes into detail regarding the possible origin and transmission of African 'Cinderella' tales, noting that surprisingly few stories emanated from Africa at this time.

Alan Dundes (1982), begins his introduction by referring to the 'astonishing research effort of Marian Roalfe Cox', declaring that 'Even today, serious students of Cinderella still have to consult this 535-page pioneering compendium.' He continues with comparisons to Anna Birgitta Rooth's *Cinderella Cycle*, and towards the end of his introduction expresses his regret that 'so many of those who have written about Cinderella failed to make use of the abundant comparative materials assembled so laboriously by Marian Roalfe Cox and later by Anna Birgitta Rooth'. Dundes gives three early versions of 'Cinderella', those of Basile, Perrault and the Grimm brothers, and continues with a series of essays

---

[1] For a discussion of the possible earlier dating of 'Cinderella' see pp. 87, 90 above.

by well-known scholars on different aspects of the 'Cinderella' story, each preceded by a short introduction.

Neil Philip (1989) uses a different approach. He wrote in the preface that his book was 'an attempt to convey the entertaining variety of the world's Cinderella stories through the stories themselves rather than analysis of them'. It is with this in mind that he offers some obscure stories, some from Cox's *Cinderella*, among the twenty-four tales included. His introduction is enlightening, giving a succinct historical perspective to the tales. Since the majority of these are not well known, it makes the book even more valuable and enjoyable to read.

Cox ended her Preface as follows:

> If the labour of which this volume is the outcome shall in any degree contribute to the settlement of several interesting questions which gather round folktales, especially the question of origin, independent or otherwise, of stories similar in their incident and widespread in their distribution, I shall in no wise begrudge the time which that labour has absorbed. There will remain the regret which invariably accompanies a work of this kind – the non-attainment of finality where materials are ever pouring in; and experience of this has reconciled me to aim at only approximate completeness.

She added several more variants to her collection, 'like Dian's kiss, unasked, unsought', in *Folk-Lore* (1907). She had written a second book, *An Introduction to Folk-Lore* (1885), but as has been said, *Cinderella* was her *magnum opus*. She died in 1916, aged 56.

A fitting tribute was written by Katharine Briggs (1976: 59):

> She was one of the women whom the nineteenth century produced: scholarly, industrious, retiring, centred in domestic life and without academic qualifications but of untiring energy and capable of great application, just such another as Charlotte M. Yonge, without her creative drive but with a more specialised application of her powers.

References

Bascom, W. (1972), 'Cinderella in Africa', *Journal of the Folklore Institute*. Bloomington, 54–70.

Blind, K. (1889), 'A Fresh Scottish Ashpitel Tale', *Archaeological Review* 3, 24–7.

Briggs, K. M. (1976), 'Two Great English Monographs', *Folk-Lore Today: A Festschrift for Richard M. Dorson*. Bloomington.

Britten, J. (1883), 'Irish Folk-Tales', *Folk-Lore Journal* 1, 54–5.

Burne, C. S. (1916), 'Obituary: Marian Emily Roalfe Cox', *Folk-Lore* 27, 434–5.

Chamberlain, A. F. (1908), 'A Macassar Version of Cinderella', *Folk-Lore* 19, 230–2.

Christiansen, R. T. (1950), 'Cinderella in Ireland', *Béaloideas* 20, 96–107.

Cox, M. E. R. (1885), *An Introduction to Folk-Lore*. London.

Cox, M. E. R. *et al.* (1889), 'Tabulations of Folktales', *Folk-Lore Journal* 7, 1–57.

—— (1890), 'Tabulations of Folktales', *Folk-Lore* 1, 123–8.

—— (1893), *Cinderella: Three Hundred and Forty-Five Variants of Cinderella, Catskin, and*

Cap O' Rushes, Abstracted and Tabulated, with a Discussion of Mediaeval Analogues, and Notes. With an Introduction by Andrew Lang. London.

—— (1907), 'Cinderella', *Folk-Lore* 18, 191–208.

Dorson, R. M. (1968), *The British Folklorists: A History.* London.

Dundes, A. (1982), *Cinderella: A Casebook.* New York.

Hunt, M. (1894) ed. and trans., *Grimm's Household Tales.* Vol. 1. London.

Jacobs, J. (1893), 'Cinderella in Britain', *Folk-Lore* 4, 269–84.

—— (1894), 'The Problem of Diffusion: Rejoinders', *Folk-Lore* 5, 129–46.

Jameson, R. D. (1932), 'Cinderella in China', *Three Lectures on Chinese Folklore*, 47–85. Peking.

Jones, W. H., and Knopf, L. (1889), *The Folk-Tales of the Magyars.* London.

Lang, A. (1893a), 'At the Sign of the Ship', *Longman's Magazine* 22, 183–5.

—— (1893b), 'Cinderella and the Diffusion of Tales', *Folk-Lore* 4, 413–33.

Linder, L. (1971), *A History of the Writings of Beatrix Potter.* London.

Newell, W. (1893), 'Review of Marian Roalfe Cox's Cinderella', *Journal of American Folk-Lore* 6, 159–61.

—— (1894), 'The Origin of Cinderella', *Journal of American Folk-Lore* 7, 70–2.

Nutt, A. (1893a), 'Cinderella and Britain', *Folk-Lore* 4, 133–41.

—— (1893b), 'Some Recent Utterances of Mr Newell and Mr Jacobs: A Criticism', *Folk-Lore* 4, 434–50.

—— (1894), 'Discussion of Mr Jacobs' Paper', *Folk-Lore* 5, 146–9.

Pedroso, C. (1882), *Portuguese Folk-tales.* London.

Philip, N. (1980), 'Cinderella's Many Guises', *Signal Magazine* 33, 130–46.

—— (1989), *The Cinderella Story.* Harmondsworth.

Ralston, W. R. S. (1879), 'Cinderella', *The Nineteenth Century*, 6, 832–53. London.

Rooth, A. B. (1977), *Askungen i öst och väst.* Uppsala.

—— (1951/1980), *The Cinderella Cycle.* New York.

Sinclair, M. (1888), 'The Snow-White Maiden, and the Fair Maid, and the Swarthy Maid, and Frizzle, or Bald Pate their Mother', *The Celtic Magazine* 13, 454–65.

Thompson, S. (1946), *The Folktale.* New York.

Thorpe, B. (1853), *Yule-Tide Stories.* London.

Ting, Nai-Tung (1974), 'The Cinderella Cycle in China and Indo-China'. FFC 213, 4–67. Helsinki.

Waley, A. (1947), 'The Chinese Cinderella Story', *Folk-Lore* 58, 226–38.

Wardrop, M. (1894), *Georgian Folk Tales.* London.

9

Hans Christian Andersen's Use of Folktales*

BENGT HOLBEK

Andersen published 156 'fairy tales and stories' by his own count. Only seven of them are manifestly taken from Danish oral tradition. There are a couple of doubtful cases as well and he also used a few legends, but they are of minor importance. Apart from that, inspiration from folktales may be traced also in several other fairy tales by Andersen. To mention but one example: the famous tale of 'The Little Mermaid' is his own invention; nevertheless, it contains a number of elements which can be traced to various sources. The plot of the tale is undoubtedly inspired by de la Motte Fouqué's *Undine*, and behind that can be glimpsed the doctrine of elementary spirits which goes back to Paracelsus. The notion of a population of sea people, the 'merfolk', stems from popular belief; besides, there is inspiration from the ballad of *Agnete and the Mermaid*, and in the scene where the mute mermaid lives in the king's palace, we are reminded of the folktale of 'The Mute Queen'. Such reminiscences may be found in many of Andersen's tales.

The number of parallels at the typological level is, however, as low as seven, i.e., three or four per cent of the entire corpus. Three of these tales belong to the category the Germans call *Zaubermärchen* and the Danes *trylleeventyr*. In English, they are called wonder tales, mythical tales, fairy tales, tales of magic etc. I shall call them tales of magic so as not to confuse them with Andersen's own tales – the alternative, 'fairy tale', is often used about literary products; but I must confess that I am not happy with the term 'magic', since the phenomenon in question has very little to do with real magic. But whatever we call them, the three tales in question are: 'The Travelling-Companion', 'The Tinder-Box' and 'The Wild Swans'. Those are the ones I shall comment upon. Before going on to do that, I ought to mention the titles of the other four tales: 'Little Claus and Big Claus', 'The Swineherd', 'All that Father Does is Right' and 'Simple Simon'.

*This article is taken from *The Telling of Stories: Approaches to a Traditional Craft*, ed. Morten Nøjgaard, Johan de Mylius, Iørn Piø and Bengt Holbek, the Proceedings of the Thirteenth International Symposium organised by the Centre for the Study of Vernacular Literature in the Middle Ages, held at the University of Odense, 21–2 November 1988. It was published in 1990 by Odense University Press, and we are most grateful for permission to publish it here. The brief introduction to the audience has been omitted, as has the translation of a story by Winther compared with part of Andersen's tale in the Appendix, together with other references to this Appendix in the text. Minimal changes to the text have been made.

Andersen says that 'The Princess and the Pea' was among the tales he remembered from his childhood, but it is not otherwise known from northern and western Europe, whereas related tales are found to the South and East as far away as India. The tale of 'The Emperor's New Clothes' belongs to folklore, but not in Denmark; Andersen had read it in *El Conde Lucanor*.

Andersen does not tell us the exact sources for the tales of 'The Travelling-Companion' and 'The Tinder-Box'. There is nothing strange in this. It appears from what is known about other storytellers that they cannot always indicate their exact sources. Often they just explain that tales used to be told on such and such occasions, and they must have heard them then. Andersen says the same thing. He refers to the picking of hops, which is slow, quiet work that can be done by several people working together, and to spinning bees, both classical occasions for storytelling. When several people are together and their hands, but not their minds, are occupied, there is time for storytelling. We have no reason to doubt Andersen's words: he *may* have heard the two tales on such occasions. Nevertheless, I have an alternative in mind; but before presenting it, I shall explain my line of reasoning.

In 1987 I published a study of the telling of magic tales in Denmark. I found, among other things, that there was a marked difference between the tales told by men and those told by women. Men very consistently preferred tales with male protagonists, whereas women gave approximately equal attention to tales with male and tales with female protagonists. Tales like 'The Travelling-Companion' and 'The Tinder-Box' have been recorded many times in Denmark, and most of the informants have been male. Men would not pick hops or spin in former times, therefore we should ask: could there be a male storyteller in Andersen's surroundings? And one must think of his father right away. In the first place, he was a shoemaker, and it is known that tailors and shoemakers were often storytellers in former times. Their work was stationary and relatively quiet, and itinerant tailors and shoemakers would often attract a crowd of children when they arrived at a farm to sell their services. In the second place, it is known that Andersen's father used to read the *Arabian Nights* and other tales to his son, and he may have told some of his own as well. In the third place, he was enrolled in the army in 1812 and served for two years. There is good evidence that the army was a hotbed for storytelling in those times; thus, there is a case of a man on Zealand who learned a tale from a Jutlander – in France, where both of them served during the Napoleonic war. In the fourth place, finally, there is some internal evidence as well, not conclusive but interesting: the tale of 'The Tinder-Box' is about a soldier who wins the princess and half the kingdom by being brave and generous, but also by insisting on having his own way; and it is known that Andersen's father impressed upon his son that he was not to let himself be confined, he was to rely on himself and to go out into the great wide world to seek his fortune for himself, which is what the soldier of that tale does. And the tale of 'The Travelling-Companion' opens with a deathbed scene: the young hero is given his father's blessing, some good advice, and the small amount of money which is precisely what he needs later on to acquire his marvellous helper. Immediately upon his father's death, the hero leaves home to wander into the wide world; Andersen did the very same: his father died when he was eleven and only three years later, at the earliest possible instant, he left home to seek his fortune in Copenhagen, the city of the king and the gate to the world.

These are the reasons why I think that he may have learned those two tales from his father. The same is not true of 'The Wild Swans', which he found in a book. One may ask: How could he find a Danish folktale in a book at a time when the collecting of folktales had not yet begun? But it was in fact possible. Selections of the French fairy tales and of the *Arabian Nights* had already appeared in the previous century; in 1816, Adam Oehlenschläger, the Danish poet, had published a selection of tales from Musäus, Tieck and a few others, and in 1821, a selection of the Grimm tales had appeared in a Danish translation. That had inspired a man from Odense to try his hand at the same task. His name was Matthias Winther and his collection appeared in 1823. It was boldly numbered vol. I, but was not followed up. The reason is not difficult to discover: the Romantic era was profoundly interested in tales, but his were not well told. The volume contains twenty tales, most of which he had heard from his nurse or from local peasants – or so he says; no precise information is given. One of the tales was called 'The Eleven Swans', and it so inspired Andersen that he retold it in his own way. It is the only one of the tales he took from folklore which features a female protagonist, and we may guess that the ultimate source was Winther's nurse or some other female informant.

A discussion of Andersen's use of folktales must therefore be based on the following: in the cases of 'The Tinder-Box' and 'The Travelling-Companion', the principal material for comparison is later records from Danish folklore – it should be mentioned that in a few cases, a limited influence from Andersen on traditional storytellers may be discerned; in the case of 'The Wild Swans', Winther's tale is the principal source, but Andersen may have known independent versions as well.

The tale of 'The Travelling-Companion' is the first tale ever published by Andersen. He published it twice. The first version, from 1830, appeared under the title 'The Dead Man. A Tale from Funen'. Andersen took no liberty with the narrative outline as he knew it from oral tradition, but he told it in a literary style which was much influenced by Musäus and other well-known writers. I shall not presume to make a translation – there may be an English translation already, although I do not know it – but a few characteristic details may be mentioned. When the hero has left home, he sleeps the first night in a field. The passage reads something like this: 'The first night he lodged in a haystack in the field and slept there like a Persian prince in his glittering chamber.' When he rewrote the tale six years later, the same passage read: 'The first night, he lay down to sleep in a haystack in the fields, for other bed he had none. But he thought it was just lovely – the king himself couldn't have a finer bed!' The elegant words and allusions are gone, everything can be readily understood by a child, the syntax is simplified and so on. At a later point in 'The Dead Man' we read: 'Our wanderers learned from the host that they were in the realm of the king of hearts, an excellent monarch and a close relative of Silvio the king of diamonds', who is well known from Carlo Gozzi's dramatic tale of 'The Three Oranges'. And further on: the princess is compared to Turandot, and about the hero himself it is said that 'It was as if he had recently read *Werther* and *Siegwarth*, he could but love and die.' In this style, the storyteller stands outside so to speak, he manages his characters as if they were puppets on strings, he reports their antics and now and then snickers a little.

The tale of 'The Dead Man' was no success. But Andersen knew that he was on to something, he went on experimenting, and five years later, in 1835, he published the first four of the tales which were to ensure his lasting fame. Two of them, the tales of 'The Tinder-Box' and 'Little Claus and Big Claus', possibly also 'The Princess and the Pea', were taken from oral tradition. The fourth one is 'Little Ida's Flowers', a delightful tale in which the student amuses the child who is unhappy because her posy of flowers is withering. The student, who is of course Andersen himself, tells her an amusing yarn about the secret night life of the flowers and thus consoles her. It may be assumed that this tale was written in the winter 1834–5, when Andersen lived in Copenhagen, next door to J. M. Thiele, the librarian and well-known editor of Danish popular legends, whose daughter little Ida was. It is probable that the tale as we know it from the edition actually reflects the story invented on the spur of the moment by the lanky student to console and entertain the little girl. The Botanical Garden, from which the flowers probably came, was right behind the house where little Ida lived, and its director, Professor Hornemann, is undoubtedly reflected in the counsellor who grumbles about the student's 'silly imagination'. But Andersen did not heed the grumbling, he had found his kingdom. From then on, his tales were for a long time told for children.

What to do? After his success with little Ida, Andersen returned to the folktales he knew from his childhood, but this time with the purpose of entertaining children, without any attempt to impress the adults with his erudition and wit. And the first he took up was 'The Tinder-Box'. For the information of those who are knowledgeable in such matters, I should add that it is Aarne–Thompson type no. 562. It is difficult and, I think, pointless, to keep it apart from type no. 561, the prototype of which is 'Aladdin'. This is no coincidence. Andersen was much attracted by that figure. Adam Oehlenschläger had published a play based on that tale as it appears in the *Arabian Nights*, but with an interesting twist at the beginning: Noureddin is looking among the children of the street for a boy who can help him get hold of the lamp. It is announced that three oranges are to be thrown to the boys. Aladdin catches the first one and also the second one. Then the other boys grab him to prevent him from getting the last one as well, but it falls right into his turban. He is favoured by luck and therefore Noureddin chooses him. Andersen, who was born in the year Oehlenschläger published *Aladdin*, interpreted his own life as a fairy tale and wrote an autobiography which is actually called *The Fairy Tale of My Life*. He saw himself as the lucky Aladdin, for which reason it cannot surprise us that he chose a Danish version of the same tale type when he began his new project of telling tales for children. At the same time, we seem to get a glimpse of his father in the strapping soldier who comes marching down the road – left, right! left, right! His father did leave home as a soldier – to return sick and broken less than two years later, it is true, but Andersen hoped to do better. There are several reminiscences of the lucky Aladdin in 'The Tinder-Box'.

The number of parallel Danish versions is not large in this case: there are fewer than twenty, but the common theme is given so many different forms that it is difficult to point to features which *must* have been invented by Andersen. It is probable that the fire-steel itself is his invention, since it is usual for the spirits to appear when *candles* are lighted. Also, the dogs with the large eyes may be his invention. It is a common feature in *legends* about treasure hunters that some sort of frightening animal is sitting on the treasure, and that it can be placated by being treated gently and respectfully. Andersen probably transferred that motif from the legends to the tale. Apart from that, he sticks closely to the traditional form. He has chosen a fairly simple form in which the soldier is found out almost immediately, but that is within the range of variation possible in oral tradition. There may be a special reason for Andersen's cutting this part of the tale short: in 'Lazy Hans', the princess is not only brought to the hero once, but every night for eight years, and she has three children when the culprit is finally caught. Andersen could not include such a coarse motif in his rendering of the tale if it was to be accepted by the children of the bourgeoisie.

This is an important point. Andersen had heard the tales in one milieu and told them in another. He had to make adjustments, one of which was that he had to disguise or obliterate all traces of overt sexuality; such matters were not then deemed fitting entertainment for the children of the bourgeoisie. I shall mention more instances of this further on. It also meant that the storyteller had a child of the city in mind when he needed material for comparison: the dog's eyes were as big as the Round Tower which every child in Copenhagen knows. The countryside is 'out there', one has to tell the child what a farmer's house looks like. But there is more to it than this kind of superficial feature, as I shall demonstrate further on.

A final remark about 'The Tinder-Box': Andersen tells it in his inimitable style, lively and humorous. There is nothing like it in the records of folktales we possess. This has led earlier commentators to the conclusion that traditional storytellers were less proficient, less gifted, than Andersen. It is said, for instance, that the folktales have no psychological depth, the style is 'simple' in the sense of 'elementary', even 'tasteless' to some of our *beaux-esprits*. And that is true enough if we look only at those ancient records. But the principal reason is that at the time when traditional storytelling was still flourishing in Denmark, the recording techniques were poor. Even the best collectors could not write nearly as fast as the tales were told. Besides, they had to record in standard Danish, not in the dialects – and much of the charm of oral storytelling hinges on the peculiarities of the dialects. When modern recording techniques were introduced, these things could be observed, but by then the ancient art had almost disappeared; but those who have worked with modern equipment in areas where storytelling has been cultivated as a living oral art form down to our time can confirm that oral narrative style is much more sophisticated than our old records indicate. This is confirmed if we read Evald Tang Kristensen's descriptions of his informants. He repeatedly emphasises that there is much more to the oral style than can be captured by even the most diligent writer. He also makes another point, namely that each storyteller has his or her own style. It is therefore hardly correct to speak of 'the' oral style. Andersen may have been a better stylist than most, but quite a number of the old storytellers might have stood up to him if we had been able to document their tales as they really sounded.

The first little volume of tales was favourably received and Andersen immediately went on to produce the next. He now rewrote the tale of 'The Dead Man', this time under the title 'The Travelling-Companion' – AT 507A; the catalogue mentions twenty-seven versions taken down from Danish oral tradition. He retained much from the earlier version, but transplanted it to the children's universe – I have given a few instances already to show the character of the changes.

The style of this tale is very different from that of 'The Tinder-Box'. It is serious and, to tell the truth, not a little sentimental. Hans Brix, one of the major Andersen scholars, discerns two classes of tales: one is told with a twinkling humour, is fast-moving, sometimes whimsical and even a little malicious at times; the other is more serious and slower. If 'The Tinder-Box' belongs to the first category, 'The Travelling-Companion' and 'The Wild Swans' belong to the second. 'The Travelling-Companion' opens with what I believe is another glimpse of Andersen's father, not, however, this time as a strapping soldier marching down the road, but as an old man on his deathbed. Deathbed scenes are found in several oral versions of this tale type and, for that matter, in other magic tales as well. It has been observed that a great many of these tales begin with the dissolution of one nuclear family and end with the formation of a new one, and that is true of this tale as well, even though it should be mentioned that there is no mother. The tale is seen exclusively from a male viewpoint.

I said earlier that Andersen took no liberty with the traditional chain of events in this tale, and that is true inasmuch as it contains the traditional series: the acquisition of a helper through a charitable deed, the helper's acquisition of magical remedies, and the winning of the princess. This series of events is present even in the oldest extant version of the tale, that in the Book of Tobit. But Andersen *adds* events which have no foundation in folklore. To mention but one instance: when the hero and his companion arrive at the inn, they see a man with a puppetshow. Andersen himself had played with puppets in his childhood and he delights in describing the play and the puppets. At night, the puppets come alive just like the flowers in 'Little Ida's Flowers', and we dwell on that scene for a while. The Companion smears some of the puppets with a life-giving ointment in return for a sabre belonging to the puppet-master, and thus the event is connected with the main course of events, since the sabre is used later on; but the scene with the night life of the puppets is given much more room for independent unfolding than would have been the case in oral storytelling.

This is actually characteristic of Andersen's way of telling stories. His talent is not really epic. The tales that are best constructed from an epic point of view are those he took from oral tradition and a few others, like 'The Ugly Duckling' and 'The Little Mermaid', whereas the majority of his own tales consist of loosely connected series of vivid images; Andersen's talent is dramatic and lyrical rather than epic. The same may be observed in 'The Wild Swans': the clear epic structure that is taken over from oral tradition is interspersed with lyric-dramatic episodes of Andersen's own invention. A folklorist may express it in this way: Andersen does not conform to Olrik's Epic Laws, according to which thoughts and feelings are expressed in action; he is free to diverge from tradition because he is not constrained by the conditions of oral storytelling.

The main event of 'The Travelling-Companion' is of course the confrontation with the princess who demands to have three questions answered on pain of death. This is where my analysis of folktales leads me to the conclusion that Andersen does not understand what they really are about; or if he understands it, he conceals it in such a way as to make it exceedingly difficult for modern people to understand. At this point, it should be emphasised that in traditional peasant communities, magic tales were principally entertainment for adult people. When they are transplanted to the world of the children of the bourgeoisie, some extremely important aspects are lost as I shall try to explain.

In my view, the tales of magic deal with the relations between ordinary people. I think that three categories of relations are described in tale after tale. In the first place, the relations between parents and children, the children's rebellion against their parents, the sometimes premature departure from home, the rivalry between siblings, the emotional attachments of children to parents and parents to children and, not infrequently, the sexual aspects of these attachments. In the second place, there are the relations between young people of opposite sexes. And in the third place, the relations between people of low and high status. All this is set out and analysed in my thesis (1987).

These relations are often painful and sometimes shameful, and they cannot always be plainly spoken of. I think that is the reason why conflicts are so to speak *displaced*, transferred wholly or in part to the never-never land east of the sun and west of the moon. Thus, there may be emotional attachments and illicit relations between mothers and sons or between fathers and daughters. This is sometimes explicitly mentioned in tales like, for instance, the Grimm tale of 'Allerleirauh' where the father wants to marry his own daughter. But more often, the relation is disguised by means of the technique which is called the *split* among psychoanalysts. For illustration I may refer to the story of *Dr Jekyll and Mr Hyde*. The two characters are opposites, but they are in reality one and the same person. I investigated a number of versions of the tale of 'The Princess on the Glass Mountain' with this in mind. The princess is placed on a glass mountain and she is to be given to the man who can scale the mountain. My question was: who put the princess in such a dangerous position? I found the following: out of twenty-three versions examined, one had no information on the point. In nine versions, the princess had been put there by a troll, a dragon, or the Devil himself. In the remaining thirteen versions, the culprit was her own *father*. It made no difference to the narrative organisation whether the princess was exposed to danger by a troll or a dragon or by her father. From this I concluded that dragons could be interpreted as poetic expressions of fathers in their threatening aspect. The argument is of course more involved than this, and there is more evidence which I could offer, but the point can be made on the strength of this example. In short, I believe that the oral versions of the tale type in question, that of the dead man as the hero's helper, present enough evidence for me to conclude that the hidden troll who helps the princess pose the riddles to her suitors is an expression of her hidden relation to her father. I think that this princess's riddle is an illicit emotional attachment to her father. If the tale is interpreted with that in mind, the riddles to be guessed acquire an ominous significance. The objects to be guessed may be her gloves or shoes or a ring or a symbol of her heart, and they may be read as symbolic aspects of herself, perhaps of her sexual aspect if the psychoanalysts are to be believed, but the third object is invariably the head of the hidden troll, i.e., her secret lover. The nature of the spell that has bound her is exposed when the hero displays the hacked-off head of the troll.

I do not know whether Andersen understood this to be the true nature of the princess's riddle. He may have done so, but in that case he must have done everything in his power to disguise a relation which he felt was not only unseemly, but also not fit to be mentioned in the company of the children of a bourgeoisie which was exceptionally careful to suppress such expressions of sexuality. But I do feel that he did not realise this aspect of the tale, and I shall explain why: if he had thought of the troll as an image of the father existing in the girl's mind, he would have done what the traditional storytellers did; they concentrate on the princess's state of mind and on her pursuer, the invisible Travelling-Companion. The Troll is mentioned and his advice to her is quoted, but that is all. Andersen, on the other hand, takes time to describe the Troll's looks and his den with its inhabitants – a whole page is spent on that. Andersen gives his imagination free rein:

> They went down a great long passage where the walls sparkled quite wonderfully – there were thousands of glowing spiders running up and down the walls and shining like fire. Then they entered a great hall built of silver and gold, with flowers as big as sunflowers shining red and blue from the walls: but no one could pick them, for the stalks were vile poisonous snakes and the flowers were the fire that flamed from their mouths. The whole ceiling was covered with shining glow-worms and sky-blue bats beating their thin wings: it looked really wonderful. In the middle of the floor there was a throne borne on the skeletons of four horses with harnesses of red fire-spiders; the throne itself was of milk-white glass, and the cushions to sit on were small black mice biting each other's tails.

And so on. Wonderful and fascinating – and completely incommensurable with all we know of traditional storytelling. None of this would be needed to describe the state of mind of a young woman who is under the spell of being attached to her father at a time when she should be ready for a husband instead. This example and others indicate to me that Andersen may use the apparatus of the traditional tales, but instead of carrying the tradition on, he gives it a new direction, undoubtedly because he is transferring it to a new environment.

The same is the case with 'The Wild Swans'. In this case, the basis of Andersen's text is known: he took it from Winther as I have already said. Some fifteen other versions of the tale are known from Danish folklore and he may have been familiar with the tale before he saw it in Winther. Nevertheless, it must be stated that even though he expanded the tale enormously, he did not add anything that would have to be explained as evidence of his acquaintance with parallel versions. Winther's tale is the main and probably the only source.

Winther's record is dull and dry. The first thirteen lines of his tale deal with the heroine's clash with her stepmother and departure from home and that is, in essence, what the entire quotation from Andersen's version is about. He not only fleshes out the bare bones of Winther's version, but also adds features of his own invention. I shall concentrate on one of these, since it will demonstrate very well the difference between Andersen and the traditional storytellers.

In traditional folktales, the qualities of the characters are not described, but demonstrated through action. The heroine of this tale is shown to be devoted to her brothers through her selfless acts: she takes it upon herself to make those shirts out of thistles and to keep silent whatever befalls her. But Andersen's heroine possesses an innate goodness which is demonstrated in an entirely different way. Her stepmother is evil, not in an ordinary way like the mother of Cinderella who merely keeps the heroine occupied with endless work and prevents her from going to a ball; that is actually what may be expected from mothers who think that their daughters should be restrained. No, Elisa's stepmother is a real witch, like the evil queen in Walt Disney's *Snow White*, and she attempts to cripple her stepdaughter out of sheer evilness. She uses toads (the most abominable creatures Andersen can think of); her kissing of the toads is an obscene act with overtones of perverted sexuality; but to no avail. The heroine overcomes her underhand attack, apparently without even consciously trying. When she emerges from the bath, the toads have been changed into red poppies. Not roses, for roses are the quintessence of perfection in Andersen's universe, and even this heroine cannot create perfection out of such depravity. They become red flowers nevertheless, and thus the heroine has won.

A similar situation occurs towards the end of the tale, where the heroine is to be burnt at the stake, but her brothers arrive in the nick of time and are transformed into human beings, thanks to the shirts. The eldest brother explains everything,

> and while he was speaking, a perfume like that of a million roses spread about them, for every stick of wood heaped about the stake had taken root and put out branches: there stood a great tall hedge fragrant with red roses. Right at the top was one flower, white and gleaming, which shone like a star.

The message seems to be that innocent goodness triumphs over evil. In Andersen's universe, the qualities of good and evil have become absolute. That is very different from what we observe in records of genuine folklore. The heroes and heroines of traditional magic tales are measured according to the qualities they need in order to function as adult, responsible members of their community. Goodness in such an absolute form as we see it in Andersen does not seem to be very useful. Instead, we observe a number of what may be called *social* virtues like helpfulness, generosity, steadfastness in danger, faithfulness, honesty and so on; but also qualities of a different sort: ability to fend for oneself, readiness to trick an opponent or swindle him out of something valuable, etc. Andersen sticks close to traditional storytelling in the tale of 'The Tinder-Box' where the hero gets away with killing the old witch who asked him to fetch the tinder-box; 'The Travelling-Companion' and 'The Wild Swans' move in a different world – the form is still that of the traditional tales, but the underlying moral attitude and view of humanity is different.

The differences between Andersen and the traditional storytellers have not been sufficiently investigated so far. My feeling is that, even though I have read all the studies of the problem which I could find and even though I have pondered it myself for quite a while, much remains to be done. I, as a folklorist, am not sufficiently schooled in literary criticism and the literary critics who have written on the subject know too little about folklore. Andersen crossed a bridge when he transferred a number of tales from folklore to literature, but we, the scholars, investigate either one or the other side of the bridge and we have not quite succeeded in describing the crossing itself.

References

Alnæs, I. (1974), 'H. C. Andersen og folkeeventyrene', *Anderseniana* 3rd series, II (1974–7), 97–119.

Askrog, S. (1987), '"Der var engang –". En genrehistorisk beskrivelse af prosaeventyret i Danmark i to perioder: som en del af folkedigtningen (folkeeventyret) og i "Guldalderen"'. MA thesis, University of Copenhagen.

Boberg, I. M. (1952), *H. C. Andersens eventyrstil*. Odense.

Brandes, G. (1899), 'H. C. Andersen som Æventyrdigter' (1869), *Samlede Skrifter* 11, 91–132. Copenhagen

Brix, H. (1907), *H. C. Andersen og hans Eventyr*. Copenhagen.

Christensen, G. (1906), 'H. C. Andersen og de danske folkeeventyr', *Danske Studier* 103–12, 161–74.

Grønbech, B. (1945), *H. C. Andersens Eventyrverden*. Copenhagen.

Holbek, B. (1987), *Interpretation of Fairy Tales: Danish Folklore in a European Perspective*. FFC 239. Helsinki.

Rubow, P. V. (1967), *H. C. Andersens eventyr*. 3rd edn. Copenhagen.

Winther, M. (1823), *Danske Folkeeventyr*. Copenhagen.

10

The Collecting and Study of Tales in Scandinavia

REIMUND KVIDELAND

In Scandinavia as elsewhere in Europe collecting and publication of folktales started in the early part of the nineteenth century. However there are folktale motifs and indications that the fairy tale existed in Scandinavia in the Middle Ages, although we have no complete texts. About 1200 Oddr Snorrason claims in the foreword to his saga of Óláfr Tryggvason (1932) that it is better to listen to his story than to stories about stepmothers told by shepherds; no one can tell whether they are true or not, and they do not tell of any glorious feats of the kings. About the same time Abbot Karl Jónsson in *Sverris saga* (7) compares the fate of King Sverri with old stories told about the children of kings who have been cursed by their stepmothers.

Most of the reminiscences of folktales found in Old Norse literature are difficult to classify as known tale types.[1] They are found in the sagas of the kings of Norway, and in the mythical-heroic sagas *(fornaldar sögur)*, as well as in the poems of the *Edda*. In the saga of Harald Fairhair as told in *Ágrip* (end of twelfth century), *Heimskringla* (early thirteenth) and *Flateyjarbók* (fourteenth century), we find three stories related to folktales: Harald makes a vow not to comb or cut his hair until he has conquered the whole of Norway (AT 314 'Goldener'); he is said to have been fostered by a giant who had stolen his father's food (AT 502: 'The Wild Man'); and he sat by the dead body of his wife Snæfríðr for three years (AT 709: 'Snow White') (Mundal 1997). In *Óláfs saga helga* (85) in *Heimskringla* the tale of the Uglier Foot is known otherwise only in modern Irish tradition, indicating Irish influence in Iceland (Almqvist 1991).

The central motif of AT 300 ('The Dragon-Slayer') is found in *Völsunga saga* and in Saxo Grammaticus, in the episode of the slaying of Fáfnir by the hero Sigurðr. In *Vigkæns saga Kúahirðis* there is a story about the hero Vigkænn who gets hold of a magic needle, kills three giants and takes all their treasures, conquers an enemy army and finally wins a princess. This cannot be classified as an international tale type, but has motifs in common with AT 314 ('Youth Transformed into a Horse') and AT 301 ('The Three Stolen Princesses'). However, it has been characterised by Schlauch (1973: 98) as 'nothing but thinly disguised *Märchen'*. There are more recognisable folktale motifs in some of the *fornaldar sögur* and Saxo Grammaticus.[2] Axel Olrik made the first

---

[1] For surveys, see E. Ól. Sveinsson (1929) and Bødker (1959).
[2] *Egils saga ok Ásmundar* has a story of two princesses carried off by giants and rescued at the end of the saga. This has been compared to AT 301 ('The Three Stolen Princesses'), as well as

serious study of folklore in Saxo's history, but we lack a modern study (Bødker 1964; Holbek 1981).

Denmark

The first Danish collection of folktales was published in 1823 by Matthias Winther. Seventeen of the twenty texts were taken from oral tradition, and the first tale is 'Hans og Grethe' from the Grimm brothers, a tale that passed into oral Danish tradition. Winther's folktales never became a popular edition of tales however (cf. p. 151 above), and in fact Denmark never had one. The probable reason is that H. C. Andersen, influenced by Winther, created his literary tales which overshadowed the folktales.

The struggle against German influences in the southern boundary region created a nationalistic atmosphere in Denmark which promoted interest in folklore. Svend Grundtvig, who was beginning work on a major publication of Danish ballads, made a public appeal for the collection of folktales. The result was about eight hundred texts, some of which he used in his *Gamle danske Minder* ('Old Danish Oral Traditions'), published in three volumes, 1854–61. Some years later he published three further volumes entitled *Danske Folkeæventyr* ('Danish Folk Tales'), intended as a national edition of Danish tales, but they were rewritten in the literary style of the period and never became popular.

The most famous Danish folklore collector was the schoolteacher Evald Tang Kristensen, who began collecting in 1868 (Rockwell 1982). He published about seventy books on folklore, including thirteen collections of folktales. He also published about 650 folktales in his journal *Skattegraveren* ('The Treasure Hunter') from 1884 to 1889. He collected about 2,500 tales himself and in addition took about 850 from other collectors. About 85 per cent remain unpublished (Holbek 1987: 607), and his enormous manuscript collection is part of the Danish Folklore Archive. His diaries and notes make it possible to trace most of his informants, and give a picture of the folktale tradition in Jutland in the nineteenth century. Compared with his, other Danish collections are small, but should not be totally forgotten. Special mention should be made of J. P. Kuhre's collection from Bornholm (1938), and that of L. Andersen from Od (1923).

AT 302 ('The Ogre's Heart in the Egg'), and AT 303 ('The Twin Brothers') because of a few common motifs (Bødker 1959: 72ff.). This case shows how difficult it is to classify folktales in Old Norse literature by the international index based on recordings of the nineteenth and twentieth centuries. *Hrólfs saga kraka* has a story similar to AT 303. Saxo Grammaticus in his *Gesta Danorum* (c.1150–1220) has used folktales as historical sources: stories of Hading and Regnilda, and of Regner can be compared to AT 300 ('The Dragon-Slayer'), that of Amleth to AT 655 ('The Wise Brother'), that of Syrintha and Othar to AT 900 ('King Thrushbeard'), and other motifs to AT 425 ('Search for the Lost Husband'), and AT 887 ('Griselda').

Norway

The classical collection of folktales in Norway is that of Peter Christen Asbjørnsen and Jørgen Moe. They originally intended to use the tales as raw material for their own poetic works, but at an early stage they came across the folktale collections of Jacob and Wilhelm Grimm, and decided to publish the folktales as they heard them. At the same time they looked on themselves as the last link in a chain of storytellers, and felt that they must tell the stories well. When necessary they combined several variants, and in order to compensate for the loss of oral performance they made the style richer, more concrete and logical, using a more oral style and vocabulary than in normal writing. In this way they changed the folktale into a literary genre that the Norwegian cultural elite and bourgeoisie could accept and use in its struggle for a Norwegian cultural identity. The editions of 1841–4 and 1852 did not sell well, and the only real success was a small collection of fourteen folktales by Asbjørnsen entitled *The Christmas Tree* (1859) which sold 23,000 copies, an unusual achievement in Norway at that time. The illustrated edition of 1879 resulted in their work becoming widely known.

In contrast to the Grimms, Asbjørnsen and Moe travelled extensively, mainly in eastern Norway but also in the rest of the country, collecting tales and other folklore. Most of the other collectors worked regionally. Many were academics, but later schoolteachers, ministers and farmers joined the growing group. The philologists Sophus Bugge and Hans Ross represented collectors who demanded exact records, but the first tales published in dialect by Andreas E. Vang in 1850 did not play an important role. Moltke Moe, the son of Jørgen Moe, made some valuable collections in Telemark, some of them published posthumously. Rikard Berge collected tens of thousands of pages of folklore in Telemark and produced some important publications of folktales, including a sampler of repertoires of storytellers (1924). Torleiv Hannaas published fifty tales from the repertoire of the last great storyteller in Norway, Olav Eivindsson Austad of Setesdal , in 1927, and Karl Braset captured the special features of the folktale in Trøndelag in 1910, while Ole T. Olsen published a collection of tales from Nordland in 1912, heavily revised by Moltke Moe.[3]

Sweden

The classical Swedish collection of folktales was published by Gunnar Olof Hyltén-Cavallius and his English friend George Stephens, known for his *Handbook of the Old-Northern Runic Monuments* (1884), who became Professor of English in the University of Copenhagen. It was entitled *Svenska folksagor och äventyr*, and since their ideal was the Icelandic sagas, they sought to give the

---

[3] The most extensive publication of folktales in Norway is *Norsk eventyrbibliotek* ('Norwegian Library of Folk Tale') edited by Bryjulf Alver, Olav Bø and Reimund Kvideland in twelve regional volumes 1967–81. A scholarly edition of erotic folktales was published by Oddbjørg Høgset in 1977.

tales an archaic medieval style and vocabulary. In later editions, especially those for children, the language was modernised, and these became very popular, but the original records are the best. They destroyed the originals of the tales which they published; the remainder are published in a scholarly edition by the Royal Gustav Adolf Academy.

August Bondeson published the outstanding collection of Swedish folk tales. He had studied the humanities and medicine at Uppsala, and became a popular author of stories of folk life. His best collection of folktales is *Historiegubbar på Dal* ('Storytellers in Dal'), where he presents four storytellers, their background and repertoires, in a surprisingly modern manner (af Klintberg 1999). Bondeson influenced Rikard Berge's *Norsk sogukunst* in Norway. Per Arvid Säve made a fine collection in Gotland, but this was not published until the 1950s. He understood the important role played by the storytellers, and made notes on over seven hundred informants (Bjersby 1964). From 1860 onwards the societies (later archives) of dialects organised the systematic collection of folklore. A good example from the twentieth century is a scholarly edition edited by Åsa Nyman of Frans Bergvall's collection, as recently as 1991. In the 1920s Waldemar Liungman in Gothenburg organised a final appeal to collectors through the local newspapers, and edited the best texts in the first of two volumes, the second containing folktales from other archives (Liungman 1949–50).[4]

Folktale Research

A great part of research on folktales has been done by scholars working on the archives and in the folklore departments of the universities. The Danish Folklore Archive in Copenhagen was founded in 1905, and on the initiative of its director, Axel Olrik, the Norwegian folklore archive was established in Oslo in 1917, and is now part of the University. In Sweden there is no national folklore archive, but archives, in some cases combined with dialect archives, were established in Lund in 1913, in Uppsala in 1914, and in Gothenburg in 1919. The Nordic Museum in Stockholm has a special folklore archive.

The first scholarly work on Scandinavian folktales was that of Jørgen Moe, in his introduction and comparative notes to the second edition of *Norwegian Folktales* in 1852. He received the first grant for folklore in the University of Oslo. Later his son Moltke Moe became the first Professor of Folklore and Norwegian dialects in Oslo in 1885 at the age of twenty-six. His first published work consisted of comparative notes to a regional collection of folktales, written from memory while he was out in the countryside and showing enormous knowledge for so young a man. His friend Axel Olrik became docent in Copenhagen in 1897, and Professor of Folklore in 1913. Among his works are his doctoral thesis on folklore in the Danish history of Saxo Grammaticus (1892), an article on 'Red Riding Hood' showing the influence of English anthropology, and a study of 'King Lindorm' in 1904 influenced by the historical-geographical method. His

---

[4] The largest collection of Swedish folktales was undertaken by the Royal Gustav Adolf Academy in Uppsala, but is not yet complete. Eleven volumes have been published.

article of 1922 on the 'Epic Laws of Folk Narrative' (Olrik 1992) has become a classic.

The next generation includes Reidar Th. Christiansen and Rikard Berge in Norway and Carl Wilhelm von Sydow in Sweden. Christiansen was devoted to the historical-geographical method all his life. His first monographs on tale types deal with an aetiological tale about the swallow (1910), and AT 613, 'The Two Travellers' (1916), AT 1655, 'The Profitable Exchange' (1931), and AT 311, 'Rescue by the Sister' (1957). He saw the weakness of the method, but did not find a better alternative, and sought a solution by making comparative studies of the whole corpus of folktale traditions in Norwegian/Scandinavian, Saami, Finnish, Scottish and Irish. His main work in this area is *Studies in Irish and Scandinavian Folktales* (1959). In *European Folklore in America* (1962) he shows how the American mentality changed the European folktale in accordance with a preference for realism and humour.

Rikard Berge studied under Moltke Moe and Axel Olrik. He worked all his life at the county museum of Telemark where he was born, and had an intimate knowledge of the region. His main contribution is an analysis of the art of storytelling, differentiating between three forms, the impersonal, personal, and rhythmical ways of relating a story. The last is built up on the principal of repetition and rhythmical rules for the form of the folktale, not to be confused with the epic rules. He argued that folktales must be studied in living tradition, and ended his analysis with a study of the repertoire of a storyteller (Berge 1924). Bjarne Hodne (1979) studied the storytellers in a community of Telemark, and Ørnulf Hodne (1979) the storytellers of Jørgen Moe, and both have analysed individual repertoires and their methods of transmission. The present author has made a survey of storytellers in Setesdal, showing how they were related and from whom they had learned their tales (Kvideland 1989).

After Olrik's death in 1917 very little folktale research took place in Denmark. The iranologist Arthur Christensen was an international expert on 'numskull' stories, and published studies of Danish material in 1939 and 1941. An institute for folktale research planned in the 1930s was never realised, but the idea was revived after the Second World War. According to a plan sketched by Paul Delarue, international centres for folktale research would be set up in Paris, Berlin/ Marburg, and Copenhagen, and the Copenhagen centre would be responsible for material from Asia and the Nordic countries, but this was never fully carried out. Laurits Bødker made an index of Indian Animal Tales (1957), and a scholarly edition appeared of the first Danish translation of *Pañcatantra* (Bødker 1951–3). Later a Nordic Institute of Folklore was founded with Laurits Bødker as Director, and he published scholarly editions of the Danish collections of N. Christensen and N. Levinsen, and a dictionary of folk literature (1965), but his work on E. T. Kristensen's storytellers was never finished.

Bengt Holbek carried on the study of the folktale in Denmark, and became famous for his *Interpretation of Fairy Tales* in 1987, basing his work on tales recorded orally. He wanted to break the code of the magic tales, and combined structural, Jungian and Freudian models in order to demonstrate the relationship between the life conditions of the storytellers and the content of the tales. His analysis shows in a convincing way that the main theme in these tales is the conflict between poor and rich, young and old. The poor and the young are in conflict with the old and rich and take over their positions. The sudden death of Holbek in 1992 was a great loss to folktale studies.

In Sweden Carl Wilhelm von Sydow was the leading scholar working on folktales. He used the historical-geographical method in his first work on AT 500 and 501, 'The Spinning Women', but further studies based on historical sources and the biology of the folktale led him to the conclusion that the folktale is a heritage of the Indo-past. He criticised the migration theory formulated by the Finnish school as too mechanistic, since folktales have been disseminated by individual storytellers and cannot be seen as a stream of tradition (von Sydow 1948: 11–43). This led him to the idea of ecotypes developing by isolation in a certain area, a theory strongly opposed by scholars of the Finnish school such as Liungman, but still used in modified form in the study of folktales (Ballard 1983; Hasan-Rokem 2000). Von Sydow found the terminology used by folklorists mechanistic and arbitrary, and for many years struggled to establish a system for categorising oral poetry in analogy with scientific systems together with an internationally understandable and acceptable terminology. He never tested this out, however, and as it was continually modified and extended it became increasingly confused. His greatest merit is that he put the question of terminology on the agenda, and some of his terms have won international acceptance; his students have continued to redefine them and some, like the *memorat*, are used today with different meanings. He was an excellent teacher, inspiring many of his students to write doctoral theses, several on folktales.[5]

Anna Birgitta Rooth produced several works on folktales, including *The Cinderella Cycle* (1951), and a study of storytelling in Northern Alaska (1976), as well as another on tales of lying (1983).[6] Åsa Nyman, who worked at the Uppsala Folklore Archive, has written on Swedish and Faroese storytellers, and compiled an index of Faroese tales (1984). Further work was done on indexes: Svend Grundtvig produced the first draft of an index of folktales taken up by Antti Aarne, and R. Th. Christiansen's Norwegian Index of 1921 was revised and enlarged by Ørnulf Hodne in 1984. Liungman has given a table of variants of five hundred types in the supplementary volume of his edition of folktales (unfortunately omitted in the German edition of 1961), and Margit Brandt edited an index of E. T. Kristensen's collection of folktales in 1974. The Norwegian corpus amounts to about 4200 variants of 450 types, and 270 types outside the AT list, including 105 fairy tales (tales of magic) with 1660 variants. Kurt Schier estimates the number of Swedish folktales as 9,700 variants of 640 types, and 2,100 variants and 130 types out of these can be classified as fairy tales. The Danish corpus is more difficult to estimate, as there is no Danish index except the one covering the collection of E. T. Kristensen (Brandt 1974). Bengt Holbek (1990: 260f.) suggests between six and ten

[5] Examples are: H. Holmström (1919) on AT 400 ('The Swan Maiden'); W. Liungman (1925) on AT 870 ('The Princess confined in the Mound'); S. Liljeblad (1927) on AT 505–8 ('The Grateful Dead'); A. B. Rooth (1951) on AT 510 ('Cinderella'); J.-Ö. Swahn (1955) on AT 425, 428 ('Cupid and Psyche').

[6] Some of her students have written doctoral theses on folktales, such as P. Peterson (1981) on AT 60 ('The Fox and the Crane Invite Each Other').

thousand variants, according to how many types of jokes, anecdotes, formula tales and versified tales are included.

It is difficult to characterise the style of folktales in the different regions of Scandinavia, since most collectors and editors translated the tales into a written and literary language. They were influenced by the Grimm brothers and by the most prominent national editors such as Asbjørnsen and Moe, and would often combine two or more texts to produce a longer story that was coherent with the literary taste. It is also difficult to distinguish between regional and individual characteristics.

In all the Scandinavian countries, however, the environment influences the folktales. Those of the coastal areas are coloured by the sea and maritime culture, and the inland areas by agriculture and forestry. Kurt Schier (1971) suggests cautiously that in Sweden the tales from Västergötaland are perhaps more realistic, and those from Gotland more fantastic and colourful than other Swedish tales. My impression is that the folktales of the eastern regions of Norway are told in a broader epic style, while in Telemark and Setesdal many storytellers consciously cultivated storytelling as a verbal art. The tales of the Trøndelag regions are shorter and told in a concise way, and those of northern Norway are more novelistic and realistic. This is indicated in the opening of the tales. One from northern Norway begins: 'Hans from Trondheim once went to New York – Hans stayed at home in Norway for a while and then he returned to America', and another: 'Henry the shoemaker was born in Norway, but how it happened or not, he roamed round for so long that he came to Russia.' It must be remembered that northern Norwegians maintained lively trade connections with northern Russia, and if they had not been to America themselves, relatives might have been or were still there.

Most collectors never mention the storytellers. The tales were looked on as collective tradition and the teller was just the person who happened to tell them. Only when they encountered extraordinary storytellers or those with physical handicaps did they describe them. Some tellers, however, were great artists in oral performance. Two examples should be sufficient to illustrate two main points: the storytellers' ability to make the listeners believe in their stories, and their ability to act out their tales (Krogvig 1920: 305):

It was as if each folk tale was a link in a row of personal experiences . . . it seemed to stand out so vividly and tangibly in her thoughts that I would not have been surprised if a listener had asked her if she remembered how the princess was dressed on that occasion, or why she had not warned the Ash-lad when the princess stole his fork.

When Jørgen Moe met a great storyteller in Telemark, he describes his acting powers (Moe 1877: 191):

One cannot say that he told his stories, because he played them; his whole body from head to toe was telling them. And when he came to the sequence where the Ash-lad had won the princess, and all the wedding guests laughed and enjoyed themselves, he danced the closing formula: 'Snipp, snapp, snute', in the steps of an old roundel.

The scattered information on the Scandinavian storytellers has never been put together and analysed. The most important contribution is Bengt Holbek's analysis of the Jutland storytellers of the nineteenth century and their repertoires. Here he shows that they have a common grammar of the folktale, but also a certain freedom to select their repertoires and to develop a personal style coloured by the living conditions and character of the individual storyteller (Holbek 1987: 140–83 and *passim*).

The indexes give some indication of the most popular tales. More than fifty variants of the following types appear:

Denmark: 'The Dragon-Slayer' (AT 300), 'The Three Stolen Princessses' (AT 301), 'The Youth who wanted to learn what Fear is' (AT 326), 'The Man on a Quest for his Lost Wife' (AT 400).

Norway: 'The Dragon-Slayer' (AT 300), 'The Three Stolen Princesses' (AT 301), 'The Twins or Blood Brothers' (AT 303), 'Rescue by the Sister' (AT 311), 'The Girl as Helper in the Hero's Flight' (AT 313), ''The Man on a Quest for his Lost Wife' (AT 400), 'The Search for the Lost Husband' (AT 425), 'The Kind and the Unkind Girls' (AT 480), 'Cinderella' (AT 510A&B), 'Strong John' (AT 650A).

Sweden: 'The Three Stolen Princesses' (AT 301), 'The Kind and the Unkind Girls' (AT 480), 'Cinderella' (AT 510), 'The Devil's Riddle' (AT 812).

This list has no claim to completeness, and could indicate tales specially requested by the collectors. However the tales given here are among the most popular of the international fairy tales.

References

Almqvist, B. (1991), 'The Uglier Foot', in *Viking Ale: Studies on Folklore Contacts between the Northern and Western Worlds*, ed. E. N. Dhuibhne-Almqvist and S. Ó Caitháin, 82–113. Aberystwyth.

Andersen, L. (1923), *Folkeeventyr indsamlede i Ods Herred*. Copenhagen.

Asbjørnsen, P. C., and Moe, J. (1843–4/1852), *Norske Folkeeventyr*. Christiania.

Ballard, L.-M. (1983), 'The Formulation of the Oicotype: A Case Study', *Fabula* 24, 233–45.

Berge, R. (1924), *Norsk sogukunst*. Kristiania.

Bergvall, F. (1991), *Sagor från Edsele*, ed. and comm. Å. Nyman and K.-H. Dahlstedt. Dialekt- och folkminnesarkivet i Uppsala. B 20. Uppsala.

Bjersby, R. (1964), *Traditionsbärare på Gotland vid 1800-talets mitt. En undersökning rörande P. A. Säves sagesmän*. Dialekt- och folkminnesarkivet i Uppsala. B 11. Uppsala.

Bødker, L. (1959), 'Eventyr', in *Kulturhistorisk leksikon for nordisk middelalder*, vol. 4, 71–6. Oslo.

—— (1964), *Dänische Volksmärchen*. Märchen der Weltliteratur. Düsseldorf/Cologne.

—— (1965), *Folk Literature (Germanic)*, International Dictionary of Regional European Ethnology and Folklore, vol. 2. Copenhagen.

Bondeson, A. (1886), *Historiegubbar på Dal*. Stockholm.

Brandt, M. (1974), *Registrant over Evald Tang Kristensens samling af eventyr*. Dansk folkemindesamlings katalog 7, NIF rapporter 1. Copenhagen/Turku.

Braset, K. (1910a) *Hollraøventyra. Svanøvenyra*. Sparbu.

—— (1910b) *Øventyr. Sagn.* Sparbu.

Christensen, A. (1939), 'Molboernes vise gjerninger', *Danmarks folkeminder* 47. Copenhagen.

—— (1941), 'Dumme folk', *Danmarks folkeminder* 50. Copenhagen.

Christensen, N. (1963–7), 'Folkeeventyr fra Kær Herred', *Danmarks folkeminder* 73.

Christiansen, R. Th. (1910), 'Die Schwalbe', *Finno-ugrische Forschungen* 10, 127–53.

—— (1916), *The Two Travellers or the Blinded Man.* FFC 24. Helsinki.

—— (1931), 'Bodach an t-Sílein', *Béaloideas* 3, 107–20 (in English).

—— (1957), 'The Sisters and the Troll', in *Studies in Folklore in Honor of Distinguished Service Professor Stith Thompson*, ed. R. W. Edson. Folklore Studies 9. Bloomington.

Hannaas, T. (1927/1989), *Sogur frå Sætesdal sagde av Olav Eivindsson Austad.* Oslo.

Hasan-Rokem, G. (2000), 'Ökotyp', in *Enzyklopädie des Märchens* 10, 258–63. Berlin.

Hodne, B. (1979), *Eventyret og tradisjonsbærerne: eventyrfortellere i en Telemarksbygd.* Oslo.

Hodne, Ø. (1979), *Jørgen Moe og folkeeventyrene.* Oslo.

—— (1984), *The Types of the Norwegian Folktale.* Inst. for sammenlignende kulturforskning B 68. Oslo.

Høgset, O. (1977) ed., *Erotiske folkeeventyr.* Oslo.

Holbek, B. (1981), 'Dänemark', in *Enzyklopädie des Märchens* 3, 273–84. Berlin

—— (1987), *Interpretation of Fairy Tales: Danish Folklore in a European Perspective.* FFC 239. Helsinki.

Holbek, B. (1990), *Dänische Volksmärchen.* Berlin.

Holmström, H. (1919), *Studier över Svanjungfrumotivet.* Malmö.

Hyltén-Cavallius, G. O., and Stephens, G. (1844–9), *Svenska folk-sagor och äfventyr.* Stockholm.

af Klintberg, B. (1999), 'Meeting the Storyteller', in *All the World's Reward: Folktales Told by Five Scandinavian Storytellers*, ed. R. Kvideland, H. K. Sehmsdorf , 203–14. Seattle.

Krogvig, A. (1920), 'Tre breve fra tegneren August Schneider til P. C. Asbjørnsen', *Edda* 13, 302–10.

Kuhre, J. P. (1938), 'Borrinjholmska Sansâger', *Danmarks folkeminder* 45. Copenhagen.

Kvideland, R. (1989), 'Olav Eivindsson Austad', in Hannaas 1989, 121–58.

Levinsen, N. (1958), 'Folkeeventyr fra Vendsyssel', *Danmarks folkeminder* 68. Copenhagen.

Liljeblad, S. (1927), *Die Tobiasgeschichte und andere Märchen mit toten Helfern.* Lund.

Liungman, W. (1925), *En traditionsstudie över sagan om prinsessan i jordkulan.* Gothenburg.

—— (1949–52), *Sveriges samtliga sagor* 1–3. Stockholm; Djursholm.

—— (1961), *Die schwedischen Volksmärchen. Herkunft und Geschichte.* Berlin.

Moe, J. (1877), 'Til Tidemands "Eventyrfortellersken"', *Norske Folkelivs-Billeder* (1854), reproduced in *Samlede skrifter* vol. 2, 187–92. Christiania.

Mundal, E. (1997), 'Kong Harald hårfagre og samejenta Snøfrid', *Nordica Bergensia* 14, 39–53.

Nyman, Å. (1984), 'Faroese Folktale Tradition', in *The Northern and Western Isles in the Viking World*, ed. A. Fenton and H. Pálsson, 292–336. Edinburgh.

Olrik, A. (1892), 'Märchen in Saxo Grammaticus', *Zeitschrift für Volkskunde* 2, 117–23, 252–8, 367–74.

—— (1922/1992), 'Epic Laws of Folk Narrative', *Principles for Oral Narrative Research.* Bloomington.

Olsen, O. T. (1912/1987), *Norske folkeeventyr og sagn samlet i Nordland.* Kristiania.

Peterson, P. (1981), *Rävens och Tranans gästabud. En studie över en djurfabel i verbal och ikonografisk tradition.* Studia Ethnologica Upsaliensia 8. Uppsala.

Rockwell, J. (1982), *Evald Tang Kristensen. A Lifelong Adventure in Folklore.* Aalborg Studies in Folk Culture 5. Aalborg.

Rooth, A. B. (1951), *The Cinderella Cycle.* Lund.

——(1976), *The Importance of Storytelling: A Study Based on Fieldwork in Northern Alaska.* Studia Ethnologica Upsaliensia 1. Uppsala.

——(1983), *Från lögnsaga till paradis.* Studia Ethnologica Upsaliensia 12. Uppsala.

Säve, P. A. (1952–5), *Gotländska sagor,* ed. H. Gustavson. Svenska sagor och sägner 10. Uppsala.

Schier, K. (1971), *Schwedische Volksmärchen.* Märchen der Weltliteratur. Düsseldorf/ Cologne.

Schlauch, M. (1973), *Romance in Iceland.* New York.

Snorrason, Oddr (1932), *Saga Óláfs Tryggvassonar af Oddr Snorrason,* ed. Finnur Jónsson. Copenhagen

Sveinsson, E. Ól. (1929), *Verzeichnis isländischer Märchenvarianten.* FFC 83. Helsinki.

Sverris saga etter Cod. AM 327 4.°, ed. G. Indrebø. Den norske kildeskriftkommission. Kristiania.

Swahn, J.-Ö. (1955), *The Tale of Cupid and Psyche.* Lund.

——(1993), 'Märchenforschung in Skandinavien', in *Märchen und Märchenforschung in Europa,* ed. D. Röth, W. Kahn. Frankfurt.

von Sydow, C. W. (1909), *Två spinnsagor.* Svenska landsmål B 3. Stockholm.

——(1948), *Selected Papers on Folklore, Published on the Occasion of his 70th Birthday.* Copenhagen

Vang, A. E. (1850/1974), *Gamla reglo aa rispo ifraa Valdres.* Christiania/Oslo.

11

The Wonder Tale in Ireland

PATRICIA LYSAGHT

In early Ireland tales were told by official storytellers at great public assemblies and storytellers also provided entertainment in noble households. These were learned and, it would appear, professional storytellers, who were rewarded for their art, and mention is made of them in various contexts in early Irish literature. In the tragic story of 'The Exile of the Sons of Uisliu', for example, dating from about the beginning of the ninth century, such a storyteller (*scélaige*) is met with. He is Feidhlimid mac Daill, the father of Deirdre (of the Sorrows) and he is the storyteller of Conchobhar Mac Nessa, king of Ulster. The story implies that Feidhlimid is a man of substance and social standing as he is entertaining the king and his retinue in his house (Windisch 1880: I, 67, lines 2–3). Other storytellers are also glimpsed in medieval Irish literature, and extant tale-lists show that the professional activity of the *file* or learned poet included storytelling, and that his repertoire consisted of a large corpus of tales for narrating 'to kings, princes and noblemen' (Mac Cana 1980: 15–16, 137; Rees 1961: 16).

While the tales appearing in medieval Irish manuscripts are grouped by scholars according to cycles (Mythological Cycle, Ulster Cycle, Fenian Cycle), the classification of tales in these surviving tale-lists is according to subject matter (Mac Cana 1980: 33–131; Rees 1961: ch. X) as in a modern-day index of folktale types, and indeed several examples of international folktales, including 'Tales of Magic', listed by Antti Aarne and Stith Thompson in the international catalogue *The Types of the Folktale* (1961), are found in medieval Irish literature and will be dealt with below.

In ancient Ireland, as in the nineteenth and twentieth centuries, storytelling appears to have taken place at night-time and during the winter or dark half of the year. In a story probably composed in the eighth century, the learned poet Forgoll, who came on visitation to an Ulster king named Mongán mac Fiachna, is said to have recited a story each night to Mongán from *Samhain* to *Bealtaine*, that is, from Halloween to May Day, thus also indicating the extensiveness of the poet's repertoire (Rees 1961: Mac Cana 1980: 14–16), an assertion which was still made about some gifted storytellers in the Irish-speaking areas of Ireland in the last century (Delargy 1945/1969: 22; Zimmerman 2001: 458)

Storytelling, then, as a form of entertainment in aristocratic circles is attested in the Early Christian period in Ireland, and it retained that role in the houses of the great into the Early Modern period. In his *History of Ireland* (1571) the English historian Edmund Campion tells that in such houses there is a 'taleteller, who bringeth his Lord on sleepe with tales vaine and frivolous' (Mac Cana 1980: 13), and a lament for the Flight of the Earls O'Neill and O'Donnell from the province of Ulster in the early seventeenth century states that as a consequence of their departure there would be 'no relating of stories at sleeping time' (14). It is not clear which stories were told on such occasions, but it has been suggested that 'certain tales or certain types of tales were considered appropriate to particular occasions and circumstances' (24). The Rees brothers have conjectured that battle-tales were told before embarking on war, tales of wooings at weddings and so on (Rees 1961: 210–11). In the nineteenth and twentieth centuries also stories appropriate to the occasion were told at wakes, seasonal gatherings, holy wells, patterns, and at other social junctures.

Apart from the learned, professional storytellers of medieval Ireland, who were the recipients of patronage and reward, there were probably also less elite practitioners of the art, more akin perhaps to the ordinary storytellers of the nineteenth and twentieth centuries, who catered for a less privileged audience. There is, however, no direct or clear information about them or their repertoire, but it is possible to suppose that the existence of 'storytellers associated with privilege and learning exerted its own influence on the style and repertoire of less distinguished performers' (Mac Cana 1980: 7–8). It is not known how these 'more humble practitioners' of the art of storytelling fared after the break-up of the old Gaelic world consequent on sixteenth- and seventeenth-century conquest, land confiscation and colonisation.

What is evident is that the learned and privileged dimension of storytelling could survive only residually after that period because of the virtual destruction of the native landed nobility, and of the learned class as a distinct social stratum, to which they had dispensed patronage. But despite 'the ruin of the old system' scholars such as Séamus Ó Duilearga stressed the remarkable continuity in the Gaelic tradition from a medieval aristocratic culture. According to Ó Duilearga, the learned and literary men of medieval Ireland, forced by circumstances to live among the ordinary people, became mediators in the transmission of some of 'the literature of the upper classes and of the written tradition of the schools of native learning' to the peasantry, effecting an enrichment of their age-old treasury of oral lore – that 'ancient, orally preserved stock of West European tradition . . . as the two streams of tradition were joined' (Delargy 1945/1969: 3–4).[1] Elements of that old, learned tradition, such as hero tales and romances, historical tradition, genealogical and place-name lore, were considered to be still reflected in the oral tradition of much of Ireland until the mid-nineteenth century, only to be lost when the crisis of the Great Famine (1845–9) accelerated linguistic change from Irish to English in much of the country. Thereafter such traditions were to be sought in areas where the Irish language survived in parts of the west and south of Ireland. Delargy states that 'the loss of the language

---

[1] This postulated social descent of the literature and learning of the upper classes to the peasantry was not viewed as involving debasement but rather heroic preservation. The term *gesunkenes Kulturgut* was coined by Hans Nauman (1922) for cultural material originating in the upper stratum of society and passed on to, or adopted by, the lower stratum, the folk. See also Bausinger (1980).

over most of Ireland brought about the destruction of the oral literature enshrined in it, leaving a gap in our knowledge of Irish folk-lore which can never be filled' (1945/1969: 4).

As the Irish language was the principal medium of storytelling, the fundamental language shift from Irish to English in parts of the east, south-east and north of Ireland, and its gradual decline in much of the remainder of the country in the course of the nineteenth century,[2] also affected both the international and native *Märchen*. These long, multi-episodic tales flourished in the Irish language, while according to Seán Ó Súilleabháin, compiler with Reidar Th. Christiansen of *The Types of the Irish Folktale* (1963) (hereafter *TIF*),[3] comparatively few have been transmitted or preserved through the medium of English, though some excellent examples of wonder tales[4] told in the English language were collected in the 1930s and 1940s.

It was in the nineteenth century that significant interest in the legends and tales of the Irish people, inspired by what was happening in that regard in other countries, arose. For most of that century this activity was carried out in the English language, and it was essentially only in its last two decades that attention was focussed on the Gaelic oral tradition. The richness of this, and the very large corpus of international folktales which it incorporated, was highlighted with the publication of *A Handbook of Irish Folklore* (Ó Súilleabháin 1942), but it was not until *TIF* appeared in 1963 that the extent of the international folktale corpus in the Irish tradition became more fully apparent.

Before touching on the folktale, and on the wonder tale in particular, in Irish writing in English in the nineteenth and early twentieth centuries, it is of interest to review aspects of an important article by Brian Earls (1992–3: 93–144), concerning the use of oral narrative genres of various kinds, including the folktale, in popular prose fiction and poetry of this period. Printed folklore in the English language, appearing in compendia, fiction, travel guides, the periodic press, and in verse, was very popular in nineteenth-century Ireland. A number of reasons have been put forward by Earls to account for this situation. He stresses the impact of romanticism and the works of Sir Walter Scott, the influence of cultural naturalism, a desire by some to provide the poorer classes with alternative reading to chapbooks and ballads of various kinds, and especially the growth of popular literacy in the English language from the late eighteenth century. The latter development encouraged the rapid expansion of commercial publishers from the early decades of the nineteenth century to serve the growing demand for printed lore from general and elite readerships in Ireland.

---

[2] For the position of the Irish language in the seventeenth century see B. Ó Cuív (1951: 14–19). For its position around 1800 see S. de Fréine (1977), and at the end of the nineteenth century, de Fréine (1977: 86), Ó Cuív (1951: 19–27) whose appendix (77–94) and the accompanying maps show the relative density of Irish speakers for the period 1851–91. See also Hindley (1990).

[3] Seán Ó Súilleabháin was the former archivist of the Irish Folklore Commission (1935–71) and of the Department of Irish Folklore from 1971 until his retirement in 1974. See P. Lysaght (1998: 137–45 and 2000b: 442–6).

[4] In this study of Irish tales, the term 'wonder tales' is preferred to 'fairy tales', in order to avoid confusion with narratives of the fairy race, which are very common in Ireland.

Earls has shown that the legend was by far the most common genre used in nineteenth-century fiction and poetry in the English language, and he has characterised the employment 'of the material of the legend for literary purposes' as 'one of the major impulses in Irish writing from the early nineteenth century onwards'. Although he had dealt with only one category of legend – migratory legends of the supernatural – his index to various legends in this category of literature is ample proof of the prominence of the genre. Earls is probably right in suggesting that the legend was preferred to the 'longer and more abstract *Märchen*' because its 'comparative brevity suited the magazine format'. In contrast to wonder tales, for example, which were told mainly by specialists in particular contexts, legends were also more widely known and could be told by almost anyone in a range of situations, even as part of ordinary conversation (Earls 1992–3: 95–6). The adaptability of the legend to changing linguistic, social and cultural situations has also been amply demonstrated by their more successful transition from the Irish language into English, from rural to urban settings, and their translation into modern forms, than was possible for the more elaborate and highly stylised folktale.

Many of the nineteenth-century sources mentioned by Earls as containing legends or legend-based fiction also employ the material of folktale. Such print-based tales not directly transcribed from oral narration might be termed 'literary folktales' (cf. Earls's term 'literary legend', 1992–3: 95). Even before the Anglo-Irish antiquarian Crofton Croker published his various works on the south of Ireland, including an important volume of legends in 1825 and others in 1829 and 1831, a collection of popular tales or *Märchen* called *The Royal Hibernian Tales: Being a Collection of the Most Entertaining Stories Now Extant* had appeared. Probably of north Antrim provenance, it is listed among three hundred chapbooks of a secular nature in the *Reports of the Commissioners of the Board of Education in Ireland* in 1825. The collection has been reprinted in *Béaloideas* (1940: 148–203) with a commentary by Séamus Ó Duilearga. Containing twelve tales, one omitted as 'entirely worthless from a folkloristic standpoint' (*Béaloideas* 1940: 149), eleven have been classified as international types, of which three are wonder tales (*Béaloideas* 1940: 200–3). Its appeal and popularity are evident from the appearance of stories from it in W. M. Thackeray's *Irish Sketch Book* (1842), in W. B. Yeats's *Fairy and Folk Tales of the Irish Peasantry* (c.1888: 299–306), and in Andrew Lang's *The Red Fairy Book* (11th impression 1912: 54).[5] It also had a considerable impact on Irish oral tradition and this was still evident in the early 1940s (*Béaloideas* 1932: 340; 1940: 200–1).

Crofton Croker scarcely touched on wonder tales, while William Carleton (1794–1869), an Irish speaker, tradition-bearer and novelist from county Tyrone, included fictionalised versions of three wonder tales (see *TIF*) in his sketches of rural life in Ireland entitled *Traits and Stories of the Irish Peasantry* (1830, 1833). In Carleton's collection of short fiction, *Tubber Derg or The Red Well*, the final story entitled 'The Three Wishes: An Irish Legend' is a literary rendering of one of the most common tales in the Irish oral tradition, 'The Smith Outwits the Devil' (AT

---

[5] Ó Duilearga was of the opinion that a tale published by Joseph Jacobs, Editor of *Folk-Lore* (1892: 47), was derived from *The Royal Hibernian Tales* (*Béaloideas* 1940: 149).

330), which resembles the Faust story, and is also the basis of an Irish-language novel *Séadna*, by Canon Peter O'Leary (1839–1920) (Ó Laoghaire 1904), chief exponent and advocate of the use of the living Irish language and folklore for the new literature emerging in Irish in the early twentieth century.

The fictionalisation of folktales continued with the Dublin-born novelist Samuel Lover (1797–1868) whose *Legends and Stories of Ireland* includes a comic version of 'The Dragon Slayer' (AT 300) (O'Donoghue 1899: 134–50). The same was true of the Limerick writer Gerald Griffin (1803–40), in whose novel *The Collegians* (1829), a story related to the well-known international folktale 'The Youth Who Wanted to Learn What Fear Is' (AT 326) is incorporated.[6] This trend towards fictionalisation was continued by a Dublin bookseller and 'library-keeper' Patrick Kennedy (1801–73) who, in a variety of contributions in periodicals and the provincial press[7] and in a series of books from the middle of the nineteenth century, retold stories heard in his youth in his native place on the borders of counties Wexford and Carlow in the southeast of Ireland (Delaney 1964, 1983, 1988). Much of this material he adapted to the conventions of Victorian prose, and he incorporated a few international or closely related wonder tales into his literary descriptions of west-Wexford rural life and customs in *Legends of Mount Leinster* (1855) and *Evenings in the Duffrey* (1869).

Nevertheless Kennedy is an important figure in folktale reporting in Ireland at that time. His two volumes, *Legendary Fictions of the Irish Celts* (1866) and *The Fireside Stories of Ireland* (1870), which are the most significant in relation to international wonder tales in the English language in Ireland at that period, are also indicative of the linguistic shift from Irish in favour of English in nineteenth-century Wexford. In Kennedy's youth the change was becoming a reality in much of the county, where, by 1851, less than one per cent of the population were Irish speakers, although, as Kennedy acknowledges, Irish was still generally spoken at the time among the older people in the parish of Killegny where he spent his formative years (Ó Cuív 1951: 23, 81). Yet it would appear that 'his knowledge of Irish was limited to a few words and phrases that were current in the English spoken in his district in his day' (Delaney 1983: 64), and his attempts to provide Irish language versions of words and phrases is not always satisfactory. Kennedy's folk narrative compilations thus reflect the transitional linguistic situation as tales and legends once told in the Irish language were crossing over into English.

The effect of this language shift on the first generation of storytellers in the English language is reflected in Kennedy's tendency often to explain anglicised forms of Irish words or dialect terms in the text itself, and to add a glossary of such terms to the respective volumes. Kennedy's awareness of the effects of the language change on the narration of different genres of folk narrative is also well illustrated in the case of one of his main narrators, Jemmy Reddy, mentioned again below. Reddy knew Fianna lore: stories of Fionn Mac Cumhail, his son

---

[6] See *TIF*. A reference in *TIF* to a version of AT 449, 'The Tsar's Dog', is unclear.
[7] Patrick Kennedy wrote for the *Dublin University Magazine*, the editor of which was his friend, the novelist Joseph Sheridan Le Fanu, during the period 1861–9 (Kennedy 1870: ix–x), *Duffy's Fireside Magazine*, and the *Wexford Independent*.

Oisín and other members of a warrior band whose exploits have delighted Irish literary and folk audiences for over a thousand years (Nagy 1985). Transmitted down the centuries through the medium of the Irish language and best preserved in those areas where that language remained vigorous, they were not so numerous in Kennedy's part of county Wexford in his youth, and the change over into the English language had adversely affected their aesthetic quality. He states (1866: 202–3):

> Of the numerous Ossianic legends found among the Irish-speaking people of The west and south, there were but two or three current in the north-west part of Wexford in the early part of this century, though the elders of families among farmers and peasants all spoke, or at least understood Irish. Jemmy Reddy . . . is our warrant for these also.

He then gives two Fianna stories in Reddy's colloquial style of English, and it is evident that the narrrator had some difficulties with both the English and the Irish languages. Kennedy's comment on this is followed by a shrewd observation about favourable parental attitudes to English (as the language of prestige and power) in the nineteenth century, when some children were even punished for speaking Irish (1866: 208–9):[8]

> The admirers of our Ossianic relics will give anything but a hearty welcome to these disfigurations of the brave old bard. But let them not blame poor Reddy too much. He understood Irish, for his father and mother spoke it pretty fluently, but they would not suffer their children to speak it. They got them taught to spell and read English, and would not allow of anything that might tend to counteract their studies. Some few of the native poetic beauties would flash out here and there, but they were stifled in the colloquial style natural to the storyteller.

Legendary Fictions was an innovative work, arranged thematically and incorporating 'household tales', in addition to supernatural legends, Ossianic and mythological narratives and hagiographical lore. Kennedy's designation of the section on international folktales as 'Household Tales' points to knowledge of the *Kinder- und Hausmärchen* of the Brothers Grimm. Indeed, familiarity not only with the Grimms' work, but also with the Norwegian collection of wonder tales by Asbjørnsen and Moe (1843), translated by Dasent in 1858, and John Francis Campbell's four-volume collection of Scottish Gaelic tales with English translations, *Popular Tales of the West Highlands* (1860–2), among other works, is evident in his comparative comments scattered through the volume. An awareness of scientific requirements in relation to faithfulness to the narrator's words and declaration of sources are also indicated, but these were not met in many cases, as will appear below.

[8] This attitude, and the use of a tally or score stick (*bata scóir*) to keep children in Irish-speaking areas from talking in Irish was highlighted by Douglas Hyde among others. It was a stick tied round a child's neck and notched or scored every time he or she spoke Irish. The child was slapped by the teacher, often a non-speaker of Irish, in proportion to the number of notches. See B. Ó Conaire (1986), S. Ó Súilleabháin (1940), also *IFC* 1318: 124, in which a man born in 1873 in Co. Galway states that he was once slapped three times in Cornamona school for speaking Irish.

A survey of *The Types of the Folktale* reveals that *Legendary Fictions* contains over a dozen wonder tales. Notable absences are 'The Smith Outwits the Devil' (AT 330) and 'Cinderella' (AT 510 A). It is not possible here to deal with each tale individually, but it is evident from *TIF* that most of them were tales still commonly told in the Irish language in the early decades of the twentieth century.

Kennedy's method of commentary on the tales was sometimes to insert comparative narratives, or learned, and at times, moralising comments between the various stories, including on occasion the name or initials and occupation of his sources, and details of the chain of transmission of the tale. The following is an example of these tendencies. In his preface to the wonder tale entitled 'Aventures of Gilla na Chrech An Gour' (*recte* Adventures of *Giolla an Chroicinn Gabhair* / 'The Adventures of the Fellow with the Goatskin') AT 571 (+650), he states (1866: 22–3):

> We heard the following household narrative only once. The narrator, Jemmy Reddy, was a young lad whose father's garden was on the line between the rented land of Ballygibbon, and the Common of the White Mountain (the boundary between Wexford and Carlow counties), consequently on the very verge of civilisation. He was gardener, ploughman, and horseboy to the Rev. Mr M[urphy] of Coolbawn, at the time of the learning of this tale. We had once the misfortune to be at a wake, when the adventures of another fellow with a goat-skin, not at all decent, were told by a boy [bachelor] with a bald head, rapidly approaching his eightieth year. Jimmy Reddy's story has nothing in common with it but the name. We recognised the other in Mr Campbell's 'Tales of the West Highlands', very much disguised; but, even in that tolerably decent garb, not worth preserving. The following avowal is made with some reluctance. Forty or fifty years since, some very vile tales – as vile as could be found in the 'Fabliaux' or the 'Decameron', or any other dirty collection, had a limited circulation among farm servants and labourers, even in the respectable county of Wexford. It was one of those that poor old T. L. told. Let us hope that it has vanished from the collections still extant in our own counties of the Pale.[9]

Kennedy left his native Wexford for Dublin in 1822, where he remained for the rest of his life. He was relying for the most part on his memory of stories heard more than forty-four years previously. The following comment by Kennedy in relation to another story told by Reddy probably reflects his *modus operandi* in his presentation of the tales' (1866: 43):

> Jimmy Reddy, Father Murphy's servant . . . told it to the occupants of the big kitchen hearth in Coolbawn, one long winter evening, nearly in the style in which it is here given, and no liberty at all has been taken with the incidents.

And referring to another narrator, Owen Jourdan, whom he describes as 'a genuine storytelling genius', be states (1866: 247–8):

---

[9] Ireland was a lordship of the English crown from the twelfth-century Anglo-Norman invasion but effective control pertained only in a limited area centred on Dublin, known as the Pale. For a map showing this and the great Gaelic and Norman lordships about 1500, see Moody and Martin (1994: 173).

We have endeavoured to retain his style of narrative, but alas! It is more than thirty years since we sat near his throne, viz., the big kitchen griddle in Tombrick.

The Fireside Stories of Ireland contain a further fourteen wonder tales. Commenting on his sources, form and style he says (Kennedy 1870: 2):

Such as they are, they may be received by our readers as obtained from *bona fide* oral sources. No changes have been made in them by us except where decency required, and they are given in as near an approach to the garb as well as the spirit of the originals as could be furnished by one to the manner born, and to whom, when young, fireside stories were as necessary as daily food and the healthy air from the neighbouring hills.

He also states that he has endeavoured to present the stories 'in a form suitable for the perusal of both sexes and of all ages' (1870: viii). His moralising tendencies evident in the above quotations have also been noted by Earls in relation to fairylore (1992–3: 103–4). Thus in the words of Douglas Hyde (1890: xii): 'We cannot be sure how much belongs to Kennedy the bookseller, and how much to the Wexford peasant'. Nevertheless, Hyde gave guarded praise to Kennedy's work, stating that he himself had heard 'in the adjoining county Wicklow' versions of two folktales collected by Kennedy in Wexford, and 'they did not differ very widely from Kennedy's' (Hyde 1890: xi). Hyde also sought to explain the persistence of Irish-language folktales in English in some eastern counties of Ireland bordering on the Pale, the sphere of English power centred on the capital Dublin (1890: xi–xii):

It is interesting to note that these counties, close to the Pale as they are, and under English influence for so long, nevertheless seem to have preserved a considerable share of the old Gaelic folk-tales in English dress . . . The reason why some of the folk-stories survive in the eastern counties is probably because the Irish language was there exchanged for English at a time when, for want of education and printed books, folk-stories (the only mental recreation of the people) *had* to transfer themselves rightly or wrongly into English. When this first took place I cannot tell, but I have heard from old people in Waterford, that when some of their fathers or grandfathers marched north to join the Wexford Irish in '98 [1798 Rebellion], they were astonished to find English nearly universally used amongst them.

Kennedy comments knowledgeably on the social function of storytelling, remarking that good storytellers are relatively few in number in any neighbourhood, and that such competent narrators are necessary for the survival of the tales. He also feared the impact of growing literacy in the English language on oral narratives, stating that 'easy access to cheap books, and the diffusion of the penny literature' was giving 'a death-blow to the oral literature of the fireside' (Kennedy 1870: vii–viii; cf. Ó Ciosáin 1977). In the Irish-speaking areas it was the decline of the language which was seen as sounding the death-knell of the narratives, especially of the long folktales.

Kennedy did not name his sources in this volume, but it is probable that they were mainly those represented in *Legendary Fictions*. Instead of inserting commentary between the stories as in the previous volume, he added a learned 'Notes and Illustrations' section in which he compared the Wexford tales with those from many cultures (Kennedy 1870: 163–71). He obviously had a command of the German language and gave references to collections of German, Hindoo, Hungarian, Italian, Polish, Russian, Scandinavian and Wendish tales (1870: 171–2). He also provided a glossary of words and terms which might prove difficult for the reader (1870: 173–4).

Patrick Kennedy was conscious of the wealth of Irish language traditions beyond his reach as he laboured in 'the comparatively barren field of a semi-English county', and stated in his introduction to *Fireside Stories* that he would rejoice 'to hear of someone gathering from a fertile district where the native tongue is still spoken, a harvest of stories racy of the Gaelic idiom' (1870: 2). His wish was to be granted in the course of the next two decades.

In 1871 an American anthropologist and linguist from Milwaukee, Wisconsin, named Jeremiah Curtin, who had an interest in myths and folklore, visited Ireland for the first time. He came again in 1872, but it was between 1887 and 1893 that he made a series of important collecting trips to Irish-speaking areas in counties Kerry, Galway and Donegal. Of Irish-speaking parents, he had acquired some knowledge of Irish, but needed the services of an interpreter while collecting, and the tales and legends which he recorded were published in English. His collecting methods have come under some unfavourable scrutiny in recent years, and his omission of the provenance of material in his initial publications has also been noted (Dunlevy 1980–1).

Curtin's visits resulted in the publication of three volumes of tales in the 1890s which provided a wealth of *Märchen*, many of which are among the most popular tales recorded from Irish oral tradition. These volumes were *Myths and Folklore of Ireland* (1890), *Hero-Tales of Ireland* (1894) and *Tales of the Fairies and of the Ghost World Collected from Oral Traditon in South-West Munster* (1895). In 1943 sixteen narratives, eleven of them wonder tales, which had originally appeared in the New York newspaper *The Sun* during the years 1892–3, were reprinted by the Folklore of Ireland Society under the title *Irish Folk-Tales* (Ó Duilearga 1943).

Further interest in recording folk narratives in the Irish language, but still publishing them in English translation, was shown by William Larminie (1849–1900), a native of county Mayo. His anthology of eighteen traditional narratives, *West Irish Folktales and Romances*, in which ten wonder-tale types are represented, appeared in 1893. With an eye to scientific requirements Larminie states in his Introduction that the tales were collected 'word for word from the dictation of the peasant narrators' during fieldwork begun as early as 1884, in the Irish-speaking areas of counties Galway, Mayo and Donegal. He names his informants and describes in general terms the varied situations in which the stories were written down. None of these appears to have been a formal storytelling occasion in the presence of narrator and audience.

An important cultural movement in the English language starting about the last decade of the nineteenth century, the so-called Anglo-Irish literary revival (1890–c.1922) (Welch 1996), was led by the poet William Butler Yeats (1865–1939), and Lady Isabella Augusta Perse Gregory (1852–1932), a member of the

Anglo-Irish aristocracy and mistress of Coole, a country estate in the barony of Kiltartan, Co. Galway, was a central figure. Both collected folklore, and produced works based on folk tradition and myth. Though they were especially interested in folk beliefs and legends, a number of *Märchen*, including tales of magic, also appear in their work, particularly in Lady Gregory's *Poets and Dreamers* (1903) and the *Kiltartan Wonder Book* (1910). While she was able to read and translate from Irish, Lady Gregory required, on her own admission, the services of an interpreter when collecting from Irish-speaking informants, and while she did not always adhere to strict editorial standards for folklore 'texts', her work remains reasonably close in content to the folk tradition (Lysaght 1999a: 65–7).

Another member of the literary revival movement, John Millington Synge (1871–1909), the Dublin playwright, visited the Aran Islands between 1898 and 1902 to learn spoken Irish, and collected material for his book *The Aran Islands* (1906). Five folktales are incorporated in the volume, including three wonder tales.

The formative recognition of the Irish-language, folk-narrative inheritance highlighted by Jeremiah Curtin and William Larminie, who nevertheless published their collections in English, was first afforded by Douglas Hyde, who spearheaded the movement for the revival of the Irish language, the Gaelic League (*Conradh na Gaeilge*), 1893,[10] a movement which directed attention to the living language and oral culture of Irish-speaking areas of Ireland. From the end of the nineteenth century until well into the twentieth, a variety of Irish-language journals and periodicals from the four provinces of Ireland, including the Gaelic League's *Irisleabhar na Gaedhilge/Gaelic Journal* and *An Claidheamh Soluis* ('The Sword of Light'), played a substantial role in the publication of folktales, including wonder tales (*TIF* 22–6).

Hyde himself collected various genres of folk narrative in the Irish language in his native Connacht, especially the folktales still remembered, though no longer performed for entertainment purposes, in the countryside.[11] *Märchen* of various kinds also appear in the Proceedings of the Oireachtas (*Imtheachtaí an Oireachtais*), a cultural festival held annually by the Gaelic League since 1897 to celebrate and promote the language and culture of the remaining Irish-speaking areas of Ireland, and in which competitive storytelling was a central element (Welch 1996: 441). Some of these were edited by Hyde, such as *Trí Sgéalta* ('Three Stories') (1905). Hyde continued to publish his collections of folktales into the twentieth century: *Ocht Sgéalta ó Choillte Mághach* ('Eight Stories from Kiltymagh'), which appeared in 1936, and *Scéalta Thomáis Uí Chathasaigh / Mayo*

[10] S. Ó Tuama (1972); see also P. Mac Aonghusa (1993); de híde (1937); Welch (1996: 208–9).

[11] These appeared in a variety of publications, the most comprehensive of which are: *Leabhar Sgeulaigheachta* ('A Book of Stories'), the first collection of folktales in the Irish language; and *Beside the Fire. A Collection of Irish Gaelic Folk Stories* (1890), in which he reviewed the work of his predecessors and the state of, and attitudes to, the Irish language (xli–xlxx): six of the fourteen tales in this volume are in the Irish language with translations into English on the facing page, and the remainder are in English. A companion volume *Cois na Teineadh* appeared in 1892, while the large and important *Märchen*-collection *An Sgeuluidhe Gaodhalach* ('The Gaelic Storyteller'), published initially with French translations by Georges Dottin in *Annales de Bretagne*, vols. 10–18 (1895–1901), was republished in book form in 1901.

Stories told by Thomas Casey (1939) represent the repertoire of a male storyteller.[12] There are around seventy wonder tales in Hyde's published collections.

Interest in the Celtic languages, generated by the rise of European philology in the latter half of the nineteenth century, brought scholars of medieval Irish to the west of Ireland, including the Aran and Blasket Islands, to learn the modern language and, as part of the learning process, they collected folklore, including wonder tales. Some or all of these collections were later published (see below). The 'Gaelicisation' policy of the new Irish State after 1922, influenced by the Gaelic League, and the sense of patriotism among the Irish people of the time, brought growing numbers of students to the west of Ireland to study modern Irish, some of whom also collected folklore and became leaders of the folklore movement in the second decade of the twentieth century. One such person was Séamus Ó Duilearga, who visited south-west Kerry to learn the Irish language and collected the repertoire of Seán Ó Conaill (1853–1931) at intervals from 1923 to 1931. This material he subsequently edited for publication in 1948.

Interest in culture contact and comparative folklore studies in north-western Europe brought Scandinavian scholars to Ireland in the 1920s to learn the Irish language. Reidar Th. Christiansen (1886–1971), then Archivist of the Norwegian Folklore Institute, came in 1921 to west Kerry (Ó Duilearga 1973: 345) and, together with Carl W. von Sydow (1878–1952), University of Lund, who also learned modern Irish and published a Swedish translation of the novel *Séadna* in 1921, greatly encouraged and supported the setting up of structures in Ireland for the collection and study of Irish folklore, which essentially began with the foundation of *An Cumann le Béaloideas Éireann* / The Folklore of Ireland Society in 1927, and the publication of its journal *Béaloideas* (Lysaght 1993, 52, 60–1; 2000a). Von Sydow's formulation of ideas on the spread of folk tradition in a lecture delivered in 1931,[13] and on 'Geography and Folk-Tale Ecotypes' (1934: 344–55; 1948: 44–59) were influenced by his knowledge of dissemination processes and geographical characteristics of the folktale in Ireland. Christiansen's contribution, in terms of classification and comparative studies, was enormous.

The Celtic scholar Kenneth Jackson (1900–91), who visited the great Blasket Island between 1932 and 1937 to learn Modern Irish, also collected tales, including five wonder tales (Jackson 1934: 301–6; 1938: nos. 1,2,35). His understanding of the aesthetics of traditional storytelling in Ireland, and of the Irish storytelling repertoire, including wonder tales, is evident in the Gregynog Lectures, published as *The International Popular Tale and Early Welsh Tradition* (1961).

The founding of the Folklore of Ireland Society in 1927 was the first major step towards the provision of institutional structures for the recording and study of Irish folklore. This had profound implications for the recording of folktales. The success of the Society especially in attracting existing collections of folklore in private possession led to the establishment of the Irish Folklore Institute

---

[12] P. Lysaght (1990: 1429–31); cf. *TIF* 14, and a list of Hyde's various publications in Dunlevy (1991).
[13] Paper read at the Nordiska Historikermötet i Helsingfors 1931. Republished in C. W von Sydow (1948: 11–42), trans. from 'Om traditionsspridning', *Scandia* V, 1932.

(1930–5), which engaged in significant collecting and published three important volumes of tales and legends in the Irish language, each of which contained wonder tales.[14] The State-sponsored Irish Folklore Commission, with Duilearga as its Honorary Director, was the premier Irish folklore institution from 1935–71, when the Department of Irish Folklore, which incorporated the Commission, was established in University College Dublin.

The appointment of collectors to record oral tradition mainly in the remaining Irish-speaking areas of the country, especially from elderly speakers, as Ó Duilearga had already done in counties Kerry and Clare from the 1920s, ensured that a very rich harvest of folktales was reaped. Although Ó Duilearga advised in an editorial in the first issue of Béaloideas (1928: 416–17) that 'shorter tales and anecdotes' should also be recorded, the long traditional folktales were still very high on the agenda of the first handbook of Irish folklore issued in Irish in 1937 (Láimh-leabhar Béaloideasa) which was prepared by Seán Ó Súilleabháin for the field collectors. He points out that no references to Irish folktales had appeared in Aarne and Thompson's The Types of the Folktale (1928), and adds that it was the responsibility of the collector to record accurately every type of tale, or even parts of tales, which he heard. He gave instructions on the contextual information to be recorded, such as biographical details of the storyteller, including social background and the degree of literacy which he and his informants enjoyed, the chain of transmission of stories, the manner of performance, the audience, the institution of storytelling, and well-known storytellers both male and female (Ó Súilleabháin 1937: 84–7).[15]

In 1942 an enlarged edition of the Láimh-leabhar in English appeared, entitled A Handbook of Irish Folklore. This volume was, at once, an outline of the general types of material already collected under the auspices of the Irish Folklore Commission, a guide for its field collectors, and a key to the indexing system for the Irish Folklore Collections. It also included summaries of about three hundred international folktales which had been found in Ireland up to that time, classified according to the international folklore register (Ó Súilleabháin 1942: 557–8).

Two further guides for collecting folklore appeared in the 1930s. These were aimed at teachers and children in primary schools whose assistance in collecting folklore was enlisted through the schools' collection scheme in 1937–8, One booklet entitled National Tradition and Folklore (1934), issued by the Department of Education to the primary schools, contained, in addition to a list of seventy topics to aid the teacher in organising the compilation of local traditions by the children, an almost equally extensive section entitled 'Folk Tales. Classified

---

[14] É. Ó Tuathail (1932), a northern collection of tales from county Tyrone; Ó Siochfhradha (1932), a miscellany of Munster material in the south-west; and Hyde (1933), representing mainly Connacht in the west. For the enumeration of wonder tales in these collections see TIF.

[15] To assist the collectors in this task he provided summaries of two hundred tales with their AT numbers. He also introduced tales found in Ireland but not listed in the AT catalogue which collectors should seek out and record (Ó Súilleabháin 1937: 84–113). He also included summaries of humorous stories, religious tales, native hero tales, Fianna narratives and other minor narrative forms.

According to Subject'. The guide for the schoolchildren themselves had no such section.

The schoolchildren made a significant contribution to the recording of folktales from adults in their communities, and thus also to our knowledge of the variety, frequency and distribution patterns of different folklore types in Ireland, especially in the English-language parts of the country where the Commission's full-time collectors rarely worked at that time. As to wonder tales, they recorded versions of most of the types listed in *TIF*, and their work underlined the popularity of such tales as 'The Dragon Slayer' (AT 300), 'The Smith Outwits the Devil' (AT 330), 'Cinderella' (AT 510A), and 'The Table, the Ass and the Stick' (AT 563). 'The Gifts of the Little People' (AT 503) was their favourite wonder tale, and the number of versions which they collected well outstripped those recorded by the adult collectors.

From its very first issue, the journal *Béaloideas* played an important part in folklore studies by publishing folktales, providing translations, or at least summaries in English, and annotating examples of tales collected in the field in Ireland. Reidar Christiansen furnished the first annotation of a wonder tale in *Béaloideas* (1: 94) (AT 130, *Die Bremer Stadtmusikanten* in the Grimms' *Kinder- und Hausmärchen*). He undertook comparative studies of a number of Irish, Scottish Gaelic and Norwegian versions of wonder tales, which also appeared in *Béaloideas*.[16]

It was early recognised that the wonder tale was the most popular genre of international folktales in Ireland and a favourite with Irish storytellers and audiences.[17] This led to attempts at classification based on the Aarne Thompson system. Kenneth Jackson made an initial attempt at classification in 1936. In an article in *Folk-Lore* (47: 263–93) on 'The International Folktale in Ireland' he surveyed the folktale against its historical, linguistic, literary, cultural and social background. He also discussed the institution of storytelling, and the 'making' of a storyteller historically and in the twentieth century, for the benefit of English folklorists. In addition he appended a type-list of Irish and Scottish folktales, arranged according to the Aarne Thompson classification system, forty-five of which were Irish wonder tales.

Christiansen also turned his thoughts towards the classification of Irish wonder tales. In an article in *Zeitchrift für Volkskunde* (vi, 1934, 3, 289–91) he identified the tale types in several published collections from the various Irish-speaking areas of Ireland, according to the Aarne Thompson system. In a number of articles in *Béaloideas* he later attempted to provide a list of Irish wonder tales. In his 1937 contribution 'Towards a Printed List of Irish Fairytales' (*Béaloideas* 7, 3–14) he acknowledged Jackson's attempt a year earlier at providing a classification but pointed out that Jackson's list was far from

---

[16] Christiansen (1928: 107–14) compared Irish, Scottish Gaelic and Norwegian versions of 'The Girl as Helper in the Hero's Flight' (AT 313) and in (1930: 235–45) he explored the relationship between Norwegian and Irish versions of 'The Black and White Bride' (AT 403).

[17] Only a few wonder tales have been studied, probably because of the rich sources, especially for the most popular tales. Cf. P. Lysaght (1991: 28off.). For later studies up to and including 1998 see *International Folklore Biography* (Bonn). For the most recent study of a wonder tale, cf. P. Lysaght (2001: 492–7).

complete due to the small number of sources on which it was based. He himself dealt with AT 300, providing a schema and list of versions, while in an article with the same title in *Béaloideas* 1938 (8, 97–105), he considered AT 301, 302 and 303 in a similar fashion. Christiansen saw the publication of Anna Birgitta Rooth's monograph *The Cinderella Cycle* (1951) as 'an immediate occasion for adding a new instalment to a couple of earlier contributions towards a list of Irish Folktales'. He accordingly dealt with AT 332 ('Godfather Death'), comparing Irish versions with those on the Continent (1953: 70–82). His major comparative work *vis-à-vis* Irish wonder tales, published by the Irish Folklore Commission, was *Studies in Irish and Scandinavian Folktales* (1959).

Christiansen's next major contribution to the study of the folktale in Ireland and to international folklore scholarship was his cooperation with Seán Ó Súilleabháin in compiling *The Types of the Irish Folktale* (1963). This catalogue showed that seven hundred or so of all the international tale types listed in the new and enlarged edition of *The Types of the Folktale* (1961) were known in Ireland, and it gave references to about forty-three thousand versions of these tales found in oral currency or in printed sources up to the end of 1956. The importance of this catalogue for international folktale scholarship is evident from the increased consideration afforded to Irish versions in monographs of individual tales. In the Irish context the catalogue has facilitated and promoted the study of a number of the international folktales attested in Ireland in oral sources and printed works, and of the interaction between oral and written tradition in Ireland from medieval to modern times.[18]

It also demonstrated the popularity of the wonder tale in Ireland. About one third of those listed by Aarne and Thompson have been recorded, and some were especially favoured in Ireland, even when compared with Gaelic Scotland. In his concise and incisive survey of the art of storytelling and the variety of genres of tales and legends in the Irish oral tradition in Irish and English, published ten years later, *Storytelling in the Irish Tradition*, Ó Súilleabháin also lists the most popular wonder tales recorded in Ireland up to this time (1973: 16–17). These include 'The Dragon Slayer', which with over six hundred and fifty recorded versions was the most common. Next came AT 313, 'The Girl as Helper in the Hero's Flight' (664 versions), while AT 326, 'The Youth Who Wanted to Learn What Fear Is' was also a favourite, as was AT 300, 'The Smith Outwits the Devil'. Popular also was AT 302, 'The Ogre's (Devil's) Heart in an Egg' and AT 303, 'The Twin or Blood Brothers', often told in combination, and AT 503, 'The Gifts of the Little People', a favourite especially with school children, and AT 510, 'Cinderella or the Cap o' Rushes'. Type 425, 'The Search for the Lost Husband', which developed an Irish ecotype, was also popular, as were AT 470, 'Friends in Life and Death', AT 471, 'The Bridge to the Other World', and AT

---

[18] Recent studies of the controversial relationship between oral and literary sources in medieval Ireland, and of how a modern folktale can throw light on a medieval text, include Barbara Hiller's doctoral dissertation on the Irish literary saga, 'The Wanderings of Ulysses Son of Laertes', one of the earliest vernacular adaptations of the *Odyssey* in medieval Europe and also an early literary attestation of the international folktale 'The Servant's Good Counsels' (AT 910B). Over two hundred and seventy Irish versions of the folktale, collected mainly from the oral tradition, have been analysed (Hillers 1977). Cf. also P. Mac Cana (1999: 149–64).

726*, 'The Dream Visit'. As we have seen, many of these and other tales have featured in various publications, particularly those in the Irish language, from the end of the nineteenth century. In the course of the twentieth century the repertoires of individual storytellers as well as other collections of folktales, large and small, have been published.[19] Almost invariably wonder tales are included in these works.

The role of the Folklore of Ireland Society in the publication of key works in Irish folklore, including *Leabhar Sheáin Í Chonaill* (1948) has already been mentioned. This volume, comprising the storyteller's collected repertoire, contains a short autobiographical account dictated by the author (xxvii–xxxii)[20] as well as folktales, including eleven wonder tales (466–8), legends, cante-fables and other traditions, was written down by Ó Duilearga between 1925 and 1931, and is a model of comparative comment and annotation.[21]

During the years 1943–4 a collection of fifty-five *Märchen* was recorded on the Ediphone recording and dictating machine from a gifted storyteller, Amhlaoibh Ó Luínse (1872–1947), Ballyvourney, county Cork, by the full-time collector Seán Ó Cróinín, and edited for publication by his brother Donncha Ó Cróinín (1971). This volume, with an English summary and notes, was also published by the Folklore of Ireland Society, and it includes twenty-three wonder tales (350–63).

The setting up of *Comhairle Béaloideas Éireann / The Folklore of Ireland Council* in 1972, which enabled the publication of a variety of folklore texts, led to the appearance of *Leabhar Stiofáin Í Ealaoire* ('Stiofán Ó hEalaoire's Book'), the repertoire of a north county-Clare storyteller (1858–1954), which Ó Duilearga recorded during the 1930s and early 1940s. This volume, also edited by him, was published posthumously in 1981. As well as hero tales, *Novella*, trickster stories, humorous tales and anecdotes, religious tales, and a large variety of legends, it also includes five wonder tales (347).

In 1981 a translation into English by Máire MacNeill of *Leabhar Sheán Í Chonaill*, entitled *Seán Ó Conaill's Book* was published by the Folklore of Ireland Council, and in 1994 an Irish-language collection of tales from the province of Connacht in the west, specifically from Inishmore (*Árainn*) of the Aran Islands, county Galway, appeared under the auspices of the Council. This volume entitled *Scéalta Mháitín Neile, bailiúchán scéalta ó Árainn* ('The Stories of Máirtín Neile. A Collection of Stories from Árainn') (Munch-Pedersen 1994), was the earliest recording of the repertoire of a single Irish-speaking storyteller. The collection was made by the renowned Danish linguist Holger Pedersen (1867–1953) who came to Inishmore in 1895 to study the Irish language. He wrote down tales from Máirtín Neile Ó Conghaile (*c*.1824–1904), the best storyteller on the island, who was known to many of the well-known writers of the time such

---

[19] Most of these publications up to 1956 are in the Bibliography to *TIF*, 10–26. cf. Lysaght (1991). Smaller collections in Irish which include wonder tales are: S. Ó Duilearga (1962: 121–55) AT 313, 425 and 449; S. Ó Catháin (1983) AT 503; S. Ó Catháin (1985) AT 302, 480.

[20] Cf. S. Ó Duilearga (1932: 101–2); P. Lysaght (1999b: 264–72).

[21] He collected about five and a half thousand pages mainly from Wexford (Index of Collectors, manuscript archive, Department of Irish Folklore). Examples of shorter items of folklore collected by him are in the recently published volume of county Wexford folklore edited by D. Ó Muirithe and D. Nuttall (1999).

as Jeremiah Curtin, Arthur Symons, John Millington Synge and Patrick Pearse (Welch 1996: 468). In this collection of thirty-nine stories eight wonder-tale types are noted (313–16, 324–5).

Also stemming from the province of Connacht is a representative anthology of the narrative repertoire of Éamon a Búrc (1866–1942), an Irish-speaking storyteller from Connemara, county Galway (Ó Ceannabháin 1983). A very large collection of material was recorded from him by the Irish Folklore Commission, and he was described by Seán Ó Súilleabháin as 'possibly the most accomplished narrator of folktales who has lived into our time'. While he was most famous as a narrator of multi-episodic hero tales (Ó Nualláin 1982), he also told international tales, and three wonder tales have been included in the selection of narratives from his repertoire which has been published (Ó Ceannabháin 1983: 303–4).

The publication of the folk narrative repertoire of storytellers in parts of the north-west of Ireland has also been undertaken. A selection of the narrative complex of a monoglot Irish-speaking community, without formal education and living in an isolated glen in the Blue Stack mountains in county Donegal, appeared in the 1980s (Ní Dhioraí 1985). In this work, the linguistic, cultural, economic and social background of the storytellers, and their repertoire, style and performance are presented. Among the international folktales included are seven wonder tales (190–1).

Mention has already been made of the contribution of schoolchildren in 1937–8 to the recording of the folktale corpus in Ireland. The results from one Irish-speaking school in Iorrus, north-west county Mayo, included nineteen folktales, nine of which are wonder tales (Ó Catháin, Uí Sheighin 1987: 167–9). The versions recorded by the schoolchildren are generally quite short when compared with those of adults.

An analysis of the content of the repertoire of an Irish-speaking storyteller in north-west Donegal, Micí Seán Néill, shows that this outstanding storyteller had a very large store of international folktales, as well as native hero tales, legends and traditional lore of various kinds (Pórtéir 1993: 78–95). His narrative repertoire includes fifty international tales. Twenty of the wonder-type tales listed in Aarne Thompson have been identified (78–85), and some have been narrated several times in different context and for different media. Thus sixty-four versions of these tales are available in various sources – printed, manuscript and tape recordings.

Although folktales in the English language have appeared from time to time in *Béaloideas*, collections of folktales in English, either recorded in English or translations from Irish, have appeared less frequently. One early collection in English was made by Ó Duilearga in north-west county Clare in December 1929–30 from Patrick Sherlock (1892–1956), an itinerant chimney-sweep from Ennistymon, a small town several miles distant. The Sherlock family had been known locally as good thatchers and chimney-sweeps for at least three generations, and as storytellers of good repute. Patrick's grandfather had told stories in the Irish language. Both Patrick and his father had served in the British army. Ó Duilearga published about half of the tales collected from Sherlock in *Béaloideas* (1962: 1–75), while four others had appeared in earlier issues of the journal (vol. 1). Of the eighteen folktales in print twelve were identified by Ó Duilearga as wonder tales.

Ó Duilearga collected four more long folktales in English from two story-tellers in north-west county Clare in 1930 and 1932, even though both narrators were Irish speakers (*Béaloideas* 32, 1964: 43–70). Two of these are wonder tales and they are of substantial length. The first (AT 313) was told by Pádraig Mac Mathúna, who had many tales in Irish, but who had apparently learnt this one in about 1900 from a travelling packman from county Roscommon who had told it in English. The second story (AT 300) was told by Máirtín Ó Súilleabháin in English as he preferred to narrate in that language due to lack of practice over the years of narrating tales in Irish (70).

In 1966 Seán Ó Sullivan published *Folktales of Ireland,* a collection of thirty-four tales drawn from the archive collection of the Department of Irish Folklore, eight of which are wonder tales (1966: 305). All but two in the collection are translations made by him from the original archive material in the Irish language. In his introduction (xxxvii) he states that English transla-tions of tales by expert storytellers such as Peig Sayers, Éamon a Búrc and others:

> give but a pale shadow of the original Irish narration. The voices, with their many modulations, are silent on the printed page; the audience is absent; only the pattern of narrative and the procession of motifs remain.

Another anthology by O'Sullivan, *The Folklore of Ireland* (1974), also consisting of tales translated from Irish, includes three wonder tales (183).

The full-time collector for the Irish Folklore Commission and its successor the Department of Irish Folklore, Michael J. Murphy, worked in a region that is sometimes referred to as 'Old Ulster', extending across the province of Ulster and southwards to the River Boyne in the province of Leinster. As an English speaker, all his collected material is in that language. His anthology of folktales *Now You're Talking . . . Folktales from the North of Ireland* (1975) aimed at being a representative sample of the folktales of this large region. The long wonder tale which was so prominent in Irish-speaking areas was still met with, even if in a somewhat truncated form, in this area, despite the loss of the Irish language. Five wonder tales are included here (177). The folktales of the northern part of Ireland are of special interest, as they may provide a link between the Irish and Scottish folktale tradition.

Another anthology of tales in the English language was published in 1978, entitled *To Shorten the Road: Traveller Folktales from Ireland.* What is different about this volume is that the tales were told by a specific social group, the Travelling people, and apart from two stories recorded by Gmelch in 1972 and 1978, they were collected for the most part by the part-time collector for the Irish Folklore Commission, the schoolmaster Pádraig Mac Gréine, who spoke *cant,* the secret language of the Travellers, between 1930 and 1932. Of the twenty-two tales in this volume, nineteen are wonder tales (Gmelch and Kroup 1978: 187).

Henry Glassie's collection, *Irish Folktales* (1985), contains twelve wonder tales mainly drawn from nineteenth- and early-twentieth-century printed sources and published anthologies. However AT 501* was collected by Glassie in county Fermanagh in 1972 and is previously unpublished (339–53).

When compared with the sheer volume, length and quality of international folktales in the Irish language, those in the English language inevitably seemed paltry in number and in length, less poetic in language and somehow less imaginative to Ó Súilleabháin and Ó Duilearga, who were so familiar with the stories of gifted storytellers in the Irish language. In *The Gaelic Storyteller* Ó Duilearga states (Delargy 1945/1969: 12): 'Some ordinary folktales did pass through the language mesh, however, but these were but faint echoes of the former glories of Irish storytelling.' It is true of course that English-language versions published in collections such as *To Shorten the Road* and *Now You're Talking* are relatively short and somewhat less robust than their counterparts in Irish, but skilful storytellers in the English language were to be found in the 1930s. They were able to combine various international themes in magic to produce long tales of wonder and imagination, and these form an important part of the rich heritage of tales from Ireland.

References

Asbjørnson, P. Ch., and Moe, J. (1843), *Norske Folkeeventyr*, 2 vols, Kristiania.

Aarne, A., and Thompson, S. (1981), *The Types of the Folktale. A Classification and Bibliography*. FFC 184. Helsinki.

Bausinger, H. (1980), 'Folklore und gesunkenes Kulturgut', in *Formen der 'Volkspoesie'*, 41–55. Berlin.

Campbell, J. F. (1860–2), *Popular Tales of the West Highlands*, I–IV, Edinburgh.

Carleton, W. (1830/1833), *Traits and Stories of the Irish Peasantry*. Dublin/London.

—— (n.d.) *Tubber Derg or the Red Well*. Dublin.

Christiansen, R. Th. (1928), 'A Gaelic Folktale in Norway', *Béaloideas* 1, 107–14.

—— (1930), 'A Norwegian Fairy-Tale in Ireland', *Béaloideas* 2, 235–45.

—— (1934), 'Neue Beiträge zur irischen Volkskunde', *Zeitschrift für Volkskunde* IV.3, 289–91.

—— (1937), 'Towards a Printed List of Irish Fairytales', *Béaloideas* 7, 3–14.

—— (1938), 'Towards a Printed List of Irish Fairytales', *Béaloideas* 8, 97–105.

—— (1950), 'Cinderella in Ireland', *Béaloideas* 20, 96–107.

—— (1953), 'Further Notes on Irish Folktales', *Béaloideas* 22, 97–105.

—— (1959), *Studies in Irish and Scandinavian Folktales*. Copenhagen.

Croker, T. C. (1825), *Fairy Legends and Traditions of the South of Ireland*. London.

—— (1829), *Legends of the Lakes or Sayings and Doings at Killarney*. London.

—— (1831), *Killarney Legends Arranged as a Guide to the Lakes*. London.

Curtin, J. (1890), *Myths and Folklore of Ireland*. Boston.

—— (1894), *Hero-Tales of Ireland*. London.

—— (1895/1970/1974), *Tales of the Fairies and of the Ghost World Collected from Oral Tradition in South-West Munster*. London; New York; Dublin.

Dasent, G. W. (1858), *Popular Tales from the Norse*. Edinburgh.

Delaney, J. G. (1964), 'Patrick Kennedy (1801–1873)', *The Past* 7, 57–8.

—— (1983), 'Patrick Kennedy, Folklorist', *The Past* 14, 55–6.

—— (1988), 'At the Foot of Mount Leinster. Collecting Folklore in Kennedy Country in 1954', *The Past* 16, 3–27.

Delargy, J. H. (1945/1969), *The Gaelic Storyteller, with Some Notes on Gaelic Folk Tales*. London; Chicago.

Dunlevy, J. W. and G. W. (1980–1), 'Jeremiah Curtin's Working Methods', *Éigse: A Journal of Irish Studies*, 67–86.

——(1991), *Douglas Hyde, a Maker of Modern Ireland*, 437–40. Berkeley/Oxford.

Earls, B. (1992–3), 'Supernatural Legends in Nineteenth-Century Irish Writing', *Béaloideas* 60–1, 93–144.

de Fréine, S. (1977), 'The Dominance of the English Language in Ireland', in *The English Language in Ireland*, ed. D. Ó Muirithe. Dublin/Cork.

Glassie, H. (1985) ed., *Irish Folktales*. London.

Gmelch, G., and Kroup, B. (1978) ed., *To Shorten the Road: Traveller Folktales from Ireland*. Dublin.

Gregory, Lady A. P. (1903/1974), *Poets and Dreamers: Studies and Translations from the Irish*. Dublin/London; Gerrards Cross.

——(1910), *The Kiltartan Wonder Book*. London.

Griffin, G. (1829), *The Collegians*. London.

——(1842), *Talis Qualis or Tales of the Jury Room*. Dublin.

Hillers, B. L. (1977), 'The Medieval Irish Odyssey. Merugud Uilixis meic Leirtis'. Doctoral dissertation, Harvard.

Hindley, R. (1990), *The Death of the Irish Language: A Qualified Obituary*. London/New York.

Hyde, D. (1889), *Leabhar Sgeulaigheachta*. Dublin.

——(1890) ed., *Beside the Fire: A Collection of Irish Gaelic Folk Stories*. London.

——(1892), *Cois na Teineadh*. Dublin.

——(1901/1933), *An Sgeuluidhe Gaodhalach*. London; Dublin.

——(1905) ed., *Trí Sgéalta*. Dublin.

——(1936), *Ocht Sgéalta Ó Choillte Mághach*. Dublin.

——(1939), *Sgéalta Thomáis Uí Chathasaigh / Mayo Stories Told by Thomas Casey*. Dublin.

de hÍde, D. (1937), *Mise agus an Connradh*. Dublin.

Jackson, K. (1934), 'Dhá scéal ón mBlascaod', *Béaloideas* 4, 301–11.

——(1936), 'The International Folktale in Ireland', *Folk-Lore* 47, 263–93.

——(1938), 'Scéalta ón mBlascaod', *Béaloideas* 8, 1–96.

——(1961), *The International Popular Tale and Early Welsh Tradition*. Cardiff.

Jacobs, J. (1892), *Celtic Fairy Tales*. London.

Kennedy, P. (1855), *Legends of Mount Leinster*. Dublin.

——(1866), *Legendary Fictions of the Irish Celts*. London.

——(1867), *The Banks of the Boro: A Chronicle of the County of Wexford*. London/Dublin.

——(1869), *Evenings in the Duffrey*. Dublin.

——(1870), *The Fireside Stories of Ireland*. Dublin/London/Edinburgh.

Lang, A. (1912), *The Red Fairy Book*. London.

Larminie, W. (1893/1972), *West Irish Folk-Tales and Romances*. London; Shannon.

Lysaght, P. (1990), 'Hyde, Douglas', in *Enzyklopädie des Märchens* 6.4/5. Berlin/New York.

——(1991), 'Irland', in *Enzyklopädie des Märchens* 7.1. Berlin.

——(1993), 'Don't Go without a Beaver Hat! Seán Ó Súilleabháin in Sweden in 1935', *Sinsear: The Folklore Journal* 7, 49–61.

——(1998), 'Seán Ó Súilleabháin (1903–96), and the Irish Folklore Commission', *Western Folklore* 57, 137–85.

——(1999a), 'Perspectives on Narrative Communication and Gender in Lady Gregory's *Visions and Beliefs in the West of Ireland* (1920)', *Fabula* 39, 59–74.

—— (1999b), 'Traditional Storytelling in Ireland in the Twentieth Century', in *Traditional Storytelling Today: An International Sourcebook*, ed. M. Read MacDonald. Chicago/London.

—— (2000a), 'Ó Duilearga, Séamus', in *Enzyklopädie des Märchens* 10.1. Berlin.

—— (2000b), Ó Súilleabháin, Séan', in *Enzyklopädie des Märchens* 10.1. Berlin.

—— (2001), 'Pan ist tot (AaTh 113 A)', in *Enzyklopädie des Märchens* 10.2. Berlin.

Mac Aonghusa, P. (1993), *Ar Son na Gaeilge. Conradh na Gaeilge 1893–1993*. Dublin.

Mac Cana, P. (1980), *The Learned Tales of Medieval Ireland*. Dublin.

—— (1999), 'The Irish Analogues of Melusine', in *Islanders and Water-Dwellers*, ed. P. Lysaght *et al*. Dublin.

Moody, T. W., and Martin, F. X. (1967/1994) ed., *The Course of Irish History*. Dublin.

Munch-Pedersen, O. (1994) ed., *Scéalta Mháirtín Neile*. Dublin.

Murphy, M. J. (1975), *Now You're Talking . . . Folktales from the North of Ireland*. Belfast.

Nagy, J. F. (1985), *The Wisdom of the Outlaw*. Berkeley.

Nauman, H. (1922), *Grundzüge der deutschen Volkskunde*. Leipzig.

Ní Dhíoraí, A. (1985) ed., *Na Cruacha: Scéalta agus Seanchas*. Dublin.

Ó Catháin, S. (1983) ed., *Scéalta Chois Cladaigh / Stories of Sea and Shore*. Dublin.

—— (1985), *Uair an Chloig Cois Teallaigh / An Hour by the Hearth*. Dublin.

—— and Uí Sheighin, C. (1987) ed., *A mhuintir Uí Chaocháin, labhraigí feasta!* Dublin.

Ó Ceannabháin, E. (1983) ed., *Éamonn A Búrc: scéalta*. Dublin.

Ó Ciosáin, N. (1977), *Print and Popular Culture in Ireland, 1750–1850*. London.

Ó Conaire, B. (1986) ed., *Douglas Hyde, Language, Lore and Lyrics. Essays and Lectures*. Dublin.

Ó Cuív, B. (1951), *Irish Dialects and Irish Speaking Districts*. Dublin.

Ó Cróinín, D. (1971) ed., *Scéalaíocht Amhlaoibh Í Lúinse*. Dublin.

O'Donoghue, D. J. (1899), *Legends and Stories of Ireland*, ed. S. Lover. London.

Ó Duilearga, S. (1932), 'In Memoriam Seán Ó Conaill, Seanchuí (1853–1931)', *Béaloideas* 3, 101–2.

—— (1943) ed., *Irish Folk-Tales Collected by Jeremiah Curtin (1835–1906)*. Dublin.

—— (1948/1964/1977) ed., *Leabhair Sheáin Í Chonaill*. Dublin.

—— (1962), 'Trí Shean-Scéal', *Béaloideas* 30, 121–55.

—— (1973), 'A Personal Tribute. Reidar Thorolf Christiansen (1886–1971)', *Béaloideas*, 37–8 (1969–70), 345–51.

—— (1981) ed., *Leabhar Stiofáin Í Ealaoire*. Dublin.

—— (1981), *Seán Ó Conaill's Book*, trans. M. MacNeill. Dublin.

Ó Laoghaire, An tAth. P. (1904), *Séadna*. Dublin.

Ó Muirithe, D. (1977) ed., *The English Language in Ireland*. Cork.

—— and Nuttall, D. (1999) ed., *Folklore of County Wexford*. Dublin.

Ó Nualláin, C. (1982), *Eochair Mac Rí in Éirinn / Eochair, A King's Son in Ireland*. Dublin.

Ó Siochfhradha, P. ('An Seabhac') (1932), *An Seanchaide Muimhneach*. Dublin.

Ó Súilleabháin, S. (1937), *Láimh-Leabhar Béaloideasa*. Dublin.

—— (1940), 'Bataí Scóir', in *Féil-Sgríbhinn Eóin Mhic Néill*, ed. J. Ryan. Dublin.

—— (1942), *A Handbook of Irish Folklore*. Dublin.

—— (1973), *Storytelling in the Irish Tradition*. Cork.

—— and Christiansen, R. Th. (1963/1968), *The Types of the Irish Folktale*. FFC 188. Helsinki.

O'Sullivan, S. (1966) ed., *Folktales of Ireland*. London.

—— (1974) ed., *The Folklore of Ireland*. London.

Ó Tuama, S. (1972) ed., *The Gaelic League Idea*. Cork.

Ó Tuathail, É. (1932), *Scéalta Mhuintir Luinigh*. Dublin.

Póirtéir, C. (1993) ed., *Micí Sheáin Néill. Scéalaí agus Scéalta*. Dublin.
Rees, A. and B. (1961), *Celtic Heritage. Ancient Tradition in Ireland and Wales*. London.
von Sydow, C. W. (1921), *Fader Peter O'Leary, Schiane*. Stockholm.
—— (1934), 'Geography and Folk-Tale Oicotypes', *Béaloideas* 4, 344–55.
—— (1948), *Selected Papers on Folklore, Published on the Occasion of his 70th Birthday*. Copenhagen.
Synge, J. M. (1906), *The Aran Islands*. Dublin.
Thackeray, W. M. (1842), *Irish Sketch Book*. London.
Welch, R. (1996), *The Oxford Companion to Irish Literature*. Oxford.
Windisch, E. (1880–1909), *Irische Texte*. 4 vols. Leipzig.
Yeats, W. B. (*c*.1888), *Fairy and Folk Tales of the Irish Peasantry*. London.
Zimmermann, G. D. (2001), *The Irish Storyteller*. Dublin.

12

Welsh Folk Narrative and the Fairy Tale

ROBIN GWYNDAF

Dwedai hen ŵr llwyd o'r gornel:
'Gan fy nhad mi glywais chwedel;
A chan ei daid y clywsai yntau;
Ac ar ei ôl mi gofiais innau . . .

(A grey-haired old man from his corner said: 'From my father I heard a tale; he
had heard it from his grandfather; and after him I too remembered it.')
(*Cerdd yr hen ŵr o'r coed* ('*Ballad of the Old Man from the Woods*'), 18th century)

Beliefs and the manner of expressing these beliefs may change from one
generation to another, but innermost desires and fears remain almost
unchanged through the ages. One of the most constant desires of men and
women was and is to avoid the routine and certainty of this world and escape
into the enchanting world of the unknown. Those in Wales are no exception.
Although Wales in recent times has not possessed professional storytellers with
a large repertoire of fairy tales of the international type, there has been an
unbroken tradition of storytelling right down to our own days.

The Religious Revivals in Wales during the eighteenth and nineteenth
centuries contributed much to the gradual disappearance of communal gatherings and of many ancient ceremonies, games and customs, yet religion did not
(contrary to the general opinion) succeed in suppressing the practice of storytelling. It continued with surprising vigour. Legends relating to ghosts, fairies
and the devil were still being recited, although we notice a distinct process of
functional adaptation, and the emphasis became increasingly moralistic and
didactic. Also the very people who endeavoured to suppress the old customs
and superstitions were indirectly responsible for a new interest in folk traditions
and antiquities. From the end of the eighteenth century onwards scores of
printed works poured out of the Welsh presses: books, chap-books, ballad
sheets, almanacs, journals and newspapers. Many contained folklore material
and tales and legends relating to the supernatural, and were read extensively.

In spite of the lack of examples in recent times, knowledge of fairy tales in
Wales clearly goes back to a very early date, as Kenneth Jackson has shown in
his discussion of tales from the *Mabinogion*. Parts of this are believed to go back
to the eleventh century, although this has not always been taken into account by
those working on fairy-tale themes (Jackson 1961: 67ff.). The tales are written in
Middle Welsh and were first given the title of *Mabinogion* by Charlotte Guest,

who translated them into English in 1838–41. They are preserved mainly in two manuscripts, the *White Book of Rhydderch* (c.1350) and the *Red Book of Hergest* (c.1400). The narratives were composed at different times, and their background and contents vary considerably (Jones 1949: introduction; Mac Cana 1977; Roberts 1988; Davies 1992).

'Culhwch and Olwen' (c.1100) is the story richest in fairy-tale motifs. The main plot is the hero's wooing of an ogre's daughter, with the aid of a team of men possessing exceptional skills (AT 513A, 'Six Go through the Whole World'), and this has been linked with Welsh legendary traditions, the hunting of the supernatural boar, the *Twrch Trwyth*, and a Welsh legend of Arthur pre-dating Geoffrey of Monmouth. Other tales which clearly contain a number of familiar motifs are the tales of Pwyll, Branwen, Manawydan and Math, the so-called 'Four Branches of the Mabinogi', probably composed 1060–1120. In spite of the masterly language and style, the confusion in the plots of several of these tales convinced Jackson that they could not have been composed in their present form by professional storytellers, but are more likely to be old tales, not wholly remembered, presented by sophisticated courtly narrators (Jackson 1961: 124ff.). This blending of international themes with native legends continued in Wales until the legendary material far outnumbered the fairy tales. A striking example of this is the legend of the Lady of Llyn y Fan Fach, which is discussed in detail below and which has continued to be enormously popular up to the present day.

In 1948 the Welsh Folk Museum, now known as the Museum of Welsh Life, in St Fagan's, Cardiff, was opened to the public, and from the outset folk studies, and particularly folk customs, were given a prominent place in its activities. As part of his work in the Museum, the author of this article was privileged during 1964–90 to undertake a survey of the Welsh folk narrative tradition. Over three thousand individuals were interviewed, mostly through the medium of Welsh, and some four hundred of these were recorded on tape, amounting to approximately 650 hours of recording and fifteen thousand brief items of narrative. In-depth studies were conducted of the narrative repertoire of certain tradition-bearers, and in particular the repertoire of Lewis T. Evans (1882–1975), who related over 350 brief folk narratives and approximately one hundred items of folk poetry (Gwyndaf 1976, 1981).

The folk narrative tradition of certain districts was also studied. One such area chosen in May 1967 was the Llanddeusant-Myddfai district, near Llandovery in Carmarthenshire, south-west Wales, where the lake known as Llyn y Fan Fach is situated. This beautiful mountain lake is associated in legend with the super-natural bride of the only son of a widow at Blaensawdde farm. When the husband broke certain taboos, she and all her animals disappeared into the lake, but she would sometimes return to teach her three children the secrets of plants, and they were said to be the founders of a long line of renowned physicians, the Physicians of Myddfai (Gwyndaf 1967a and b; 1992–3).

In studying Welsh folk narratives we notice a remarkable continuity of tradition from very early times to the present. The reason is that the tradition was, and to a great extent still is, a living tradition. From time to time the form and content of the narratives may have altered, but the actual function of many remained almost unchanged. No living folk narrative tradition belongs merely to the past, for there is a creative force at work which ensures that it continuously changes, developing as the nature of society changes. This explains why so many of the Welsh legends survived the eighteenth- and nineteenth-century Religious Revivals. A study of the morphology of Welsh folk narratives shows not only how old motifs may be combined in one tale, but also how they may be adapted to a new environment in a later period. Although examples of the international fairy tales are very scarce in Wales, many recognised fairy-tale motifs can be found in Welsh legends, such as that of the Lady of Llyn y Fan Fach.

Today few of the old tales of romance (*Novella*) or the traditional fairy tales still exist in current Welsh oral tradition, and those that do are considerably shortened versions. When Jacobs published his collection of *Celtic Fairytales* at the end of the nineteenth century, he could only find two Welsh tales to include, one the Lady of Llyn y Fan Fach and the other from the medieval *Mabinogion*. Even so, the Welsh legends of magic give us a brief glimpse of the ever-present atmosphere of enchantment (*hud a lledrith*), which was so characteristic of the medieval world. We find the magic ring which gives a poor boy everything he wishes (AT 560), the magic mill which still grinds salt at the bottom of the Welsh Sea (AT 565), and the tale of the monk of Maes-glas (Greenfield, Flintshire), who listened to a nightingale's song, and when he returned to his monastery found it in ruins and all his colleagues long since dead (AT 471A).

The Llyn y Fan Fach legend may be classified as a migratory legend, that is, a localised story with similar versions in other countries. A legend can be distinguished from a fairy tale because it deals with named persons and/or places, and is told for true. However this legend is closely related to fairy tales in the motifs which form part of it. The most attractive genres in Wales today are brief jokes and anecdotes, related in an informal, day-to-day context. The emphasis is on chronicates, 'true' narratives, and many of the jokes are recited 'as if they were true'. Yet the Llyn y Fan Fach legend with its emphasis on magic and the supernatural is as popular as ever, constantly retold and illustrated.

However detailed the narrative material recorded in print and archives may be, the folktale scholar will always benefit by spending as much time as possible in actual fieldwork. To understand fully the lore of the people he must first understand something about the 'people of the lore'. Context is just as important as text. In the case of the Llyn y Fan Fach legend, collectors and editors have concentrated mainly on presenting the text. During a week of fieldwork in the Llanddeusant-Myddfai district in 1967, much valuable information was gathered about the inhabitants themselves, and how they regarded the legend today. Their attitude and world-view, the mystery which still surrounds the mountain lake, and various current folk traditions about the lake and the legend and about the Physicians of Myddfai were recorded (Gwyndaf 1967a and b). Whether this particular story is regarded as a tale of magic, a legend, a fabulate or 'just a story' is not the crucial question, but whether it has a meaningful function and a relevant message to specific people at a specific moment in time. To consider this question, we must first look at the narrative itself.[1]

---

[1] The retelling of the legend is based on the version by William Rees of Tonn, Llandovery, Carmarthenshire. See also the papers of William Rees in the City and County of Cardiff Library (Cardiff MS 3.376).

The eventful struggle of the Princes of South Wales to preserve the independence of their country was drawing to a close in the twelfth century. At that time there lived at Blaensawdde farm in Llanddeusant, Carmarthenshire, a widow whose husband had been killed in one of these wars. One day when her only son was tending his mother's cattle on the banks of a small lake, Llyn y Fan Fach, on the Black Mountain, he saw a beautiful maiden sitting on the surface of the water, combing her hair. She was more beautiful than any girl he had ever seen before. Bewildered by a feeling of love and admiration, the youth held out his hand towards the maiden and offered her barley bread, but she said, 'Hard is thy bread, / 'Tis not easy to catch me.' Then she sank into the water. The love-stricken youth returned home, and his mother advised him to take moist bread with him the next day. After waiting for many hours, the maiden appeared. He once more offered her bread, and she said, 'Moist is thy bread, / I do not want thee.' Smiling, she again vanished.

The mother then suggested slightly baked bread. The following day the young man again waited and waited. As the sun was almost setting and he was on the point of going home, he cast a sad and final farewell glance over the lake, at which moment he saw, to his astonishment, cattle walking on the surface of the water, followed by the maiden. This time she accepted the bread and consented to be his wife, but on one condition. 'If you strike me three causeless blows', she told him, 'I will leave you for ever.' Suddenly the maiden plunged into the water, and after a while a strongly built, hoary-headed man came out of the lake with two beautiful identical girls. 'I will give you my daughter in marriage if you can tell me which of the two you love', said the hoary-headed man. They were so much alike that the youth was on the point of saying that he could not, when the one with a star on her sandal thrust her foot forward just a little, and he pointed to the girl he loved. 'You have chosen rightly', said her father, 'I will give you as dowry as many sheep, cattle, goats and horses as she can count of each with one breath.' Then she began counting as rapidly as she could, by fives: *un, dau, tri, pedwar, pump; un, dau, tri, pedwar, pump* . . . and the exact number of animals counted each time came out of the lake. The young couple were married and lived happily in great prosperity for many years on the farm of Esgair Llaethdy, Myddfai, nearby, and had three sons.

One day they had been invited to a christening in the neighbourhood. The husband told his wife to fetch a pony from the field, and he went to the house for her gloves. When he returned she was still standing in the same place, and the husband tapped her playfully with one of the gloves and said, 'Go, go!' It was then that she reminded him of the 'three blows without a cause', and warned him to be careful. Some time later they were at a wedding when the wife suddenly burst into tears. Her husband again tapped her on the shoulder and asked her why she was weeping, and she answered: 'I weep because the young couple's troubles are now beginning, and so are ours too, for this is the second causeless blow.'

The years passed by, but at a funeral one day the wife began to laugh most gaily. Touching her arm, her husband urged her to be quiet, but she replied: 'When people die, their troubles are over, and so, dear husband, is our marriage. This is the third causeless blow. Farewell for ever.' She walked towards Esgair Llaethdy and called her cattle and all the other animals by their names:

> Mu wlfrech, Moelfrech,
> Mu olfrech, Gwynfrech,
> Pedair cae tonn-frech,
> Yr hen Wynebwen,
> A'r las Geingen,
> Gyda'r Tarw Gwyn
> O lys y Brenin,
> A'r llo du bach
> Sydd ar y bach,
> Dere dithe, yn iach adre!
> Pedwar eidion glas
> Sydd ar y maes,
> Deuwch chwithe
> Yn iach adre!

> Brindled cow, white speckled,
> Spotted cow, bold freckled,
> The four field sward mottled,
> The old white-faced,
> And the grey Geingen
> With the white bull
> From the King's court,
> And the little black calf
> Suspended on the hook,
> Come thou also, quite well, home!
> The four grey oxen
> That are on the field,
> You too come
> Quite well, home!

They all followed her, even the little black calf, though slaughtered and hung upon a hook. Four oxen ploughing in a field on the mountainside were also called, and they dragged the plough with them, making a deep furrow which remains to this day. Led by the lady, all the animals disappeared into the Fan Fach lake.

The husband was broken-hearted, and the sons wandered long, searching for their mother. One day at a mountain gate near Dôl Hywel, now called Llidiart y Meddygon (the 'physician's gate'), the mother suddenly appeared to Rhiwallon, her eldest son, told him that his mission on earth was to heal the sick, and gave him a bag full of medical prescriptions. On several occasions she met her three sons on the bank of the lake, and once she even accompanied them on their return home as far as the place still called Pant y Meddygon (the 'physician's dingle'), where she revealed to them the medicinal qualities of various plants and herbs. Rhiwallon and his three sons, Cadwgan, Gruffudd and Einion, became physicians to Prince Rhys Gryg, Lord of Dinefwr, who gave them lands and privileges. They wrote down their knowledge in manuscripts, and their fame as physicians soon spread throughout the whole country, and has continued among their descendants to this day.

This is a retelling of one of the best known and best loved of all Welsh folk narratives since the *Mabinogion*. The legend was first recorded in print as recently as 1821, by Siencyn ab Tydvil. The more detailed and best known version was printed in 1861 by the Reverend John Williams, 'Ab Ithel', in his introduction to *The Physicians of Myddvai* (*Meddygon Myddfai*), which includes the text and translation into English of one of the three medieval manuscripts of the Physicians' herbal remedies (Williams 1861). The legend had been written down for him by William Rees of Tonn, Llanymddyfri (Llandovery), from the oral testimony of three elderly natives of Myddfai in 1841. Since that time the legend has been included in almost every published collection of Welsh folktales. It is worthwhile to consider briefly the reasons for its wide and enduring popularity.

First, the legend gives pleasure because of its aesthetic qualities. Although the version published by Williams in 1861 is somewhat static and flowery in style, it reflects the art of a good storyteller in its form, pattern and structure. The use of rhyme (*cante fable*) and rhythm to express the maiden's response to the youth's offer of bread has an important mnemonic function, and helps the listener to grasp the significance of the words, while emphasising the mystery of her refusal. There is a similar function in the use of rhyme in the long cattle-call run, to which there are parallels in tales of otherworld cattle from Norway (Davidson 1996: 101).

Interesting use is made in this legend of formulaic numbers and patterns, and of various motifs found in international popular tales, and described by Axel Olrik as the 'epic laws of folk narrative' (Olrik 1965: 129–41). The hero is the only son of a widow, as is frequent in fairy tales. Another familiar motif is the 'Law of Twins'. Here two girls appear who seem identical (though in many tales it is three or more), and one helps the hero to pick her out from her companions. Similarly we notice the 'Law of Contrast', when the lady cries at a wedding and laughs at a funeral. Much use is made of the formula number three, which sustains the sense of anticipation and contrast. The youth waits for three days to see the lake maiden and offers her three kinds of bread. When they marry they have three sons, as does also Rhiwallon, the eldest. The fairy wife stipulates that she must not be struck three causeless blows, and when she is struck three times it is at the three crucial festivals in human life important in the rites of passage, birth, marriage and death (Owen 1974: 142ff.).

The storyteller's art and the human imagination at work is very evident also in the legend's structure. From the fourteenth century onwards the fame of the Myddfai Physicians is well attested in Welsh literature. Yet there is no recorded tradition connecting them with fairy descent prior to the printed version published in 1821 and that of Williams in 1861. What we have here therefore is an interesting example of the blending of tradition and history. The narrative is a fusion of two local legends. The first is an early lake legend based on the motif of the supernatural bride, the fairy water-maiden marrying a mortal man (Motif F302.2). The second is a much later local onomastic tale relating to place-names with medical associations and centred round the Physicians of Myddfai.

The water-bride theme is of course a version of a very popular migratory legend. Sir John Rhŷs (1901: 17ff.) gave a number of examples from various lakes in Wales with information about the people from whom he heard the tales, and the subject has been further discussed by Juliette Wood who points out that this Welsh tale differs from others of the same type in that it is the fairy bride herself who makes the conditions under which she will remain in the world of mortals, and that she brings material prosperity (Wood 1992: 66). It seems, however, that the onomastic legend associated with the water-bride's descendants, the Physicians, does not exist as an independent tale in Welsh tradition, and this is the only known version. The earlier lake legend and the later onomastic legend have been combined with the introduction of three well-attested related motifs, namely 'Gifted Descendant of Fairy-mortal Marriage' (Motifs F241.2.3, 302, 302.6, 384.3); 'Fairy Mother bestows Magic Power upon Half-mortal Son' (F305.1.1), and 'Fairy Mother returns to visit Son' (305.1.2).

The addition of these motifs has greatly enhanced the legend and given it a new meaning. The various other versions of the lake legend end tragically with the fairy wife returning to the lake. In some versions she occasionally revisits the children, sometimes speaking a verse, but usually only to give clothes or money, and no more is heard of them. It is the end of the story. The wisdom and knowledge imparted to the Physicians of Myddfai, however, were to benefit mankind for generations to come, so that the tale was a source of satisfaction and hope.

In the Laws of Hywel Dda (d. 950) there is a reference to the white cattle at the Royal Court of Dinefwr, and white cattle have been part of the estate up to the present day. It is possible that there was some connection in people's minds between the white bull of the lake legend and the white cattle of the nearby Royal Court of Dinefwr. At a later stage in the oral tradition the Physicians of Myddfai, who were the official physicians to Rhys Gryg, Lord of Dinefwr, could have been fused with the water-bride theme of the earlier lake legend. Giving them a mother of supernatural origin was a means of explaining the source of their wisdom and powers of healing.

In an important article in *Studia Celtica* (1975–6: 232), Morfydd E. Owen has shown that all three medieval manuscripts containing the herbal remedies of the Myddfai Physicians derive from a period about a century and a half after Rhys Gryg, who died in 1233. The earliest surviving manuscript (BM Add. MS 14912) belongs to the second half of the fourteenth century. Owen points out that the texts are distinguished by 'the frequent use of stylistic devices, such as numerical groupings, pairs of antithetical statements, alliteration, and rhymes', which owe their origin undoubtedly to 'the oral nature of Welsh learned tradition and had a mnemonic function'.

The English translation of the colophon in the *Red Book of Hergest*'s version (MS CX1, c.1400) reads as follows (cf. Owen 1975–6: 215):

Here with the help of God, the almighty Lord, are shown the most important and essential remedies for man's body. And those who caused them to be written down in this manner were Rhiwallon, the doctor, and his sons, Cadwgan, Gruffudd and Einion; for they were the best and leading doctors of their time and of the time of Rhys Gryg, their lord and Lord of Dinefwr, the man who safeguarded their status and privilege completely and honourably as was their due. And the reason they caused the rules of their art to be written down in this way was lest there be no one who knew them as well as they did after their days.

Rhys Gryg ('The Stammerer') was one of the eight sons of Rhys ap Gruffudd ap Rhys, Arglwydd (Lord) Rhys (d. 1197), one of the last and most important of the Welsh native princes. He and his family were well known for their patronage of the church, the arts and learning. It would be quite in character, therefore, for one of its members, Rhys Gryg, 'to support a family of medical men, particularly at a time when medical studies were gaining prominence in Europe, as they were in the twelfth and thirteenth centuries' (Owen 1975–6: 216).

Early Irish and Welsh laws testify to the high status given to the physician in society. Herbs were specially cultivated for him. During the thirteenth century Myddfai was a royal manor under the lordship of Dinefwr. Morfydd Owen (1975–6: 219) suggests that

> lands in Myddfai could have been held by a family of lay physicians, originally mediciners of the Lords of Dinefwr, subsequently of the Anglo-Norman Lords of Llanymyddyfri, and if the continuity of popular tradition be accepted, finally a family of country physicians famous for their remedies and their healings.

The last of the direct line of hereditary physicians who practised at Myddfai, it seems, were a father and son who died in 1719 and 1739 respectively, but direct descendants of the family continued to practise medicine in the twentieth century. Photographs of two recent upholders of the tradition were published in the *Welsh Medical Gazette* in 1971.[2]

Pant y Meddygon ('physicians' dingle'), mentioned in the legend, is situated on the south facing slope of Mynydd Myddfai. It is an area rich in ferns, bog plants and herbs. Local tradition firmly testifies to the belief that certain farms in Myddfai parish once belonged to the Physicians, in particular Esgair Llaethdy ('dairy ridge'), where the youth and maiden went to live. The onomastic element in the name is obvious when one remembers that the fairy cattle brought the couple great prosperity. Other farms are Llwyn Ifan Feddyg ('Grove of Evan, the physician') and Llwyn Maredudd Feddyg ('Grove of Meredith, the physician') (Gwyndaf 1967a: tapes MWL 1528–37).

The Llyn y Fan Fach legend is interesting in its form and structure and its fusion of history and tradition, but above all, as in the fairy tale, we have interaction between the natural and the supernatural, the rational and irrational. The youth belongs to this world and the lake-lady to the supernatural one, but they are not completely apart and there are bridges which assist the characters

---

[2] 'Profile: Two Descendants of the Physicians of Myddfai', in *Cylchgrawn Meddygol Cymru – Welsh Medical Gazette* 12 (Winter 1971), 6. These are Surgeon-Major Edward Hopkins, Carreg Cennen, Carmarthenshire, south-west Wales, and Dr John Edward Powell, The Norton, Tenby, Pembrokeshire, who died in 1970, aged 95: 'He was descended in the female line from the Physicians of Myddfai through his great-grandmother, who was Joan Jones, niece of the John Jones, Surgeon, whose tombstone stands in the porch of Myddfai church.'

to cross from one realm to another. We have what Alwyn and Brinley Rees (1961: 345–6) have called 'the union of opposites', which seems to be symbolised by the different types of bread offered to the lake-maiden. She chooses lightly baked bread, which is between the baked and the unbaked, thus bridging the gulf between the two worlds. This is a particularly powerful symbol when the form of the tale is a local legend rather than a fairy tale, and both the setting and the characters are well known to the local inhabitants. In some of the versions of the Fairy Bride legend there is a distinct process of rationalisation. The maiden always returns to the lake in the end, but sometimes this is explained as an accident and she is not a supernatural character. In the Llyn y Fan Fach version, however, she is a figure of considerable power, deciding whether to accept the bread, and laying down the conditions under which she will remain with her husband. She brings the wonderful animals which assure their prosperity, and the gift of healing which she bestows on her sons enhances her power.

In English the wife is referred to as the 'lady', 'maiden' or 'woman' of the lake. In Welsh oral tradition she is invariably referred to as *y forwyn* ('maid', 'maiden', 'virgin'). She is not called a fairy, but she counted in fives, as the fairies did, and in some versions of the story she seems to be afraid of iron, like the fairies. It has been pointed out that her reluctance to attend a christening may have been because this was the rite separating a human being from the supernatural world (Rees 1961: 344–5). She differs from the usual Welsh fairies, represented as small and dainty, since she is a dignified, grown woman, with a hint of the goddess about her. Katharine Briggs suggested that such fairy brides 'of human size and more than human beauty' were perhaps particularly characteristic of Wales (1967: III, 88). But although the maiden came into the life of the Myddfai youth from a supernatural world, she had all the qualities and characteristics of a mortal woman, helping to account for the legend's appeal. According to a popular verse, Myddfai parish was celebrated for its beautiful girls (Williams 1861: xxii). Moreover while other versions of the tale of the bride from a lake end tragically, this one finishes on a triumphant note, and in one sense there is no end. Some of the magic and goodness of the woman from the lake is re-enacted in her own children and her children's children.

For over seven hundred years the memory of the Physicians was kept alive in the Myddfai district. The legend is presented in photographs and prints on the walls of the nearby Llanddeusant Youth Hostel, and in the 1950s the farmer of Esgair Llaethdy called some of his cattle by the names recorded in the legend. The present family of Llwyn Maredudd Feddyg are very proud of their herbal garden, said to have belonged to one of the Physicians, and at Afon-wen, near Caerwys, Flintshire, a young couple have named their plant centre Perlysiau Myddfai ('Myddfai herbs') in honour of the thirteenth-century physicians.

In some of the versions of the tale found elsewhere in Wales, the wife returned to the lake to become a moaning spirit, or led men attracted by her beauty to destruction, so that they were drowned or wounded (Trevelyan 1909: 9, 12), and their lakes were places to avoid. But at Llyn y Fan Fach people believed (or wished to believe) that the maiden still presided over the lake as a source of guidance and inspiration. She returned to the kingdom whence she came, the land beneath the waves, *Annwfn* (literally 'the deep'), the Underworld. Welsh fairies were sometimes called *Plant Annwfn* ('children of the underworld') or *Gwragedd Annwfn* ('women of the underworld'). In legend and tradition the lake came to be regarded as a doorway to the underworld, the other world of youth and bliss, like that visited by Brân (Rees 1961: 343):

> Without grief, without sorrow, without death,
> Without sickness, without debility

During the nineteenth century scores of people used to visit Llyn y Fan Fach every year at the beginning of August, especially on the first Sunday or Monday of that month, for the coming of the Lady of the Lake. It is said that some even took potato peelings to offer to the Lady (Gwyndaf 1967a: tapes MWL 1528, 1533, 1535). Local inhabitants still relate some of the traditions and beliefs they have heard (Llywelyn 1997–8; Pugh 1997–8). It is said, for example, that when the fairy wife returned to the lake the husband and sons endeavoured to drain it, but a hairy monster arose from below the waves to prevent them. Another tradition is that the Devil attempted in vain to destroy the lady by throwing a cauldron into the lake (Tape MWL 1530). It is also said that the lake is bottomless, that there are seven echoes between the banks known as Tyle Gwyn and Gwter Goch, and that there is suction in the surrounding rocks, so that stones thrown from them will never reach the water below (Gwyndaf 1967b).

We have a unique example here of the effectiveness of international popular motifs as found in the fairy tale when linked with local traditions about outstanding people who once lived in the district. There seems every reason to believe that such motifs entered Wales early, perhaps even in the period of Roman occupation (Jackson 1961: 74), since a number can be found in the *Mabinogion*. The much loved story of the Lady of Llyn y Fan Fach then, is a vivid illustration of the successful blending of fairy tale and local legend, which has ensured its survival up to the present day.

References

Briggs, K. M. (1967), *The Fairies in Tradition and Literature*. London.
Davidson, H. E. (1996), 'Milk and the Northern Goddess', in *The Concept of the Goddess*, ed. S. Billington and M. Green, 91–106. London.
Davies, S. (1992), 'Storytelling in Medieval Wales', *Oral Tradition* 7, 231–57.
Gwyndaf, R. (1967a), Transcript of Museum of Welsh Life (MWL) sound tapes: nos.1528–38, relating to the Myddfai–Llanddeusant district.
—— (1967b), Fieldwork, diary and notes, relating to the Myddfai–Llanddeusant district, 22–6 May.
—— (1976), 'The Prose Narrative Repertoire of a Passive Tradition-Bearer in a Welsh Rural Community', Part 1, in *Folk Narrative Research. Studia Fennica* 20, 283–93. Helsinki.
—— (1981), 'The Prose Narrative Repertoire . . .', Part 2, *Fabula* 22, 28–54.
—— (1992–3), 'A Welsh Lake Legend and the Famous Physicians of Myddfai', *Béaloideas* 60–1, 241–66.

Jacobs, J. (1892), *Celtic Fairy Tales*, London.

Jackson, K. H. (1961), *The International Popular Tale and Early Welsh Tradition*. Cardiff.

Jones G. and T. (1949), *The Mabinogion*. London.

Llywelyn, H. (1997–8), 'The Physicians of Myddfai: Pilgrimage and Colloquy', *Cambria: National Magazine for Wales* 1, 54–8.

Mac Cana, P. (1977), *The Mabinogi*. Cardiff.

Olrik, A. (1965), 'Epic Laws of Folk Narrative', in *The Study of Folklore*, ed. A. Dundes. Englefield Cliffs, NJ.

Owen, M. E. (1975–6), 'Meddygon Myddfai: A Preliminary Survey of Some Medieval Medical Writing in Welsh', *Studia Celtica* 10/11, 210–33.

Owen, T. M. (1974), *Welsh Folk Customs*. Cardiff.

Pugh, R. (1997–8), 'The Physicians of Myddfai: Myth and Reality', *Cambria: National Magazine for Wales*, 48–53.

Rees, A. and B. (1961), *Celtic Heritage: Ancient Tradition in Ireland and Wales*. London.

Rhŷs, Sir J. (1901), *Celtic Folklore, Welsh and Manx*. 2 vols. Oxford.

Roberts, B. F. (1988), 'Oral Tradition and Welsh Literature: A Description and a Survey', *Oral Tradition* 3, 61–87.

Trevelyan, M. (1909), *Folk-Lore and Folk Stories of Wales*. London.

ab Tydvil, S. (1821), 'The Legend of Meddygon Myddvai', *The Cambro-Briton* 2, 313–15.

Williams, J. (Ab Ithel) (1861), *The Physicians of Myddfai, Meddygon Myddfai*, trans. J. Pugh. Llandovery (facsimile reprint, Llannerch 1993).

Wood, J. (1992), 'The Fairy Bride Legend in Wales', *Folklore* 103, 56–72.

13

The Ossetic Oral Narrative Tradition: Fairy Tales in the Context of Other Forms of Traditional Literature

ANNA CHAUDHRI

> . . . and Oræzmæg says to the people: 'Shall I tell you an old tale or
> a new one?' So they said to him, 'We would indeed have listened
> to an old tale, but tell us a new one!'   (Gardanti[1] 1927: 12)

Ossetia is a small land in the central north Caucasus, the inhabitants of which speak an Indo-European language, unlike their Caucasian neighbours, to whom they are only culturally related. The speakers of the two main dialects of northern Ossetic, Digoron and Iron, are divided from the speakers of the southern dialect by the Caucasus range itself. The written language developed only after the Russian conquest of the Caucasus and the first texts published in Ossetic appeared at the end of the eighteenth century. After brief experiments with both the Roman and the Georgian alphabet, Ossetic continues to be written in the Cyrillic script.

Ossetes are justly proud of their oral tradition and cultural heritage. Since the later part of the nineteenth century a fine written literature has developed in all the main areas of drama, prose and poetry, but it is the large corpus of orally transmitted traditional material which has given many Ossetic writers their inspiration. Kh. N. Ardasenov (1959: 51–3) stresses the importance of traditional prose and poetry, in all its variety, as a source of subject matter, rich language and form for Ossetic writers; written literature in Ossetia developed within the context of a still thriving oral tradition. In 1934 the Digoron poet Maliti compared himself to the legendary Nart musician, Atsæmæz: 'I wish, Mama, I could become for you, like Atsæmæz, a wonderful *fændyr*-player . . . I would play wondrous songs' (Maliti 1986: 50).

The fairy tale (Ossetic *aryau*) is well represented in Ossetic and an attempt was made to list and classify Ossetic animal and fairy tales, according to the system of Aarne and Andreev, in 1958 by A. Kh. Biazyrov. The tales classified as *Volshebnye Skazki* 'wonder tales', types 300–749, are subdivided into the familiar

---

[1] Ossetic names are normally written surname first e.g. Gardanti Mikhal, 'Michael of the Gardantæ family'. Where an Ossetic name is written in full it will be written in this correct way. Where, however, only initials and surname are given, these will be given in the English style e.g. G. A. Dzagurti. In some cases the Russianised version of the name is given if this is the form of the name which appears in the published work, e.g. T. A. Khæmitsaeva.

categories of Supernatural Enemies, Tasks, Helpers and Objects and there are good Ossetic examples of many very well-known tales, including 'The Dragon Slayer', 'The Two Brothers', 'Rapunzel', 'Magic Flight', 'The Swan Maiden', 'The Princess in the Skin of a Frog', 'The Serpent Prince', 'Little Brother and Little Sister', 'Puss-in-Boots', 'The Golden Bird' and many others. Many Ossetic fairy tales are complex and multi-episodic, often combining several tale-types and a wide range of motifs. They are characterised by their emphasis on the wonderful and the supernatural and the term 'wonder tale' seems far more appropriate to them than 'fairy tale'. The Biazyrov Index has the great merit of using sources where, in many cases, the actual narrator from whom the tale was recorded, is listed. Many collections of Ossetic tales have been published but these are collections based on oral accounts from the archives rather than recorded verbatim from the narrators.[2] Biazyrov uses very authoratative sources and indicates that the fairy tale has long been part of the oral tradition alongside epic legends and ritual texts.

In his study of the Russian folktale, J. V. Haney also prefers the term 'wonder tale' to 'fairy tale' and he defines this form as one among many types of the folktale. Haney regards the folktale as 'an orally derived, traditional verbal art form' (1999: 4). Within the broader category of the folktale, the 'wondertale is basically an oral story about a young man's, or less often a young girl's, initial venture into the frightening adult world' (92). The hero or heroine is tested physically or spiritually, assisted by supernatural agents, whose help, however, is often subject to strict taboo. Through these trials the hero or heroine is transformed to become a different person by the end of the tale, able to take up a new, usually elevated, social position.

From about the middle of the nineteenth century scholars began to collect recordings of Ossetic narrators and singers and to organise and classify the material in archives and a series of publications. Schiefner's *Osetinskie teksty* appeared in 1868, comprising a selection of ritual texts, songs and tales published in Ossetic with Russian translation and commentary. Two series published in Tbilisi in the later part of the nineteenth century, *Sbornik svedenii o Kavkazskikh Gortsakh* (from 1870) and *Sbornik materialov dlia opisaniia Mestnostei i Plemen Kavkaza* (from 1881) also included recordings of Ossetic tales amongst other ethnographic and folklore articles from Ossetia and other parts of the Caucasus region. Particularly noteworthy were the contributions of the Shanaevs (e.g. 1871, 1876).

The outstanding contribution to the collection and study of Ossetic oral literature and the language itself was made by Vsevolod Miller in the nineteenth and early twentieth century. With R. von Stackelberg he published five Digoron stories in 1891; a large number of tales and traditional material of various kinds was included in his three-volume work *Osetinskie etiudy* (1881–7), and a further selection of tales was published in *Digorskie skazaniia* (1902). All of these publications are extensively commentated with linguistic and ethnographic

---

[2] The author does not have access to all the published collections in Ossetic and Russian translation but the particular contribution of S. Britaev and G. Kaloev should be noted (1951, 1959, 1960). These writers have done much to focus attention on the fairy tale within Ossetic oral tradition.

notes, as well as provided with translation into German (Miller and von Stackelberg 1891) or Russian. Additionally, Miller always gives details of the narrators from whom he made his recordings.

In the early twentieth century the study of Ossetic oral material took on a greater impetus. This mirrored the vigorous trend elsewhere within the newly formed Soviet Union, where the collection of folklore was now pursued with a strong emphasis on accurate recording from individual narrators, replacing the earlier tendency to edit collected material (Haney 1999: 35). Scholarly expeditions to the mountain valleys were organised from the research institutes in North and South Ossetia; further material was recorded and classified in the extensive archives, and large folklore collections were published. The greatest of these are the series *Pamiatniki narodnogo tvorchestva Osetin*, published in four volumes between 1925–30 and the three-volume South Ossetic collection, *Khussar iron adæmy uatsmystæ* (1929–31), the third volume of which is devoted to fairy tales and proverbs. These collections contain a wealth of authentic material, including epic legends, folktales, ritual texts, songs, historic stories and prayers. They are scrupulously recorded with translations and notes and their great value is that they are recorded in the original language and dialect of the narrators.[3]

Further edited selections of legends and folktales were published during the course of the twentieth century. An accessible and scholarly source of fairy tales for the European reader is the collection of B. Munkácsi (1927/1932). This scholar recorded tales and songs and other authentic oral material from prisoners of war in Hungary between the years of 1915–17, and in the resulting publication he provided each accurately recorded text with a German translation and commentary. The tales are characterised by their relatively complex plots and abundance of miraculous motifs. They contain many features and characters common to fairy tales the world over but they are nevertheless lively oral accounts by Ossetes living at the time.

After the Second World War the oral tradition began to decline but a landmark in the publication of Ossetic folklore was Z. Salægaty's vast two-volume work, which appeared in 1961. This collection is compiled from archive recordings and some previously published texts. A large portion of the second volume is devoted to fairy tales and after each Ossetic text full details of sources are given.

The most famous oral works of the Ossetes are the epic legends of the Nart heroes. These have been collected in all three main dialects of Ossetic and many editions of the Nart legends have appeared in Ossetic with Russian translation. In 1965 G. Dumézil published a French translation and the best comparative study of the variants of all the legends is that of Khæmitsaeva and Biazyrov (1989–91). In the third volume Khæmitsaeva has included a short article on the Ossetic narrators of the late nineteenth and early twentieth century (1991: 135–53). She has concentrated exclusively on the oral delivery of the Nart legends in her article but the narrators she describes would have also been skilled in many

---

[3] Volume 1 of the North Ossetic series (Dzagurti, 1925) is in Russian, based on recordings of the previous century.

other forms of oral expression. Indeed the great popularity of the Nart legends has somewhat overshadowed the many other forms of traditional Ossetic literature. Gardanti's 1927 collection is a good and typical selection of an Ossetic narrator's output. Here prominence is given to the twenty-five Nart legends but there are also fairy tales, historic tales, funerary texts of horse dedication, wonderful laments and ritual songs and prayers. When examining Ossetic literature it is necessary to take all these forms into account, to understand the full context of the oral tradition.

The narrator in Ossetic society was a person of great importance. As Khæmitsaeva observes, no social function would be complete without him, whether he were simply entertaining listeners on the village assembly place (Ossetic *nykhas*) with a fairy tale or a gripping Nart legend, or performing a lament at a funeral, or a eulogy at a wedding (Khæmitsaeva and Biazyrov 1991: 135–6). The narrators could be drawn from all social classes, since literacy was not a prerequisite and narrators might learn their material from relatives or friends and neighbours within the village community. Many narrators would be active participants in village life, particularly in the capacity of mediator. Being an eloquent man, a storyteller might be called upon to assist in the adjudication of financial matters or family disputes. Nevertheless, as Khæmitsaeva stresses, it was their talent alone which gave them their prominence (Khæmitsaeva and Biazyrov 1991: 136). Nor should the knowledge of their listeners be under-estimated. Ossetes have always been, and remain, extremely knowledgeable about their rich oral tradition. Many sayings still in current use reflect awareness of folk tradition. In the past it seems that storytelling competitions took place on the occasions of the numerous popular festivals in the ritual calendar of the Ossetes. Narrators came from different villages and valleys and recounted their tales to large, enthusiastic audiences and if a narrator was performing badly or misrepresenting a tale in the opinion of his listeners, they would cut him short and another would be called upon to take his place (Khæmitsaeva and Biazyrov 1991: 136). This point is a very important one to bear in mind when considering the oral transmission of tales. Traditional narrators were gifted with excellent memory and although each retelling of a story might vary slightly, particularly with the active participation and reaction of the audience, nevertheless the plot of a tale would have remained fairly stable within a narrator's repertoire. On the other hand, each narrator would have brought something individual to the tales he told. Some narrators would be particularly famed for their renditions of a certain tale or cycle of tales. In a vibrant oral tradition such as that which flourished in Ossetia, people were constantly hearing tales of all kinds and would have done so for generations. In the mouths of the narrators the content and emphasis of those tales would vary and both listeners and narrator would combine to create new versions of tales. This spring of oral creativity seems to have started to run dry only after 1945 in Ossetia (Khæmitsaeva and Biazyrov 1991: 138).

It is important to consider the impact of written literature on any oral tradition and Ossetia is no exception. The intensive collection and study of the oral tradition coincided with the birth and rapid growth of written literature. Ardasenov points out that some writers such as Kanukov and

Kubalov began to publish and rework popular tales; the novelist and short-story writer, Gædiaty Sek'a, showed the deep influence of the oral tradition in his style and imagery. Furthermore, the works of some Ossetic writers, such as the great Khetægkaty K'osta, because of their strong links with popular tradition, were recited widely alongside genuinely oral works, as if they too were part of that tradition (Ardasenov 1959: 49–51). Nevertheless, this influence from literature should not be over-emphasised in the case of Ossetia where, although it is impossible to date the source of much oral material, there is no doubt that the local narrator must have been the means of transmission and preservation of tradition over many centuries. The epic cycles of the Narts, which are thought to be very ancient in origin, contain many well-known fairy tales, as will be seen below.

J. V. Haney (1999: 4) stresses the importance of the oral tradition in Russia and comments that each telling of a tale was an event which could never be repeated exactly. The narrator on each occasion would give a unique performance, using varied intonation, gestures, facial expressions, and the audience would respond; none of this could be recorded in writing. Additionally, as Haney rightly observes, storytellers improvise and borrow from each other, thus creating new tales with a new combination of motifs (1999: 12). The resulting tale may or may not require a new classification. Fairy tales seem to have been particularly susceptible to this, as a glance at the Aarne Thompson Index will show. Often their plots are multi-episodic and contain many motifs; Haney goes on to discuss a Russian narrative, recorded by Afanas'ev which contains eight tale types (1999: 16–17).

He comments further on the importance of the narrator's art which, he observes, was not always well understood by the early collectors of the Russian folktale (1999: 19–20):

> In order to tell a tale successfully, the raconteur must not only know the structure of Russian folktales, . . . and the plots of tales, . . . but also possess the storyteller's art. In the natural setting the teller is an ad-lib actor with a well-known script whose success depends not just on knowing the story but on telling it in an appropriate way. The ability to use the voice, facial gestures, and body language is part of a good performance. So, too, is the characteristic language of the narrator.

Although the language of the fairy tale is often formulaic with many stock expressions to describe, for example, the beauty of the heroine or the distance the hero has to travel, every narrator would have given a familiar tale a unique sound and appeal to the audience. The formulaic expressions may in many cases be very old, predating some of the fairy tales themselves. Haney points out the importance of formulaic expression in the composition of epic poetry and indicates that certain stock phrases have survived in oral prose as fixed epithets that aid composition and comprehension (1999: 21). Undoubtedly the familiarity of such expressions would have enhanced the tale, as well as placing it firmly in the realm of fantasy.

Now it is necessary to look at the work of the Ossetic narrators in a little more detail. In her description of these men, Khæmitsaeva quotes G. A. Dzagurti's description of the performance of Mudoïty Sabe (Khæmitsaeva and Biazyrov 1991: 140):

> All my life I will remember . . . the fervour with which Sabe was gripped when, on 26 March, 1909, he recounted to me with extraordinary artistry, in the presence of other listeners, the best of his Nart tales, 'The Tale of the Skin of the Black Fox'. I sat by him spellbound and listened to the tale to the end, without stopping him or interrupting him with questions, so as not to spoil his poetic inspiration. . . . The tale was recorded by me, word for word, without any changes.

Dzagurti, who had known the narrator since childhood, described his appearance and how he used gesticulation, facial expressions and a variety of different voice tones to enhance his narratives. He paid tribute to Sabe's narrative skill and inspiration and indicated how the other listeners present, who were neighbours of the storyteller, and included a well-known local hunter, listened with equally rapt attention. The tale in question is published as text 95 in Salægaty (1961: I, 312–22).

The tale of the Skin of the Black Fox is very well known among the Ossetic Nart legends (Khæmitsaeva and Biazyrov 1991: 110–11) and it was recorded by M. Gardanti in the Digoron village of Mækhchesk on 26 September, 1903 from another great narrator, Kertibiti Kertibi (Gardanti 1927: 37–42). The style and content of the two versions is rather different but the tale, although categorised as a Nart epic tale, is in fact a series of fairy tales told within the framework of a hunting legend.

G. A. Dzagurti has been of particular importance in the collection of Ossetic oral material, in that he has provided much information about the narrators themselves. He gives an excellent short biographical introduction to the work of the narrator Kertibiti Kertibi in his Introduction to Gardanti's collection (1927: ix–xiii). Kertibi was born in 1834 in the Digoron village of Uæqæs, where he died in 1914. His mother Dzotzo was married into the aristocratic Tuganov family as a concubine (*qumaiæg uosæ*) but, because of her inferior social status, she lived in poverty and her children achieved no rise in social status through their father. At the age of fourteen, Kertibi became independent of his father's family and adopted his first name as his surname also, thus founding his own family name. He gradually acquired some livestock for himself and lived modestly. As his reputation as a narrator grew, he played an ever fuller part in the life of the village.

He is said to have learned some of his material from his mother who was an enthusiast for the traditional stories and lays, but he also acquired his art and repertoire from other village elders while he was still young. Kertibi was a master of the Digoron dialect and his stories are always rich in content. He was particularly strong in relating Nart epic legends but he also included historic stories, fairy tales, hunting tales and a variety of fine ritual songs and laments among his repertoire. Dzagurti describes his style as unusually easy (Gardanti 1927: xiii) but it is clear from some of the omissions or brevity of expression in many of his narratives, that Kertibi expected his audience to know the tales he was recounting. They would only require a brief reference to some details. A good example can be found at the beginning of his tale of Ækhsaræ and Ækhsærtægk (Gardanti 1927: 5):

There came a time when the Boriatæ descended on the Ækhsærtægkatæ and left none of their male progeny alive apart from Bayodza. But he was, as you yourself may know, such a useless blundering, low-born man. But still one of the women of the Ækhsærtægkatæ, the daughter of a poor man, went away to her parental home with troubled heart. God alone knows what happened, then twins, two sons were born to her.

The reference to low birth would have struck a chord with the listeners, since Kertibi himself was of that social class. Moreover, here the narrator appeals directly to the knowledge of his listeners. He often performed his stories to the accompaniment of a two-stringed *fændyr*, a traditional Ossetic instrument, and the whole village would turn out to hear him, old and young. According to Dzagurti, the performances were so absorbing that the listeners would stay all day long and express their regret when Kertibi grew tired (Gardanti 1927: xiii).

Dzagurti regrets that Gardanti did not record the whole of the repertoire of this great storyteller and remarks that when he visited Kertibi in 1910, to try to record further material, the narrator had by then grown too old to remember his stories well. Thus the 1927 collection is only a selection of Kertibi's large repertoire, recorded when his memory was still excellent, but it is good enough to give us a clear idea of the great art of this man.

In the tale of the Black Fox, three heroes set out together to hunt the elusive and remarkable animal, but they cannot agree on who should have its pelt as a trophy. They start a storytelling competition to decide the prize. The hero Oræzmæg tells the tale of the hunter who is transformed into a dog by an enchantress and who is then sold into the service of various people, where he distinguishes himself by his exceptional cleverness and skill. He finally gets his revenge by turning the enchantress herself into a bitch, who gives birth to his two hunting hounds, and then a mare, who gives birth to his great heroic horse.

This tale can be classified as AT 449, 'The Tsar's Dog', and it is an extremely popular one in Ossetia (Biazyrov 1958: 332) and, indeed, elsewhere in the Caucasus. It is often attached to the legendary hunter Tsopan and is told very widely and in great detail. Its popularity is no doubt in part due to its association with hunting lore. It is usually told as the tale of a hunter who chases a marvellous animal who turns out to be an enchantress in animal form. There are probably traces of an old belief in a hunting goddess here which have been discussed elsewhere (Chaudhri 1996: 175). Munkácsi (1927: 48–57) recorded a detailed variant from Zakhari Kokoev in 1917, where the motif of the unfaithful wife is introduced and the unfortunate hunter is eventually released from his enchantment through the aid of a goose-maiden.

The second tale in the competition is told by Khæmits, who relates the tale of his marriage to a beautiful woman, which incurs the jealousy of his other wives. They curse the girl, who sickens and dies, but Khæmits resurrects her from the grave by rubbing a jewel from a serpent's head upon her body. In Mudoïty Sabe's version of the Black Fox tale, Khæmits relates the other story which is often associated with him in the epic cycles, but is also a very widely known fairy tale, namely that of his marriage with a frog who sheds her skin at night to become a beautiful maiden. Khæmits, however, becomes impatient with the arrangement and throws the frog-skin upon the fire, whereupon his wife, said in this text to be a daughter of the Water Guardian (Ossetic *Donbettyr*), is at once compelled to return to the water but she leaves him pregnant with their son, by spitting between his shoulders. In the epic cycles this is the story of the birth of the great hero Batraz, who is cut from his father's back but, once again, this is also recognisable as the text of a well-known fairy tale (Biazyrov 1958: 329).

The third tale in the competition is told by the hero Soslan who relates a hunting tale of how he and his foster-brother were out hunting. When they had killed a hare the foster-brother started to cook it on top of an anthill but the hare came back to life and ran away. Soslan then kills himself and enters the world of the dead. Once he has sought a wife for himself from among the dead, the foster-brother rolls him on the anthill and he too is restored to life. Soslan wins the fox pelt, since he is deemed to have had a witness to his activities.

Storytelling practices, including the competition, are reflected within the oral tradition itself. In the epic cycles of the Narts a famous story recounts how the heroes were competing in storytelling for the *Uatsamongæ*, a miraculous cup which can reveal the truth of a hero's account of his valour (Salægaty 1961: 253–4). This has been compared by several commentators (e.g. Abaev 1945: 65) to Herodotus's account of a bowl among the Scythian warriors and is one of the features of the Nart cycles which many consider to be very archaic because of the Sarmatian ancestry of the Ossetes (Herodotus IV, 66; trans. A. D. Godley):

> Moreover once in every year each governor of a province brews a bowl of wine in his own province, whereof those Scythians drink who have slain enemies; those who have not achieved this taste not this wine but sit apart dishonoured; and this they count a very great disgrace; but as many as have slain not one but many enemies, they have each two cups and so drink of them both.

It is impossible to say how old the Nart epic traditions are. Although they contain many apparently archaic features, yet it is impossible, with the lack of written evidence, to say how old the material is. It is certainly difficult to envisage an oral tradition reaching down through the centuries and passed from generation to generation till very recent times, yet this would seem to be the case. The Nart cycles are known elsewhere in the Caucasus, notably among the Circassian peoples, where they have also been handed down in an oral tradition.

It is interesting to examine in a little more detail the art of the two narrators of the Black Fox story. Kertibi, renowned for his economical style, does indeed present the more succinct text. Typical of his style are the many rhetorical questions he addresses to his audience. When describing the encounter with the enchantress, he uses a series of wishes of Uoræzmæg (Gardanti 1927: 38–9):

> Uoræzmæg said, . . . Then evening brought me to a house. I sat down in the room and I said with feeling, 'Would that there were a fire for me!' A fire appeared for me. Then I said, 'If only there would appear by the fire a round table full for me!' A round table appeared for me and I sated myself. 'Ah well,

now if only, amid all this abundance, there were a bed for me!' A bed appeared for me and I lay down. Then a woman came along and lay at the foot of the couch. Sleep no longer came to me. I stirred and the woman said, 'Hey! My sated guest, be still!' The second time it was also like that but the third time I remained upon her. Saying, 'May God not pardon you!' she took out a felt whip from her pillow and brushed me with it, 'As I wish, so become the ox of Begendi!' I became an ox.

One may imagine the effect this series of wishes would have had on his audience. Simply expressed, they would have appealed directly to the hearts of the listeners. Any visitor to an Ossetic household would at once be offered food and treated with great honour as a guest, with the best of all the household could offer. Certainly in popular lore it would be incumbent on a woman, in the absence of male members of the household, to entertain a passing guest. It would also be incumbent on the guest to behave with honour. Kertibi brings out the humour of the situation with his simple statements: 'Then a woman came along . . .'. The hero expresses no surprise at this. 'Sleep no longer came to me' and for his understandable misbehaviour, Uoræzmæg is punished by his far-from-ordinary hostess.

Let us compare this with Mudoïty Sabe's account. First of all, Sabe spends much more time on the episode of the actual shooting of the black fox. It must be remembered that on the occasion of this narration a very renowned hunter was present. The three heroes argue about who shot the fox, with which weapon (Salægaty 1961: 313):

> Then they spoke to each other, all three at once:'Indeed I shot its thigh!'Another, however, said, 'Indeed I shot its neck!' While another said, 'Indeed I shot its middle!' So they began to quarrel. They sat down and said, 'What shall we do? Indeed we shall remain without supper.'

Sabe's account is full of dialogue and he thereby introduces a note of humour and also pays tribute to the established and sacred hunting customs which would require a strict order in the allocation of the prey (Chaudhri 1996: 167). The preamble about who shot and who should have the pelt of the fox is much longer than Kertibi's account. Finally the three heroes decide on the storytelling competition. Again Sabe's account is full of questions to his audience. He describes Oræzmæg's encounter with the beautiful girl, 'a golden girl' (Salægaty 1961: 316):

> When half the night had passed, then I no longer held back and I would touch her. So the girl said:
> 'What are you doing? Why are you doing this? Leave me alone!'
> How could I leave her alone? Once again I touched her.

It is at this point that the sorceress seizes her whip and changes Oræzmæg into a dog. The narrator continues in Oræzmæg's own words: 'What happened, God knows, then I mated and when my day came, she took me outside and on a mat I gave birth to two hunting hounds.'

Sabe includes the reaction of the audience: 'The people were therefore amazed. "We have never heard anything more extraordinary than this! So now how will the fox skin be taken from him?"'

Mudoïty Sabe's style is earthy, simple and direct, in the best tradition of Ossetic narrators, and one can well understand how his narrative must have appealed to his audience and why Dzagurti was so impressed by it. He uses stock phrases to great effect but his style is also unique. Particularly striking is his use of repetetive direct speech throughout the narrative.

In the second account of Khæmits, Sabe spends much time again on the hunting etiquette of dividing up the spoils and sharing with any chance-comer. No doubt many of his listeners that day were adept hunters or at least fully aware of the very strict etiquette of hunting. The hero meets a tiny man in the forest 'a span tall' and of a similar width: 'O God what will this turn out to be' (Salægaty 1961: 317). This is typical of the lively style of the narrator, exemplified by Sabe: the heroes when they see trouble approaching often pose such a question, as if anticipating the thoughts of the listeners.

Another fine example of a fairy tale which also has currency as a Nart legend is the tale of the Nart progenitors, Ækhsaræ and Ækhsærtæg, which is a good rendition of the widespread tale of the Two Brothers. Kurt Ranke had already noted Kertibi's version in his great 1934 study of this widespread tale (1934: 104). Once again it is worth comparing the account of Kertibi, recorded 30 September, 1903 in Mækhchesk (Gardanti 1927: 5–8), with that of another narrator, Qarati Myrzabeg, recorded 28 August, 1933 in the village of Lesken (Salægaty 1961: 21–7). The latter account gives more detail than the former and explains circumstances more fully. A good point of comparison is the episode where the first of the brothers meets his wife-to-be. On the previous night, while guarding an apple tree, the hero shoots a bird which has been attacking the tree; the bird flies away but the hero keeps a little drop of its blood and sets out on its trail. Kertibi then describes what follows (Gardanti 1927: 6):

> Then he arrived at the village of a Khan. The Khan's daughter was on the verge of death and people had gathered round her. The girl was she whom Ækhsærtæg had shot that night. Ækhsærtæg stood at the edge of the crowd; he took from his purse the drop of blood on the leaf of the tree; he smeared her wound with this and the girl became as good as if newly born from her mother. The Khan gave her to him as his wife.

Kertibi's listeners would have had no difficulty in understanding this episode, although it is expressed with minimal detail; the audience would have known the story and followed the narrative thread easily, as long as Kertibi omitted no detail of importance.

Qarati Myrzabeg's description is much more elaborate. The hero finds an old man and woman inside a burial mound watching over their dying daughter and a dialogue ensues between the hero and the couple. They explain that they only had daughters and that the girls were bringing them apples from somewhere so that they could retain their sight but that now the girl has returned wounded. The hero asks (Salægaty 1961: 23):

'And is there no medicine at all for her illness?'

They said to him, 'Certainly there is a cure for her: if her wound were to be smeared with a drop of her own blood, then she would get better.'

'In that case, it is not difficult,' said Ækhsaræ and he took the droplets of blood from his purse and smeared the wound of the sick girl. Immediately the girl became as good as if newly born from her mother. When the mother and father saw this, then they said, 'You have rescued our daughter from doom; well now, probably God has considered her worthy of you and so may our gift to you be as God's gift.' What better thing could Ækhsaræ have asked of God? And he began to live there with them.

Qarati's tale also gives a description of the woman whom the hero meets when out on the hunt: 'a woman, with one fang reaching to the ground, another reaching the sky, came up to him'. This monstrous female is reminiscent of the Russian Baba Yaga. In Kertibi's account no description of the woman is given. The two tales end rather differently. Both include the motif of the arrow of truth. Suspicion comes between the two brothers on account of the wife of the first hero who cannot tell the twins apart. In Kertibi's version, the arrow simply chops off one of the fingers of Ækhsærtæg's hand because he had doubted his brother. This gives the tale symmetry, since Ækhsaræ had lost a finger earlier in the tale when he had failed to guard the apple tree. In Qarati's version, the arrow divides and strikes both brothers dead, leaving the pregnant wife of Ækhsaræ to mourn, a powerful image which has been much favoured by illustrators. Her twin sons grow up to restart the family line.

Here is a good example of how variant tales arise but also that one cannot be said to be a more valid version than the other. In many respects these two variants of the story resemble each other closely, even in some of the turns of phrase used, but the style of the two narrators is very different and the preferred endings represent two separate lines of tradition.

The story of the Two Brothers is a very popular one in Ossetia and is told outside the context of the Nart Epos. Once again its popularity might, at least in part, be accounted for because of the strong hunting background to the tale. Biazyrov (1958: 323–4) lists several variants where the heroes of the tale are differently named. The story of Saui and Budzi, for example, combines the tale with that of the Dragon-Slayer; such a combination is very common throughout Europe. Saui, after parting from his brother, slays a serpent which is devouring the maidens of a village. With the help of friendly wild animals, Saui overcomes the monster and his evil master, and marries the girl he rescues. Then follows the episode of his meeting the enchantress in the forest and his rescue by his twin brother. In a Russian translation of this story (Britaev and Kazbekov 1951: 204–12), Saui slays his brother in a fit of jealousy over the wife but the slain twin is resurrected by the helpful animals and the brothers are reconciled. Also the story starts much more within the usual frame of the fairy tale: the two brothers are said to be the sons of poor parents. When their loving mother dies, the father remarries but the boys are mistreated by their stepmother and they decide to run away. It is at this point of crisis, typical of the fairy tale, that the boys start to meet with their adventures.

Up to this point attention has been drawn to fairy tales which also appear as part of the epic Nart cycles. In a living oral tradition it is impossible to keep the forms apart. Fairy tale, folktale, epic legend, ritual poetry and prose mutually influence and inform each other. However, not just any fairy tale that has a Nart name attached to it can be considered a Nart legend. A good case in point is that of Asægo. This is the first of the five Ossetic tales recorded by Miller and Von Stackelberg from Tukkati Masiko (1891: 1–15). The tale is described in the introduction as a Nart legend but the commentators have difficulty in placing it, since the hero Asægo is unknown as a Nart hero and this tale is not recounted elsewhere in the epic cycles. It is multi-episodic and complex and also rather long. It begins in true fairy-tale style with a childless old man and woman. The beloved baby is left in a forest and discovered by a giant who takes him home to rear. The child grows up exceptonally strong and eventually rediscovers his parents and the secret of his upbringing. He wins a beautiful wife by virtue of his exceptionl strength but then a malicious old woman sows discontent between the boy and his parents. The parents keep demanding that the youth bring his wife to them to keep house but he refuses. The youth sets out, meets two other strong companions and they encounter three strong maidens in a field. They wrestle with them and while the elder two are defeated, Asægo wins the younger, a golden-haired beauty. At this point we seem to lose track of his original wife. The two go on together and camp by a waterside. While Asægo is away hunting one day, his wife is discovered by a local noble who covets her. By treachery one of his servants finds out that Asægo's soul is kept in the nape of his neck and, after two attempts, succeeds in killing the great hero by simply removing the soul while he sleeps and drowning it. The nobleman then has the wife brought to him but she stalls his advances by asking leave to mourn her husband in the traditional way for a year. This is granted. Meanwhile, by means of a life token, the erstwhile companions of the hero see a spring flow with blood and understand that he has died. They seek and find him and resuscitate him by catching the fish who has swallowed his soul. The wife is then restored to him.

This tale, overladen with episode and marvel and a little illogical in structure, is classified as AT 465, 'The man persecuted because of his beautiful wife' (Biazyrov 1958: 333–4). It certainly is not a Nart legend but a detailed fairy tale, comprising at least two plots and a large number of typical fairy-tale motifs.

Such complex plots are characteristic of the fairy tale in Ossetic. Even Kertibi's fairy tales which are told outside the context of the Nart cycles, are more intricate and emphasise magical help. They also involve much more repetition. For example, his version of the Magic Flight story, 'The Khan's Son' (Gardanti 1927: 105–8), involves the flight of the hero from a wolf who has sworn to eat him on his wedding day. The youth flees and comes upon supernatural women in three towers who offer him aid in the form of magical objects, but who also say that their power alone is not sufficient to rid the boy of his pursuer. In each case they say he must go to a more powerful older sister. With the aid of the magic objects – a comb, two loaves of bread and a strand of hair which can become a bridge – the hero meets a monstrous woman with fangs who emerges from a burial mound. These motifs are reminiscent of Russian traditions about the Baba Yaga and her sisters. One very interesting detail in this tale is the second appearance of the wolf. When the boy sets off to the house of his betrothed, the young women in the house are making dough figurines, in accordance with custom. One girl makes the figure of a wolf which comes to life and pursues the boy. This is a good example of Ossetic culture reflected in the tale, since the making of such figurines in the shape of people and animals, to ensure prosperity, would have been customary on the occasion of a wedding (Gardanti 1927: 105), as it was on festival days such as New Year.

Another example of the complexity of the Ossetic fairy tale is the tale of the 'Bronze Maiden in the Copper Tower' (Britaev and Kazbekov 1951: 117–29). This tale begins with the abandonment of three sisters in a forest; the trio are discovered by a nobleman who marries the youngest because she promises to bear him two beautiful children. The older sisters grow envious and substitute two puppies for the children, at which the husband is enraged and banishes his hapless wife. The children are kept in isolation by their jealous aunts who incite the boy to go on an impossible quest to seek the Bronze Maiden. When he succeeds in this, they send him on a second quest to seek a miraculous, animated fur coat. With the aid of supernatural animals and objects he succeeds in this too. Eventually the treachery of the aunts is discovered and the nobleman welcomes his children and banished wife back. In his introduction to this collection of tales, Britaev stresses the artistry of the Ossetic fairy tale and describes it as a more popular, more accessible form than other types of oral tradition. In comparing the fairy tales with the animal tales which are also common in Ossetic, he indicates that the more laconic style of the latter marks them out as older, and that the fantastic plots and complex composition of the fairy tales indicate that they are a less ancient form of narrative (Britaev and Kazbekov 1951: 5–6). Haney makes a similar point in the case of the Russian tales, suggesting that the wonder tale seems to have arisen later, 'from a common cultural milieu in Europe' (Haney 1999: 89, 92).

There is no doubt that in Ossetia, even though some fairy tales are preserved within the Nart epic cycles, the fairy tale forms a separate genre with its peculiar characteristics of form and subject matter. It is, however, impossible to say with any certainty, and without further research into the possible influences on the tale from sources outside Ossetia, in particular Russia, how old the genre is. The Ossetic tales do seem to have their own flavour, influenced by their own rich cultural context, particularly the hunting tradition; certain other aspects of Ossetic ritual and culture, and the high regard for the epic tradition, may account for the popularity of certain tale types. The most important feature of the Ossetic fairy tale is, however, that it is an oral form. Its transmission through generations of narrators skilled in various forms of traditional narrative has meant that the form has remained fluid until very recent times, and that it has both affected, and been strongly affected by, many other forms of oral tradition.

References

Aarne, A., and Thompson, S. (1981), *The Types of the Folktale. A Classification and Bibliography*. FFC 184. Helsinki.

Abaev, V. I. (1945), 'Nartovskii epos', *Izvestiia Severo-osetinskogo nauchno-issledovatel'skogo instituta* X.i. Dzaudzhyqæu.

Ardasenov, Kh. N. (1959), *Ocherk razvitiia osetinskoi literatury.* Ordzhonikidze.

Biazyrov, A. Kh. (1958), 'Opyt klassifikatsii osetinskikh narodnykh skazok po sisteme Aarne–Andreeva', *Izvestiia Iugo-osetinskogo nauchno-issledovatel'skogo instituta Akademii nauk Gruzinskoi SSR* 9.

Britaev, S., and Kazbekov, K. (1951) trans., *Osetinskie narodnye skazki.* Moscow.

Britaev, S., and Kaloev, G. (1959), *Osetinskie narodnye skazki.* Moscow.

——(1960), *Iron adæmy aræutæ.* Ordzhonikidze.

Chaudhri, A. (1996), 'The Caucasian Hunting-Divinity, Male and Female: Traces of the Hunting-Goddess in Ossetic Folklore', in *The Concept of the Goddess,* ed. S. Billington and M. Green. London/New York.

Dumézil, G. (1965), *Le Livre des héros.* Paris.

Dzagurti, G. (1925), *Pamiatniki narodnogo tvorchestva Osetin* 1. Vladikavkaz.

Gardanti, M. (1927), *Pamiatniki narodnogo tvorchestva Osetin* 2, with introduction, Russian translation and commentary by G. A. Dzagurti. Vladikavkaz.

Haney, J. V. (1999), *An Introduction to the Russian Folktale.* New York/London.

Herodotus (1982), trans. A. D. Godley. Loeb Classical Library. Cambridge, MA/ London.

Khæmitsaeva, T. A., and Biazyrov, A. Kh. (1989–91), *Narty. Osetinskii geroicheskii epos.* 3 vols. Moscow.

Maliti, G. (1986), *Iræf.* Ordzhonikidze.

Miller, V. (1881–7), *Osetinskie etiudy.* 3 vols. Moscow.

——(1902), *Digorskie skazaniia.* Moscow.

Miller, V., and von Stackelberg, R. (1891), *Fünf ossetische Erzählungen in digorischem Dialect.* St Petersburg.

Munkácsi, B. (1927/1932), 'Blüten der ossetischen Volksdichtung', *Keleti szemle* xx. Budapest.

Ranke, K. (1934), *Die zwei Brüder.* FFC 114. Helsinki.

Salægaty, Z. (1961), *Iron adæmy sfældystad.* 2 vols. Ordzhonikidze.

Schiefner, A. (1868), *Osetinskie teksty.* St Petersburg.

Shanaev, Dzh. (1871), 'Narodnyia skazaniia Kavkazskikh Gortsev: osetinskiia narodnyia skazaniia', *Sbornik svedenii o Kavkazskikh Gortsakh.* Tbilisi.

Shanaev, G. (1876), 'Narodnyia skazaniia Kavkazskikh Gortsev: iz osetinskikh skazanii o Nartakh', *Sbornik svedenii o Kavkazskikh Gortsakh.* Tbilisi.

14

Russian Fairy Tales and Their Collectors

JAMES RIORDAN

When the eastern Slavs trekked north and eastwards from south central Europe some fifteen hundred years ago, they found themselves in a strange terrain, flat and marshy, interspersed with broad rivers. Some tribes headed south from Kiev through a tree-less steppe of feather grass so high it could conceal a horse and rider, a country which Nikolai Gogol describes in *Taras Bulba* as 'a land of the tall embrace, of a greenish-yellow ocean sprinkled with millions of spring flowers.'

Other tribes went due east, clearing a way by axe and fire through a forest of fir, pine, silver birch and larch, well watered by bog and lake, nourishing great numbers of wild animals: elk and wolf, bear and wild boar, and many fur-bearing rodents. Still others paddled their canoes along the Volga and Dvina rivers northwards, past Novgorod and Pskov, through solid pine forests to lakes Ladoga and Onega. All these varied lands settled by the eastern Slavs became known as *Rus* or Russia. Initially three of the tribes were called according to hair colour: red, black and white Russians. The white Russians – *Belorus* – retain their name to this day; the black Russians became 'Little' or 'Minor Russians', and then the people living on the borderlands (*okraina*) – 'Ukrainians'. The red Russians became 'Great Russians', then simply Russians.

According to Russian historian Vasili Kliuchevskii (1841–1911), we must learn about the Russian forest, river and steppe in order to understand the Russian people. In his *Course of Russian History* (written down by his students at Moscow University from his lecture notes), he wrote (Kliuchevskii 1901: I, 27):

> The forest provided the Russian with oak and pine to build his house, it warmed him with aspen and birch, it lit his hut with birchwood splinters, it shod him in birch bast sandals, it gave him plates and dishes, clothed him in hides and furs and fed him honey. The forest was the best shelter from his enemies.

But life in the forest was tough and dangerous; a way had to be hacked through the thick undergrowth; trees had to be cut down to make a clearing for huts and cattle; wolves and bears stalked man and beast. It was an awe-inspiring world of weird sounds and menacing shadows. The forest taught caution and kindled fantasy.

Kliuchevskii observes (36–7):

The silence of the sleepy, dense forest frightened the Russian. It seemed to harbour something evil in the fearful, soundless twilight of its ancient summits. The momentary expectation of sudden, unexpected, unforeseen danger strained his nerves, excited his imagination. And the ancient Russian peopled the forest with all kinds of fantastic creatures. It was the dark realm of the one-eyed woodsprite who would amuse himself by leading men astray.

The steppe put quite a different imprint on the Russian soul. Its endless expanse gave the feeling of vast horizons and distant dreams. Yet it was even more menacing than the forest, for it offered no hiding place from the marauding nomads and the dreaded Tatars. The forest and steppe, therefore, evinced conflicting feelings, were both friend and foe. Not so the Russian river (Kliuchevskii 1901: I, 39–40):

> He loved his river. There is no other feature of the land so fondly sung of in folklore. And for good reason. In his meanderings, she showed him the way; in his settlements, she was his constant companion. He placed his home upon her banks. For most of the year she fed him. For the trader she was the perfect summer and winter road. She taught the Russian order and sociability; she made men brothers, made them feel part of society, taught them to respect the customs of others, to trade goods and experience, to invent and to adapt.

The rivers and lakes, too, had their mysteries. In a world inhabited by demons, it is easy to understand how primitive Russians thought the spirit of the river murmured when pleased or roared when angry. The continual motion of water naturally suggested that it was alive. So each river had its spirit – old, ugly, green-bearded – who, when drunk, made the rivers overflow; when pleased, guided the fish into the fishermen's nets; when cross, raised storms, sank boats, seized and strangled sailors, tore traps and lines. In the depths of the waters lived the *rusalka* or water nymph, a lovely naked girl with skin the colour of moonlight, silken hair and emerald eyes. She so charmed passers-by with her laughter and song that some would drown themselves for her sake.

Here, then, are the principal offspring of Mother Nature that formed the Russian soul and lent Russian folklore its special flavour and imagery. Much of the subject matter is, of course, common to folktales throughout the world. But the style is purely Russian, a faithful mirroring of customs, fears, prejudices and dreams, all nurtured by the Russian habitat.

The unique artistry of Russian folktales must in part be attributed to the storytellers (*skomorokhi*), who cultivated their storytelling art and passed down stories by word of mouth from generation to generation. These minstrels, jesters, blind pedlars, vagabonds of every sort, masters of the telling of a tale, were most welcome in the strung-out settlements. Some were so adept at their craft that they were 'able to relate tales not only the whole night through, but for several days on end' writes Yuri Sokolov (1950: 7).

At a time when modern life had not yet spread into the remotest corners of the countryside, storytelling was a favourite entertainment in the quietness and monotony of the long winter evenings, in a land where snow covers the earth for half the year. As recently as 1915, the Sokolov brothers could describe the following scene (1915: 57–8):

> In the winter, in the depths of the forest, far from any habitation, there is often a whole village gathered together – peasants, their wives and children. By day there is the heavy toil, but, when it begins to grow dark, there is the well-deserved repose beside a blazing hearth. In the forest they build a camp – that is, a spacious mud hut with a hearth in the middle. The people are packed in and here they warm their chilled limbs and satisfy their hunger and thirst. They then begin to while away the long winter evening.
>
> What a valuable person, then, does the storyteller prove to be. In the midst of the dense forest, with trees crackling from the frost, to the accompaniment of the howling of wolves, beside the blazing fire – what an apt setting, what a wonderful atmosphere for a folk tale full of every imaginable kind of terror. And here the storyteller comes on to the scene, the jester, the merry fellow, whose witticisms and mockery pour forth as from a horn of plenty. The entire audience listens with bated breath, and unanimously and rapturously acclaims his diverting story.

When the Sokolov brothers were recording folktales, they recalled that fishermen would come and bargain with the storyteller who pleased them most, promising him a portion of their catch if he would accompany them on their fishing expeditions. Naturally, the storyteller did not work for nothing, and it is a device of their craft that they would frequently begin their story with a *priskazka* – a prelude to the story, hinting that they needed a drink to recall the story itself; and they would finish the tale with a humorous rhyme calling for their reward (another drink) (Sokolov 1915: 76):

> It was at the feast I heard this tale,
> There it was I drank mead ale.
> Though it flowed down my beard, my mouth stayed dry,
> For never a drop passed my lips swear I!

It is interesting that in Russia folktales were for so long not simply tales to amuse the common people, but to entertain gentlefolk too. A good storyteller was a much prized possession in many wealthy homes, including that of the tsar himself. The first Russian tsar, Ivan IV ('The Terrible'), was said to be a great admirer of folktales and had at Court three blind men who would take turns at his bedside, telling stories to lull him to sleep. The Russian poet Alexander Pushkin acknowledges his debt to his childhood nurse Ariana Rodionovna for his great love of folktales. Count Leo Tolstoy, as a child, fell asleep to the stories told by an old man who had been purchased by his grandfather for his storytelling skill. Folk stories recounted by serf nurses to young aristocratic gentlefolk provided themes for innumerable Russian masterpieces, from the music of Tchaikovsky (*Sleeping Beauty, Swan Lake, Nutcracker*), Rimsky-Korsakov (*Sadko, The Snow Maiden, The Golden Cockerel*) and Stravinsky (*The Firebird, Petrushka*), to the writings of Pushkin, Gogol and Aksakov. Indeed, there can scarcely have been a Russian writer or composer of any stature whose work was not inspired at one time or another by memories of folktales told in childhood.

But storytellers had not always been so welcome. The tsar Alexei Mikhailo-vich, father of Peter the Great, had the *skomorokhi* rounded up and their tongues cut out. In the famous royal edict of 1649 it was proclaimed: 'Many persons stupidly believe in dreams, in the evil eye and birdsong, and they propound riddles and tell fairy stories. By idle talk and merry-making and blasphemy, they destroy their souls.'

Ironically enough, it was during the reign of Tsar Alexei Mikhailovich that the first records of oral Russian tales were made. But they were not published in Russia or in their mother tongue. Ten tales were recorded by an English-man, Samuel Collins (1619–70), who worked in Moscow as royal physician during the 1660s. His stories, along with travel notes, were published in London in 1671 under the title *The Present State of Russia*. It was to be nearly two centuries, however, before a collection of Russian folktales was published in Russia.[1]

Why, in the land of its birth, were records of the Russian folktale so late in appearing? After all, Charles Perrault began publishing his French fairy tales in 1697 and the brothers Jacob and Wilhelm Grimm their German tales in 1812. The answer to this Russian riddle also explains why Russia's voice was silent for so long in literature generally; it was only in the nineteenth century that Russian literature and music came to life. An explanation for this late start must be sought partly in the role of the Church in Russia.

It has to be said that, unlike the Sumerians, Egyptians, ancient Greeks and Aztecs, the Slavs generally left no written record of their folktales. Only after their christianisation in the late tenth century did literacy and literature appear. When Christianity (the eastern branch of the Catholic church – Greek, then Russian, Orthodoxy) came to Russia, it outlawed the pagan Slav gods, although some of their features reappeared in the legendary feats of the saints. But the old cults continued: either they were adopted by the new Church as its own rites, or they became magic. Thus, Perun, the god of thunder and lightning, became Ilya the Prophet; Volos, guardian of herds and flocks, became St Vlasia; Kupalnitsa, goddess of rivers and lakes, became St Agrippina; the spring rites now coincided with Easter, the winter Calendae was replaced by Christmas, and the Festival of Yarilo, god of the sun and all earthly life, became St John's Day. Nevertheless, the memory of local gods persisted and the fear of them degenerated into superstition. At this stage of disorganisation of local custom, the magic of folktales became half-fantastic, half-conventional; transmitted as they were, orally and under the ban of the Church, the tales became diluted with faint memories of real history, lost folk songs and laments, Christian legend and superstitions dating back to earlier times.

The Church, by its control of printed literature in Russia, was for several centuries able to prevent the literate from reading the 'fables of men'; they were not to be deflected from the 'Divine Scriptures'. In any case, the idea of using written Russian, so intimately associated with the Church Slavonic, for the coarse peasant language of the oral tales was alien to the Russian tradition. Even

---

[1] For a detailed account of the early recording and collection of Russian folktales see Haney (1999: 23–36).

when Russia's first poet of note, Alexander Pushkin (1799–1837), attempted to imitate the folktale, he was condemned for intruding peasant vulgarity into refined aristocratic society. Like other writers to follow, he was compelled to 'prettify' the folktale, draw on west European, not Russian sources, before it could be accepted. It was perhaps hardly surprising that the priests and the nobility should find themselves lampooned by the folk whose lore they sought to suppress, or even by eminent Russian writers in their stylised folktales. For example, Pushkin's satire on the clergy, *The Priest and His Workman Balde*, was banned during his short lifetime, then published four years after his death (in a duel) as *The Merchant Ostolop and His Workman Balde*, and was only restored to its original version some forty years later.

Despite the dead hand of Church censorship, the nineteenth century saw the intensive recording and study of folktales. In 1838 there appeared the first attempt at a collection of true folktales – five stories under the title *Russian Folk Tales*, by Bogdan Bronnitsyn, taken down, the preface says, 'from the words of an itinerant storyteller, a peasant from the Moscow region, to whom they had been related by an old man, his father' (Bronnitsyn 1838: iii).

But the first significant and unsurpassed collection of Russian folktales was that made by Alexander Afanas'ev (1826–71), whose vast enterprise appeared in eight volumes between 1855 and 1867 and contained as many as 640 tales, by far the largest collection of folktales by one man anywhere in the world. Unlike the Grimm tales, most of Afanas'ev's stories were taken down second-hand, from the records of other people. Only about a dozen stories were recorded by Afanas'ev himself. Yet the modest lawyer from the Voronezh region became one of the most influential figures in Russian national culture. Generations of Russian authors, composers, artists and sculptors have drawn upon his subject matter and been inspired by it. As the writer and humanist Maxim Gorky said (1968: 77):

> In the tales, people fly through the air on a magic carpet, walk in seven-league strides, build castles overnight. The tales opened up for me a new world where some free and fearless power reigned and inspired in me the dream of a better life. The immortal oral poetry of the common people, at a time when poet and peasant were one, has greatly helped me to understand the fascinating beauty and wealth of our language.

Afanas'ev's interest and pride in the intrinsic beauty of Russian peasant language, at a time when aristocratic Russian society was aping foreign fashions and conversing in French, brought him to admire folklore for its rich musical quality, its poetic artistry, sincerity, purity and childlike simplicity. He would surely have agreed with Pushkin (1841: 73) that

> Our language is inherently beautiful and nowhere has it such breadth of expression as in folk tales. How marvellous they are – each one a poem! We must learn to speak and love Russian, not simply to admire it in tales.

To Afanas'ev folktales were primitive people's story of nature: the heroes are the gods of sun, sky, light, thunder and water, while their foes are the gods of

darkness, winter, cold, storms, mountains and caves. Because of this mythological approach, Afanas'ev attached no value to information concerning the
storytellers from whom the tales had been taken. He regarded his texts as
inviolable, however illiterate they might seem. So, unlike the Grimms, he makes
no attempt to 'prettify' his stories, to make them interesting for children. In at
least a third of the tales, he does not even indicate where the tales come from.
However, his biographer, Vladimir Porudominskii (1974: 2) writes:

> If we take a map of Russia and colour in the provinces from which Afanas'ev's
> tales come, we have an area stretching eastwards from the western borders to
> the Ural Mountains, from the northern regions down through the Volga almost
> to the Caucasus. Over thirty provinces sent their storytelling envoys to him:
> they came from Vologda and Astrakhan, Oryol and Perm, Grodno and
> Orenberg, Kazan and Kharkov.

In his search for material, Afanas'ev had much assistance from the Russian
Geographical Society, founded in 1848. At the end of his day's clerical work in
the Moscow archives of the Imperial Foreign Ministry, he was able to work in its
library, sifting through the notebooks on folklore; the Society also sponsored
expeditions to distant regions of the country in order to record and gather tales
from peasant storytellers. As his publishing mission became known, he received
collections sent by village teachers, provincial governors, army officers and
others who had recorded tales for their own amusement and stored them away.

Soon he had accumulated as many as 125 stories, which he edited and
published in three volumes between 1855 and 1858. This was only the
beginning. By the end of the 1850s, however, the sources seemed to be drying
up. The Geographical Society called off its expeditions owing to lack of funds
and officialdom began to have second thoughts about publishing folktales. In
desperation, Afanas'ev wrote to an elderly scholar, Vladimir Dal', living in the
old market town of Nizhny Novgorod, whom he knew to be an ardent collector
of tales. His proposal was that a new book of tales should be published,
collected by Dal' and edited by Afanas'ev. Dal' replied to his letter at once
(1862: 7):

> I accept your suggestion wholeheartedly. Let me explain. I have several
> hundred tales. Of course, they contain much rubbish and repetition. I haven't
> the time to publish them myself as I have too much work (my Russian
> dictionary). I do not want any credit at all save to ask you to mention in
> general that such-and-such book of tales was given to you. That is only
> because there has been some talk about the tales and people have a right to
> demand to expect something from me on that matter. Therefore I am giving
> you my entire collection and you may do what you like with it.

After carefully editing this valuable collection, Afanas'ev was able to
publish a further 228 tales in two volumes. Besides the fairy stories, the
new work contained many satirical animal tales and anecdotes. Not all of
them evaded the censor and those that were published stirred up opposition
in some quarters. The Moscow Metropolitan Filaret declared: 'The legends
published by Afanas'ev are thoroughly blasphemous and immoral. They

offend pious sentiment and propriety. Religion must be safeguarded from such profanity.'

To this Afanas'ev replied indignantly and incautiously, 'There is a million times more morality, truth and human love in my folk legends than in the sanctimonious sermons delivered by Your Holiness!'

But the tide of official encouragement was now turning and many in authority inclined to the view that the folktales tended to corrupt by their coarseness, their satire (particularly against the clergy and nobility) and their peasant wit. It has to be remembered that Russia in the 1860s was in the throes of radical social and economic change: peasant uprisings, a radical intelligentsia and industrial development had all combined to force the tsar to free the peasants from serfdom in 1861. Although this freedom from slavery was long overdue, its immediate effect was to produce even greater violence and discontent in virtually all sections of society. For Afanas'ev trouble was brewing. In 1860 the censor responsible for vetting his works was dismissed and the police raided the printing works which published the tales. The owner, Grachev, was arrested and the second edition of the tales, then in preparation, was confiscated and later burned.

Dismayed and embittered at this brutish treatment of his life's work, Afanas'ev sought permission to take a holiday abroad. Although his health was failing, it was not for this reason that he went on a European tour, for, during his three months' tour (July–October 1860) of Germany, Belgium, England, France, Switzerland, Italy, Austria and Poland, he arranged for publication abroad of several works that would clearly not please the Russian censor. In London he handed to a publisher notebooks of tales rejected by the Russian censor and in Geneva, he published a highly amusing and very bawdy collection of folk wit under the title *Sacred Tales*, which contained a biting satire on the clergy and nobility (Afanas'ev 1992).

It was printed under the fictitious authorship of 'Balaam, by the Typographical Art of the Monastic Fraternity in the Year of Obscurantism.' The Preface explains (iv):

Our book is appearing as a fortuitous and simple collection of that aspect of Russian folk humour for which there has hitherto been no room. Under the extreme conditions of Russian censorship, with its distorted understanding of ethics and morals, our book has been quietly printed in that cloister far removed from the disturbances of the world, into which there still has not penetrated the sacrilegious hand of any kind of censorship.

Not long after Afanas'ev's return from abroad, his house was searched by the police and he was summoned to the capital, St Petersburg, to appear before a special investigating committee. Although this body was unable to produce any evidence of his involvement in revolutionary or other subversive activities, its chairman, Prince Golitsyn, recommended to Alexander II (Porudominskii: 26):

Considering that the accused civil servant, employed in the archives of the Ministry of Foreign Affairs, may collaborate with people of evil intent to obtain from the Archives documents which should not be opened without government permission, I deem it necessary to draw the attention of the Foreign Minister to this circumstance so that he may take appropriate measures.

To this the tsar appended just one word, in pencil, in the margin: 'ABSO-LUTELY!'

Consequently, Afanas'ev found himself disgraced, dismissed from his job and deprived of his Moscow house where he had resided for the previous thirteen years. For the next three years he vainly sought employment and was forced to sell his priceless library in order to live. He commented wryly: 'Books once nourished me with ideas, now – with bread.'

At the end of 1865 Russia's greatest folklorist and eminent historian at last found work as a humble assistant clerk in a Moscow court. Two years later he was promoted to clerk to the Congress of Commune Judges in the Second Parish of the City of Moscow, where he spent his days filing reports, filling in forms and registering visitors. No other work was available to a man who had fallen under the shadow of the tsar himself. His home was now a cramped and damp room and this, along with his hard work, caused his health to suffer. He contracted consumption, which he used to laugh off as a 'mild lung disorder'.

Despite his illness and poverty, Afanas'ev was not idle. During the period of penury he spent every free moment on a monumental new work: *The Poetic Interpretations of Nature by the Slavs*, which ran to over 2,500 pages in three thick volumes. Here he expounded his theories of the symbols of folk mythology in folktales. Aided by the press censorship reforms of 1865, he managed to get his work published (Afanas'ev 1865–9) and received an award from the Russian Academy of Sciences. Though unable to publish any more genuine folktales, he did produce two volumes of *Russian Children's Tales* in 1870. But this was to be his last undertaking.

Attitudes towards him seemed to be changing once more as Russian writers, eminent or unknown, acknowledged their debt to the man who had brought to light the prodigious repertoire of tales of the Russian people. In the spring of 1872 the famous writer Ivan Turgenev wrote a letter from Paris to the Russian authorities, declaring that Afanas'ev's literary works gave him the right to receive financial assistance 'for security from hunger, cold and his other discomforts'.

Turgenev could not have known that Alexander Afanas'ev had died in poverty and virtual obscurity six months previously. He was forty-five.

References

Afanas'ev, A. N. (1865–9), *Poeticheskie vozzreniia slavian na prirodu. Opyt sravnitel'nogo izucheniia slavianskikh predanii i verovanii, v sviazi s mificheskimi skazaniiami drugikh rodsvennykh narodov*. 3 vols. Moscow.
—— (1945), *Russian Fairy Tales*, trans. N. Guterman. New York.
—— (1992), *Russkie zavetnye skazki*, ed. E. Grachev and T. Mazepov. Moscow/Paris.
Bronnitsyn, B. (1838), *Russkie narodnye skazki*. Moscow/St Petersburg.
Collins, S. (1671), *The Present State of Russia*. London.

Dal', V. I. (1862), *Poslovitsy russkogo naroda: sbornik.* Moscow.

Gorky, M. (1968), *O detskoi literature,* ed. N. B. Medvedeva. Moscow.

Haney, J. V. (1999), *An Introduction to the Russian Folktale.* New York/London.

Kliuchchevskii, V. (1901), *Kurs russkoi istorii.* Moscow.

Porudominskii, V. (1974), *A rasskazhu vam skazku?* Moscow.

Pushkin, A. (1841), *Russkie skazki.* Moscow/St Petersburg.

Sokolov, B. and Yu. (1915), *Skazki i pesni rayona Belozerskogo kraiia.* Moscow.

Sokolov, Yu. M. (1950/1966), *Russian Folklore,* trans. C. R. Smith. Folklore Associates. Hatboro, PA.

15

Fairy-Tale Motifs from the Caucasus[1]

DAVID HUNT

The Caucasus area not only contains the highest and least accessible mountain region of Europe, but is also one of the main land routes between Europe and the Middle East, and has been frequently overrun by various peoples of other cultures. Constant pressure from peoples coming from Central Asia and through southern Russia, from pre-Christian times onwards, drove the dwellers on the northern plains deeper into the mountain valleys. Successive incursions of different groups of people left their mark on the local folk culture, so that we have here a wide range of languages, customs and beliefs within a relatively small region, and this has been largely cut off from later developments in western Europe. Within the Caucasus it is possible to identify some common cultural elements, although neighbouring peoples may be speakers of languages from two entirely different language groups. Moreover, because of the inaccessibility of some of the high mountain areas, communication between villages or valleys has not always been easy. This is reflected in the great number of dialects within the languages spoken here.

Against such a background, it is perhaps not surprising that the Caucasus is very rich in folklore and literature of all kinds. Georgia, for example, could boast a very fine literature by the thirteenth century. Christianised already in the fifth century, it developed a literature of sacred texts, chronicles, and poetry, a masterpiece of which is *The Knight in the Panther's Skin* by the twelfth-century poet, Shota Rustaveli. In many areas, however, even within the mountainous districts of Georgia itself, heroic poetry and prose, folktale and ritual song were preserved orally and only collected from about the mid-nineteenth century onwards. An additional factor was the reversal in cultural development suffered throughout the Caucasus after the many foreign invasions, and especially the devastating onslaught of the Mongols in the thirteenth century.

Systematic collection and recording of oral material became more prolific in the early twentieth century and during the early Soviet era much work was done on recording the culture and literature of the region. Successive ethnographic expeditions were sent out to the mountain areas to record folklore and epic lays from known narrators, and a great number of publications in the original languages and in Russian translation were the

[1] I should like to thank Hilda Ellis Davidson and Anna Chaudhri for their help and advice in compiling this paper and for drawing my attention to a number of useful references.

result. Fairy tales were recorded alongside epic material and ritual poetry and one sees constant cross-fertilisation in all branches of traditional literature. Moreover the same folklore and epic traditions of the region are often retained by different ethnic groups (Rayfield 1994: 218):

> If literature draws the Georgians close to the major cultures around them – Greek, Persian and Russian – folk poetry ties them to their Caucasian neighbours, to the unwritten lore of the nations to the north and the northwest – to Svan, Mingrelian, Abkhaz, Circassian, . . . Chechen, Ingush . . . and Ossetic poetry.

In a region where such a strong oral tradition existed, fairy tales were certainly not exclusively for children, and a good narrator would have had a repertoire comprising these alongside heroic legends and myths. Some tales give the impression of having degenerated from legends, and belief in supernatural agents has survived until recent times. Storytelling was a popular means of entertainment. Chikovani (1971: 6–7) writing about Georgia says:

> The telling of tales, even in our days, continues to remain one of the favourite entertainments of village life during leisure hours . . . In the long winter evenings men and women gather in the family of one of the villagers. There is a predominance of women, who bring with them various items of needlework. The men, in turns, tell stories. At the end of the narration, a gift of fruit is given. The best [gift] is received by the one who tells the most fascinating tale. In the telling of tales, women also take part. On these evenings, in most cases the tales are followed by songs, playing on the *chonguri* (a stringed instrument) and dances . . . Tales are told on traditional feast days, during field work, in the forest, at the mill, on journeys and so on . . . Oral fiction is a favourite occupation of the shepherds on the mountain . . . Their oral competitions frequently continue until dawn.

Malsagov, writing in 1983 about tales among the Ingush and Chechens, specifically states that the legends and traditions are nearly always narrated by men, but that fairy tales and animal tales are primarily told by women (Malsagov 1983: 17). He quotes one of his narrators:

> At the time of my childhood people knew many tales. They were related especially often when livestock were being pastured or when people were spending the night in the fields at the time of ploughing, sowing or weeding. It was boring, and in order to while away the time we would tell each other what we knew. Often we would entertain guests with tales.

In Malsagov's collection (1983: 231) there is a tale of three brothers who meet a dragon in turn, and the two elder ones are eaten because they are unable to tell a story. However the youngest brother overcomes the dragon and rescues his brothers by telling an absorbing tale. Other tales include storytelling competitions. In spite of the richness of Caucasian folk-culture, it is difficult to find fairy-tale types which are independent of those listed in the international tale type indexes. However the special conditions of the Caucasus have favoured certain motifs, and a few of the more interesting will be considered here.

Hospitality and blood revenge play a frequent part in the tales. In the less accessible mountainous regions there was no strong feudal system, and people were governed mainly by custom and by the head of the family. It was important to gain strength by the survival of many sons, and to develop extended ties by marriage, adoption and hospitality, and this is reflected in the tales. There is a considerable difference in the attitude towards sons and daughters, since a daughter will be married off and absorbed into another family. If she marries with her father's consent, this will cement a new relationship, but if kidnapped, as often happened in the past, this could result in violence and perhaps a blood vendetta. Thus the birth of a boy was more desirable, and might be celebrated by the firing of guns. An orphan was in a precarious situation throughout life, as there was no one to avenge his death, and in a number of tales orphan boys are brought up by animals. Such boys need heroic qualities to survive. Orphan girls could gain a family through marriage, but would have little choice of suitors.

Horses are still of great importance in the Caucasus. They are used for personal transport between remote villages in the mountain regions and in the steppe regions of the north, and as pack animals to transport goods over mountain trails. For the hero the horse was an extension of a young man's virility, and helped him to fight his enemies, while for the ordinary traveller a reliable horse might make the difference between life and death. There was a well-developed horse culture, epitomised in the exploits of the *jigits*, dare-devil riders who practise stunts such as picking up a ring from the ground while the horse is at full gallop.

Tales of wonder horses are more prominent in the plains area, such as the Kabardan Plain, the coastal regions of Daghestan, and the low-lying parts of Georgia. The classic heroic legendary cycles of the Caucasus region are the Nart sagas, diffused throughout the North Caucasus and even beyond the crest of the mountains, and the legends of Andemyrkan, the Kabardan hero considered to be the illegitimate son of a prince, who spent his life fighting with the feudal princes and was finally treacherously murdered. In both these cycles the hero has a wonderful horse with heroic qualities similar to his own.

The tales contain several of the international tale types and motifs involving wonder horses. Type 530, 'The Princess on the Glass Mountain', and 531, 'Ferdinand the True and Ferdinand the False', are both well represented, with emphasis on the importance of the hero's horse. In the former the hero is the youngest of three brothers requested by their father's will to guard his grave in turn for three nights. The two eldest brothers, however, neglect to do this and the youngest guards it every night. Each night a different wonder horse comes down to attack the grave, but the hero manages to capture and tame each one of them, acquiring a token that can summon the horse at will. Here the horse appears out of the air. In the tales which fit Type 531, the father's horse and armour are buried underground to be ready for the young hero to grow up and be able to use them, and so here the horse appears from below the earth. In the Ingush tale, 'The Son of a Nart' (Malsagov 1983: 87) the young hero is told by his mother: 'If you dig up the earth in the yard, then you will see nine holes with nine doors; if you break open all the doors, you will see the horse.' The hero then collects his father's armour and rides into the yard.

A recurring motif, especially from the North Caucasus, is the obtaining of horses from the sea. In some of the Andemyrkan legends the hero gets his wonderful horse Jemansharyk in this way. He may find him on the seashore, or a mare may come out of the sea to foal, sometimes abandoning her colt in the reeds, or the horse runs into the sea with the hero clinging to him, or the colt is born as the result of a magnificent stallion coming out of the sea and covering a mare (Sokolov 1936: 283ff.). It is generally assumed that the setting for such tales is the low-lying swampy ground bordering the Caspian Sea, especially in the vicinity of the River Kuma and possibly the Terek. This vast area is known as the *Prikaspiyskaya Nizmennost* (Caspian-Littoral Lowlands), and much of it lies below sea level.

Similar motifs occur also in the fairy tales of the region. In several of them the hero, usually with a cowardly partner, steals horses from a sea-ogre, who then emerges from the sea and is killed by the hero. Sometimes this ogre has killed his father. Evidently the best horses are not obtained by careful breeding of stock, but from one of the elements, air, earth or water. There seems to be no clear distinction between the qualities of the horses from different elements, though those from the air seem to jump high and sometimes fly (Motifs B412 and B587.1). Those from the sea sometimes make long sea crossings. There are various formulae for describing the hero departing on his horse. In one tale he 'set his horse at a gallop and broke to pieces the porcelain walls and gates', 'porcelain' indicating richness and strength. In others he races his horse and jumps three times over a stone, or fences, or a gate (Motif F989.1). Such details are testimonies of the quality of the horse. Others are its ability to fly, and its attempts to remove its rider by crushing him against the sky. The best horses can also foretell the future and read the minds of villains (Type 531). Since they can also speak, they can give warning to the hero, which may save his life.

The Georgian tale 'The Horse Lurja' (Chikovani 1971: 49) has been assigned its own type number 538* (Kurdovanidze 2000). 'Lurja' is a typical Georgian name for a horse, meaning 'blue-grey'. The heroine of this tale is about to be slaughtered by her parents, who intend to rejuvenate themselves by eating her heart and liver. Her horse tells her to dress as a man and ride away, and she becomes the guest of a prince, who believes that she is really a girl in spite of her male attire. He puts her to various tests, such as selecting weapons, trick riding and a drinking competition, and the horse helps her to pass the first two, and in the drinking test stands behind her chair; every time she drinks a toast she is supposed to say: 'I am drinking, but Lurja is getting drunk', but she forgets to do this at the last toast, becomes tipsy and falls asleep. When she wakes she is in bed with women's clothes beside her. She marries the prince, and the tale then continues as Type 707 II, in which she is accused of having given birth to an animal and is about to be put to death. The horse Lurja escapes from the stable, but loses a leg in the process, and he rescues the heroine and takes her into the mountains. He persuades her that he is useless with only three legs, and that she must sacrifice him and say: 'In the name of the integrity and honesty of my Lurja, let there be a temple here, worthy of his service and devotion.' As she utters these words, a temple is miraculously raised on the spot (Motif V12.4.9). The horse's head continues to work miracles, and eventually the truth is revealed and the married couple reunited.

The emphasis on marvellous horses is no doubt strongly influenced by Caucasian heroic literature. In the north Caucasian Nart epic, for instance, heroes are constantly advised by their horses, which child-heroes frequently inherit from their fathers. The horses are given names; they are gifted with supernatural strength and guile, the gift of speech and great valour, all qualities possessed by heroic horses throughout world literature. Another important factor, however, is the existence of a horse cult within the region, closely connected with the realm of the dead. In Ossetia, for example, funeral texts dedicating a horse to the deceased to carry him to the next world have been recorded. Horse races were run on the occasion of a funeral and many particular rites were associated with the horse in many parts of the Caucasus. These have been discussed in detail by Bleichsteiner (1936) and by Lipets (1984).

The hero's wonderful horse is normally large, strong and swift. However, in a few tales there are dwarf horses that are even swifter, known as *gulings*, owned by an exceptionally strong dwarf master. In the Ingush tale 'Ovdilg', the hero's wife is kidnapped by a dwarf with a three-legged *guling* and taken to his distant home. The hero uses his wonder horse to try and retrieve her:

> For sixty-three days he rode over burdock thorns; for sixty-three days he rode over corn-stalks; for sixty-three days he rode over sharp stones, until his saddle had stuck to the horse and he himself had become rooted to the saddle.

However, although the dwarf sleeps for six more days after the hero has snatched his wife back, his wonderful horse is no match for the *guling*: 'Do we catch them after dinner or do we catch them without dining?' the villain asks. 'We will catch them without dinner or after dinner', replies the three-legged horse, and of course they succeed. After two failed attempts the hero is advised by his brother-in-law to obtain a four-legged *guling*. This may be obtained from a special mare who comes to a bald mountain once a year to give birth to a *guling*, but the foal will be immediately eaten by predators unless the hero scatters meat for them, and even then a wolf will eat one leg unless the hero gives some of his own flesh to satisfy its hunger. A special ointment heals the hero's flesh, and he goes on his four-legged *guling* to rescue his wife. This time the dwarf's horse tells his master: 'This time whether we have dined or whether we have not dined, we will still not catch them.' During the chase the three-legged horse makes a pathetic plea to the hero's four-legged one: 'Take pity on me. Wait a little, after all we are from the same mother. Do not let me die a cruel death.' The two horses hatch a plan in which the villain is thrown off and killed. These supernatural horses with an unusual number of legs call to mind the horses of the Baba Yaga and Koshchey the Deathless in Russian fairy tales; both of these are figures connected with the world of the dead (see pp. 117–18 above).

Heroes reared by animals are found in many countries in Europe, and in Thompson's Motif Index we have, for example: B35, Animal Nurse; F611.2.1, Strong hero suckled by animal; T611.10, Man suckled by dog/wolf; S352,

Animal aids abandoned children. Among them is the well-known tale of Romulus and Remus. The 'Bear's Son', AT 301, which is found over a large area of Europe, gives the hero an animal father and there are also examples of 'Son of a man and a she-bear or cow'. This is a particularly interesting motif in the Caucasus on account of the custom of fostering children. Among some ethnic groups fostering has been the norm, and in the past this applied throughout the North Caucasus, especially in the upper classes (Piotrovskii 1988: 475). In earlier times the foster parents would generally be of the same rank as the parents, but later a prince might give his children to members of the gentry, and a member of the gentry might give his to a peasant. The foster parents would feed, clothe and educate the child without payment, and he would return to his own home, either in adolescence or at maturity. Klaproth (1814) mentions this custom among the Tcherkess. The custom of fostering resulted in the extension of the family group, and provided protection for its members by forging powerful alliances between families; this in turn helped to maintain law and order in the absence of central government.

The traditional method of adoption was for the adoptive son to suck the breast of his new 'mother'. This would often be an old lady and the procedure would be merely a ritual. Such a ceremony could also be used in the adoption of adults and might be a means of avoiding or settling blood feuds: once the guilty man had been adopted, he would be under the protection of the family. The son of a prince might be sent round to all the villages for suckling by all the nursing mothers, thus becoming part of all the families in the region and putting them under the obligation to protect him from violence. In the Ingush tale, 'Brave Pakhtat', the hero puts his mouth to the breast of the cannibal ogress, where-upon she exclaims: 'Ach, you son of a bitch, now you have become my son, and I had intended to eat you up.' In the Avar tale, 'The Sea Horse', the cannibal ogress demonstrates how she would have treated him if he had not sucked at her breast: 'There and then she seized the cat, fried it over the fire and swallowed it down.' By analogy, the sucking of milk from a domestic or wild animal means that the hero becomes part of the community of that animal, or adopts that animal totem.

Horses were not only faithful servants and friends of heroes, they might also rear them or even give birth to them. In 'Brave Pakhtat' the hero was born from a mare in the herd of a childless couple, and his brother from a cow belonging to the same couple (Malsagov 1983: 47). The hero is relatively invincible because his soul lives outside of his body, beneath his cranium, which was considered as external: 'Beneath my cranium there is a tiny box. In this tiny box there are three fledglings. Only after they have been killed can I lose my life.' Another Ingush tale, 'The Boy with the Sun in his Mouth and the Moon between his shoulders', begins as Type 707 II, when a witch takes the newborn son and puts a puppy in its place. She throws him to some sheep 'so that they would eat him up', but instead 'the boy sucked the milk of a ewe, and he rode around on a ram, and like that he grew up'. The witch then throws him into a herd of horses, but 'he sucked the milk of a mule and rode round on a stallion and grew even more'.

Heroes are reared by different animals in other tales. In the Georgian tale, 'Olenok and Elena the Beautiful' (Chikovani 1971: 152), and the Abkhazian tale,

'Jamkhukh the Deer's Son' (Bgazhba 1985: 171), the heroes are brought up by a deer after being abandoned in the forest. In the Ingush tale, 'How Black Nege Was Defeated' (Malsagov 1983: 137), the hero is abandoned in the forest as a newborn baby when his mother dies. Fortunately he has some unusual qualities: he has the sun beneath his armpit and 'out of one finger flowed water; out of another milk; out of a third oil; out of a fourth honey'. In the forest he sucked his fingers and so fed himself. Later he tames a wolf which takes him on its back to its master, who becomes the boy's foster father, and appears to be a master of animals. He gives him the name of 'Wolfheart'.

Stories belonging to the 'Bear's Son' theme are found in many parts of Europe and among the native Americans in North America (Davidson 1978: 128–9). In the Ingush tale, 'Chaitong, the Son of a Bear' (Malsagov 1983: 33), a girl is kidnapped by a bear and gives birth to the hero, who is exceptionally strong. He later takes his mother back to her parents. The Avar tale, 'Bear's Ear' (Atayev 1972: 89), has a similar beginning but the hero kills his bear-father before taking his mother home (AT 301). These motifs have an interesting association with the custom requiring the father to give his daughter away to an approved bride-groom; although 'marriage by capture' used to take place in the Caucasus as late as the end of the nineteenth century, involving the family honour and perhaps a life and death chase. Once the marriage had been consummated, however, the families would usually be reconciled after some negotiated settlement and the payment of a bride price.

Another animal playing an important part in the tales is the ox. It may rescue one or more adolescent children from a wicked parent or an evil cannibal man (Motif B411.2, Helpful Ox). In the Chechen tale, 'Akhkepig', the cannibal figure has killed and eaten the children's parents, but they escape and are carried across the sea on the ox's back. Then the ox tells them to sacrifice it, describing the benefits that will result: its skin will become a farm; the intestines the fence and gates; the legs four towers (defensive towers were common in Chechnya and throughout the Caucasus); the ears will provide workpeople; the eyes brave hounds; liver and heart gold and silver weapons and powder, and the liver also gold coins; the gall will cause the hounds to hate their enemies and the kidneys will become a horse that can 'keep pace with the morning dawn', with a saddle of gold and silver. Later in the tale, the girl marries the cannibal villain and so, transferring her loyalties, becomes part of his family and tries to destroy her brother. Eventually he is saved by the two hounds, which kill the villain. The hero was unable to kill his treacherous sister because they were 'brother and sister from the same womb', but he curses her so that she changes herself 'into a thorn that can lodge in the hand'.

The ox performs a similar role in the Georgian tale, 'Tsikara' (or 'Krasnukh'). In one version it saves the boy from being killed by his father, since the boy's wicked stepmother had wanted to eat his heart and liver. They escape and the ox leaves the boy in a tree, playing on either a joyful or a distressful pipe, according to his mood. The ox goes off to graze but finally dies, and the boy finds him with his eyes pecked out by vultures and carrion crows. He then 'played no more, either on the joyful pipe or the distressful pipe'. This is a very poetic tale about the growing up of an adolescent (Motif F562.1, Boy lives on ox.

Never walks on ground). In another Georgian tale, 'The Little Boy and the Oxen', it is the oxen, Tsikara and Nikora, who are about to be killed by the malicious father. The boy loves the oxen, so he lets them out of the shed and rides away on one of them, but when crossing a river he is swept away and drowns and the oxen are unable to revive him. These tales of the beneficent ox are characterised by tragedy set against the selfless nature of the ox. The ox is still an important sacrificial animal in the Caucasus and many folk beliefs surround it. Black oxen were traditionally thought to be of particular value.

The figure of a devouring sister is widespread through the Caucasus region. It fits AT type 315A, which is only listed as found in India. The hero is generally the only one who recognises that his young sister is a cannibal. He flees, but in spite of his warnings the rest of his family or his village is devoured, and he may return to find the whole village deserted except for his sister. There is usually a sequence where the sister keeps going out of the house, eating part of his horse and returning to say: 'Do you mean, dear brother, that you rode here on a horse with three legs . . . two legs . . . one leg?' and finally, 'Dear little brother, do you mean to say that you came here on foot?' After this the sister goes out to sharpen her teeth in order to eat her brother. He may be warned by an animal, or else he realises the danger and runs away. The sister chases him but he escapes, usually with the help of animals.

In an Abkhazian tale, 'Why is there a spot on the Moon?' (Bgazhba 1985: 36), the sister is about to eat the hero, when a little rat comes in and plays on an *apkhyartsa* (two-stringed guitar) and sings a warning. There is a desperate chase, in which the girl is led along false trails by a helpful woodpecker and a helpful witch. Then the hero throws a magic ring to his moon-wife, who sends down dogs to attack the sister. She escapes from these and manages to tear off one of the hero's legs before he climbs up to his wife's house in the moon. The story concludes: 'If you carefully study the outlines of the spot on the moon, you will see the outline of a one-legged man: it is he!'

In a Karachay tale, 'The Monster' (Kavkazsky Dom 1995), the hero hinders the pursuing sister by magic objects thrown behind him. The third object is an awl, which changes into an iron tree 'of nine to ten girths', which he climbs. The sister begins gnawing through the tree, and the hero asks passing birds to bring his hunting dogs to help. Eventually he is saved by his parents' dogs and the girl in fear begins to climb up to the sky while the dogs pursue her. She is said to be responsible whenever there is an eclipse of the moon or the sun. In an Ingush tale (Malsagov 1983: 181), the sister becomes a cat-like ogre, and the hero is warned by a cat that jumps in through the window; he takes the cat away on his shoulder when he runs away. He again throws magic objects behind him, the third of which, three needles, change into cast-iron pillars up which he climbs. His sister gnaws through these one by one, but the hero is saved at the last minute by his hounds.

It is noticeable that in the Karachay tale the girl is born after nine brothers, and in the Abkhazian tale after three. These are significant numbers in the Caucasian tales, indicating completeness. According to Bardavelidze (1992), in some mountain areas the counting system was not decimal but based on nine, and the shepherd would count his sheep by one nine, two nines and so on. The cannibal girl is number ten and number four in the family and is therefore superfluous. In an Avar version she is the hero's stepsister. In the Ingush version there is only one brother but the father has died away from home, so the girl's background is abnormal. If a girl did not marry, she would stay at home and her contribution to the household would be considered as menial, and in all these tales the girl is at home and unmarried. She is said in three tales to begin by eating lambs, before going on to devour human beings. Her demanding appetite and her being a hostile force within the family in the tales reflect perhaps the real-life position of an unwelcome extra mouth to feed within a poor family. The role of the dogs in the tales is also of importance, suggesting a sheep-herding and hunting community. The motif of the dog as faithful assistant and protector of the hero against female assailants is very well developed in the rich hunting lore of the Caucasus (Chaudhri 1996). In one Avar tale the hero is rescued by two little dragons which he has reared from birth, and which 'helped him to pasture his sheep and cheered him up when he was sad'.

The concept of a dead person, particularly a mother, returning in another form such as a bird or animal is found in a number of European fairy tales (Motif E600–E699), but is particularly frequent in the Caucasus, where she often takes the form of material objects. It is sufficiently developed in Georgia for a specific tale-type to be invented for it in the Index of Georgian folktale plot types, listed as 403D*, 'Substituted Wife', with ten examples (Kurdovanidze 2000). A typical tale of this type is 'The Three Sisters' (Chikovani 1971: 105). Here a huge dragon (*gveleshapi*) wraps itself round a family's grain stack and demands to marry one of the daughters. The first two refuse, but the youngest agrees. As soon as they start off for the dragon's home, he throws off his skin and becomes a handsome prince. She later returns to her family home to give birth to a baby son. The envious eldest sister asks to return with her and in the forest persuades the heroine to change clothes and then to climb a tree to pick apples, while she holds the baby. The eldest sister then joins the prince, who accepts her as his wife, while the heroine remains marooned in the tree. Her sister cannot feed the baby, who is given cow's milk, and when he is old enough takes the cow out to graze. Meanwhile the heroine weeps until she loses all her substance in tears, and there is nothing left in the tree, but 'where her tears and blood spilled, there grew up out of the earth reeds like a forest, and a thousand kinds of flowers and grasses'. The boy plucks a reed, makes a pipe and starts playing it. The pipe sings: 'It is your mother weeping, my son!' The boy presses the pipe to his heart, takes it home and keeps playing on it. The false wife seizes it, breaks it and burns it, and the ashes pile up and form a portrait of the heroine on the side of the stove. The false wife rakes out the ashes and scatters them on the roof, where they grow into a beautiful poplar tree, and when the husband spreads his bed under it at night its branches embrace him. The false wife has it cut down, and an old woman finds a piece of the wood and takes it home. Each time she leaves the house, the slab of wood changes into the heroine, who does the housework. The old woman discovers her and adopts her as a daughter. The prince's family is invited to dinner, and the truth is revealed during the toasts.

Here we find most of the basic elements of the Cinderella story (AT 510), but linked in an unusual way. The tale contains a prince, a wicked stepmother, one or two unpleasant sisters, a downtrodden heroine, ashes, and final recognition of the heroine. It also contains a number of transformations: dragon to prince, the series of transformations of the wife to tears and blood, a reed pipe, the portrait in the ashes, a poplar tree, a slab of wood, a girl, and finally back to wife and mother. The way in which the cheated mother remains present in the pipe and the poplar tree to watch over her son and husband recalls the mother's influence in the Cinderella story, where she protects her daughter in the form of a tree growing on the grave (Motif E631). In Afanas'ev's version of 'Cinderella', the mother is present as a little doll, to be carried by the heroine as a protective charm (Afanas'ev 1945: 439–47). Some further related motifs are K1911.3.4, 'True Bride Reincarnated as Reed Reveals Truth' (also from India); E632, 'Reincarnation as a Musical Instrument', found also in Europe, India and Japan; and E648, 'Reincarnation Man–Object–Man', listed from India and Europe.

The reincarnation motif is found in other parts of the Caucasus, for instance in the Ingush tale, 'Gombot and his Wife' (Malsagov 1983: 164). Here the wife, after being drowned, is transformed into a green shoot, a tree, a balalaika, ashes, hemp, a cake and then a girl, who is restored as wife. When the husband plays the balalaika, it keeps on singing: 'Chaki-Chak! In Gombot's embraces is a bald head!' so that the false wife burns it and throws out the ashes; this part of the tale is an instance of Motif 632, where a musical instrument reveals a crime.

Other similar tales are two from Ossetia, one from Adygea and one from Daghestan. There are two Abkhazian tales, the first of which, 'Santa Saaja and Safa Saaja', is long and contains many motifs (Bgazhba 1985: 194). The wife is finally changed into a frog and burned by the false wife. She survives in a single bone from the frog, which changes into a fish in the river and is caught and eaten by the substitute wife. However, one fin is saved and grows into a big handsome tree, which is cut down and burned. One wood chip is taken home by an old woman and this changes back into the girl. In the second tale, 'The Prince's Youngest Daughter' (Bgazhba 1985: 149), the tale begins with Motif K2115, 'Animal Birth Slander', but in this case it is the baby who is killed and then cooked by the wife's sisters. The fat from the baby is thrown out into the yard and the baby is transformed from this into an aspen tree, chips of which are put on to the fire; a hot coal rolls out, which becomes a gold coin, which is put into a chest, and this is restored to the form of the baby again. The true wife is then reinstated into her husband's household.

Another Caucasian tale which is found more than once is 'The Little Girl and the Lamb' (AT 450). This involves the heroine's brother being transformed into an animal after drinking water from a puddle. The girl then marries a prince, but a witch throws her into water to drown, so that her own ugly daughter can take her place as the prince's wife. The brother is then to be killed to hide the crime. In an Armenian version, 'Brother Lamb', the brother in animal form divulges the truth and the girl is found alive and well with her newborn baby inside a large fish (Surmelian 1968: 186). This ending is close to one of the standard versions of AT 450. However in a Karachay-Balkar version, the body of the drowned wife is buried in the cemetery and during the night a golden tree grows from her grave. The tree is cut down but an old woman finds, when she digs beneath it 'at a great depth' a little golden root, which she takes home and puts in a chest. The next morning this turns into the girl again.

In these tales, the series of transformations takes place when an attempt is made to kill a young wife and mother, and all are female except in the case of the baby referred to above. A tree is one of the forms taken, and a piece from this is taken home by an old woman and placed in a chest. Fire and ashes and a musical instrument, which reveals the truth, are present in a number of tales. The tale of 'The Juniper Tree' (AT 720), recorded by the Grimms, forms an interesting parallel.

The fairy tales of the Caucasus region are very rich in motifs and this brief survey focuses only on a few tale complexes which are particularly common. Social practices and local factors can account in part at least for the popularity of some of these tale types and motifs. In the examples cited the region shows a wide range of multi-episodic tales which seem to be characterised often by much wonder and miracle. Indeed, even within the context of the fairy tale, some of these Caucasian tales can be said to be fantastic.

References

Those marked with an asterisk are collections which the author has translated into English. These translations are all available in the Folklore Society Library, London.

Aarne, A., and Thompson, S. (1981), *The Types of the Folktale. A Classification and Biography*. FFC 184. Helsinki.

Afanas'ev, A. (1945/1975), *Russian Fairy Tales*, trans N. Guterman. New York.

Atayev, D. (1972), *Avarskie narodnye skazki*. Moscow.*

Bardavelidze, J. (1992), Private communication.

Bgazhba, Kh. (1985), *Abkhazskie skazki*. Sukhumi.*

Bleichsteiner, R. (1936), 'Rossweihe und Pferderennen im Totenkult der kaukasischen Völker', *Wiener Beiträge zur Kulturgeschichte und Linguistik*. Wien.

Briggs, K. M. (1970), *A Dictionary of British Folk-Tales*. London.

Chaudhri, A. (1996), 'The Caucasian Hunting Divinity, Male and Female: Traces of the Hunting-Goddess in Ossetic Folklore', in *The Concept of the Goddess*, ed. S. Billington and M. Green. London/New York.

Chikovani, M. (1971) ed., *Gruzinskie narodye skazki. Sto skazok*. Tbilisi.*

Davidson, H. R. E. (1978), 'Shape changing in the old Norse sagas', *Animals in Folklore*. Ipswich.

Kavkazsky Dom. (1995), *Karachayevo-balkarskii fol'klor*. Tbilisi.*

Klaproth, J. (1812/1814), *Reise in den Kaukasus und nach Georgien*. London.

Kurdovanidze, T. (2000), *The Index of Georgian Folktale Plot Types*. Tbilisi.

Lipets, R. (1984), *Obrazy Batyra i ego konia v tiurko-mongol'skom epos*. Moscow.

Malsagov, A. (1983), *Skazki i legendy Ingushei i Chechentsev*. Moscow.*

Piotrovskii, B. B. (1988) ed., *Istoriia narodov severnogo Kavkaza*. Moscow.

Rayfield, D. (1994), *The Literature of Georgia: A History*. Oxford.

Semyonov, N. (1882), *Skazki i legendy Chechentsev*. Vladikavkaz.

Sokolov, Iu. M. (1936), *Kabardinskii fol'klor*. Moscow.

Surmelian, L. (1968), *Apples of Immortality*. Aylesbury.

Thompson, S. (1955), *Motif Index of Folk-Literature*. Indianapolis.

Virsaladze, E. B. (1973), *Gruzinskie narodnye predaniia i legendy*. Moscow.*

16

The Fairy Tale in South Asia: The Same Only Different

MARY BROCKINGTON

No longer is it a truth universally acknowledged that all fairy tales are of Indic origin. The area now collectively known as South Asia (Bangladesh, India, Nepal, Pakistan, Sri Lanka, and in this context Tibet) has undoubtedly transmitted many tales to neighbouring regions, but it has also received, preserved and transformed others. The task of determining the direction of transmission is at best demanding and painstaking, and at worst arid, subjective or even impossible; a more rewarding line of enquiry is to investigate what changes are made when a given tale, story unit or motif is transmitted from one culture to another, in whichever direction. A third category – those tales which have not, or not yet, been reported outside the area – deserves much more study than it has so far received. Do any of these tales have distinctive features which betray their South Asian origin, or could they theoretically have been composed elsewhere? An essay of this length cannot hope to deal comprehensively with every question; I shall therefore concentrate firstly on a few representative tales, and secondly on patterns of research, past and future, perforce leaving aside vast areas and numerous major authorities.[1]

Use of terminology devised to be appropriate to Europe complicates any enquiry into South Asian tales. In the Indic context, 'oral' cannot be equated with 'folk', nor 'written' with 'literary'. Texts which, by European standards, are clearly 'literary', 'religious' or even 'philosophical' in nature have been transmitted without the aid of writing, or alongside written versions, and also alongside texts which can be defined as 'folktales', and the degree of cross-fertilisation should not be underestimated or disregarded. Whatever may be the case elsewhere, the major Indic literary creations contain a considerable amount of so-called 'folk material' and, more importantly, are themselves the source of a great many folk narratives. The problem is to decide which is which.

---

[1] An extensive bibliography of the subject is given by Blackburn and Ramanujan (1986); a comprehensive listing can be found in Handoo (1977), while the history of earlier folktale collection in South Asia is outlined by Mazharul Islam (1982). One topic which regrettably cannot be explored here is that of the animal fable, exemplified by the influential *Pañcatantra* collection but pervading all Indian tradition. Animal tales were classified by Bødker (1957) and have also been studied by Brown (1978: 123–48) and others. The *Kathāsaritsāgara* collection of tales also deserves a far more thorough treatment than I am able to give it here; its influence on subsequent European collections has been repeatedly documented and Penzer's detailed notes pointing to parallel themes elsewhere have had a considerable effect on international narrative research (Penzer 1923–8). For a classification of its stories by genre, see Sudyka (1995).

Nor should South Asia be regarded as in any sense homogeneous. Only from the outside has the area ever been seen as a unit. No unifying factor has ever been present: a multiplicity of languages within two major linguistic families, extremes of climate and geography, several major religions, diverse social customs, conquest by, and trading relations with, many alien forces, fragmented and changing political divisions (even the British, who came nearest to imposing a single overall administrative structure, ruled India and Ceylon as separate colonies), all ensured that South Asia has from early times been a multi-cultural society. It has been united only by a grudging acceptance of its diversity often mistaken for tolerance, an acceptance which has greatly facilitated the inter-penetration of the differing cultures and differing oral traditions. In short, variants of the same tale, one adapted to a Hindu context, one to a Muslim, can exist quite happily side by side and pass easily from one culture to another. Susette Taylor (1895: 399) says of her informant, an old Hindu *ayah* from Central India, 'in telling me the tales she would one moment use the word *rajah* (Hindu term) and the next *pacha* (Mohammedan) for the same person.' Successive incidents in the story of Rājā Rasālū, collected from a village accountant from Rawalpindi (now in northern Pakistan), involve a *yogi* and a cremation ritual, presupposing a Hindu setting, and a corpse which cannot rest in its grave, implying Muslim burial customs (Temple 1884–6: I, 31–40); these incidents are adapted as 'How Raja Rasālu became a jogi' and 'How Raja Rasālu journeyed to the city of King Sarkap' (Steel and Temple 1973: 170–3, 174–5).

Fairy-tale material has been recorded in South Asia from a much earlier date than in most cultures, preserved in writing in literary texts dating very roughly from the beginning of this era but with an earlier long and fluid oral history. Another important source is the Vedic corpus, transmitted since perhaps 1000 BC by punctilious memorisation of the words themselves, a technique quite different in concept and effect from the re-creation of episodes practised by the traditional storyteller. Valuable collections of traditional tales of all sorts, including many animal fables, such as the *Pañcatantra*, the *Kathāsaritsāgara* and the Buddhist *jātakas*, were put together in the second part of the first millennium AD, and have since been enthusiastically imitated and widely translated throughout Asia and Europe. However, the temptation to regard these tales as necessarily native to India, and also the source of all similar tales just because they were recorded there earlier than elsewhere, should be resisted unless any more positive evidence can be adduced (cf. the judicious assessments by Brown (1978: 176–9; 186–200)). Tales can be lent as well as borrowed, and motifs can be devised independently in different places to meet similar narrative needs. From the first half of the first millennium BC, Indra defeats the demon Namuci with a thunderbolt made of foam, at dawn, which is 'neither dry nor wet . . . neither by day nor by night' (*Śatapatha Brāhmaṇa* 12,7.3.1–3).[2] This stratagem at once suggests Thompson's motif M 367.1 (neutralisation of an enemy's apparent invulnerability by use of a paradox, the specifically Indic form of the familiar 'Paradoxical Task' motifs H 1050–77). The requirement to circumvent a prophecy, oath, prohibition or magic power by such means is

---

[2] A fuller account of the story alluded to in *Ṛgveda* 8,14.13; reported by Soifer (1991), 38–9.

surely common to any narrative tradition, and only if the precise details of the trick can be identified elsewhere need we consider any possibility of direct influence. Even within India the later (though still early) popular literary stories of Viṣṇu in his form as Narasiṃha defeating the demon Hiraṇyakaśipu by a form of this trick, use a similar concept, but different, ever developing details (Brockington forthcoming).

Texts, tales and motifs

While much of early Indic literature contains fairy-tale elements, the *Rāmāyaṇa* can in itself be considered a Sanskrit fairy tale: the story of a mortal's triumphant encounter with the supernatural, where the hero's familiarity with the Other emphasises his special nature as a human being. This heroic romance was conceived several centuries BC and was continuously modified and enlarged to become a vast religious epic. In origin it is the story of Prince Rāma, who is banished from court by the intrigue of a jealous stepmother; he wanders in a forest until his wife Sītā is abducted by a demon, and is helped by grateful animals to kill the demon, recover his wife and return home in triumph. Other fairy-tale elements are advice from a preternaturally ancient bird, the triumph of the human hero over fearsome ogres, and the possession by the villain of various magic powers, including the ability to change shape, and (in some parts only of the text) ten heads, each of which re-grows when severed until the hero strikes him in the heart. Later authors add the heroes' miraculous births, the winning of princesses in marriage, and the eventual deaths of heroine and hero (finally regarded as divine). As a literary work, both oral and written, the *Rāmāyaṇa* has given rise to countless adaptations, including folk versions reflecting their origin in subcultures outside mainstream Hinduism, uninhibited by Rāma's modern status as God; such tales often change the emphasis, as well as the details, of the orthodox story. Taylor's brief version, with its simplified, more unified plot structure, retains the fairy-tale atmosphere and accords divine status to the monkey-helper, Hanumān (Taylor 1896: 84–5, 85–6; cf. also Brockington 2001a). In this case, the process is towards the divinisation of a supernatural helper, rather than the degradation of an ancient god, a process comparable to that observed in the case of both hero and villain of the Sanskrit *Rāmāyaṇa* (Brockington 2001b). In Taylor's version, Rāma is portrayed as a relatively undistinguished human, but a Bhil tribal version examined by Komal Kothari shows a much greater reversal of status (Kothari 1989: 115–16). A seminar edited by Singh and Datta (1993) gives reports of numerous folk *Rāmāyaṇas*.

The *Rāmāyaṇa's* influence on independent folk narratives has been considerable. Among the Santal tribe the names of Rāma and his companion brother are used for the heroes of 'The Ogre and the Dom', a straightforward version of 'The Dragon-Slayer' with many variants in India, and unrelated to the plot of the *Rāmāyaṇa* (AT 300; Bodding 1925–9: II, 284–8, no. 62). The same names appear as the heroes of a variant of 'Faithful John' (AT 516; 'Rama and Luxman; or The Learned Owl', Frere 1868: 72–86, no. 5), another type with many South Asian variants. The association is not all one-sided and can lead in turn to the absorption into later versions of the *Rāmāyaṇa* of elements suggested by the folktales.

A few detailed remarks, taking as an example type AT 303, 'The Two Brothers' / 'The Twins', will illustrate this point. This widely collected tale tells of the birth of identical boys to impoverished childless parents after supernatural intervention. One boy has an adventure which leads to marriage with a princess, but is subsequently bewitched by a malevolent being. His twin seeks him, is at first mistaken for his brother, but then succeeds in disenchanting the victim, only to suffer unjust suspicion over his relationship with his jealous brother's wife. The nature, origin and diffusion of this putative base text (*Urform*) of AT 303 was examined by Kurt Ranke (1934), who concluded that it was compiled in western Europe, whence it eventually spread to most parts of the world, including South Asia. Later scholars have identified a distinctive Indic subform, TR 303, collected in many diverse parts of India, and also in Sri Lanka, in which the opening episodes (magic birth from eating a fish, fight with a dragon) are replaced by the Indic version of type 1121: a malicious sage procures the birth, with the condition that one of the boys be given up to him, but is thwarted in his attempt to sacrifice the hero when the boy pretends not to know the correct position to take up and tricks the sage into becoming the sacrificial victim himself (the 'show-me-how' motif).[3] The 'Dragon-Slayer' episode, AT 300, commonly found in the *Urform* as the boy's first adventure, which this new opening has displaced, has already been mentioned. As frequently in Europe, it is nevertheless found as an independent tale or as a component of longer tales. Its climax is the outwitting of a low-class imposter who has claimed the reward of the bride; in the Indian context, the threat of enforced marriage to an imposter who is a sweeper is even more horrific.

Indian social conventions have had a still greater effect on the outline of 'The Two Brothers', for a 'fairy-tale marriage' between a princess and a pauper, so welcome to a European audience, would be inconceivable in India; South Asian tales regularly involve princes as heroes, even where their activities seem inconsistent with this status. For example, Indian variants of 'Aladdin' incongruously replace the poverty-stricken ne'er-do-well hero with a prince, although Steel's spendthrift prince attempts to combine the two themes in 'The Wonderful Ring' (Steel and Temple 1973: 124–9). In 'A Sage's Word' (Ramanujan 1997: 152–4, no. 55), a cook's son can marry a princess only when he has himself become a prince. The hero of TR 303 is accordingly a prince, but this rise in status presents another problem: the childless father is obliged by Hindu religious practice to accept food only from someone of equal or higher social status; now that he is a king, the only person with sufficient authority to give him the impregnating food is a sage, and it ought to be vegetarian, not fish; the frequent choice is a mango. The motif of childless king + sage + mango had been found in literary form as early as India's other epic, the *Mahābhārata*, this

---

[3] For a more detailed exploration of TR 303 see Brockington (1995a) and Smith (1996); for a full list of Indic variants see Brockington (1998); on the nature and sources of the sage's subsequent malice and defeat, see Bloomfield (1924).

episode probably no earlier than the first century BC, and it now forms a common opening episode to a wide variety of tales (cf. Brockington 2000).

As this modified form of the tale type 303 became current in South Asia, it would have been narrated and heard against a well-established background of recitations of Indic material, particularly the *Rāmāyaṇa* and the *Mahābhārata*. The *Rāmāyaṇa* opens with an episode in which the hero and his brothers are born to a long-childless king, after their mothers are given special food by a mysterious figure emerging from a sacrifice; in an unconnected sequel, an irascible sage turns up to demand that the youthful hero and one brother go with him to the forest to fight dangerous monsters, after which they win brides for all four. The general similarity of type 303 to this familiar outline would, subconsciously at least, have influenced successive narrators as they dealt with the consequences necessitated by the new form. The subtle process of continuous re-creation involved should not, however, mislead the unwary into making tortuous claims that the *Rāmāyaṇa* and 'The Two Brothers' are in origin the same tale; Heino Gehrts's attempts to do just this (1967; 1977) are not convincing to an Indologist. Details of plot and characterisation, and even reminiscences of wording, each one insignificant in itself, in total indicate the extent to which the developed variants of TR 303 are dependent on the *Rāmāyaṇa*. The climax, in Europe an encounter with a witch, is in some Indian variants a dice-game against a cheating opponent, this time reflecting the central episode of the *Mahābhārata*. This episode is found commonly in unrelated modern tales, for example TR 217, 'The Cat and the Candle'.

Once the Indic form of 'The Two Brothers' had become established, it was reflected back towards the West, carried by Arabs and other Muslims in ever more attenuated form as it was re-adapted to different cultures and re-absorbed into the older form. For instance, the mango becomes a pomegranate in Persia and an apple in Greece and the Balkans, and the dice-game becomes in Persia a wrestling-match with a beautiful fairy, a motif already found in a variant collected in Sri Lanka, 'The Story of the Gamarāla's Son' (Parker 1910–14: III, 78–83, no. 196). The recension current in Arabic North Africa, with an opening episode classified as a separate tale, AT 516*E (Jason 1975), has its hero sent out into the world by the jealousy of his stepmother. It can even be argued that it is from the *Rāmāyaṇa* too that the redactors of this recension have drawn the curious motif of friendship between the half-brothers, rather than the hostility normally to be found in such a well-worn plot element, for the theme of unity between the half-brothers in the face of the intrigue of the mother of one of them is prominent in the *Rāmāyaṇa* (Brockington 1998).

Confirmation of this symbiotic relationship is provided by a number of 'Two Brothers' details which appear in later or vernacular versions of the *Rāmāyaṇa*; the most significant is the 'Show-me-how' motif inserted, often rather clumsily, into a number of versions of the Rāma story composed in the north-east, the region where the interaction between the two works appears to have taken place. A tale appearing in the *Kathāsaritsāgara*, a compilation of perhaps the eleventh century (7, 58, 'Story of King Parityāgasena, His Wicked Wife and His Two Sons', Penzer 1923–8: III), may be seen as marking a transitional stage in the process of mutual influence. While the plot belongs to neither tradition, it draws many of its motifs from the *Rāmāyaṇa*. Conversely, Ruth Norton (1920: 220–1) drew attention to the comparative rarity of its passive form of the Life Index in South Asia. Since several of the examples she did cite are from variants of 'The Two Brothers' or related tales, it may be speculated that this motif was popularised in the region by TR 303; to the examples she gave may be added, significantly, one from a late version of the *Rāmāyaṇa* (Brockington 1995a: 268).

A telling example of the different meanings attached to the same motif in Europe and South Asia is provided by T 11.4.1, 'Love on Sight of Golden Hair'. In Europe it appears as almost realistic, reflecting an ideal of female beauty. But no South Asian has naturally golden hair. When the motif is employed, the image it evokes is of a mysterious, alien being and the compulsion it exercises is not just physical and aesthetic but obsessive and can even be sinister. In 'Sona and Rupa' (Ramanujan 1991: 12–14; Parmar 1998: 7–12), a prince is driven to demand an incestuous double marriage, and his horrified golden- and silver-haired sisters escape by magic means within their own special tree: clearly they should be thought of as tree-spirits. 'The Wonderful Ring', Steel's variant of types 560 + 516B (Steel and Temple 1973: 124–9), goes even further: the princess with the golden hair has had herself actually turned into gold by the magic ring, although in other respects she remains human; we may suspect that in this variant the transformation has been introduced, along with the fact that the marvellous palace is itself made of gold, to explain the golden hair motif found in its source. In 'Hanchi' (Ramanujan 1991: 285–90; 1997: 74–9), the heroine's golden hair is again a wonder inspiring incestuous lust; 'Prince Lionheart and his three friends' (Steel and Temple 1973: 33–44) also includes type 516B, but not the extension that the princess is made of gold. There is a hint that golden hair was beginning to be considered inauspicious as early as the *Mahābhārata* (12, 329.14, 1–2): the god Indra is cursed to have a gold beard as a punishment for adultery, though his regular description, 'golden-bearded' in the much earlier *Ṛgveda* had no negative implications (Söhnen-Thieme 1996: 46–9). A generalised shining or golden resplendence is associated with divine figures, but hair-colour is not particularly mentioned in ancient Indian literature, nor is the motif discussed in Penzer's copious notes to the *Kathāsaritsāgara*. Whether this indicates that the motif has been imported from Europe, emerged independently in both areas, or was devised in South Asia at a relatively late date as a straightforward expression of an Otherworld marvel and then attenuated when carried to the West, cannot be determined. Any transmission to Europe would have to be early enough for the motif to appear in literary form in the twelfth-century Middle High German *Tristrant* by Eilhart von Oberge where, ironically, the colour of the hair is not mentioned (Thomas 1978: 64), and in the fourteenth-century *Göngu-Hrolfssaga* (Pálsson and Edwards 1980: 50–1). A further refinement would have the motif devised in another black-haired area and transmitted to South Asia; this might particularly fit its association with Aladdin-type stories, brought into India by Arabs. In an Egyptian tale recorded *c*.1250 BC it is the scent, not the colour, of a lock of hair which betrays its owner's supernatural origin (AT 318; Lichtheim 1973–80: II, 203–11).

Another tale-type collected in both India and Europe and in Jewish Yemeni sources (Jason 1965) is 'Six Brothers Seek Seven Sisters as Wives' (AT 303A).

Once again, the direction of influence is unclear and is far less interesting than the significant adaptations made to make the story appropriate to the social customs of the area. In the European variants, the brothers win their brides and are taking them back home to be married when the party is attacked by a wizard and eventually disenchanted by the youngest brother, who had stayed at home. There are two Indian examples, 'The Sons of the Kherohuri Raja' (Bompas 1909: 251–4, no. 84) and 'The Bride of the Sword' (Shovona Devi 1915: 117–26). Shovona's tale, which has a suspiciously literary feel, is closer in detail to the European variants than is Bompas's tribal version. In both, the couples are married early in the tale and the attack takes place as the wedding procession is making its way back, in typical Indian fashion, to the princes' kingdom after the ceremony. This poses a narrative problem not faced by the European narrators: how is the hero to escape the attack? The problem is solved by the use of an even more esoteric motif. One princess is married to her prince by proxy and in both variants he sends his sword to act as his representative in his absence, a practice attested in India but little studied (Brockington 1995b).[4] Narrators of both variants make further use of the sword. In Bompas's version it serves as a recognition token (the prince has, after all, not yet seen his bride) and also as a practical weapon. Shovona's sword is invested with pathetic symbolism and brings about a tragic ending to the tale, determined by the introduction of another motif exclusive to Indian social customs, that of a declaration of symbolic brother- and sisterhood between hero and unrecognised heroine that ensures the speaker's safety but cannot be revoked to allow the consummation of the marriage when their identity is established. The heroine has already protected herself from her captor by declaring herself his 'daughter', mirroring the fateful declaration by her husband. A similar declaration is made between the spirits Kordabbu and Tani Maniga in the Tulu living oral traditional epic, *Kordabbu*, recorded in coastal Karnataka (Blackburn 1989: 235). No magic charm or talisman is needed: will-power, albeit reinforced by implied supernatural sanction, is sufficient.

The type known in Europe as 'Faithful John' (AT 516) provides a good example of the need for caution when discussing sources and diffusion. Several modern South Asian variants tell how a servant, warned by talking birds, saves the life of a king and queen at the expense of being turned to stone, to be disenchanted by the king decapitating his own son, who is subsequently restored to life.[5] Ramanujan's comment on a Sindhi variant, 'Told from Portugal to India and often considered to be of Indian origin, this tale appears in the eleventh century in the *Kathasaritsagara*' (Ramanujan 1991: 345), is here misleading, for only the motif of the sacrifice of a son to obtain benefit for another is common to the two tales. The narratives are of completely different types and even the motifs are not identical; see 'The Adventures of Vīravara' (Penzer

---

[4] To the references cited there add 'The Two Friends' (Taylor 1895: 399–403). The practice also occurs in the Indic form of 'Saif ul-Muluk' (Kincaid 1922: 38) but not in the Persian form appearing in the *Arabian Nights* (Lane 1981: III, 283–351), which has no proxy marriage.

[5] For example 'The Eighth Key' (Ramanujan 1991: 312–18), very close to the Grimms' version; 'Rama and Luxman' (Frere 1868: 72–86, no. 5); 'The King and His Faithful Minister' (King 1926: no. 14), with less savage endings; and 'Untold Stories', Ramanujan's Gondi variant (1991: 4–5, reprinted from Elwin 1944) which has a bitter twist to it.

1923–8: VI, 191–8) where the servant's whole family is sacrificed to ensure long life for the king. There is no reason to link the complete tale-type to this literary *Kathāsaritsāgara* tale any more than to a roughly contemporary Latin poem from western Europe, *Ad Bernardum*, which also applies the child-sacrfice theme to a friendship story of a totally different nature. This Latin poem is the earliest extant version of the *Amicus et Amelius* stories, although its eleventh-century author, Radulphus Tortarius, is probably retelling an older tradition: Amelius kills his children to cure his friend's leprosy, then finds them restored to life (Monteverdi 1928; trans. Leach 1937: 101–5). The point is that all three stories involve the sacrifice of what is dearest to the hero, and all three original authors, understandably, make the same choice.

Collection and analysis

Fallacious and hasty though earlier assumptions about India as the source of all fairy tales may have been, they have had the beneficial effect of focusing the attention of western scholars on the oral traditions of South Asia since the middle of the nineteenth century. Benfey's famous assertion that, 'My research in the area of fables, fairy tales and stories of both the West and the East has convinced me that few fables but a great number of fairy tales and stories have been spread from India throughout the world' (1859: I, xxii) was greeted with great positive acclaim (and subsequently generalised as if it applied to folk material which Benfey had then no opportunity of studying) by scholars still excited by the implications of Sir William Jones's proclamation of the relationship between Sanskrit and the European classical languages. That proclamation of 1786 had drawn widespread scholarly attention to the relationship of the Indo-European languages, although similar ideas had been put forward virtually unnoticed during the preceding two hundred years. Benfey's invaluable work on the *Pañcatantra* was published before the explosion of folktale collection in Europe and elsewhere in the second half of the nineteenth century, and his belief in the Indian origin of many (not all) tales was based on his study only of literary collections, whether Asian or European. The Indic sources he used were of a date sufficiently early to make his belief reasonable; tales not attested until one or two thousand years later are a different matter.

It is striking how many of the early collectors of South Asian tales were women, a fact which tends to obscure the equally significant point that a similar proportion were clergymen, both being classes of people who had more access to the native population through their servants and more interest in them as individuals than did the colonial administrators; indeed it is R. C. Temple, an army officer, who is unusual. He collected a few tales himself but chiefly analysed and published those collected by others, especially Flora Steel, identifying and classifying types and motifs known from European analogues long before the work of Aarne, Thompson and their successors (cf. Steeland Temple 1973: 204–308). The main period for British collecting activity was the second half of the nineteenth century, at a time when Europeans were beginning to view India with more detachment, no longer seeking to live as Indians but to present Indian culture to a western audience. At this period a British woman, even if born in India, was unlikely to have grown up there. To live in India as wife or sister-housekeeper was a matter of conscious choice, and a woman who made that choice must have been a person of enterprise and initiative; once there, she would find little outlet for her energies. Several describe how, in their enforced isolation, they collected stories from their women servants, traditional tellers of tales to children; Flora Steel tells of the much greater lengths to which she went in actively seeking out tales from Indian village children (Steel and Temple 1973: Preface). The work of these British women was continued by native Indians, again including women: valuable collections were published by Sunity Devee, Maharani of Cooch Behar (1923) and by Shovona Devi (1915). Shovona was clearly a frustrated novelist, cowed by her overpowering family of western-influenced Bengali literary men, including her uncle Rabindranath Tagore. She admitted to collecting and publishing folktales as the only outlet open to her and the possibility cannot be excluded that she exercised her talents on some of the tales, though they are obviously genuine in outline.

Collections of tales produced for the modern western child reader tend to reproduce the work of the nineteenth-century collectors, sometimes bringing their archaic diction up to date in a continuation of the narratorial tradition. Within India strenuous efforts have been made in recent years to record and preserve the corpus of oral narratives for South Asian readers, with large numbers of versions published. Prominent among these is the series of twenty-one volumes of folktales published in Delhi between 1969 and 1977 by Sterling Publishers, which forms an excellent introduction to the tales of each state, although there is regrettably little information provided on the sources. Heda Jason (1989) has made a valiant attempt to give it some value to scholars by classifying the tale types: she was able to add seventy to the types listed by Aarne and Thompson, twenty-eight of them newly devised.

The work of collecting and studying these oral narratives has too often been regarded as a discipline separate from Indology, with the inevitable result that folktale-analysts have looked largely to the West for analogues, often unaware of the indigenous context. Penzer's monumental annotation of the Kathā-saritsāgara is a case in point: for example, his detailed exploration of the international context of the heads which re-grow when severed until the hero learns the effective method of killing his enemy (Penzer 1923–8: III, 268–9) is here inapposite, for that motif is only one of the many drawn by this tale from the Sanskrit Rāmāyaṇa (6,96). Conversely, Indologists miss much by ignoring the oral narratives and their social and international dimensions. Rigorous scientific study to continue the pioneering work of Temple was carried out in the first decades of the twentieth century by Norman Brown, rare in his field in that he combined the skills of the Sanskritist with those of the oral narrative specialist, and so was able to demonstrate the interdependence of the two classes of literature; his example has not been followed and Indology is the poorer for it. His article on the Pañcatantra (1978: 123–48) concludes with the first detailed bibliography of the subject and remains a valuable research tool; other useful articles include investigations of the 'Tar-baby' motif (176–9), the 'Silence Wager' (186–200), and 'Change of Sex' (201–11). Different insights from a social anthropology perspective were provided by scholars such as Elwin and Emeneau, who not only collected tales, but investigated their meaning in their tribal contexts. Among their many publications, particularly valuable are Elwin's *Folktales of Mahakoshal* (1944) and Emeneau's *Kota Texts* (1944-6).

If western collectors were at first understandably mesmerised by finding so many tale type parallels to European types, more recently indigenous scholars have been able to point to the rich treasury of tales which have not yet been identified outside South Asia. Chief among these was A. K. Ramanujan, who worked both in India and the USA, producing much perceptive analysis and two collections of tales, namely *Folktales from India* and *A Flowering Tree*. The latter was made in his home state of Karnataka, and published posthumously. Its editors report that as many as thirty-two of its seventy-seven tales are unrecorded in the international indices, vastly expanding our knowledge of these tales (1997: xiv). Ramanujan pleaded for more work to be done in this field, pointing to the distinctive nature of tales chronicling the mutual antagonism of mothers-in-law and daughters-in-law, rooted as it is in South Asian social customs (an analogue to the traditional European rivalry of stepmothers and stepdaughters (1997: 236-7)). More distinctive still are those tales where stories themselves are anthropomorphised, for which Ramanujan suggests new motif- and type-numbers (1997: 228). In the tale chosen to open the 1997 collection, 'A Story and a Song', the *dramatis personae* are songs, stories and lamp-flames, and the non-material world they inhabit symbolises the necessity of preserving the oral tradition of tale-telling (see also Ramanujan 1991: 4-5); the message is universal, but the form in which it is expressed finds parallels as far back as the Vedic concept of Vāc, the speech principle given substance as a goddess.

Ramanujan's lively and sensitive translations, whether of tales adapted from earlier collections or of others collected by himself or recollected from his own childhood, together with his commentaries, all testify to his deep personal love for the medium, as well as his rigorous scholarly commitment to it. It is instructive to compare, for instance, his telling of 'Bopoluchi' with its source (Ramanujan 1991: 7-11; Steel and Temple 1973: 48-51). Many of the tales portray with vivid realism the everyday experience of the people of India, and so fall outside the scope of this study. In others, such as 'The Rain King's Wife' and 'Sister Crow and Sister Sparrow' (Ramanujan 1997: 145-8; 161-3), the protagonists are only ostensibly supernatural, their nature laying a superficial veneer of fantasy over all-too-human problems. This strain of realism and immediacy is maintained even in what could be termed 'true' fairy tales, where the most extreme fantasy is made believable: consider merely the title of 'The Prince who married his own left half' (1991: 293-6; 1997: 142-5). 'A Flowering Tree' (1991: 110-19; 1997: 53-62) is the tale of a girl who is able at will, and with no explanation, to turn herself into a tree. No attempt is made to set the tales in any mysterious, ethereal realm of the Other – a down-to-earth approach which runs completely counter to misconceived western notions of the 'mystic East'.

The lack of inhibition in both language and topics treated in the modern collections, compared with the nineteenth-century pioneering classics should not lead us to condemn the earlier scholars too harshly for prudery. The retellings by Steel and many of her contemporaries were intended specifically for children, and their value lay in the delight in things Indian with which they enthused their readers; indeed, since many of Steel's informants were children themselves, any bowdlerisation may have been due as much to the original narrator as to the collector. Nevertheless, more than one third of *Tales of the Punjab* is devoted to Temple's notes, and scholarly versions of many of the tales published for children in *Wide-awake Stories* and *Tales of the Punjab* had first been printed in a journal, *The Indian Antiquary* (Steel and Temple 1880–3).

Ramanujan not only had a different readership in mind, he had a different persona as a collector; inevitably different tales will be told in different language to a man of the teller's own nationality, from those told to a woman representative of an alien occupying power, or to a pious missionary. He also contributed a useful summary of the whole subject in his Foreword to Brenda Beck's *Folktales of India* (1987), a careful collection of tales, with detailed bibliography and indices of tale-types and motifs, which provides much valuable material in the traditional mould.

In recent years, the emphasis has switched from the collecting and classifying of tales for its own sake to the study of the concept of orality, and a great deal of fieldwork has been done on the techniques of performance, both by indigenous researchers and in particular by American and Finnish scholars, work which is still in progress. The Central Institute for Indian Languages at Mysore provides a focus for such research within India, and in 1995 was host to a wide-ranging international conference on Folk Narrative Research (Handoo 1998). A notable emphasis is placed on the so-called 'oral epics' (Blackburn 1989) and on the study of women's tales, now seen as a special genre with its own characteristics of content and form. Ramanujan, among others, has explored the different meanings of the same tale told from a man's or a woman's perspective. Little work has been carried out on the content of the tales themselves, with a few notable exceptions, such as Stuart Blackburn's study of animal-husband tales (1995). The fairy tale in South Asia is now rather the preserve of the social scientist and social anthropologist, and there is need for their perspectives and understanding to be complemented by, and applied to, a closer study of the content of tales in their literary context. When Sanskritists no longer feel demeaned by the word 'folktale', and their social science colleagues no longer feel threatened by historical linguistic research, but each discipline admits the validity of the other, we may yet, in cooperation, arrive at a true and fully rounded appreciation of this enduring and vital form of expression.

References

Aarne, A., and Thompson, S. (1961), *The Types of the Folk-Tale. A Classification and Bibliography*. FFC 184. Helsinki.

Beck, B. E. F. (1987) ed., *Folktales of India*. Chicago.

Benfey, T. (1859) trans., *Pantschatantra: fünf Bücher indischer Fabeln, Märchen und Erzählungen*. 2 vols. Leipzig.

Blackburn, S. H. (1989) ed., *Oral Epics in India*. Berkeley.

—— (1995), 'Coming out of His Shell: Animal-Husband Tales from India', in *Syllables of Sky: Studies in South Indian Civilization in Honour of Velcheru Narayana Rao*, ed. D. Shulman, 43–75. Delhi.

—— and Ramanujan, A. K. (1986) ed., *Another Harmony: New Essays on the Folklore of India*. Berkeley.

Bloomfield, M. (1924), 'On False Ascetics and Nuns in Hindu Fiction', *Journal of the American Oriental Society* 44, 202–42.

Bodding, P. O. (1925–9), *Santal Folk Tales*. 3 vols. Oslo.

Bødker, L. (1957), *Indian Animal Tales: A Preliminary Survey*. FFC 170. Helsinki.

Bompas, C. H. (1909), *Folklore of the Santal Parganas*. London.

Brockington, M. (1995a), 'The Indic Version of The Two Brothers and Its Relationship to the *Rāmāyaṇa*', *Fabula* 36, 259–72.

—— (1995b), 'The Sword as a Symbol in Indian Literature and Folk Tales', in Galewicz (1995), 81–9.

— (1998), 'The Relationship of the *Rāmāyaṇa* to the Indic Form of The Two Brothers and to the Stepmother Redaction', in *The Epic: Oral and Written*, ed. L. Honko, ISFNR Congress Papers V, 139–50. Mysore.

— (2000), 'Jarāsaṃdha and the Magic Mango: Causes and Consequences in Epic and Oral Tales', in *On the Understanding of Other Cultures*, ed. P. Balcerowicz and M. Mejor. Proceedings of the International Conference on Sanskrit and Related Studies, 85–94. Warsaw.

—— (2001a), 'Once upon a Time . . .: The *Rāmāyaṇa* in Traditional Tales', in *Indian Epic Traditions – Past and Present*. 16th European Conference on Modern South Asian Studies. *Rocznik Orientalistyczny* 54.1, 133–58.

—— (2001b), 'Indian Ogres: Tradition versus Artistry', in *Supernatural Enemies*, ed. H. Ellis Davidson and A. Chaudhri. Durham, NC.

—— (forthcoming), 'Indian gods as helpers: the non-human *avatāras*', in *Supernatural Helpers*, ed. A. Chaudhri and H. Ellis Davidson. Durham, NC.

Brown, W. N. (1978), *India and Indology: Selected Articles*, ed. R. Rocher. Delhi.

Elwin, V. (1944), *Folk-Tales of Mahakoshal*. Oxford.

Emeneau, M. B. (1944–6), *Kota Texts*. 4 vols. Berkeley.

Frere, M. (1868/1967), *Old Deccan Days: Or, Hindoo Fairy Legends Current in Southern India Collected from Oral Tradition*. London/New York.

Galewicz, C. (1995) ed., *Proceedings of the International Conference on Sanskrit and Related Studies, September 23–26, 1993*. Cracow Indological Studies 1. Kraków.

Gehrts, H. (1967), *Das Märchen und das Opfer. Untersuchungen zum europäischen Brüdermärchen*. Bonn.

—— (1977), *Rāmāyaṇa: Brüder und Braut im Märchen-Epos*, Abhandlungen zur Kunst-, Musik- und Literaturwissenschaft 255. Bonn.

Goldman, R. P. (1984–) ed. and trans., *The Rāmāyaṇa of Vālmīki: An Epic of Ancient India*. Princeton.

Handoo, J. (1977), *A Bibliography of Indian Folk Literature*. Mysore.

—— (1998) ed., *ISFNR Xth Congress Papers*, 6 vols. Mysore.

Islam, M. (1982), *A History of Folktale Collections in India, Bangladesh and Pakistan*. 2nd edn. Calcutta.

Jason, H. (1965), 'Types of Jewish-Oriental Oral Tales', *Fabula* 7, 115–224.

—— (1975), *Types of Oral Tales in Israel*, part 2. Israel Ethnographic Society. Jerusalem.

—— (1989), *Types of Indic Oral Tales: A Supplement*. FFC 242. Helsinki.

Kincaid, C. A. (1922), *Tales of Old Sind*. London.

King, L. V. (1926), 'Panjab Folktales', *Folklore* 37, 84–9.

Kothari, K. (1989), 'Performers, Gods and Heroes in the Oral Epics of Rajasthan', in *Oral Epics in India*, ed. S. H. Blackburn, 102–17. Berkeley.

Lane, E. W. (1859/1981) trans., *The Thousand and One Nights*. 3 vols. London.

Leach, M. (1937) ed., *Amis and Amiloune*. Early English Text Society, o.s. 203. London.

Lichtheim, M. (1973–80), *Ancient Egyptian Literature: A Book of Readings*. 3 vols. Berkeley.

Monteverdi, A. (1928), 'Rodolfo Tortario e la sua epistola "Ad Bernardum"', *Studi Romanzi* 19, 7–45.

Norton, R. (1920), 'The Life Index: A Hindu Fiction-Motif', in *Studies in Honor of Maurice Bloomfield*, 211–24. New Haven.

Pálsson, H., and Edwards, P. (1980) trans., *Göngu-Hrolfs Saga*. Edinburgh.

Parker, H. (1910–14), *Village Folk-Tales of Ceylon*. 3 vols. London.

Parmar, S. (1973/1998), *Folk Tales of Madhya Pradesh*. New Delhi.

Penzer, N. M. (1923–8/1968), *The Ocean of Story: Being C. H. Tawney's Translation of Somadeva's Kathā Sarit Sāgara*. 10 vols. London/Delhi.

Ramanujan, A. K. (1991/1993), *Folktales from India: A Selection of Oral Tales from Twenty-Two Languages*. New York/ New Delhi.

—— (1997), *A Flowering Tree and Other Oral Tales from India*, ed. S. Blackburn and A. Dundes. Berkeley.

Rāmāyaṇa – see Goldman (1984–).

Ranke, K. (1934), *Die zwei Brüder*. FFC 114. Helsinki.

Shovona Devi (1915), *The Orient Pearls*. London.

Singh, K. S., and Datta, B. (1993), eds. *Rama-katha in Tribal and Folk Traditions of India: Proceedings of a Seminar*. Anthropological Survey of India. Calcutta.

Smith, W. L. (1996), 'Two Nepalese Versions of the Mahīrāvaṇa Tale', in *Change and Continuity: Studies in the Nepalese Culture of the Kathmandu Valley*, ed. S. Lienhard. Turin. 379–85.

Söhnen-Thieme, R. (1996), 'The Ahalyā story through the Ages', in *Myth and Mythmaking*, ed. J. Leslie. Collected Papers on South Asia 12. London. 87–105.

Soifer, D. A. (1991), *The Myths of Narasiṃha and Vāmana: Two Avatars in Cosmological Perspective*. New York.

Steel, F. A., and Temple, R. C. (1880–3), 'Folklore in the Panjāb' and 'Folklore from Kashmir', *Indian Antiquary* 9–12.

—— (1884), *Wide-Awake Stories*. Bombay.

—— (1894/1973/1984), *Tales of the Punjab Told by the People*: reprints of 1884, above. London.

Sudyka, L. (1995), 'Genres in the Kathāsaritsāgara', in Galewicz (1995), 253–69.

Sunity Devee (1923), *Indian Fairy Tales*. London.

Taylor, S. M. (1895, 1896), 'Indian Folktales', *Folk-Lore* 6, 399–406; 7, 83–8.

Temple, R. C. (1884–6), *The Legends of the Panjāb*. 3 vols. London.

Thomas, J. W. (1978), trans. *Tristrant*, Eilhart von Oberge. Lincoln, NE.

Thompson, S., and Balys, J. (1958), *The Oral Tales of India*. Bloomington.

—— and Roberts, W. E. (1960), *Types of Indic Oral Tales: India, Pakistan and Ceylon*. FFC 180. Helsinki.

Rewriting the Core: Transformations of the Fairy Tale in Contemporary Writing

TOM SHIPPEY

One of the surprise best-sellers of 1994 was James Finn Garner's *Politically Correct Bedtime Stories*, which retold a number of traditional fairy tales in satirical form, using the language of the fashionable 'politically correct' world of American universities. The Norwegian tale of 'The Billy-Goats Gruff' thus reappears as 'The Three Codependent Goats Gruff', and in it the billy-goats, instead of deceiving and finally defeating the troll, insist in turn on their own culpability and eventually fall into the ravine with the troll, all still fighting desperately for the right to feel 'guiltier than thou'. In Garner's version of H. C. Andersen's 'The Emperor's New Clothes', the new suit is said to be visible only to 'enlightened people with healthy lifestyles', who 'don't smoke, drink, laugh at sexist jokes, watch too much television, listen to country music, or barbecue'; and when the little boy calls out 'The emperor is naked!' a quick-witted bystander replies, 'No, he isn't! The emperor is merely endorsing a clothing-optional lifestyle!', so that folly is never exposed at all. Similar treatments are given to a dozen familiar fairy tales, with Grandma cutting off the woodcutter-person's head in 'Little Red Riding Hood', for being sexist and speciesist, 'The Three Little Pigs' becoming *porcinistas* to destroy wolvish colonialism, Snow White and her stepmother chasing away the dwarves and the prince to set up a women's spa and conference-centre, and so on.

The joke was received with considerable *hauteur* by academic fairy-tale scholars, Jack Zipes for instance classing it among 'opportunistic books . . . that mock politics and the fairy tale itself' (Zipes 1994: 26). Zipes's criticisms are more annoyed than accurate. Garner's book was a commercial success, but that alone does not prove it particularly 'opportunistic'. It contains no criticism of politics in general, and its mockery is not of the fairy tale but of what academic commentary might do to it, indeed already had done to it: Zipes's complaint about people using the fairy tale opportunistically had, by 1994, more than a hint of trying to stuff the djinn back into the bottle. What Garner's collections and the critical response to them really show is that, by the 1990s, the traditional fairy tale had become a contested site, viewed by many as an actual or potential means of social comment, social control, or social change. This development was both a recent and an academic one, brought about when new modes of criticism exposed long-familiar fairy tales as transparent, suggestive, and above all, pliable.

A further surprise might well be how long it took for this to become obvious to English-speaking critics. The European explosion in fairy-tale collections, set off by the Grimm brothers' *Kinder- und Hausmärchen* of 1812, and very often associated with quests for national identity, rapidly reached Britain and America, with the Grimms translated by Edgar Taylor in 1823, the Norwegian collection of Asbjørnsen and Moe by G. W. Dasent in 1859, selections from the Icelandic collection of Jón Árnason by George E. J. Powell and Eiríkur Magnússon in 1864–6, the literary tales of H. C. Andersen almost as they came out from the 1830s, and many more, the whole activity memorably consolidated by Andrew Lang's eclectic collection of 1889, *The Blue Fairy Book*, with its eleven differently coloured successors. The serious interest of the Grimms and their successors in mythical history, language variation, and national identity as revealed or defined in fairy tale, however, found very little response in England, at that time perhaps the most secure of all the European powers in its own role and its own boundaries. Possibly as a result, the popular activity of adding new fairy tales to the corpus remained, in the English-speaking world, at best light-hearted.

One can see this easily by looking through such recent collections as Alison Lurie's *The Oxford Book of Modern Fairy Tales* (1993), or Sara and Stephen Corrin's *Faber Book of Modern Fairy Tales* (1981). The *Oxford Book*, which is organised chronologically, contains forty stories, beginning in 1839 and going on to 1990. The list of contributors for the nineteenth and early twentieth century is extraordinarily distinguished, and includes major writers like Hawthorne, Dickens, Wilde and Wells, 'Victorian sages' like Ruskin and George Macdonald, and prominent children's writers like Robert Louis Stevenson, Kenneth Grahame, of *The Wind in the Willows*, E. E. Nesbit, and Frank Baum, creator of the 'Oz' sequence. The Faber collection adds to the latter group A. A. Milne, creator of 'Winnie the Pooh,' F. Anstey, author of the Victorian children's classic *Vice Versa* (1882), and Alison Uttley, of the 'Little Grey Rabbit' books. Other major authors who wrote fairy tales which appear in neither collection include Thackeray, with his 'The Rose and the Ring' (1855), Oscar Wilde, with *The Happy Prince* (1888), and Andrew Lang, who included in his collections some of his own fairy-tale 'Chronicles of Pantouflia', published in several volumes from 1884 to 1906.[1]

Nevertheless, in spite of the distinction and one might say venerability of the author-list, these early literary fairy tales now make a curious impression. They are consistently non-serious, but in a heavily elaborate or even patronising way, as if the authors were not sure what tone to take with their audience (implicitly a childish one), or worse, not sure that they should be writing in what they took to be a children's mode at all. George Macdonald's 'The Light Princess' (1864) is about a princess who is cursed at birth by a wicked fairy to have no weight, but the author develops this with a string of leaden jokes about gravitation, education, proper pronunciation, and other schoolroom topics. It is perhaps

---

[1] A third collection is Jack Zipes's *Victorian Fairy Tales* (1987). This adds Lewis Carroll and Rudyard Kipling to the list of distinguished names, and stresses the value of fairy tale as a means of covert social comment and social resistance.

characteristic of Dickens to centre his 'The Magic Fishbone' (1868) on a shabby-genteel king who does his own shopping and looks forward to Quarter Day as the day when he gets paid, but A. A. Milne uses much the same strategy in his 'Prince Rabbit' of 1925, with its strikingly bourgeois domestic ending: "Very well, dear,' said the Princess'. Kenneth Grahame's 'The Reluctant Dragon' (1898) deals with a pacific and poetry-loving dragon forced to fight a good-natured St George by the demands of the crowd, who are offering 'six to four on the dragon'.[2]

All these stories are, in a word, anachronistic: they never lose the sense of the Victorian/Edwardian world of their tellers in the timeless world of the fairy tale. They are also consistently condescending. J. R. R. Tolkien summed them up well in his influential 1947 essay 'On Fairy-Stories', where he said (speaking of Andrew Lang in particular), 'I will not accuse [him] of sniggering, but certainly too often he had an eye on the faces of other clever people over the heads of his child-audience' (Tolkien 1997: 136). Lang's laborious 'Preface' to his Green Fairy Book of 1892 only confirms Tolkien's analysis. Addressed 'to the friendly reader,' who is clearly imagined as a child, Lang explains Darwinistically that although fairy tales were not created by children, they are old, and 'men were much like children in their minds long ago'; 'as the world became grown-up,' the tales were forgotten except by 'old grannies' who 'told them to the little grand-children'; now 'they amuse children still, and also grown-up people who have not forgotten how they once were children' (Lang 1892/1978: 390). In Lang's account fairy tales are thrust to the periphery in several respects: they are essentially childish, transmitted by the old, female and powerless, and can be appreciated by adults only through a deliberate exercise of memory – and yet of all Victorian Englishmen Lang was perhaps the fairy tale's greatest defender! The contrast with fairy tales as viewed a century later could not be greater.

Exactly when attitudes changed is impossible to determine. Cristina Bacchilega, in her interesting account of Postmodern Fairy Tales: Gender and Narrative Strategies (1997) remarks that while Italo Calvino's collection of Italian Folktales (1956, but not translated into English till 1980) cannot be called 'postmodern', Angela Carter's Virago Book of Fairy Tales (1990) can (Bacchilega 1997: 21). A similar exercise in chronological 'bracketing' could be carried out by looking at 'Bluebeard' stories. This tale has formed the basis for some of the most characteristic and influential postmodern and feminist fairy-tale retellings, notably the title story of Angela Carter's The Bloody Chamber (1979), and Margaret Atwood's 'Bluebeard's Egg' (1983). Sylvia Townsend Warner's story 'Bluebeard's Daughter', from 1940 (cf. Lurie 1993), is however quite devoid of the serious concerns that will surface in Carter and Atwood, and remains locked into the Victorian tradition of jocularity. Her story opens after Bluebeard has been killed, when it transpires that he left a daughter, and a will, and a family solicitor to safeguard the daughter's rights of inheritance and arrange for her 'a public school education' and a suitable marriage. The joke throughout the story is that it is the daughter Djamileh's idiotic husband who is desperate to break into the locked chamber, only to hurt himself, discover the dangers of curiosity,

[2] The Milne story is to be found in the Corrins' anthology, the other three in Alison Lurie's.

and be rescued by the superior intelligence of his wife. The story ends with much the same domestic suppression as Milne's 'Prince Rabbit'. But there is no sign that Warner is aware of this, or sees in it any ironic point.

In between Warner's quasi-Victorian humour and Carter/Atwood's developed seriousness, one might note Donald Barthelme's story 'Bluebeard'. This was not printed till Barthelme brought out his inclusive collection *Forty Stories* in 1987, but seems likely to have been written much earlier – Barthelme published a surprisingly 'postmodern' novel-length version of *Snow White* twenty years before *Forty Stories*. Like Carter's 'Bloody Chamber', Barthelme's 'Bluebeard' is a first-person narrative told by Bluebeard's wife, whose untraditional self-awareness is obvious from the first few lines of the story: 'I had a very good idea of what lay on the other side of the door and no interest at all in opening it.' Like Warner, on the other hand, Barthelme remains insistently jocular, the joke in this case being that Bluebeard keeps pressing his wife to open the door, in which she continues to profess 'no interest' – though she can afford to claim this, since she has in any case had fourteen duplicate keys made. Barthelme's ending is violently bathetic: the locked room, finally entered by the wife under extreme and untimely pressure from Bluebeard, contains, 'hanging on hooks, gleaming in decay and wearing Coco Chanel gowns, seven zebras', clearly an early example of 'performance art'. As in Atwood's story and to a lesser extent Carter's, the ending leaves one uncertain what to think; but like Warner and unlike the later authors Barthelme shows no interest in probing the inner meaning of the original story, still regarded perhaps as primitive, non-adult.

One might conclude that attitudes had changed unmistakably by the 1980s, and might be seen beginning to change ten or fifteen years before. As is appropriate for a genre which was to become so heavily academic, the lead was given by a string of critical works. In 1970 Alison Lurie wrote a piece in the *New York Review of Books* which praised traditional fairy tales as 'one of the few sorts of classic children's literature of which a feminist would approve', celebrating the power of both fairy godmothers and wicked stepmothers (Lurie 1970: 42). The piece, with its more defensive sequel, was however attacked by Marcia K. Lieberman in the journal *College English*.[3] Lieberman analysed the tales selected in Andrew Lang's *Blue Fairy Book* (to which Lurie had referred) to show that they created thoroughly unwelcome female stereotypes: the equation of beauty with virtue, and of virtue with docility, the passive heroine who has no ambitions beyond marriage, the imprisoned maiden who has to wait to be rescued. Lieberman ended by saying, 'one may wonder to what extent [these stories] reflect female attributes, or to what extent they serve as training manuals for girls' (Zipes 1986: 200). Most of her readers were in no such doubt. Fairy tales, at least as collected by nineteenth-century European males, existed to teach and to reinforce the lessons of patriarchal power.

Studies developing this line of thought rapidly became legion. One response was to blame the 'patriarchal' nineteenth-century collectors, and to try to break through their layers of editorship to the earlier female collectors or the

---

[3] The article was later to gain wider circulation through being reprinted in Jack Zipes's 1986 anthology, *Don't Bet on the Prince*.

patriarchs' female informants, the 'old grannies' whom Lang had dismissed. Attacks on the Grimms as editors included, for instance, John Ellis's *One Fairy-Story Too Many* (1983), Ruth Bottigheimer's *Grimms' Bad Girls and Bold Boys* (1987), and parts of Marina Warner's *From the Beast to the Blonde* (1994), while one particularly thorough attempt to get back to an original or pre-patriarchal form of a tale, in which the heroine does not have to be rescued but rescues herself, is Jack Zipes's *The Trials and Tribulations of Little Red Riding Hood* (1983b). Concurrently, female authors with little interest in fairy tales as such nevertheless took up the point that women had had their heads turned by the insidious pressure of fairy tale, especially in America, and especially as mediated by the highly successful film-cartoon versions of Walt Disney: the ground-breaking *Snow White and the Seven Dwarfs* in 1937, *Cinderella* in 1950, *Sleeping Beauty* in 1959, *Beauty and the Beast* in 1991.[4] In the first of these one sees Snow White, assisted by the woodland animals, turning into the perfect house-wife as she gaily dusts and sweeps and cleans. Far too many young women (it came to be thought thirty years later) had seen her and her successors as characteristically unambitious and self-effacing role models. Their titles and subtitles alone accordingly explain the point of popular and successful works like Madonna Kolbenschlag's *Kiss Sleeping Beauty Goodbye: Breaking the Spell of Feminine Myths and Models* (1979) or Colette Dowling's *The Cinderella Complex: Women's Hidden Fear of Independence* (1981). The feminist movement, in short, during the 1970s and 1980s turned a penetrating gaze on the tacit assumptions of fairy tales as traditionally transmitted, and for the most part found them very much wanting. It is in this sense that the fairy tale during this period became, as claimed above, 'transparent'.

However it also became 'suggestive'. Here the decisive academic study may well have been Bruno Bettelheim's *The Uses of Enchantment: the Meaning and Importance of Fairy Tales*, published in book form in 1975, but originating from a series of articles in the *New Yorker* a few years earlier. Bettelheim's book has been much criticised since, especially for its lack of awareness of issues of gender (cf. Zipes 1979: 160–82), and its interpretations are indeed often weird or doctrinaire. They were, however, based on case studies of actual patients, and had an avowedly therapeutic purpose. Bettelheim moreover took the bold step of insisting that fairy tales were not all surface, that they were in fact concerned with and vital for the whole process of reaching maturity. Even more critically, he introduced to many readers the idea of 'transformation' – of characters appearing twice over, as doubles or as splits, with the same sort of shifting but powerful significance that they have in dreams. In Bettelheim's view, for instance, 'Snow White' is about escaping from 'oedipal entanglements'. The girl-heroine here is really competing with her mother (of whom the wicked stepmother is merely a disguised transformation), while her father appears in double guise as the characteristically weak or absent father of so many fairy tales, and (transformed again) as the strong and protecting hunter. Snow White's period with the dwarves is a kind of arrested adolescent development,

[4] Disney had produced several short fairy-tale cartoons before *Snow White*, including *Little Red Riding Hood* (1922) and *Puss in Boots* (1924), but these did not have the same impact or continuing life.

significantly broken by the threatening gifts, associated with sexual attraction, of stay-laces, a hair-comb, and finally the traditional red apple of temptation (Bettelheim 1975/1991: 194–214).

But what about Snow White's glass coffin, and the wicked queen's ultimate red-hot shoes? Any commentator worth his or her salt can probably find a suitable answer to questions like these. Once one has grasped the Bettelheim method, with its unspoken rules – characters can be doublets or triplets of each other, all objects have symbolic meaning – not only do fairy tales become quite easy to interpret, they also provoke and reward interpretation. To give some simple examples: who dominates the story of 'Cinderella', with its (dead) mother, (wicked step)mother and (fairy god)mother? Surely it is the mother's ghost, and surely the story is about vampiric maternal ambition, which goes to the length (in the Grimmian version) of amputating daughters' feet to make them 'fit in', to make them catch a man: so says Angela Carter in her 1987 story 'Ashputtle, or The Mother's Ghost' (which begins as a parody of an academic lecture).[5] What dominates the story of 'Snow White'? Surely it is the voice of the magic mirror, the counterpart of the glass coffin, and surely this stands for the voice of the father/king/patriarch, for ever judging females by their beauty or lack of it, and provoking eternal competitive insecurity: this is the argument of Sandra M. Gilbert and Susan Gubar, in their 1979 study, *The Mad Woman in the Attic*.[6] This is a game that anyone can now play, though its rules would have been completely obscure to Jacob Grimm or Andrew Lang. As said above, it has made fairy tales suddenly and irrevocably 'suggestive', but also, once more, non-childish and non-peripheral.

The third quality of the fairy tale in the contemporary world is 'pliability', which follows on from the other two just discussed. Fairy tales may be transparently patriarchal, but once this is grasped they need be so no more: they can be rewritten with an entirely different, or inverted, orientation. They may suggest strange and unwelcome things about anorexia, menstruation, incest and self-doubt, but they can be rewritten to be therapeutic, or exploratory, to penetrate and illuminate the psyche in areas where the novel of bourgeois realism cannot readily go. They can also, as said in the first paragraph above, serve more than one mistress, or master. Books like Dowling's and Kolbenschlag's were complemented, in a way, by Robert Bly's *Iron John* (1990), a work which saw in a Grimm fairy tale a fable for the means by which men could recover their masculinity in a world perceived as increasingly female-dominated. Like the *Politically Correct Bedtime Stories*, this was not well received by *bien pensant* fairy-tale critics, Zipes once again devoting time and effort to showing that Bly was no scholar, that 'Iron John' is not a proper fairy tale, and that the tale has been both 'twisted' and 'milked' for political, or rather (in his view) anti-political purposes (Zipes 1994: 96–118). But as with the *Bedtime Stories*, this response is beside the point. *Of course* Bly is using fairy tales for his own purposes. Everybody does, nowadays, *because they*

---

[5] This appeared first in the *Virago Book of Ghost Stories* (1987), and was reprinted in Carter's collection *American Ghosts and Other Wonders* (1993). All Carter's works mentioned here are cited from *Burning Your Boats: Collected Short Stories* (1996).

[6] Cited here from the section reprinted as 'The Queen's Looking Glass' in Zipes 1986: 201–8.

have been shown how to. To repeat the formulations given above, the contemporary fairy tale is 'transparent, suggestive, and above all pliable': that is what makes it a 'contested site'.

The most straightforward way of engaging in the contest was to write new stories which would provide girl-children with more active and more positive role models than Sleeping Beauty or Disney's domesticated Cinderella. A paradigm story is Jeanne Desy's 'The Princess Who Stood On Her Own Two Feet', from 1982, given the lead position in Zipes's 1986 anthology *Don't Bet on the Prince.* Desy's princess is 'tall and bright as a sunflower'. When a prince is found for her, though, she turns out to be taller than he is, which he finds humiliating, as he does her superiority in riding. She deals with this in the manner which used to be recommended to women by advice columns and Hollywood musicals, i.e. by feigning incompetence and remaining lying down, but the price of this strategy eventually becomes too much. The princess is saved by her enchanted dog, who turns out to be a more understanding (but no taller) lover, and declares 'It is a pleasure to look up to a proud and beautiful lady.' The story ends with a traditional moral, 'sometimes one must sacrifice for love', countered by an anti-moral, 'sometimes one must *refuse* to sacrifice' (Zipes 1986: 47). In similar style and in the same collection, Tanith Lee's 'Prince Amilec' (1972) centres, seemingly more traditionally, on a prince who enlists the aid of a witch to win the love of a spoiled princess who sets her suitors impossible tasks; the twist here is that in the end, not only does he decide that he prefers the witch, but the princess decides to go out in the world and look for a prince of her own, which leads, as the story ends, to her enlisting the aid of an enchanter. As if taking up where Lee's story ends, Jay Williams's 'Petronella' (1979) centres on a princess who is born instead of a prince (her parents meant to call him 'Peter'), but who insists on taking the quest intended for her brother. However, like Lee's hero but with genders reversed, she too rejects the spoiled and bone-idle prince she meets on her quest, and rides off with the wicked enchanter instead.

Such stories make their point. Indeed, if one were to offer a criticism, it is that they are all point. The moral determines the story as powerfully as in some Victorian examples, and is accompanied by much the same self-conscious humour.[7] Slightly more depth is provided by writers who adopt the strategy of taking a traditional tale and rejecting its climax, or asking what its central scene really implies. Still in the Zipes collection, Sara Henderson Hay's 'Rapunzel' (1982) presents Rapunzel as a girl seduced and abandoned after she has twisted 'Her heartstrings to a rope for him to climb' – a traditional theme in folksong, but not in fairy tale. In more developed form, Joanna Russ's 'Russalka, or the Seacoast of Bohemia' (1978) retells H. C. Andersen's 'The Little Mermaid', but has the mer-princess becoming human and marrying the prince, only to find that they are totally incompatible.[8] The prince hires a wizard

---

[7] To be found also in such collections as Jay Williams's *The Practical Princess and Other Liberating Fairy Tales* (1978), Babette Cole's *Princess Smartypants* (1986), or Judy Corbalis's *The Wrestling Princess and Other Stories* (1986).

[8] Russ's story is printed separately in Zipes 1986, but is excerpted there from Russ's fantasy novel, *Kittatiny: A Tale of Magic* (New York, 1978). For other versions of the same story, including Dvorak's 1901 opera *Rusalka*, see Warner 1994: 396–9.

to return her to her own shape (which he assumes will be ideally beautiful) only to find that in true shape she cannot live on land: she dies saying 'Fool', by which she means both of them. Like Hay, but unlike some of the more propagandist writers, Russ is prepared to have a female character representing, not 'strong women', but women whose weaknesses are used against them. Tanith Lee's 'Red as Blood', in her collection of the same name, meanwhile uses what was to become a very standard device by recentring 'Snow White' on the 'wicked stepmother', who proves in this version to be entirely benevolent, with her stepdaughter Bianca and the dwarves as the villains of the piece.[9]

The most suggestive work in this mode, however, is perhaps Anne Sexton's collection of poems, *Transformations* (1971). The title is itself suggestive. Fairy tales themselves contain transformations – frog to prince, beast to husband, etc. – and Sexton's poems further transform the fairy tales. In the 1970s, however, Sexton's title might well have suggested Noam Chomsky's 'transformational-generative grammar', a theory which seemed to give deep insights into human ability to create language by being at once rule-bound and creative: the classic example is the transformation of active to passive constructions by a short set of rewrite rules. Could this apparently universal human quality be extended from grammar to narrative? The thought is provoked by several of the fairy-tale rewritings discussed below, and becomes stronger the more one reads. But Sexton's poems further introduced darker thoughts about the psychic origins of fairy tale. Her version of 'Briar Rose (Sleeping Beauty)' thus begins with what seems to be a girl being psychoanalysed, trying to recover hidden memories of sitting on her father's knee. From this opening the poem goes on to tell the traditional story, up to the moment of the kiss, when Sleeping Beauty wakes crying 'Daddy! Daddy!' The poem then continues by saying that Sleeping Beauty, married to the prince, becomes an insomniac who is afraid to sleep. Why? 'There was a theft', she says. She does not say what it was, but the suggestion is that it was sexual abuse of the girl-child by her father. Sexton's poem challenges one to consider whether there was not some element of sexual abuse all along in the traditional story. Commentators have pointed out that in versions before Perrault's politely censored one, the sleeping girl is in fact 'deflowered' by the prince, not kissed (cf. Warner 1994: 220), while the image of the rose among the thorns is a traditional and continuing image of virginity. As for the father's role, one could argue that even in Perrault the father is chokingly protective, that the fear of the princess being 'pricked' has strong phallic suggestions, that fathers with incestuous desires do figure in fairy tale, even though nineteenth-century collectors were likely to censor them. So Sexton's interpretation is not entirely baseless: far from distorting or modernising the fairy tale, she could be said to be revealing its turbid heart, in ways quite horrific for admirers of Walt Disney.

There is a further thought which arises from any survey of contemporary

---

[9] Politicised retellings are also common. Zipes includes in *Don't Bet on the Prince* a 'Snow White' version of 1972 by the Merseyside Fairy Story Collective in which the wicked queen is ousted by popular revolution. Among stories he discusses in his *Fairy Tales and the Art of Subversion* is a German version of 'The Magic Table' in which collective Utopia is achieved by the advice of an elf called 'Xram' – an especially easy reversal to spot (Zipes 1983a: 61).

rewritings of fairy tale, which is that the tales selected continually recur. Enormous numbers of fairy tales have been recorded, and made available in countless anthologies from the time of Andrew Lang and before. However, allowing for exceptions and reactions like *Iron John*, one finds oneself dealing over the last three decades of the twentieth century with a rather small core-group of familiar stories. 'Bluebeard', 'Snow White', 'Cinderella', 'Little Red Riding Hood', 'Sleeping Beauty', and 'Rapunzel', have already been mentioned. A seventh member of the core group is certainly 'Beauty and the Beast', with 'The Frog Prince' also popular, and 'Snow White and Rose Red' on the margin. There is naturally nothing *officially* canonical about this group, but it does in practice form a kind of canon. Angela Carter's collection *The Bloody Chamber* (1979) consists of ten stories, the title story a version of 'Bluebeard', with two more versions of 'Beauty and the Beast', and two (or perhaps three) versions of 'Little Red Riding Hood', as well as repeated reference to 'Sleeping Beauty'. Tanith Lee's 1983 collection contains nine stories, seven of them from the core-group. The eight sections of Bettelheim's book which centre on individual tales feature 'Snow White' (twice), 'Little Red Riding Hood', 'Cinderella' and 'Sleeping Beauty', with 'Goldilocks', 'Hansel and Gretel' and 'Jack and the Beanstalk' in support. Cristina Bacchilega's four central chapters deal with retellings of 'Snow White', 'Little Red Riding Hood', 'Beauty and the Beast', and 'Bluebeard'. Four of this core group became Disney cartoons. What is their linking factor? It does not seem to be connected with their ultimate origin: four of them are from the Perrault collection, four from the Grimms, and one, 'Beauty and the Beast', from Mme de Beaumont. Nor is it any particular quality in the way they are told. The first English versions of all of them are to be found in the Opies' 1974 collection. But in contemporary rewritings one might well conclude that exact texts are not important, as the stories have been reprinted and retold too often for anyone, scholars included, to be sure where they first read or heard them; it may well have been from one of the many cheap commercial children's retellings such as the Ladybird Books series.[10] The true linking factor, surely, is one of situation: a threatened female protagonist, surrounded by wolves, witches, stepmothers, beasts and husbands, always rescued, always triumphant.

There are other features which connect this group of tales in less determinable ways: the feeble or impotent father-figures, the aggressive and threatening female fairies and stepmothers, the pricked fingers and drops of blood, the thorns which protect Sleeping Beauty but scratch the eyes out of Rapunzel's lover. Reversing, or 'transforming' traditional tales may be seen as a modern and anachronistic strategy, but there is an evident reversal between 'Bluebeard' and 'Beauty and the Beast', the one a tale of the ideal husband who becomes a monster, the other a tale of the monster who turns into an ideal husband. The enchanted Sleeping Beauty has to be kissed into life by the prince, but the enchanted prince-turned-Beast has to be loved into human shape by Beauty. Are female-protagonist fairy-tales, then, all versions of each other? In Chomsky's terms, transformations of the same 'deep structure'? Or maybe alternative

---

[10] Carter comments that the version of 'Red Riding Hood' told her by her grandmother 'followed almost word for word the text first printed in this country in 1729' (Carter 1990: xv), but this must be unusual, see Zipes 1983 *passim*.

endings for the same story, as in a modern 'interactive' role-playing book? Vladimir Propp had after all notoriously demonstrated that all the tales in Afanas'ev's Russian collection were at bottom structurally the same, an academic finding that became well-known after his work was translated into English in 1958. Considerations such as these may account for some of the most bewildering and provocative qualities of the best contemporary rewritings.

Of these the most interesting, inexplicable and 'postmodern' is certainly Angela Carter's 1979 collection of ten tales, *The Bloody Chamber and Other Stories*, which makes transformation into a dominating principle. As one reads through the collection, one feels a continuous but growing sense that there are more connections present than anyone can assimilate at once. Attempts to pin this down, to focus on one set, immediately force others to go out of focus. Any critical account is therefore even more than usual bound to be reductive, but one might begin with the apparently non-canonical story, seventh in the set, 'The Lady of the House of Love'.

On the face of it, this is not even a fairy story, but a reversed vampire story. A young English officer, cycling through Romania just before the outbreak of the First World War, is offered hospitality by a female vampire. She means to eat him, but his own innocence – when she cuts her finger he 'kisses it better' – preserves him: as vampire-bite turns humans into vampires, so human-kiss, it seems, turns vampires into humans. The story is however full of references to fairy tale. The English officer himself is compared to the hero of the Grimms' story, 'The Boy Who Set Out to Learn Fear'; being English, he is also in a way the hero of 'Jack and the Beanstalk', with the giant's rhyme twice quoted, 'Fee fi fo fum, / I smell the blood of an Englishman'; the vampire lives in a garden surrounded by a wall of rose-thorns, and the narrator repeats that 'A single kiss woke up the Sleeping Beauty in the Wood'; suggestions that the vampire is like a girl dressed up in her mother's wedding dress recall not only Dickens and Miss Havisham but the Grimms' Cinderella-version 'Ashputtle', later to be retold by Carter with commentary.

So 'The Lady of the House of Love' is in one sense a wicked 'Sleeping Beauty', a demonstration of female desire and female power. Its images, however, relate laterally, not to other fairy tales but to other stories in the collection. The officer comes away with a rose as a memento, a rose which revives (like a vampire) in 'corrupt, brilliant, baleful splendour' after it seems to be dead. The plucked rose is also a central image in 'Beauty and the Beast'. It is what delivers the father, and so Beauty, into the power of the Beast, and in this there is a kind of symbolic logic: if a 'white, perfect rose' is a symbol of virginity, then the father's theft of one from the Beast has to be compensated by the repayment to the Beast of its symbolic equivalent, Beauty's virginity. In polite versions of the tale this repayment is only hinted, not exacted. However, in the second of Carter's retellings of this tale, 'The Tiger's Bride', it is not the father who gives a rose to Beauty, but Beauty who gives one to her careless and foolish father, who has lost her at cards; but as she picks the rose, 'to show that I forgive him . . . I prick my finger and so he gets his rose all smeared with blood' (Carter 1996: 158). Meanwhile, in the shortest of Carter's ten stories, 'The Snow Child', a rose is again central. The story is less than five hundred words long, and has no immediate fairy-tale analogue, but it begins with a strong reminiscence of 'Snow White': a Count, not his Countess, wishing for a girl as white as snow, as red as blood, as black as a raven. The wish creates the snow-child, the 'child of his desire', and the Countess is instantly jealous. Her first two attempts to humiliate the girl fail, in the third she asks for a rose. The girl picks it, pricks her finger, bleeds and dies. The Count copulates with her, acting out the necrophiliac hints of 'Sleeping Beauty'. Then he hands the rose to the Countess, who drops it: 'It bites!'

The bloody rose, or the vampire-rose, is thus consistent as an image in all three Carter stories. But is there any consistency in its meaning, or in the stories, as one feels there may be at the heart of the Beauty/Snow White/Cinderella corpus? There is no clear answer to this, but one may say, first, that Carter's stories go much closer to acting out the negatives only hinted at in fairy tale (cannibalism, deflowering, necrophilia, rape), and second, that the focus of her stories is, again much more explicitly than in fairy tale, the fears, desires and fantasies of the pubescent girl.

The first paragraph of the lead story, 'The Bloody Chamber', looks indeed very like a deliberate recreation/parody of the style of modern commercial female romance:[11] the young girl 'in a tender, delicious ecstasy of excitement', cheek burning, heart pounding, listening to the 'great pistons ceaselessly thrusting' of the train taking her on her honeymoon, and, with banal obviousness, anticipating another form of ceaseless thrusting from her Bluebeard husband. The deflowering does indeed take place, and is described in detail, as it would not be either in Perrault or in modern commercial romance, but the questions that power 'The Bloody Chamber' are those which previous 'Bluebeard' versions had always shirked. Why does Bluebeard kill, and keep, his wives? Is he a freak, or a timeless element in the male psyche, or in the female? Carter responds to this with many of the insights becoming common, in the 1970s, in feminist argument. For her, Bluebeard is less a brute than a collector. Female beauty is for him something to be looked at, a picture (he collects pornographic pictures), a mirror (the marital chamber is surrounded by mirrors so that he can watch multiple deflowerings), a specimen (the bloody chamber is an exhibition-case). He wants his wives dead so that they stay passive. He is a projection, to use a Bettelheim term, of female awareness of the male appraising gaze, to which all women are meat, 'cuts on the slab . . . bare as a lamb chop' (Carter 1996: 115, 119).

However, Carter's story contains further disturbing elements not present in the original Perrault version, detectable perhaps if one starts to consider 'Bluebeard' as an inversion or transformation of 'Sleeping Beauty' or 'Beauty and the Beast'. A strong element of female complicity has been introduced to 'The Bloody Chamber'. Not only does Bluebeard have a loyal female housekeeper, well aware of what he has been doing, but his virgin bride's old nurse feels 'incredulous joy' at her fosterling's 'marital coup' (Carter 1996: 113). The heroine, too, responds sexually, if guiltily, to her husband's gourmand rituals: 'I

---

[11] The 'intertextuality' of Carter's story is discussed by Bacchilega (1997: 119–29), though this study concentrates on other 'Bluebeard' narratives.

was aghast to feel myself stirring . . . I longed for him. And he disgusted me'
(119, 125). The romantic/pornographic tone of the first paragraph is, in other
words, not dismissed as completely false. There is a *female* fantasy of power
lurking in Perrault's story, Carter suggests, as in other Perrault stories. That is
how Bluebeard got so many wives. That is why Beauty goes back to the Beast.[12]

Two other non-traditional elements in Carter's retelling show her even-
handedness, or multivalency. In the Perrault story the heroine is saved at the
last moment by 'sister Anne', who keeps watch, and her brothers, who break in
and kill Bluebeard. In Carter, 'sister Anne' is replaced by a blind male piano-
tuner, with whom the heroine later sets up house, but whom she does not
marry, while the brothers are replaced by the heroine's mother, a tiger-hunter
who breaks in and shoots Bluebeard dead with her husband's old revolver. Both
changes could be seen as strengthening the element of female fantasy: if the
mother is an embodiment of female rage and power, the piano-tuner is a male
opposite of Bluebeard, unable to use the pornographic appraising male gaze
because he is blind, sensitive to nuance because he is a piano-tuner, weak, poor
and eventually dependent. But if he and Bluebeard are the two male extremes,
the two halves, one might say, of Charlotte Brontë's Mr Rochester, what is the
beau idéal?

Other stories in 'The Bloody Chamber' seem to explore this issue, and do so
by stepping outside what I have indicated as the modern canonical core. 'Puss-
in-Boots' (narrated by the tomcat) appears to be very much a male fantasy, of
relentless seductions by both Puss and his master, but it climaxes in a traditional
image of male horror, as a sexually dominant female straddles her new lover on
the floor next to her husband's corpse, before seizing the keys, the cash, and the
reins of power.[13] 'The Erl-King' makes more radical changes to a traditional
figure. In the story as made canonical by Goethe's poem, *Der Erlkönig*, the Erl-
King is both the elf-king and the alder-king, the woodland figure who steals the
life of a boy-child out of his father's arms. He is threatening, but not sexually so.
In the Carter story, however, he has become an image of male ruthlessness, still
living in the wood, but now a seducer who strips girls as he skins rabbits, and
whistles doves out of the air, 'those silly, fat, trusting woodies with the pretty
wedding rings round their necks' (Carter 1996: 189), which he then keeps in
cages to sing for him, like Disney housewives. The girl-narrator means to
strangle him in the end with his own hair, and then she (the pronoun changes
at this point from 'I') will string a fiddle with five threads of it, and the fiddle
will cry out by itself, 'Mother, mother, you have murdered me!' (192). Don Juans
have a power of enchantment, then, but the power comes from an inner
weakness. Carter's 'Erl-King' exactly reverses Bettelheim's theory about breaking free of 'oedipal entanglements'; oedipal entanglement is what kills the Erl-
King.

---

[12] Carter has accordingly been criticised as insufficiently feminist by feminist critics. She is
defended from charges of (for instance) sympathising with female masochism by Bacchilega
(1997: 50–1, and again 123–4).

[13] She acts out the accusation levelled against wives by the husband of Chaucer's Wife of Bath:
'somme han slayn hir housbondes in hir bed, / And lete hir lecchour dighte hire al the nyght,
/ Whan that the corps lay in the floor upright', see 'Wife of Bath's Prologue' lines 766–8.

The other two major transformations in the Carter collection are of 'Beauty and the Beast' and 'Little Red Riding Hood'. Each traditional story is told twice, as if to explore alternatives within the story, while all three of the collection's core-group stories (the two just mentioned and 'Bluebeard') could also be seen as transformations of each other. 'Beauty and the Beast' appears as both 'The Courtship of Mr Lyon' and 'The Tiger's Bride'. In 'Mr Lyon', the story is relatively traditional, the Beast saved from death by love, and Beauty saved from self-absorption by care. It ends furthermore with an almost Victorian image of happily married domesticity: 'Mr and Mrs Lyon walk in the garden; the old spaniel drowses on the grass, in a drift of fallen petals' (Carter 1996: 153). 'The Tiger's Bride', however, is another inversion. Instead of the Beast being changed back to human shape by Beauty, Beauty is slowly licked into her true non-human tiger shape by the Beast. The latter story also picks up the motifs of 'The Bloody Chamber', with the tigress-heroine this time defeating the power of the pornographic gaze. In both stories a major role is played by new subsidiary figures: the spaniel-guide in 'Mr Lyon', the male animal-valet and the female clockwork-maid in 'Tiger's Bride'. The first perhaps acts as an *alter ego* of both hero and heroine – what Beauty is by tradition (gentle and loyal), what the Beast will become. Meanwhile the valet/maid pair perhaps function as horrific alternatives to the happy ending, the male turned into a beast, his sable-fur gift transformed into 'black squeaking rats', the female reduced to a simulacrum without personality. In this version there is no mention of marriage or domesticity, and the moral is (not dissimilar to Jeanne Desy's formulation above), 'The tiger will never lie down with the lamb . . . The lamb must learn to run with the tigers' (Carter 1996: 166). Unless, of course, in the logic of transformation, both prefer to be spaniels.

Carter's transformations of 'Little Red Riding Hood' are relatively easy to describe, for in the earliest-known story as told by Perrault there are only three active characters, the girl, the granny, and the wolf, and the story ends with girl and granny both gobbled up. The Grimms patriarchally added a rescuing father-figure in the shape of the woodcutter with his axe. Zipes postulates a more feminist ur-version in which the girl saves herself by scatological trickery abetted by strip-tease (the pornographic gaze used against itself, Zipes 1986: 228–9). But if one sticks with Perrault, the possibilities for transformation remain limited, if shocking. Briefly, in Carter's 'The Werewolf', granny is also the wolf; but the girl exposes granny as a werewolf, has her killed, and then in a sense becomes granny: 'Now the child lived in her grandmother's house; she prospered' (Carter 1996: 211). But the girl may also in a sense be the wolf, for if one does not believe in werewolves, or in the old-woman witches whom the peasants also seek out and kill, then there *was* no wolf except in the girl's accusation: the tale is one of generational conflict.

This version however removes the sexual element at the centre of all other versions of the story, in which the wolf is very clearly an image of the male seducer, the path off which Red Riding Hood must not stray is the straight and narrow path of sexual propriety, and the vital 'what big eyes you have' scene has a strong suggestion of sexual initiation. Mothers, fathers and grannies, of course, mean to save girls from this; but in doing so their versions of the story ignore female complicity, which Carter's 'The Company of Wolves' restores, as in other stories discussed above. In 'Company of Wolves' the werewolf is very clearly a male seducer, and Red Riding Hood's shawl marks her as virgin, but pubescent. The wolf gobbles the granny, Red Riding Hood carries out the striptease of Zipes's 'oral' version, but then gleefully accepts sexual initiation against all (grand)-parental fears and prohibitions. In the end, 'sweet and sound she sleeps in granny's bed, between the paws of the tender wolf' (Carter 1996: 220).[14]

In both Carter's stories the girl wins, but granny loses. One final aspect of the kaleidoscopic quality of fairy-tale transformation is that stories remain open for others to transform. Not only may traditional tales be seen as versions of each other, not only can authors rewrite their own scripts, authors can rewrite each other's scripts: the contemporary fairy tale is in this way as much a continuum as the traditional or pre-literary one. What would happen to 'Little Red Riding Hood' if *granny* won? The answer to this is Tanith Lee's 'Wolfland', included in her 1983 collection *Red as Blood*. Here granny is once again a werewolf, but she is not exposed to peasant vengeance, as she is in Carter's 'Werewolf'. Like Carter's Bluebeard, Lee's granny is too rich and too powerful, and like Carter's Bluebeard again, she has loyal and feudally complicit servants of the opposite sex, especially the dwarf called, not 'Beauty' but 'Beautiful'. Nor does she mean to 'gobble up' the Little Red Riding Hood analogue, she means to turn her into a werewolf too and make her (as in Carter's 'The Werewolf', but complicitly) her successor. The person gobbled up is the Grimms' father-figure, granny's abusive and sadistic husband, whose pistol fails him where the tiger-hunting mother's, in 'The Bloody Chamber', did not. Meanwhile the third wolf-story in Carter's collection is 'Wolf-Alice', the tale of a female wolf-child kept in the castle of a lycanthrope duke. In the end the wolf-girl licks the man-wolf lovingly into human shape, reversing the endings of 'The Tiger's Bride' and 'Company of Wolves' at once. But by this stage one may feel that the echoes and inversions of the contemporary fairy tale have become as literally unmanageable as the myriad retellings of the traditional tales: the stories have taken over. Alternatively one might say that the authors have seen and released in the stories a potential that was there all along.

Rewritings as extensive as 'Wolfland' – some twelve thousand words compared with the less than one thousand of the Perrault story – raise a further issue for contemporary audiences and authors. The traditional fairy tale has neither history nor geography. Events take place notoriously 'Once upon a time', or long ago. They are set against a background of forests and peasants and kings of nameless countries. To many readers brought up, not on fairy tale, but on the conventions of the realist novel (not to mention the TV soap opera), this lack of verisimilitude is incomprehensible or unacceptable. They like the stories, but they want background. Satisfying this demand, though, means changing many things. As Carter says, in the 'academic lecture' part of her 'Ashputtle', answering the obvious realist questions about motivation 'would mean I'd have

---

[14] *Company of Wolves* was filmed in 1984 by the director Neil Jordan, at a time when werewolf-movies were already an established genre, with prominence given to the themes of male threat and female complicity.

to provide a past for all these people . . . It would transform "Ashputtle" from the bare necessity of fairy tale . . . to the emotional and technical complexity of bourgeois realism' (Carter 1996: 392).

Some writers have done just that. The publishing firm TOR has thus commissioned and printed a sequence of novel-length rewritings of fairy tale, each of them provided with a realistic setting. Patricia C. Wrede rewrote *Snow-White and Rose-Red* (1989) as a fantasy set on the edge of fairyland, but still in Elizabethan England, with a background of witch-trials and historically real alchemists. Jane Yolen turned *Briar Rose* (or 'Sleeping Beauty') into a post-Holocaust story (1992), in which the 'princess' is a dead woman with no past, and a grand-daughter determined to discover why the 'princess' continually retold the old fairy tale as if she had been the centre of it. Charles de Lint rewrote *Jack the Giant-killer* as an urban fable in modern Canada (1987), with a sequel, *Drink Down the Moon*, in 1990. There have been no less than three novel-length retellings of the fairy ballad *Tam Lin*: Pamela Dean's *Tam Lin* (1991) in the TOR series, Ellen Kushner's *Thomas the Rhymer* (1991), set in the Scottish border country of the ballad, and Diana Wynne Jones's *Fire and Hemlock* (1985), put in a firmly contemporary setting of divorce and neurosis and genuinely threatening stepmothers. The controlling device of Tanith Lee's collection mentioned several times above is to give each of her nine tales a different place and time, from 'Paid Piper' in Asia just before the birth of Christ, to 'Beauty', a science fiction story in which the Beasts are a race of extra-terrestrial aliens, who appear to be taking off human children for unknown, but (we discover in the end) ultimately benevolent purposes. Furthermore, while such crossings of the fairy tale with 'bourgeois realism' may be just a device for making the reader feel easy, they can also bring to the fore the questions raised again and again by the analytic academic criticism so influential on the genre.[15] The best example of this is Margaret Atwood's story, 'Bluebeard's Egg' (first published 1983, reprinted in Zipes 1986: 160–82).

This is not a fairy tale in itself, rather a rumination on why fairy tales should seem so relevant to the real-life situation of modern women. Its central character is Sally, a married woman in a prosperous suburb of a modern city. Her situation is in many ways markedly different from that of the wife in Perrault's story, or in Carter's 'The Bloody Chamber'. She has full civil rights and the protection of a modern state. There is no locked room in her comfortable house, no strange prohibition from her husband, and her husband is not a serial killer. The only overt connection with 'Bluebeard' is that Sally is taking an evening course on 'Forms of Narrative Fiction', and has been given, as an exercise, the task of rewriting the story from the point of view of 'anyone or anything in the story'. Sally's decision – she never actually writes the story – is to tell it from the viewpoint of 'Bluebeard's egg', an object which in the version she has been told takes the role of Perrault's key with the ineradicable stain. The question as to why she decides this is obviously provoked by Atwood's story, and in some

---

[15] Science fiction began to draw on fairy tale at an early date, one should note. A forgotten masterpiece is Philip José Farmer's highly Oedipal retelling of 'The Wolf and the Three Little Pigs' as 'Mother' and 'Daughter'. The two stories first appeared in *Thrilling Wonder Stories* for April 1953 and Winter 1954, and were reprinted in Farmer's 1960 collection, *Strange Relations*.

ways Atwood's story parallels the story Sally never writes. However, Atwood's story, the story *about* Sally, contradicts the physical differences between it and the traditional tale by showing a string of uncomfortable and unwelcome analogies.

The main one is that though Sally's husband Ed is not a serial killer, he is a serial husband. There have been two wives before Sally, both now divorced. Is Ed going to divorce her? Ed is a heart surgeon, rich, and strongly attractive to women. Sally fears the women who want, she tells Ed, to 'gobble you up' – like the wolf in 'Little Red Riding Hood', but gender-reversed. There is no physical locked chamber in the Sally–Ed household, but there is something Sally cannot get into just the same, and it is Ed's mind. Especially threatening is Sally's close friend Marylynn, who is everything that Sally is not: a divorcée, with her own business, confident and independent. She ought to be on Sally's side, a sister and a feminist – the two women share the joke that Ed does not even know the word, but says 'femininist'. But the moment of anagnorisis in 'Bluebeard's Egg' is not Sally entering the locked chamber, but Sally seeing Ed fondling Marylynn, and Marylynn certainly not moving away. It is a very qualified anagnorisis, because Sally is not quite sure what she has seen, nor what it might mean. Maybe nothing. But 'it could mean something more sinister . . . If this is it, Sally has been wrong about Ed, for years, forever' (Zipes 1986: 181). In which case, though neither Sally nor Atwood says this, Sally may find herself disposed of like Ed's two previous wives, hanging in the modern equivalent of Bluebeard's bloody chamber. The closest analogue between the traditional story and the modern rewrite is fear.

The fear, in a feminist world, would of course not be there. Sally would not be dependent on Ed, financially or emotionally: this was the point of books like Kolbenschlag's or Dowling's, mentioned above. Sally and Marylynn would also be allies, not potential rivals. But just as Cinderella and Snow White find their real competition from stepsisters and stepmothers, so Sally's threat is not Bluebeard, but Bluebeard's next wife: maybe she is not the heroine of the Bluebeard story, but the wife *before* the heroine, a character normally ignored. Atwood's story in fact highlights the problem of female complicity, like Carter's 'Bloody Chamber' and 'Company of Wolves'. There is, finally, the question of the egg, with which the story ends. Eggs hatch. The last words of the story are 'But what will come out of it?' (Zipes 1986: 182).

It is possible to see this ending positively, and critics have preferred to do so. Zipes sees the egg as Sally, ready to take a first step towards liberation (Zipes 1986: 26). Bacchilega offers three possible scenarios, all positive: Sally may break Ed's egg/life in order to survive herself; or Ed might hatch out, which would mark 'the frightening but potentially promising renewal of their relationship'; or perhaps Sally 'could be witnessing the beginnings of her own rebirth, as a woman no longer under the spell of Bluebeard' (Bacchilega 1997: 115). But these all look ominously like forms of denial. The really plausible scenario in Sally's mind at the end of the story, highly unwelcome though this may be, is that Ed is going to ditch her for Marylynn and leave her to make her own way in the world of work, which she already knows will 'end up leading nowhere', with her as 'a nothing' (Zipes 1986: 165).

'Bluebeard's Egg' is a highly academic work, with a carefully described academic course as part of its scenario and a familiar academic exercise at its core. It also fits contemporary academic fashion in its multivalency, its obscurity, its concern with alternative texts, its feminist interests. Yet there is a sense in which all these are rejected. Sally is not interested in variant texts, she never completes her exercise, and she regards her middle-aged counter-culture course-instructor Bertha as a comic failure, with nothing to tell her about success in life or in fiction. Yet Sally is fascinated by one fairy tale, and by the method she has been taught for reading it. She represents the new audience for fairy tales brought into being from the 1970s, and the new relevance that audience saw behind the fairy tales' archaic scenarios and non-realist narration. What Atwood does is to take the nucleus of a traditional tale, its own inner egg, and transfer it to the quite different culture of 'bourgeois realism', with all its (Carter's phrase) 'emotional and technical complexity'. It is a striking demonstration of how and why fairy tales, and in particular a core-group of them, have come alive for feminist and post-feminist generations.

Once created, the taste for transformations has proved a lasting one. In 1993 Ellen Datlow and Terri Windling, already well-known as anthologists in the area of fantasy and horror-story, brought out a collection of twenty modern rewritings of fairy tale, *Snow White, Blood Red*. This has been followed by five further collections with similar titles between 1994 and 2000, as well as a children's collection, *A Wolf at the Door* (2000b), the whole creating an *oeuvre* comparable to the Victorian 'fairy-book' series of Andrew Lang. The tales brought together by Datlow and Windling on the whole reinforce the conclusions arrived at above. The many authors represented of course all aim at originality, and frequently achieve it; nevertheless there is a sense that they are operating within the boundaries of what is now a familiar genre. The core-group of stories continues to figure prominently, with eight of the twenty items in *Snow White, Blood Red* deriving from it. Motifs and methods reappear. 'Goldilocks and the Three Bears' is rewritten satirically as a child-abuse story in Scott Bradfield's 'Goldilocks Tells All', in *Black Heart, Ivory Bones* (2000a). The same theme is picked up more seriously and menacingly in Wendy Wheeler's 'Little Red', in the 1993 collection: this time it is Little Red Riding Hood who has the big eyes, and the big ears, for her stalking stepfather. In *Black Thorn, White Rose* (1994) Peter Straub creates another academically oriented 'Ashputtle'. Tanith Lee has developed a technique of crossing one story with another, thus recognising their intrinsic connections: 'Snowdrop', in the 1993 collection, fuses 'Snow White' with 'Bluebeard', while 'The Beast', in the 1995 collection *Ruby Slippers, Golden Tears*, has a Bluebeard figure dying not at the hands of vengeful relatives, but because Beauty refuses to come back to him. Particularly frequent in the Datlow and Windling anthologies are rewritings of both 'Rapunzel' and 'The Frog Prince', with different-viewpoint stories of the kind that Atwood's Sally is asked to write prominent among them. Gahan Wilson's 'The Frog Prince' (1993) tells one story from the viewpoint of the frog, who is being psychoanalysed for his princess-delusions; Gregory Frost's 'The Root of the Matter', in the same collection, offers multiple viewpoints on 'Rapunzel' from witch, maiden, and prince, while Anne Bishop's 'Rapunzel', in *Black Swan, White Raven* (1997), gives a love-redemption alternative. Susan Wade's 'Like a Red, Red Rose', in *Snow White, Blood Red*, picks up the connection between rose-colour and sexual awakening hinted at in the Carter stories discussed above, to create a story of Freudian suggestion matched only, perhaps, by Margaret Atwood's second version of 'Bluebeard', the essay/story 'Alien Territory' in her 1992 collection *Good Bones*.

Common to all the above is the strong concern with sex- and gender-issues, the most striking feature of literary fairy tale in the post-Bettelheim and post-Carter era. It is not surprising, however, that another postmodern issue has begun to appear, through attention to the self-reflexive quality of narrative. This is not absent from the Datlow and Windling collections, but features more prominently in the writings of authors established outside the field of fantasy. A. S. Byatt's collection *The Djinn in the Nightingale's Eye* (1997) thus contains 'The Story of the Eldest Princess', whose heroine is aware that in fairy tale it is traditional for the elder brothers and sisters to fail, and for the youngest to succeed. She learns that stories can be changed, with a liberation-moral similar to Jeanne Desy's story discussed above. The heroine of the title-story in Byatt's collection is meanwhile a narratologist, shifting from academic conference to academic conference discussing stories, re-interpreting stories, her main example being the story of 'Patient Griselda', a 'Bluebeard'-variant with a notoriously unsatisfactory and patriarchal happy ending. In the end she is herself caught up in a story, the tale of 'Aladdin's Lamp'. Salman Rushdie has also attempted to reach out beyond the Western/feminist core-group, with his *Haroun and the Sea of Stories* (1990) based on both the *Arabian Nights* and on the eleventh-century collection the *Kathā Sarit Sāgara*, or 'Ocean of the Sea of Story', translated into English by C. H. Tawney in the 1920s. In Rushdie's allegory the Sea of Story is being poisoned, so that storytellers turn mute and writers fall silent. Strangely enough, in view of the theme, Rushdie has reverted in this to the jocular/facetious mode of Victorian rewriters, as if not sure whether fairy tale is after all a suitable adult mode.

If Rushdie were not sure about this, or if he had any real fear of the 'Ocean of Story' drying up, a glance at the Datlow and Windling collections ought to reassure him. The literary fairy tale is now characteristically not the independent invention of Victorian or Edwardian writers, but a traditional fairy tale 'transformed', i.e. rewritten in a different setting, and leading above all to a novel interpretation. In this kind of transformation, commentary is as important as narrative: the mode is in origin a highly academic one. There remains, however, no shortage of willing writers and readers, as one can see from the bibliographies included every year in a further series of anthologies from Datlow and Windling, *The Year's Best Fantasy and Horror*, published annually from 1988.[16] A small selection from items mentioned in recent years would include Susan Wilson's *Beauty* (1996) and Robin McKinley's *Beauty* (1978) and *Rose Daughter* (1996), all three novel-length versions of 'Beauty and the Beast'; Robert Coover's *Briar Rose* (1996) and Susanna Moore's *Sleeping Beauties* (1993);

[16] The collections began as *The Year's Best Fantasy: the First Annual Collection*, in 1988 (for 1987), the words *and Horror* being added to collections from the third (1990, for 1989).

and David Henry Wilson's *The Coachman Rat* (1989), 'Cinderella' seen from the viewpoint of the pumpkin-driver. Story collections with titles and subtitles of familiar type include Emma Donoghue's *Kissing the Witch: Old Tales in New Skins* (1997), Shahrukh Husain's *Women Who Wear the Breeches: Delicious and Dangerous Tales*, Priscilla Galloway's *Truly Grim Tales*, and Vivien Vande Velde's *Tales from the Brothers Grimm and the Sisters Weird* (all three 1995).

One final and somewhat contrarian point, however, deserves to be made about fairy-tale reception in the later twentieth and twenty-first centuries. The critical, and to some extent the creative, traditions described above are markedly anti-Grimm. The Grimm brothers are routinely criticised for their editing of fairy tales, and for suppressing the voices of their female informants; the core group of female-protagonist tales now most familiar derives in large part from French tradition, seen as dominated by women collectors before Perrault and underlying the Grimms' collection to an extent they refused to recognise; Tanith Lee opposes 'the Sisters Grimmer' to 'the Brothers Grimm', and is followed by Galloway and Vande Velde just above. These criticisms, however, focus on a very small part of the Grimms' lifetime work, controlled as this was by a clear agenda. The Grimms' interest in fairy tale was philological and mythological. In their overall project of discovering at once the history of the Germanic languages, the old texts written in ancient forms of those languages, and the mythology which they felt must have underlain those old texts and the many more texts which had not survived the centuries, the fairy tales functioned for the Grimms above all as vestiges: clues to what had not survived mythologically, or had been excluded from standard German linguistically.

This project has no interest for most of the writers discussed above. It was in many ways paralleled, however, in England in the twentieth century by the writings of J. R. R. Tolkien, who can be seen as an 'English Grimm'. It is true that Tolkien had many differences with the Grimms at every level. In a letter since published, Tolkien half-apologises for the influence of the Grimms' *Kinder-märchen* on early chapters of *The Hobbit* (Tolkien 1981: 26) – chapter 2, the encounter with the trolls, has strong similarities with the Grimms' 'Brave Little Tailor', and Bilbo Baggins's dwarf-companions could be seen as owing a debt to 'Snow White'. They owe a much greater debt, however, to the old texts of which the Grimms thought, or hoped, their fairy tales might be vestiges, texts such as the Old English *Beowulf* and the Old Norse poems of the *Elder Edda*. Tolkien was trying, in very brief summary, not to modernise fairy tales, like Carter or Atwood or Lee, but to make them more antique, and so in his and the Grimms' view more genuine.

In this endeavour his interest was not in the story patterns of fairy tales but in their personnel, one might say, in their stage props: dwarves, trolls, magic rings, wizards, dragons, werewolves and werebears, fairies and goblins rewritten as elves and orcs. In his essay 'On Fairy-Stories' already mentioned – which one can now see, with hindsight, to have been largely self-referential and self-justifying – he remarked that 'fairy stories are not in normal English usage stories *about* fairies or elves, but stories about Fairy, that is *Faërie*, the realm or state in which fairies have their being' (Tolkien 1997: 113). This latter was indeed his own subject. In a *tour de force* of 'bourgeois realism' – for hobbits are

archetypally bourgeois – Tolkien supplied Fairyland, or Middle-earth, with all
the things which traditional fairy tales lacked: history in the form of annals and
chronicles; geography in the form of maps; languages and linguistic relationships; a guide to non-human species. Ever since there has been passionate
dispute about whether this was a wise or a justifiable thing to do, but one
undeniable result has been the creation of a literary genre of epic fantasy, as
popular as anything done by Walt Disney, operating recognisably within
Tolkien's terms. Tolkien made the material of traditional fairy tale, and in
particular fairy tale within the Germanic tradition of the Grimms, once more
completely familiar, part of the 'cultural wallpaper'. To the modernising urge of
post-1970 feminist fairy-tale rewriters, there is then an archaising counterpart,
more popular, less academic (at least on the surface), more independent of its
narrative models, and derived from an entirely different (indeed now almost
forgotten) interpretive tradition.[17] Yet this too is part of the twentieth century's
long and complex response to the rehabilitation of the fairy tale in the nineteenth
century. Which part of the response will prove strongest in the twenty-first
century remains to be seen.

References

Atwood, M. (1983), *Bluebeard's Egg and Other Stories*. Toronto.
—— (1992), *Good Bones*. Toronto.
Bacchilega, C. (1997), *Postmodern Fairy Tales: Gender and Narrative Strategies*. Phila-
      delphia, PA.
Barthelme, D. (1967), *Snow White* (repr. New York 1987).
—— (1987), *Forty Stories*. New York.
Bettelheim, B. (1975), *The Uses of Enchantment: The Meaning and Importance of Fairy
      Tales* (repr. Harmondsworth 1991).
Bly, R. (1990), *Iron John: A Book about Men*. Reading, MA.
Bottigheimer, R. (1987), *Grimms' Bad Girls and Bold Boys: The Moral and Social Vision of
      the Tales*. New Haven.
Byatt, A. S. (1997), *The Djinn in the Nightingale's Eye: Five Fairy Stories*. New York.
Carter, A. (1979), *The Bloody Chamber and Other Stories*. London.
—— (1990), *The Virago Book of Fairy Tales*. London.
—— (1995), *Burning Your Boats: Collected Short Stories*. London (repr. 1996).
Cole, B. (1986), *Princess Smartypants*. London.
Coover, R. (1996), *Briar Rose*. New York.
Corbalis, J. (1986), *The Wrestling Princess and Other Stories*. London.
Corrin, S. and S. (1981) ed., *The Faber Book of Modern Fairy Tales*. London/Boston.
Datlow, E., and Windling, T. (1988 onwards) ed., *The Year's Best Fantasy and Horror*.
      New York.
—— (1993), *Snow White, Blood Red*. New York.
—— (1994), *Black Thorn, White Rose*. New York.
—— (1995), *Ruby Slippers, Golden Tears*. New York.
—— (1997), *Black Swan, White Raven*. New York.

---

[17] That of comparative philology, see chapters 1 and 2 of my *The Road to Middle-earth* (1982,
      1993).

——(1999), *Silver Birch, Blood Moon*. New York.

——(2000a), *Black Heart, Ivory Bones*. New York.

——(2000b), *A Wolf at the Door and Other Retold Fairy Tales*. New York.

Dean, P. (1991), *Tam Lin*. New York.

de Lint, C. (1987), *Jack the Giant-Killer*. New York.

——(1990), *Drink Down the Moon*. New York.

Donoghue, E. (1997), *Kissing the Witch: Old Tales in New Skins*. London.

Dowling, C. (1981), *The Cinderella Complex: Women's Hidden Fear of Independence*. New York.

Ellis, J. M. (1983), *One Fairy-Story Too Many: The Brothers Grimm and Their Tales*. Chicago.

Farmer, P. J. (1960), *Strange Relations*. New York.

Galloway, P. (1995), *Truly Grim Tales*. New York.

Garner, J. F. (1994), *Politically Correct Bedtime Stories*. New York.

Gilbert, S. and Gubar, S. (1979), *The Mad Woman in the Attic: The Woman Writer and the Nineteenth Century Imagination*. New Haven.

Husain, S. (1995), *Women Who Wear the Breeches: Delicious and Dangerous Tales*. London.

Jones, D. W. (1985), *Fire and Hemlock*. London.

Kolbenschlag, M. (1979), *Kiss Sleeping Beauty Goodbye: Breaking the Spell of Feminine Myths and Models*. New York.

Kushner, E. (1991), *Thomas the Rhymer*. London.

Lang, A. (1892), ed. *Green Fairy Book*. (repr New York, 1978.)

Lee, T. (1983), *Red as Blood, or Tales from the Sisters Grimmer*. New York.

Lieberman, M. K. (1972), 'Some Day My Prince Will Come: Female Acculturation through the Fairy Tale', *College English* 34, 383–95 (repr. Zipes 1986, 185–200).

Lurie, A. (1970), 'Fairy Tale Liberation', *The New York Review of Books*, 17 Dec., 42.

——(1971), 'Witches and Fairies: Fitzgerald to Updike', *The New York Review of Books*, 2 Dec., 6.

——(1993) ed., *The Oxford Book of Modern Fairy Tales*. Oxford.

McKinley, R. (1978), *Beauty*. New York.

——(1997), *Rose Daughter*. New York.

Moore, S. (1993), *Sleeping Beauties*. New York.

Opie, I. and P. (1974), *The Classic Fairy Tales*. Oxford.

Propp, V. (1958), *The Morphology of the Folktale*, trans. L. Scott. Austin, TX.

Rushdie, S. (1990), *Haroun and the Sea of Stories*. London.

Russ, J. (1978), *Kittatiny: A Tale of Magic*. New York.

Sexton, A. (1971), *Transformations*. Boston.

Shippey, T. (1982), *The Road to Middle-earth*. London (rev. edn 1993).

Tolkien, J. R. R. (1947), 'On Fairy Stories', in *The Monsters and the Critics and Other Essays*, ed. C. Tolkien. London (repr. 1997).

——(1981), *Letters of J. R. R. Tolkien*, ed. H. Carpenter and C. Tolkien. London.

Vande Velde, V. (1995), *Tales from the Brothers Grimm and the Sisters Weird*. San Diego.

Warner, M. (1994), *From the Beast to the Blonde: On Fairy Tales and Their Tellers*. London.

Williams, J. (1978), *The Practical Princess and Other Liberating Fairy Tales*. New York.

Wilson, D. (1985), *The Coachman Rat*. New York.

Wilson, S. (1996), *Beauty*. New York.

Wrede, P. (1989), *Snow White and Rose Red*. New York.

Yolen, J. (1992), *Briar Rose*. New York.

Zipes, J. (1979), *Breaking the Magic Spell: Radical Theories of Folk and Fairy Tales*. Austin, TX.

——(1983a) *Fairy Tales and the Art of Subversion: The Classical Genre for Children and the Process of Civilization*. New York.

——(1983b/1993), *The Trials and Tribulations of Little Red Riding Hood: Versions of the Tale in a Socio-historical Context*. New York.

——(1986) ed., *Don't Bet on the Prince: Contemporary Feminist Fairy Tales in North America and England*. New York. Includes 'A Second Gaze at Red Riding Hood's Trials and Tribulations'.

——(1987) ed., *Victorian Fairy Tales: The Revolt of the Fairies and Elves*. London/New York.

——(1994), *Fairy Tale as Myth / Myth as Fairy Tale*. Lexington, KY.

General Index

Index of main tales and tale-types

Note: this includes modern rewritings of traditional tales, and 'literary' fairy tales.

Printed in the USA
CPSIA information can be obtained
at www.ICGtesting.com
JSHW011454150823
46583JS00003B/224